Additional Praise for
Fixed Income Securities:
Tools for Today's Markets, 2nd Edition

"In my opinion, this edition of Tuckman's book has no match in terms of clarity, accessibility and applicability to today's bond markets."

—Vineer Bhansali, Ph.D.
Executive Vice President
Head of Portfolio Analytics
PIMCO

"Tuckman's book is a must for the bookshelf of anyone interested in the concepts of fixed income markets and their application. Throughout the book, the basic concepts are illustrated with numerical examples that make them easier to apply from a practical perspective."

—Marti G. Subrahmanyam
Charles E. Merrill Professor of Finance, Economics
and International Business
Stern School of Business, New York University

John Wiley & Sons

Founded in 1807, John Wiley & Sons is the oldest independent publishing company in the United States. With offices in North America, Europe, Australia and Asia, Wiley is globally committed to developing and marketing print and electronic products and services for our customers' professional and personal knowledge and understanding.

The Wiley Finance series contains books written specifically for finance and investment professionals as well as sophisticated individual investors and their financial advisors. Book topics range from portfolio management to e-commerce, risk management, financial engineering, valuation and financial instrument analysis, as well as much more.

For a list of available titles, please visit our web site at www.WileyFinance.com.

Fixed Income
Securities

Tools for Today's Markets

Second Edition

BRUCE TUCKMAN

John Wiley & Sons, Inc.

Published by John Wiley & Sons, Inc., Hoboken, New Jersey.
Published simultaneously in Canada.

For general information on our other products and services, or technical support,
please contact our Customer Care Department within the United States at
800-762-2974, outside the United States at 317-572-3993 or fax 317-572-4002.

Wiley also publishes its books in a variety of electronic formats. Some content that
appears in print may not be available in electronic books.

Lehman Brothers is not responsible for any statements or conclusions herein, and
no opinions, theories, or techniques presented herein in any way represent the position
of Lehman Brothers.

Library of Congress Cataloging-in-Publication Data:
Tuckman, Bruce.
    Fixed income securities : tools for today's market / Bruce Tuckman.—
2nd ed.
        p.   cm.—(Wiley finance series)
    ISBN 0-471-06317-7 (cloth)
    ISBN 0-471-06322-3 (paperback)
        1. Fixed income securities.   I. Title.   II. Series.
    HG4650 .T83   2002
    332.63'2044—dc21   2002005425

Printed in the United States of America.

10   9   8   7   6   5   4   3   2

CONTENTS

INTRODUCTION

The goal of this edition is the same as that of the first: to present the conceptual framework used for the pricing and hedging of fixed income securities in an intuitive and mathematically simple manner. But, in striving to fulfil this goal, this edition substantially revises and expands the first.

Many concepts developed by expert practitioners and academics remain mysterious or only partially understood by many. Examples include convexity, risk-neutral pricing, risk premium, mean reversion, the futures-forward effect, and the financing tail. While many books explain these and other concepts quite elegantly, the largely mathematical presentations are beyond the reach of much of the interested audience. This state of affairs is particularly regrettable because the essential ideas developed in industry and academics can be conveyed intuitively and by example. While this book is quantitatively demanding, like the field of fixed income itself, the level of mathematics has been confined mostly to simple algebra. On the occasions when the calculus is invoked, the reader is escorted through the equations, a term at a time, toward an understanding of the underlying concepts.

The book is full of examples. These range from simple examples that introduce ideas to the 15 detailed applications and trading case studies showing how these ideas are applied in practice. This "spoonful of sugar" approach makes the material easier to understand and more fun to study. Equally important, it gives readers a sense of orders of magnitude. After working to understand the coupon effect, for example, one should also have a good idea of when the effect is large and when it is insignificant. In a complex, competitive, and fast-moving field like fixed income, it is crucial to develop the ability to distinguish between issues that require immediate attention and those that may be reflected upon at leisure.

Part One of the book presents the relationships among bond prices, spot rates, forward rates, and yields. The fundamental notion of arbitrage pricing is introduced in the context of securities with fixed cash flows.

Part Two describes various ways to measure interest rate risks for the purpose of quantifying and hedging these risks. The chapters cover basic and commonly used measures, like DV01, duration, and simple regression-based measures, as well as several more sophisticated measures. These include measures based on pricing models, multi-factor measures, and two-factor regression-based measures.

Part Three introduces the arbitrage-based, term structure models used to price fixed income derivatives, that is, securities whose cash flows depend on the level of interest rates. Many well-known models are discussed, like the Vasicek or Black-Karasinski models, but since there are many models in use and many more potential models, the chapters in this part have two broader aims: First, to explain the roles of expectations, volatility, and risk premium in the determination of the term structure and in the construction of term structure models; Second, to explain how the fundamental building blocks of term structure models, namely, drift, volatility structure, and distribution, are assembled to create models with different characteristics. Some multi-factor models are also discussed. Finally, this part describes how term structure models are applied to trading and investment decisions.

Part Four uses the concepts of the first three parts to analyze several major securities in fixed income markets. These are important subjects in their own right: repurchase agreements, forwards, futures, options, swaps, and mortgages. In addition, however, the exercise of using the fixed income tool kit to analyze these securities in detail develops the skills required to attack unfamiliar and challenging problems.

This book is meant to help current practitioners deepen their understanding of various subjects; to introduce newcomers to this complex field; and to serve as a useful reference after an initial reading. As a result of these multiple objectives, the book does mention certain subjects before they are formally treated. For example, a relevant point about swaps may be made in an early chapter even though swaps are not discussed in detail until Chapter 18. Current practitioners and readers using the book as a reference will not find this a problem. Hopefully, with a willingness to take some points on faith during a first reading or with the enterprise to use the index, newcomers to the field will eventually appreciate this organization.

ACKNOWLEDGMENTS

I thank Guillaume Gimonet, Andrew Kalotay, Vinay Pande, Fidelio Tata, and especially Jeffrey Rosenbluth for extremely helpful discussions on the subject matter of this book, and I thank Helen Edersheim for carefully reviewing the manuscript. All errors are, of course, my own. I am indebted to Bill Falloon at John Wiley & Sons for his support throughout the planning, writing, and production stages. Finally, I thank my wife Katherine and my two boys, Teddy and P.J., for the sacrifices they made in allowing me the time to write this book and for reminding me that the field of fixed income is, after all, a very small part of life.

The Relative Pricing of Fixed Income Securities with Fixed Cash Flows

Bond Prices, Discount Factors, and Arbitrage

THE TIME VALUE OF MONEY

How much are people willing to pay today in order to receive $1,000 one year from today? One person might be willing to pay up to $960 because throwing a $960 party today would be as pleasurable as having to wait a year before throwing a $1,000 party. Another person might be willing to pay up to $950 because the enjoyment of a $950 stereo system starting today is worth as much as enjoying a $1,000 stereo system starting one year from today. Finally, a third person might be willing to pay up to $940 because $940 invested in a business would generate $1,000 at the end of a year. In all these cases people are willing to pay less than $1,000 today in order to receive $1,000 in a year. This is the principle of the *time value of money*: Receiving a dollar in the future is not so good as receiving a dollar today. Similarly, paying a dollar in the future is better than paying a dollar today.

While the three people in the examples are willing to pay different amounts for $1,000 next year, there exists only one market price for this $1,000. If that price turns out to be $950 then the first person will pay $950 today to fund a $1,000 party in a year. The second person would be indifferent between buying the $950 stereo system today and putting away $950 to purchase the $1,000 stereo system next year. Finally, the third person would refuse to pay $950 for $1,000 in a year because the business can transform $940 today into $1,000 over the year. In fact, it is the collection of these individual decisions that determines the market price for $1,000 next year in the first place.

Quantifying the time value of money is certainly not restricted to the pricing of $1,000 to be received in one year. What is the price of $500 to be received in 10 years? What is the price of $50 a year for the next 30 years? More generally, what is the price of a fixed income security that provides a particular set of cash flows?

This chapter demonstrates how to extract the time value of money implicit in U.S. Treasury bond prices. While investors may ultimately choose to disagree with these market prices, viewing some securities as undervalued and some as overvalued, they should first process and understand all of the information contained in market prices. It should be noted that measures of the time value of money are often extracted from securities other than U.S. Treasuries (e.g., U.S. agency debt, government debt outside the United States, and *interest rate swaps* in a variety of currencies). Since the financial principles and calculations employed are similar across all these markets, there is little lost in considering U.S. Treasuries alone in Part One.

The discussion to follow assumes that securities are *default-free*, meaning that any and all promised payments will certainly be made. This is quite a good assumption with respect to bonds sold by the U.S. Treasury but is far less reasonable an assumption with respect to financially weak corporations that may very well default on their obligations to pay. In any case, investors interested in pricing corporate debt must first understand how to value certain or default-free payments. The value of $50 promised by a corporation can be thought of as the value of a certain payment of $50 minus a default penalty. In this sense, the time value of money implied by default-free obligations is a foundation for pricing securities with *credit risk*, that is, with a reasonable likelihood of default.

TREASURY BOND QUOTATIONS

The cash flows from most Treasury bonds are completely defined by *face value* or *par value*, *coupon rate*, and *maturity date*. For example, buying a Treasury bond with a $10,000 face value, a coupon rate of $5^1/_4\%$, and a maturity date of August 15, 2003, entitles the owner to an interest payment of $10,000 \times 5^1/_4\%$ or $525 every year until August 15, 2003, and a $10,000 principal payment on that date. By convention, however, the $525 due each year is paid *semiannually*, that is, in installments of $262.50 every six months. In fact, in August 1998 the Treasury did sell a bond with this coupon and maturity; Figure 1.1 illustrates the cash paid in the past and to be paid in the future on $10,000 face amount of this bond.

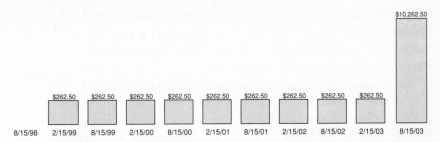

FIGURE 1.1 The Cash Flows of the 5.25s of August 15, 2003

An investor purchasing a Treasury bond on a particular date must usually pay for the bond on the following business day. Similarly, the investor selling the bond on that date must usually deliver the bond on the following business day. The practice of *delivery* or *settlement* one day after a transaction is known as *T+1 settle*. Table 1.1 reports the prices of several Treasury bonds at the close of business on February 14, 2001, for settlement on February 15, 2001.

The bonds in Table 1.1 were chosen because they pay coupons in even six-month intervals from the settlement date.[1] The columns of the table give the coupon rate, the maturity date, and the price. Note that prices are expressed as a percent of face value and that numbers after the hyphens denote 32nds, often called *ticks*. In fact, by convention, whenever a dollar or other currency symbol does not appear, a price should be interpreted as a

TABLE 1.1 Selected Treasury Bond Prices for Settlement on February 15, 2001

Coupon	Maturity	Price
7.875%	8/15/01	101-12³/₄
14.250%	2/15/02	108-31+
6.375%	8/15/02	102-5
6.250%	2/15/03	102-18¹/₈
5.250%	8/15/03	100-27

---

[1]Chapter 4 will generalize the discussion of Chapters 1 to 3 to bonds that pay coupons and principal on any set of dates.

percent of face value. Hence, for the $7^7/_8$s of August 15, 2001, the price of 101-12$^3/_4$ means $101+^{12.75}/_{32}$% of face value or approximately 101.3984%. Selling \$10,000 face of this bond would generate \$10,000×1.013984 or \$10,139.84. For the $14^1/_4$s of February 15, 2002, the symbol "+" denotes half a tick. Thus the quote of 108-31+ would mean $108+^{31.5}/_{32}$.

DISCOUNT FACTORS

The *discount factor* for a particular term gives the value today, or the *present value* of one unit of currency to be received at the end of that term. The discount factor for t years is written $d(t)$. So, for example, if $d(.5)=.97557$, the present value of \$1 to be received in six months is 97.557 cents. Continuing with this example, one can price a security that pays \$105 six months from now. Since \$1 to be received in six months is worth \$.97557 today, \$105 to be received in six months is worth .97557×\$105 or \$102.43.[2]

Discount factors can be used to compute *future values* as well as present values. Since \$.97557 invested today grows to \$1 in six months, \$1 invested today grows to \$1/$d(.5)$ or \$1/.97557 or \$1.025 in six months. Therefore \$1/$d(.5)$ is the future value of \$1 invested for six months.

Since Treasury bonds promise future cash flows, discount factors can be extracted from Treasury bond prices. According to the first row of Table 1.1, the value of the $7^7/_8$s due August 15, 2001, is 101-12$^3/_4$. Furthermore, since the bond matures in six months, on August 15, 2001, it will make the last interest payment of half of $7^7/_8$ or 3.9375 plus the principal payment of 100 for a total of 103.9375 on that date. Therefore, the present value of this 103.9375 is 101-12$^3/_4$. Mathematically expressed in terms of discount factors,

$$101 + 12\,{}^3\!/_4\,/\,32 = 103.9375d(.5) \tag{1.1}$$

Solving reveals that $d(.5) = .97557$.

---

[2]For easy reading prices throughout this book are often rounded. Calculations, however, are usually carried to greater precision.

The discount factor for cash flows to be received in one year can be found from the next bond in Table 1.1, the $14^1/_4$s due February 15, 2002. Payments from this bond are an interest payment of half of $14^1/_4$ or 7.125 in six months, and an interest and principal payment of 7.125+100 or 107.125 in one year. The present value of these payments may be obtained by multiplying the six-month payment by $d(.5)$ and the one-year payment by $d(1)$. Finally, since the present value of the bond's payments should equal the bond's price of 108-31+, it must be that

$$108 + 31.5 / 32 = 7.125d(.5) + 107.125d(1) \qquad (1.2)$$

Knowing that $d(.5)$ = .97557 from equation (1.1), equation (1.2) can be solved for $d(1)$ to reveal that $d(1)$ = .95247.

Continuing in this fashion, the prices in Table 1.1 can be used to solve for discount factors, in six-month intervals, out to two and one-half years. The resulting values are given in Table 1.2. Because of the time value of money, discount factors fall with maturity. The longer the payment of $1 is delayed, the less it is worth today.

Applying techniques to be described in Chapter 4, Figure 1.2 graphs the collection of discount factors, or the *discount function* for settlement on February 15, 2001. It is clear from this figure as well that discount factors fall with maturity. Note how substantially discounting lowers the value of $1 to be received in the distant future. According to the graph, $1 to be received in 30 years is worth about 19 cents today.

TABLE 1.2 Discount Factors Derived from Bond Prices Given in Table 1.1

Time to Maturity	Discount Factor
0.5	0.97557
1	0.95247
1.5	0.93045
2	0.90796
2.5	0.88630

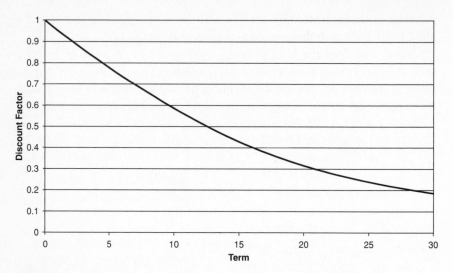

FIGURE 1.2   The Discount Function in the Treasury Market on February 15, 2001

THE LAW OF ONE PRICE

In the previous section the value of $d(.5)$ derived from the $7^7/_8$s of August 15, 2001, is used to discount the first coupon payment of the $14^1/_4$s of February 15, 2002. This procedure implicitly assumes that $d(.5)$ is the same for these two securities or, in other words, that the value of $1 to be received in six months does not depend on where that dollar comes from. This assumption is a special case of the *law of one price* which states that, absent confounding factors (e.g., liquidity, special financing rates,[3] taxes, credit risk), two securities (or portfolios of securities) with exactly the same cash flows should sell for the same price.

The law of one price certainly makes economic sense. An investor should not care whether $1 on a particular date comes from one bond or another. More generally, fixing a set of cash flows to be received on any set of dates, an investor should not care about how those cash flows were assembled from traded securities. Therefore, it is reasonable to assume that

[3]See Chapter 15.

discount factors extracted from one set of bonds may be used to price any other bond with cash flows on the same set of dates.

How well does the law of one price describe prices in the Treasury market for settlement on February 15, 2001? Consider the four bonds listed in Table 1.3. Like the bonds listed in Table 1.1, these four bonds make payments on one or more of the dates August 15, 2001, February 15, 2002, August 15, 2002, February 15, 2003, and August 15, 2003. But, unlike the bonds listed in Table 1.1, these four bonds are not used to derive the discount factors in Table 1.2. Therefore, to test the law of one price, compare the market prices of these four bonds to their present values computed with the discount factors of Table 1.2.

Table 1.3 lists the cash flows of the four new bonds and the present value of each cash flow. For example, on February 15, 2003, the $5^3/_4$s of August 15, 2003, make a coupon payment of 2.875. The present value of this payment to be received in two years is 2.875×$d(2)$ or 2.875×.90796 or 2.610, where $d(2)$ is taken from Table 1.2. Table 1.3 then sums the present value of each bond's cash flows to obtain the value or predicted price of each bond. Finally, Table 1.3 gives the market price of each bond.

According to Table 1.3, the law of one price predicts the price of the $13^3/_8$s of August 15, 2001, and the price of the $5^3/_4$s of August 15, 2003, very well. The prices of the other two bonds, the $10^3/_4$s of February 15, 2003, and the $11^1/_8$s of August 15, 2003, are about .10 and .13 lower, respectively, than their predicted prices. In trader jargon, these two bonds are or trade *cheap* relative to the pricing framework being used. (Were their

TABLE 1.3   Testing the Law of One Price Using the Discount Factors of Table 1.2

Date	13.375s 8/15/01 Cash Flow	13.375s 8/15/01 Present Value	10.75s 2/15/03 Cash Flow	10.75s 2/15/03 Present Value	5.75s 8/15/03 Cash Flow	5.75s 8/15/03 Present Value	11.125s 8/15/03 Cash Flow	11.125s 8/15/03 Present Value
8/15/01	106.688	104.081	5.375	5.244	2.875	2.805	5.563	5.427
2/15/02	0.000	0.000	5.375	5.120	2.875	2.738	5.563	5.298
8/15/02	0.000	0.000	5.375	5.001	2.875	2.675	5.563	5.176
2/15/03	0.000	0.000	105.375	95.677	2.875	2.610	5.563	5.051
8/15/03	0.000	0.000	0.000	0.000	102.875	91.178	105.563	93.560
Predicted price		104.081		111.041		102.007		114.511
Market price		104.080		110.938		102.020		114.375

prices higher than expected, it would be said that they trade *rich*.) The empirical deviations of the prices of high coupon bonds from the law of one price will be revisited in Appendix 1B. Now, to introduce the notion of arbitrage, the discussion turns to how an arbitrageur might attempt to profit from a violation of the law of one price—in particular, from the cheapness of the $10^3/_4$s of February 15, 2003.

ARBITRAGE AND THE LAW OF ONE PRICE

The law of one price can be defended on stronger grounds than the argument that investors should not care about the source of $1. As it turns out, a violation of the law of one price implies the existence of an *arbitrage opportunity*, that is, a trade that generates or that might generate profits without any risk.[4] But, for reasons to be made explicit, such arbitrage opportunities rarely exist. Therefore, the law of one price usually describes security prices quite well.

Table 1.4 describes an arbitrage trade in which one buys the cheap $10^3/_4$s of February 15, 2003, while simultaneously *shorting*[5] or selling its *replicating portfolio*, a specially designed portfolio of four of the bonds listed in Table 1.1. The reason for the name "replicating portfolio" will soon become clear.

The row labeled "Face amount" gives the face value of each bond bought or sold in the arbitrage. The trade shorts about 2 face of the $7^7/_8$s of August 15, 2001, the $14^1/_4$s of February 15, 2002, and the $6^3/_8$s of August 15, 2002; shorts about 102 face of the $6^1/_4$s of February 15, 2003; and buys 100 face of the $10^3/_4$s of February 15, 2003.

The first four columns of the "Cash Flows" section of Table 1.4 show the cash flows that result from each bond position. For example, a short of 2.114 of the $6^3/_8$s of August 15, 2002, incurs an obligation of $2.114 \times 6^3/_8\%/2$

---

[4]Market participants often use the term "arbitrage" more broadly to encompass trades that, while they can lose money, seem to promise large profits relative to the risk borne.

[5]To "short" a security means to sell a security one does not own. The mechanics of short selling bonds will be discussed in Chapter 15. For now, assume that when a trader shorts a bond he receives the price of the bond and is obliged to pay all coupon flows. In other words, assume that the cash flows from shorting a bond are the negatives of the cash flows from buying a bond.

or .067 on November 15, 2001, and May 15, 2002, and an obligation of $2.114\times(100\%+6^3/_8\%/2)$ or 2.182 on November 15, 2002.

The fifth column sums the cash flows across bonds for each date to obtain the cash flow from the sale of the portfolio as a whole. Note that the portfolio's cash flows exactly offset the cash flows of the $10^3/_4$s of February 15, 2003. This explains why the special portfolio sold in the arbitrage trade is called the replicating portfolio of the $10^3/_4$s. Appendix 1A shows how to derive the bond holdings that make up this replicating portfolio. The important point here, however, is that the arbitrage trade does not generate any cash flows, positive or negative, in the future.

The "Proceeds" row of Table 1.4 shows how much cash is raised or spent in establishing the arbitrage trade. For example, the sale of 1.974 face amount of the $14^1/_4$s of February 15, 2002, generates 1.974 times the price of the bond per dollar face value, that is, $1.974\times(108+^{31.5}/_{32})\%$ or 2.151. However, the purchase of 100 face value of the $10^3/_4$s costs 110.938 and is, therefore, recorded as a negative number.

The total proceeds raised from selling the replicating portfolio are 111.041, exactly the present value of the $10^3/_4$s reported in Table 1.3. This is not a coincidence. One way to value the $10^3/_4$s is to derive discount factors from four bond prices and then compute a present value. Another way is to price the portfolio of four bonds that replicates the cash flows of the

TABLE 1.4 An Arbitrage Trade: Buy the 10.75s of February 15, 2003, and Sell Their Replicating Portfolio

	7.875s 8/15/01	14.25s 2/15/02	6.375s 8/15/02	6.25s 2/15/03	−Replicating Portfolio	10.75s 2/15/03
Face amount	−1.899	−1.974	−2.114	−102.182		100.000
Date			Cash Flows			
8/15/01	−1.974	−0.141	−0.067	−3.193	−5.375	5.375
2/15/02	0.000	−2.114	−0.067	−3.193	−5.375	5.375
8/15/02	0.000	0.000	−2.182	−3.193	−5.375	5.375
2/15/03	0.000	0.000	0.000	−105.375	−105.375	105.375
Price	101-12¾	108-31+	102-5	102-18⅛		110-30
Proceeds	1.926	2.151	2.160	104.804	111.041	−110.938
Net proceeds	0.103					

$10^3/_4$s. So long as both methods use the same four bonds, both methods will assign the same value to the $10^3/_4$s.

The net proceeds from the arbitrage trade are the amount received from selling the replicating portfolio minus the amount paid when purchasing the $10^3/_4$s. As shown in Table 1.4, these net proceeds equal .103. In summary, then, one can buy 100 face of the $10^3/_4$s, sell the replicating portfolio, collect .103 today, and incur no net obligations at any future date. This profit might sound small, but the trade can be scaled up. For $500 million face of the $10^3/_4$s, which is not an abnormally large block, the profit rises to $515,000.

Absent any confounding factors, arbitrageurs would do as much of this trade as possible or, in trader jargon, they would do the trade all day. But since so many arbitrageurs would wish to buy the $10^3/_4$s and sell the replicating portfolio at the prices of Table 1.4, the price of the $10^3/_4$s would be driven up and/or the price of the replicating portfolio would be driven down. Furthermore, this process would continue until the arbitrage opportunity disappeared and the law of one price obtained. In fact, as many arbitrageurs would relate, prices would probably *gap*, or jump directly, to levels consistent with the law of one price. As a result, very few arbitrageurs, or possibly none at all, would be able to execute, or, more colloquially, put on the trade described.

The fact that the market price of the $10^3/_4$s remains below that of the replicating portfolio strongly indicates that some set of confounding factors inhibits arbitrage activity. The financing costs of this type of arbitrage will be discussed in Chapter 15. Also, the $10^3/_4$s, like many other high coupon bonds, were issued as 20-year bonds quite a while ago and, as a result, have become relatively illiquid. In any case, Appendix 1B uses another type of replicating portfolio to examine the magnitude and persistence of the deviations of high coupon bond prices from the law of one price.

TREASURY STRIPS

In contrast to coupon bonds that make payments every six months, *zero coupon* bonds make no payments until maturity. Zero coupon bonds issued by the U.S. Treasury are called *STRIPS* (separate trading of registered interest and principal securities). For example, $1,000 face value of a STRIPS maturing on August 15, 2003, promises only one payment: $1,000 on August 15, 2003. STRIPS are created when someone delivers a particular coupon bond to the Treasury and asks for it to be "stripped" into its principal and coupon components. Figure 1.3 illustrates the stripping of $10,000 face value of the 5³/₄s of August 15, 2003, as of February 15, 2001, to create five coupon or interest STRIPS, called *TINTs*, *INTs*, or *C-STRIPS*, and one principal STRIPS, called a *TP*, a *P*, or a *P-STRIPS*.

The Treasury not only creates STRIPS but also retires them. For example, an investor can deliver the set of STRIPS in Figure 1.3 and ask the Treasury to *reconstitute* the $10,000 face amount of the 5³/₄s of August 15, 2003. It is important to note that C-STRIPS are fungible, while P-STRIPS are not. In particular, when reconstituting a bond, any C-STRIPS maturing on a particular coupon payment date may be used as that bond's coupon payment. P-STRIPS, however, are identified with particular bonds: P-STRIPS created from the stripping of a particular bond may be used to reconstitute only that bond. This difference implies that P-STRIPS inherit the cheapness or richness of the bonds from which they are derived.

Investors like zero coupon bonds for at least two reasons. First, they make it easy to construct any required sequence of cash flows. One simple and important example is the case of a family saving for the expense of a college education. If the family invested in a coupon bond, the coupons

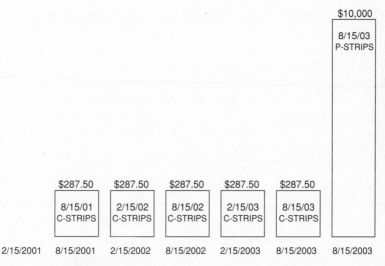

FIGURE 1.3 Stripping the 5.75s of August 15, 2003

would have to be reinvested, at uncertain rates, until the funds are required. By contrast, investing in zeros that mature when a child is expected to begin college eliminates the hassle and risk of reinvestment. Another example would be the case of a property and casualty insurance company that knows with reasonable certainty how much it will have to pay out in claims each quarter over the next few years. With the funds it has collected in premiums the insurance company can buy a sequence of zeros that match these future liabilities. This practice is called *immunization*. Any alternative investment strategy, as will be seen in Part Two, exposes the insurance company to interest rate risk.

The second main attraction of zeros, particularly long-term zeros, is that per dollar invested they have much greater sensitivity to interest rates than coupon bonds. In fact, an insurance company with very long-term liabilities, like obligations to pay life insurance claims, might find it difficult to find any coupon bond that would hedge these long-term liabilities.[6] Once again, these hedging issues will be discussed in Part Two.

Table 1.5 lists the prices of five short-term C- and P-STRIPS as of February 15, 2001, along with the discount factors derived in Table 1.2. Since 100 face value of a STRIPS pays 100 at maturity, dividing the price of that STRIPS by 100 gives the value of one unit of currency payable at that maturity (i.e., the discount factor of that maturity). Table 1.5, therefore, essentially shows three sets of discount factors: one implied from the coupon bonds listed in Table 1.1, one implied from C-STRIPS, and one implied from

TABLE 1.5 STRIPS Prices for February 15, 2001,
Settlement and the Discount Factors from Table 1.2

Maturity	C-STRIPS Price	P-STRIPS Price	Discount Factor
8/15/01	97.577	97.550	0.97557
2/15/02	95.865	95.532	0.95247
8/15/02	93.252	93.015	0.93045
2/15/03	90.810	90.775	0.90796
8/15/03	88.798	88.594	0.88630

[6]Asset-liability managers requiring very long-term assets may very well turn to equity markets.

P-STRIPS. According to the law of one price, these columns of discount factors should be identical: why should an investor care whether $1 comes from a portfolio of bonds, a coupon payment, or a principal payment?[7]

Since STRIPS can be very illiquid, so that quoted prices may not accurately reflect executable prices, only broad conclusions can be drawn from the prices in Table 1.5. First, with the exception of the February 15, 2002, maturity, the P-STRIPS prices are reasonably consistent with the discount factors extracted from coupon bonds. Second, the C-STRIPS prices in Table 1.5 all exceed the matched-maturity P-STRIPS prices. To examine these observations in the STRIPS market for February 15, 2001, settlement, Figure 1.4 shows the difference between discount factors from Figure 1.2 (which were extracted from coupon bond prices) and discount factors implied from C- and P-STRIPS prices. A value of 25 means that a $100 STRIPS payment synthetically created by coupon payments costs 25 cents more than $100 face value of the STRIPS. In other words, that STRIPS is 25 cents cheap relative to coupon bonds. Again,

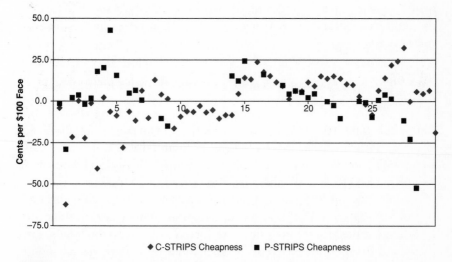

◆ C-STRIPS Cheapness   ■ P-STRIPS Cheapness

FIGURE 1.4 Discount Factors Implied by Coupon Bonds Minus Those Implied by STRIPS on February 15, 2001

---

[7]C-STRIPS and P-STRIPS are taxed alike.

while recognizing the limitations of some price quotations in the STRIPS market, Figure 1.4 does suggest that shorter-term C-STRIPS traded rich, longer-term C-STRIPS traded cheap, and P-STRIPS traded closer to fair. Some P-STRIPS, like the longest three shown in Figure 1.4, traded rich because the bonds associated with those STRIPS traded rich (that these particular bonds trade rich will be discussed in Chapter 4). The 10- and 30-year P-STRIPS, cut off by the scale of the vertical axis in Figure 1.4, traded extremely rich because the associated bonds enjoyed financing advantages and were particularly liquid. These factors will be discussed in Chapter 15.

The previous section shows how to construct a replicating portfolio and price a bond by arbitrage. The construction of a portfolio of STRIPS that replicates a coupon bond is a particularly simple example of this procedure. To replicate 100 face value of the $5^3/4$s of August 15, 2003, for example, buy $^{5.75}/_2$ or 2.875 face value of each STRIPS in Table 1.5 to replicate the coupon payments and buy an additional 100 face value of August 15, 2003, STRIPS to replicate the principal payment. Since one may choose between a C- and a P-STRIPS on each cash flow date, there are many ways to replicate the $5^3/4$s of August 15, 2003, and, therefore, to compute its arbitrage price. Using only P-STRIPS, for example, the arbitrage price is

$$\frac{5.75}{2}\left[.97550 + .95532 + .93015 + .90775 + .88594\right] + 88.594 = 101.976 \quad (1.3)$$

This is below the 102.020 market price of the $5^3/4$s of August 15, 2003. So, in theory, if the prices in Table 1.5 were executable and if transaction costs were small enough, one could profitably arbitrage this price difference by buying the P-STRIPS and selling the $5^3/4$s of August 15, 2003.

While most market players cannot profit from the price differences between P-STRIPS, C-STRIPS, and coupon bonds, some make a business of it. At times these professionals find it profitable to buy coupon bonds, strip them, and then sell the STRIPS. At other times these professionals find it profitable to buy the STRIPS, reconstitute them, and then sell the bonds. On the other hand, a small investor wanting a STRIPS of a particular maturity would never find it profitable to buy a coupon bond and have it stripped, for the investor would then have to sell the rest of the newly created STRIPS. Similarly, a small investor wanting to sell a particular STRIPS would never find it profitable to buy the remaining set of required STRIPS, reconstitute a coupon bond, and then sell the whole bond.

Given that investors find zeros useful relative to coupon bonds, it is not surprising some professionals can profit from differences between the two. Since most investors cannot cost-effectively strip and reconstitute by themselves, they are presumably willing to pay something for having it done for them. Therefore, when investors want more zeros they are willing to pay a premium for zeros over coupon bonds, and professionals will find it profitable to strip bonds. Similarly, when investors want fewer zeros, they are willing to pay a premium for coupon bonds over zeros and professionals will find it profitable to reconstitute bonds.

APPENDIX 1A
DERIVING THE REPLICATING PORTFOLIO

Four bonds are required to replicate the cash flows of the $10^3/_4$s of February 15, 2003. Let F_i be the face amount of bond i used in the replicating portfolio where the bonds are ordered as in Table 1.4. In problems of this structure, it is most convenient to start from the last date. In order for the portfolio to replicate the payment of 105.375 made on February 15, 2003, by the $10^3/_4$s, it must be the case that

$$\left[F_1 \times 0 + F_2 \times 0 + F_3 \times 0 + F_4 \times \left(100 + \frac{6\frac{1}{4}}{2}\right)\% \right] = 105.375 \qquad (1.4)$$

The face amounts of the first three bonds are multiplied by zero because these bonds make no payments on February 15, 2003. The advantage of starting from the end becomes apparent as equation (1.4) is easily solved:

$$F_4 = 102.182 \qquad (1.5)$$

Intuitively, one needs to buy more than 100 face value of the $6^1/_4$s of February 15, 2003, to replicate 100 face of the $10^3/_4$s of February 15, 2003, because the coupon of the $6^1/_4$s is smaller. But, since equation (1.4) matches the principal plus coupon payments of the two bonds, the coupon payments alone do not match. On any date before maturity, 100 of the $10^3/_4$s makes a payment of 5.375, while the 102.182 face of the $6^{1}/_{4}$s makes a payment of $102.182 \times 6^{1}/_{4}\%/2$ or 3.193. Therefore, the other bonds listed in Table 1.4 are required to raise the intermediate payments of the replicating portfolio to the required 5.375. And, of course, the only way to raise these intermediate payments is to buy other bonds.

Having matched the February 15, 2003, cash flow of the replicating portfolio, proceed to the August 15, 2002, cash flow. The governing equation here is

$$\left[F_1 \times 0 + F_2 \times 0 + F_3 \times \left(100 + \frac{6\frac{3}{8}}{2}\right)\% + F_4 \frac{6\frac{1}{4}\%}{2} \right] = 5.375 \qquad (1.6)$$

Since F_4 is already known, equation (1.6) can be solved showing that $F_3 = -2.114$. Continuing in this fashion, the next equations, for the cash flows on February 15, 2002, and August 15, 2001, respectively, are

$$\left[F_1 \times 0 + F_2 \times \left(100 + \frac{14\frac{1}{4}}{2}\right)\% + F_3 \times \frac{6\frac{3}{8}\%}{2} + F_4 \frac{6\frac{1}{4}\%}{2} \right] = 5.375 \qquad (1.7)$$

$$\left[F_1 \times \left(100 + \frac{7\frac{7}{8}}{2}\right)\% + F_2 \times \frac{14\frac{1}{4}\%}{2} + F_3 \times \frac{6\frac{3}{8}\%}{2} + F_4 \frac{6\frac{1}{4}\%}{2} \right] = 5.375 \qquad (1.8)$$

When solving equation (1.7), F_3 and F_4 are already known. When solving equation (1.8), F_2 is also known.

Note that if the derivation had started by matching the first cash payment on August 15, 2001, the first equation to be solved would have been (1.8). This is not possible, of course, since there are four unknowns. Therefore, one would have to solve equations (1.4), (1.6), (1.7), and (1.8) as a system of four equations and four unknowns. There is nothing wrong with proceeding in this way, but, if solving for the replicating portfolio by hand, starting from the end proves simpler.

APPENDIX 1B
APPLICATION: Treasury Triplets and High Coupon Bonds

On February 15, 2001, there were six sets of "triplets" in the Treasury market where each triplet consists of three bonds maturing on the same day. Table 1.6 lists these bonds along with their terms at issue. For example, the Treasury sale of a 20-year bond on July 5, 1983 (maturing August 15, 2003), a 10-year bond on August 16, 1993 (maturing August 15, 2003), and a five-year bond on August 17, 1998 (maturing August 15, 2003), resulted in three bonds maturing on one date.

The text of this chapter shows that to replicate a bond with cash flows on a given set of dates requires a portfolio of other bonds with cash flows on the same set of dates. Replicating a bond with 10 remaining cash flows, for example, requires a portfolio of 10 bonds with cash flows on the same set of dates. In the special case of a triplet of any maturity, however, a portfolio of two of the bonds in the triplet can replicate the cash flows of the third.

Let c_1, c_2, and c_3 be the coupon rates of the three bonds in the triplet. Consider constructing a portfolio of F_1 face amount of the first bond and F_3 face amount of the third bond to replicate one unit face amount of the second bond. For the principal payment of the replicating portfolio to equal the principal payment of the second bond, it must be the case that

$$F_1 + F_3 = 1 \qquad (1.9)$$

TABLE 1.6 Treasury Triplets as of February 15, 2001

Triplet	Coupon	Maturity	Original Term
	5.625%	5/15/01	3
May-01	8.000%	5/15/01	10
	13.125%	5/15/01	20
	5.250%	8/15/03	5
Aug-03	5.750%	8/15/03	10
	11.125%	8/15/03	20
	5.250%	5/15/04	5
May-04	7.250%	5/15/04	10
	12.375%	5/15/04	20
	6.000%	8/15/04	5
Aug-04	7.250%	8/15/04	10
	13.750%	8/15/04	20
	5.875%	11/15/04	5
Nov-04	7.875%	11/15/04	10
	11.625%	11/15/04	20
	6.500%	5/15/05	5
May-05	6.750%	5/15/05	10
	12.000%	5/15/05	20

For the interest payments of the replicating portfolio to match the coupon payments of the second bond, it must be the case that

$$c_1 F_1 + c_3 F_3 = c_2 \tag{1.10}$$

Solving equations (1.9) and (1.10) shows that

$$F_1 = \frac{c_2 - c_3}{c_1 - c_3}$$
$$F_2 = \frac{c_1 - c_2}{c_1 - c_3} \tag{1.11}$$

Applying (1.11) to the Aug-03 triplet by letting c_1=11.125%, c_2=5.75%, and c_3=5.25% shows that F_1=8.51% and F_3=91.49%. In words, a portfolio with 8.51% of its face value in the 11.125s and 91.49% of its value in the 5.25s will replicate one unit face value of the 5.75s.

Now, let P_1, P_2, and P_3 be the prices of the three bonds in the triplet. Since the portfolio described by (1.11) replicates the second bond, the arbitrage price of the second bond is given by the following equation:

$$P_2 = F_1 P_1 + F_3 P_3 \tag{1.12}$$

Continuing with the example of the Aug-03 triplet, if the prices of the bonds in descending coupon order are 114-12, 102.020, and 100-27, then the arbitrage equation predicts that

$$P_2 = 8.51\% \times (114 + 12/32) + 91.49\% \times (100 + 27/32)$$
$$= 101.995 \tag{1.13}$$

In this example, then, the market price of the middle bond is .025 greater than predicted by the arbitrage relationship (1.12).

Like all arbitrage relationships, equation (1.12) gives the prices of bonds relative to one another. Therefore, in this example it is as meaningful to say that the high coupon bond is cheap relative to the other two bonds as it is to say that the middle bond is rich relative to the other two bonds. This observation, then, allows for the investigation of the pricing of high coupon bonds. Figures 1.5 and 1.6 chart the price of the replicating portfolio minus the price of the middle bond for the May-01, Aug-03, May-04, Aug-04, and Nov-04 triplets

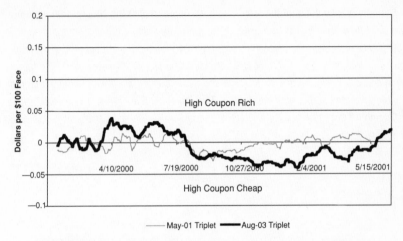

FIGURE 1.5   The Mispricing of May-01 and Aug-03 Treasury Triplets

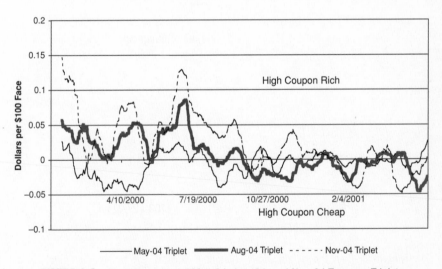

FIGURE 1.6   The Mispricing of May-04, Aug-04, and Nov-04 Treasury Triplets

from January 2000 to June 2001. The May-05 triplet was omitted because, over that time period, its middle bond was the most recently issued five-year Treasury bond. As such, this bond enjoyed financing advantages and commanded a liquidity premium. (See Chapter 15.)

A positive value in the figures means that the middle bond is cheap relative to the others, or, equivalently, that the high coupon bond is rich relative to the others. The charts show that the high coupon bonds can be both rich and cheap, although the extremes of deviations from the law of one price occur when the high coupon bonds are rich. The charts also indicate that triplets of shorter maturity tend to deviate by less than do triplets of longer maturity. The May-01 triplet, in particular, deviates very little from the law of one price. The longer the horizon of a trade, the more risky and costly it is to take advantage of deviations from fair value. Therefore, market forces do not eradicate the deviations of longer-maturity triplets from fair value so efficiently as those of the shorter-maturity triplets.

CHAPTER 2

Bond Prices, Spot Rates, and Forward Rates

While discount factors can be used to describe bond prices, investors often find it more intuitive to quantify the time value of money with rates of interest. This chapter defines spot and forward rates, shows how they can be derived from bond prices, and explains why they are useful to investors.

SEMIANNUAL COMPOUNDING

An investment of $100 at an annual rate of 5% earns $5 over the year, but when is the $5 paid? The investment is worth less if the $5 is paid at the end of the year than if $2.50 is paid after six months and another $2.50 is paid at the end of the year. In the latter case, the $2.50 paid after six months can be reinvested for six months so that the investor accumulates more than $105 by year's end.

A complete description of a fixed income investment includes the annual rate and how often that rate will be *compounded* during the year. An annual rate of 5%, compounded semiannually, means that the investor receives $^{.05}/_2$ or 2.50% every six months, which interest is reinvested at the same rate to compound the interest—that is, to earn interest on interest. An annual rate of 5% compounded quarterly means that the investor receives $^{.05}/_4$ or 1.25% every quarter while the same 5% compounded monthly means that the investor receives $^{.05}/_{12}$, or approximately .42%, every month. Because most U.S. bonds pay one-half of their annual coupons every six months, bond investors in the United States focus particularly on the case of semiannual compounding.

Investing $100 at an annual rate of 5% compounded semiannually for six months generates

$$\$100 \times \left(1 + \frac{.05}{2}\right) = \$102.50 \tag{2.1}$$

The term $(1+{.05}/{2})$ represents the per-dollar payment of principal and semiannual interest. Investing $100 at the same rate for one year instead generates

$$\$100 \times \left(1 + \frac{.05}{2}\right)^2 = \$105.0625 \tag{2.2}$$

at the end of the year. The squared term results from taking the principal amount available at the end of six months per-dollar invested, namely $(1+{.05}/{2})$, and reinvesting it for another six months, that is, multiplying again by $(1+{.05}/{2})$. Note that total funds at the end of the year are $105.0625, 6.25 cents greater than the proceeds from 5% paid annually. This 6.25 cents is compounded interest, or interest on interest.

In general, investing x at an annual rate of r compounded semiannually for T years generates

$$x\left(1 + \frac{r}{2}\right)^{2T} \tag{2.3}$$

at the end of those T years. Note that the power in this expression is $2T$ since an investment for T years compounded semiannually is, in fact, an investment for $2T$ six-month periods. For example, investing $100 for 10 years at an annual rate of 5% compounded semiannually will, after 10 years, be worth

$$\$100\left(1 + \frac{.05}{2}\right)^{20} = \$163.86 \tag{2.4}$$

Equation (2.3) can also be used to calculate a semiannually compounded *holding period* return. What is the semiannually compounded return from investing x for T years and having w at the end? Letting r be the answer, one needs to solve the following equation:

$$w = x\left(1 + \frac{r}{2}\right)^{2T} \tag{2.5}$$

Solving shows that

$$r = 2\left[\left(\frac{w}{x}\right)^{\frac{1}{2T}} - 1\right] \qquad (2.6)$$

So, for example, an initial investment of $100 that grew to $250 after 15 years earned

$$2\left[\left(\frac{250}{100}\right)^{\frac{1}{30}} - 1\right] = 6.20\% \qquad (2.7)$$

SPOT RATES

The *spot rate* is the rate on a *spot loan*, a loan agreement in which the lender gives money to the borrower at the time of the agreement. The t-year spot rate is denoted $\hat{r}(t)$. While spot rates may be defined with respect to any compounding frequency, this discussion will assume that rates are compounded semiannually.

The rate $\hat{r}(t)$ may be thought of as the semiannually compounded return from investing in a zero coupon bond that matures t years from now. For example, the C-STRIPS maturing on February 15, 2011, was quoted at 58.779 on February 15, 2001. Using equation (2.6), this implies a semiannually compounded rate of return of

$$2\left[\left(\frac{100}{58.779}\right)^{\frac{1}{20}} - 1\right] = 5.385\% \qquad (2.8)$$

Hence, the price of this particular STRIPS implies that $\hat{r}(10)=5.385\%$.

Since the price of one unit of currency maturing in t years is given by $d(t)$,

$$\hat{r}(t) = 2\left[\left(\frac{1}{d(t)}\right)^{\frac{1}{2t}} - 1\right] \qquad (2.9)$$

Rearranging terms,

$$d(t) = \frac{1}{\left(1 + \dfrac{\hat{r}(t)}{2}\right)^{2t}}$$

$$(2.10)$$

In words, equation (2.10) says that $d(t)$ equals the value of one unit of currency *discounted* for t years at the semiannually compounded rate $\hat{r}(t)$.

Table 2.1 calculates spot rates based on the discount factors reported in Table 1.2. The resulting spot rates start at about 5%, decrease to 4.886% at a maturity of two years, and then increase slowly. The relationship between spot rates and maturity, or term, is called the *term structure* of spot rates. When spot rates decrease with maturity, as in most of Table 2.1, the term structure is said to be *downward-sloping* or *inverted*. Conversely, when spot rates increase with maturity, the term structure is said to be *upward-sloping*.

Figure 2.1 graphs the *spot rate curve*, which is the collection of spot rates of all available terms, for settlement on February 15, 2001. (The construction of this graph will be discussed in Chapter 4.) Table 2.1 shows that the very start of the spot rate curve is downward-sloping. Figure 2.1 shows that the curve is upward-sloping from then until a bit past 20 years, at which point the curve slopes downward.

It is important to emphasize that spot rates of different terms are indeed different. Alternatively, the market provides different holding period returns from investments in five-year zero coupon bonds and from investments in 10-year zero coupon bonds. Furthermore, since a coupon bond

TABLE 2.1   Spot Rates Derived from the Discount Factors of Table 1.2

Time to Maturity	Discount Factor	Spot Rate
0.5	0.97557	5.008%
1	0.95247	4.929%
1.5	0.93045	4.864%
2	0.90796	4.886%
2.5	0.88630	4.887%

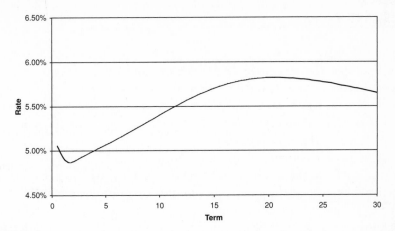

FIGURE 2.1   The Spot Rate Curve in the Treasury Market on February 15, 2001

may be viewed as a particular portfolio of zeros, the existence of a term structure of spot rates implies that each of a bond's payments must be discounted at a different rate.

To elaborate on this point, recall from Chapter 1 and equation (1.2) that the price of the $14^1/_4$s of February 15, 2002, could be expressed as follows:

$$108 + 31.5/32 = 7.125d(.5) + 107.125d(1) \tag{2.11}$$

Using the relationship between discount factors and spot rates given in equation (2.10), the price equation can also be written as

$$108 + 31.5/32 = \frac{7.125}{\left(1 + \dfrac{\hat{r}(.5)}{2}\right)} + \frac{107.125}{\left(1 + \dfrac{\hat{r}(1)}{2}\right)^2} \tag{2.12}$$

Writing a bond price in this way clearly shows that each cash flow is discounted at a rate appropriate for that cash flow's payment date. Alternatively, an investor earns a different rate of return on bond cash flows received on different dates.

FORWARD RATES

Table 2.1 shows that the six-month spot rate was about 5.01% and the one-year spot rate was about 4.93%. This means that an investor in a six-month zero would earn one-half of 5.01% over the coming six months. Similarly, an investor in a one-year zero would earn one-half of 4.93% over the coming six months. But why do two investors earn different rates of interest over the same six months?

The answer is that the one-year zero earns a different rate because the investor and the issuer of the bond have committed to roll over the principal balance at the end of six months for another six months. This type of commitment is an example of a *forward loan*. More generally, a forward loan is an agreement made to lend money at some future date. The rate of interest on a forward loan, specified at the time of the agreement as opposed to the time of the loan, is called a *forward rate*. An investor in a one-year zero can be said to have simultaneously made a spot loan for six months and a loan, six months forward, with a term of six months.

Define $r(t)$ to be the semiannually compounded rate earned on a six-month loan $t-.5$ years forward. For example, $r(4.5)$ is the semiannually compounded rate on a six-month loan, four years forward (i.e., the rate is agreed upon today, the loan is made in four years, and the loan is repaid in four years and six months). The following diagram illustrates the difference between spot rates and forward rates over the next one and one-half years: Spot rates are applicable from now to some future date, while forward rates are applicable from some future date to six months beyond that future date. For the purposes of this chapter, all forward rates are taken to be six-month rates some number of semiannual periods forward. Forward rates, however, can be defined with any term and any forward start—for example, a three-month rate two years forward, or a five-year rate 10 years forward.

$$
\left.\begin{array}{l}
\left.\begin{array}{l}
02/15/01 \text{ to } 08/15/01\}r(.5) \equiv \hat{r}(.5) \\
08/15/01 \text{ to } 02/15/02\}r(1)
\end{array}\right\}\hat{r}(1) \\
02/15/02 \text{ to } 08/15/02\}r(1.5)
\end{array}\right\}\hat{r}(1.5)
$$

The discussion now turns to the computation of forward rates given spot rates. As shown in the preceding diagram, a six-month loan zero years forward is simply a six-month spot loan. Therefore,

$$r(.5) = \hat{r}(.5) = 5.008\% \tag{2.13}$$

The second equality simply reports a result of Table 2.1. The next forward rate, $r(1)$, is computed as follows: Since the one-year spot rate is $\hat{r}(1)$, a one-year investment of \$1 grows to $[1+\hat{r}(1)/2]^2$ dollars at the end of the year. Alternatively, this investment can be viewed as a combination of a six-month loan zero years forward at an annual rate of $r(.5)$ and a six-month loan six months forward at an annual rate of $r(1)$. Viewed this way, a one-year investment of one unit of currency grows to $[1+r(.5)/2]\times[1+r(1)/2]$. Spot rates and forward rates will be consistent measures of return only if the unit investment grows to the same amount regardless of which measure is used. Therefore, $r(1)$ is determined by the following equation:

$$\left(1+\frac{r(.5)}{2}\right)\times\left(1+\frac{r(1)}{2}\right)=\left(1+\frac{\hat{r}(1)}{2}\right)^2 \tag{2.14}$$

Since $r(.5)$ and $\hat{r}(1)$ are known, equation (2.14) can be solved to show that $r(1)$ is about 4.851%.

Before proceeding with these calculations, the rates of return on six-month and one-year zeros can now be reinterpreted. According to the spot rate interpretation of the previous section, six-month zeros earn an annual 5.008% over the next six months and one-year zeros earn an annual 4.949% over the next year. The forward rate interpretation is that both six-month and one-year zeros earn an annual 5.008% over the next six months. One-year zeros, however, go on to earn an annual 4.851% over the following six months. The one-year spot rate of 4.949%, therefore, is a blend of its two forward rate components, as shown in equation (2.14).

The same procedure used to calculate $r(1)$ may be used to calculate $r(1.5)$. Investing one unit of currency for 1.5 years at the spot rate $\hat{r}(1.5)$ must result in the same final payment as investing for six months at $r(.5)$, for six months, six months forward at $r(1)$, and for six months, one year forward at $r(1.5)$. Mathematically,

$$\left(1+\frac{r(.5)}{2}\right)\times\left(1+\frac{r(1)}{2}\right)\times\left(1+\frac{r(1.5)}{2}\right)=\left(1+\frac{\hat{r}(1.5)}{2}\right)^{3} \tag{2.15}$$

Since $r(.5)$, $r(1)$, and $\hat{r}(1.5)$ are known, this equation can be solved to reveal that $r(1.5)=4.734\%$.

Generalizing this reasoning to any term t, the algebraic relationship between forward and spot rates is

$$\left(1+\frac{r(.5)}{2}\right)\times\cdots\times\left(1+\frac{r(t)}{2}\right)=\left(1+\frac{\hat{r}(t)}{2}\right)^{2t} \tag{2.16}$$

Table 2.2 reports the values of the first five six-month forward rates based on equation (2.16) and the spot rates in Table 2.1. Figure 2.2, created using the techniques of Chapter 4, graphs the spot and forward rate curves from the Treasury market for settle on February 15, 2001. Note that when the forward rate curve is above the spot rate curve, the spot rate curve is rising or sloping upward. But, when the forward rate curve is below the spot rate curve, the spot rate curve slopes downward or is falling. An algebraic proof of these propositions can be found in Appendix 2A. The text, however, continues with a more intuitive explanation.

Equation (2.16) can be rewritten in the following form:

$$\left(1+\frac{\hat{r}(t-.5)}{2}\right)^{2t-1}\times\left(1+\frac{r(t)}{2}\right)=\left(1+\frac{\hat{r}(t)}{2}\right)^{2t} \tag{2.17}$$

TABLE 2.2 · Forward Rates Derived from the Spot Rates of Table 2.1

Time to Maturity	Spot Rate	Forward Rate
0.5	5.008%	5.008%
1	4.929%	4.851%
1.5	4.864%	4.734%
2	4.886%	4.953%
2.5	4.887%	4.888%

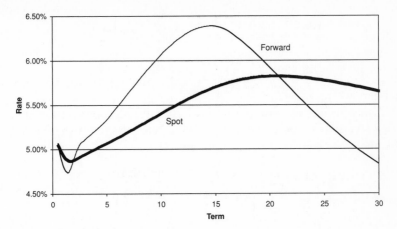

6.50%

6.00%

Rate 5.50%

5.00%

4.50%

0   5   10   15   20   25   30

Term

Forward

Spot

FIGURE 2.2   Spot and Forward Rate Curves in the Treasury Market on February 15, 2001

For expositional ease, let $t=2.5$ so that equation (2.17) becomes

$$\left(1+\frac{\hat{r}(2)}{2}\right)^{4}\times\left(1+\frac{r(2.5)}{2}\right)=\left(1+\frac{\hat{r}(2.5)}{2}\right)^{5} \qquad (2.18)$$

The intuition behind equation (2.18) is that the proceeds from a unit investment over the next 2.5 years (the right-hand side) must equal the proceeds from a spot loan over the next two years combined with a six-month loan two years forward (the left-hand side). Thus, the 2.5-year spot rate is a blend of the two-year spot rate and the six-month rate two years forward.

If $r(2.5)$ is above $\hat{r}(2)$, any blend of the two will be above $\hat{r}(2)$, and, therefore, $\hat{r}(2.5) > \hat{r}(2)$. In words, if the forward rate is above the spot rate, the spot rate curve is increasing. Similarly, if $r(2.5)$ is below $\hat{r}(2)$, any blend will be below $\hat{r}(2)$, and, therefore, $\hat{r}(2.5) < \hat{r}(2)$. In words, if the forward rate is below the spot rate, the spot rate curve is decreasing.

This section concludes by returning to bond pricing equations. In previous sections, bond prices have been expressed in terms of discount factors and in terms of spot rates. Since forward rates are just another measure of the time value of money, bond prices can be expressed in terms of forward rates as well. To review, the price of the $14\frac{1}{4}$s of February 15, 2002, may be written in either of these two ways:

$$108 + 31.5 / 32 = 7.125d(.5) + 107.125d(1) \qquad (2.19)$$

$$108 + 31.5 / 32 = \frac{7.125}{\left(1 + \dfrac{\hat{r}(.5)}{2}\right)} + \frac{107.125}{\left(1 + \dfrac{\hat{r}(1)}{2}\right)^2} \qquad (2.20)$$

Using equation (2.16) that relates forward rates to spot rates, the forward rate analog of these two pricing equations is

$$108 + 31.5 / 32 = \frac{7.125}{\left(1 + \dfrac{r(.5)}{2}\right)} + \frac{107.125}{\left(1 + \dfrac{r(.5)}{2}\right)\left(1 + \dfrac{r(1)}{2}\right)} \qquad (2.21)$$

These three bond pricing equations have slightly different interpretations, but they all serve the purpose of transforming future cash flows into a price to be paid or received today. And, by construction, all three discounting procedures produce the same market price.

MATURITY AND BOND PRICE

When are bonds of longer maturity worth more than bonds of shorter maturity, and when is the reverse true?

To gain insight into the relationship between maturity and bond price, first focus on the following more structured question. Consider five imaginary $4^7/_8\%$ coupon bonds with terms from six months to two and one-half years. As of February 15, 2001, which bond would have the greatest price?

This question can be answered, of course, by calculating the price of each of the five bonds using the discount factors in Table 1.2. Doing so produces Table 2.3 and reveals that the one and one-half year bond (August 15, 2002) has the greatest price. But why is that the case? (The forward rates, copied from Table 2.2, will be referenced shortly.)

To begin, why do the $4^7/_8$s of August 15, 2001, have a price less than 100? Since the forward rate for the first six-month period is 5.008%, a bond with a 5.008% coupon would sell for exactly 100:

$$\frac{102.504}{1 + \dfrac{.05008}{2}} = 100 \qquad (2.22)$$

TABLE 2.3 Prices of 4.875s of Various Maturities Using the Discount Factors of Table 1.2

Maturity	Price	Forward
8/15/01	99.935	5.008%
2/15/02	99.947	4.851%
8/15/02	100.012	4.734%
2/15/03	99.977	4.953%
8/15/03	99.971	4.888%

Intuitively, when a bond pays exactly the market rate of interest, an investor will not require a principal payment greater than the initial investment and will not accept any principal payment less than the initial investment.

The bond being priced, however, earns only $4^7/_8\%$ in interest. An investor buying this bond will accept this below-market rate of interest only in exchange for a principal payment greater than the initial investment. In other words, the $4^7/_8$s of August 15, 2001, will have a price less than face value. In particular, an investor buys 100 of the bond for 99.935, accepting a below-market rate of interest, but then receives a 100 principal payment at maturity.

Extending maturity from six months to one year, the coupon rate earned over the additional six-month period is $4^7/_8\%$, but the forward rate for six-month loans, six months forward, is only 4.851%. So by extending maturity from six months to one year investors earn an above-market return on that forward loan. This makes the one-year bond more desirable than the six-month bond and, equivalently, makes the one-year bond price of 99.947 greater than the six-month bond price of 99.935.

The same argument holds for extending maturity from one year to one and one-half years. The coupon rate of $4^7/_8\%$ exceeds the rate on a six-month loan one year forward, at 4.734%. As a result the August 15, 2002, bond has a higher price than the February 15, 2002, bond.

This argument works in reverse, however, when extending maturity for yet another six months. The rate on a six-month loan one and one-half years forward is 4.953%, which is greater than the $4^7/_8\%$ coupon rate. Therefore, extending maturity from August 15, 2002, to February 15, 2003, implicitly makes a forward loan at below-market rates. As a result, the price of the February 15, 2003, bonds is less than the price of the August 15, 2002, bonds.

More generally, price increases with maturity whenever the coupon rate exceeds the forward rate over the period of maturity extension. Price decreases as maturity increases whenever the coupon rate is less than the relevant forward rate.

MATURITY AND BOND RETURN

When do short-term bonds prove a better investment than long-term bonds, and when is the reverse true?

Consider the following more structured problem. Investor A decides to invest $10,000 by rolling six-month STRIPS for two and one-half years. Investor B decides to invest $10,000 in the 5¹/₄s of August 15, 2003, and to roll coupon receipts into six-month STRIPS. Starting these investments on February 15, 2001, under which scenarios will investor A have more money in two and one-half years, and under which scenarios will investor B have more money?

Refer to Table 2.2 for forward rates as of February 15, 2001. The six-month rate is known and is equal to 5.008%. Now assume for the moment that the forward rates as of February 15, 2001, are realized; that is, future six-month rates happen to match these forward rates. For example, assume that the six-month rate on February 15, 2003, will equal the six-month rate two years forward as of February 15, 2001, or 4.886%.

Under this very particular interest rate scenario, the text computes the investment results of investors A and B after two and one-half years.

Since the six-month rate at the start of the contest is 5.008%, on August 15, 2001, investor A will have

$$\$10,000 \times \left(1 + \frac{5.008\%}{2}\right) = \$10,250.40 \tag{2.23}$$

Under the assumption that forward rates are realized, the six-month rate on August 15, 2001, will have changed to 4.851%. Rolling the proceeds for the next six months at this rate, on February 15, 2002, investor A will have

$$\$10{,}250.40 \times \left(1 + \frac{4.851\%}{2}\right) = \$10{,}499.01 \qquad (2.24)$$

Applying this logic over the full two and one-half years, on August 15, 2003, investor A will have

$$\$10{,}000\left(1 + 5.008\%/_2\right)\left(1 + 4.851\%/_2\right)\left(1 + 4.734\%/_2\right)\left(1 + 4.953\%/_2\right)\left(1 + 4.888\%/_2\right) = \$11{,}282.83 \ (2.25)$$

The discussion now turns to investor B, who, on February 15, 2001, buys the $5^1/_4$s of August 15, 2003. At 100-27, the price reported in Table 1.1, \$10,000 buys \$9,916.33 face value of the bond. August 15, 2001, brings a coupon payment of

$$\$9{,}916.33 \times \frac{5.25\%}{2} = \$260.30 \qquad (2.26)$$

Investor B will reinvest this interest payment, reinvest the proceeds on February 15, 2002, reinvest those proceeds on August 15, 2002, and so on, until August 15, 2003. Under the assumption that the original forward rates are realized, investor B's total income from the \$260.30 received on August 15, 2001, is

$$\$260.30\left(1 + 4.851\%/_2\right)\left(1 + 4.734\%/_2\right)\left(1 + 4.953\%/_2\right)\left(1 + 4.887\%/_2\right) = \$286.52 \qquad (2.27)$$

Investor B will receive another coupon payment of \$260.30 on February 15, 2002. This payment will also be reinvested to August 15, 2003, growing to

$$\$260.30\left(1 + 4.734\%/_2\right)\left(1 + 4.953\%/_2\right)\left(1 + 4.887\%/_2\right) = \$279.74 \qquad (2.28)$$

Proceeding in this fashion, the coupon payments received on August 15, 2002, and February 15, 2003, grow to \$273.27 and \$266.67, respectively. The coupon payment of \$260.30 received on August 15, 2003, of course, has no time to earn interest on interest.

On August 15, 2003, investor B will receive a principal payment of \$9,916.33 from the $5^1/_4$s of August 15, 2003, and collect the accumulated proceeds from coupon income of \$286.52+\$279.74+\$273.27+\$266.67+

$260.30 or $1,366.50. In total, then, investor B will receive $9,916.33+ $1,366.50 or $11,282.83. As shown in equation (2.25), investor A will accumulate exactly the same amount.

It is no coincidence that when the six-month rate evolves according to the initial forward rate curve investors rolling short-term bonds and investors buying long-term bonds perform equally well. Recall that an investment in a bond is equivalent to a series of forward loans at rates given by the forward rate curve. In the preceding example, the $5^1/_4$s of August 15, 2003, lock in a six-month rate of 5.008% on February 15, 2001, a six-month rate of 4.851% on August 15, 2001, and so on. Therefore, if the six-month rate does turn out to be 4.851% on August 15, 2001, and so on, the $5^1/_4$s of August 15, 2003, lock in the actual succession of six-month rates. Equivalently, investors in this bond do exactly as well as investors who roll over short-term bonds.

When does investor A, the investor who rolls over six-month investments, do better than B, the bond investor? Say, for example, that the six-month rate remains at its initial value of 5.008% through August 15, 2003. Then investor A earns a semiannual rate of 5.008% every six months while investor B locked in the forward rates of Table 2.2, all at or below 5.008%. Investor B does get to reinvest coupon payments at 5.008%, but still winds up behind investor A.

When does investor B do better than investor A? Say, for example, that on the day after the initial investments (i.e., February 16, 2001) the six-month rate fell to 4.75% and stayed there through August 15, 2003. Then investor B, who has locked in the now relatively high forward rates of Table 2.2, will do better than investor A, who must roll over the investment at 4.75%.

In general, investors who roll over short-term investments do better than investors in longer-term bonds when the realized short-term rates exceed the forward rates built into bond prices. Investors in bonds do better when the realized short-term rates fall below these forward rates. There are, of course, intermediate situations in which some of the realized rates are higher than the respective forward rates and some are lower. In these cases more detailed calculations are required to determine which investor class does better.

Investors with a view on short-term rates—that is, with an opinion on the direction of future short-term rates—may use the insight of this section to choose among bonds with different maturity dates. Comparing the forward rate curve with views on rates by inspection or by more careful computations will reveal which bonds are cheap and which bonds are rich with respect to forecasts. It should be noted that the interest rate risk of long-term bonds differs from that of short-term bonds. This point will be studied extensively in Part Two.

TREASURY STRIPS, CONTINUED

In the context of the law of one price, Chapter 1 compared the discount factors implied by C-STRIPS, P-STRIPS, and coupon bonds. With the definitions of this chapter, spot rates can be compared. Figure 2.3 graphs the spot rates implied from C- and P-STRIPS prices for settlement on February 15, 2001. The graph shows in terms of rate what Figure 1.4 showed in terms of price. The shorter-maturity C-STRIPS are a bit rich (lower spot rates) while the longer-maturity C-STRIPS are very slightly cheap (higher spot rates). Notice that the longer C-STRIPS appear at first to be cheaper in Figure 1.4 than in Figure 2.3. As will become clear in Part Two, small changes in the spot rates of longer-maturity zeros result in large price differences. Hence the relatively small rate cheapness of the longer-maturity C-STRIPS in Figure 2.3 is magnified into large price cheapness in Figure 1.4.

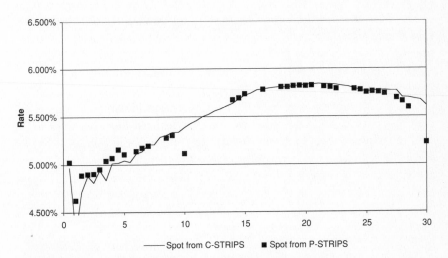

FIGURE 2.3 Spot Curves Implied by C-STRIPS and P-STRIPS Prices on February 15, 2001

The two very rich P-STRIPS in Figure 2.3, one with 10 and one with 30 years to maturity, derive from the most recently issued bonds in their respective maturity ranges. As mentioned in Chapter 1 and as to be discussed in Chapter 15, the richness of these bonds and their underlying P-STRIPS is due to liquidity and financing advantages.

Chapter 4 will show a spot rate curve derived from coupon bonds (shown earlier as Figure 2.1) that very much resembles the spot rate curve derived from C-STRIPS. This evidence for the law of one price is deferred to that chapter, which also discusses curve fitting and smoothness: As can be seen by comparing Figures 2.1 and 2.3, the curve implied from the raw C-STRIPS data is much less smooth than the curve constructed using the techniques of Chapter 4.

APPENDIX 2A
THE RELATION BETWEEN SPOT AND FORWARD RATES AND THE SLOPE OF THE TERM STRUCTURE

The following proposition formalizes the notion that the term structure of spot rates slopes upward when forward rates are above spot rates. Similarly, the term structure of spot rates slopes downward when forward rates are below spot rates.

Proposition 1: If the forward rate from time t to time $t+.5$ exceeds the spot rate to time t, then the spot rate to time $t+.5$ exceeds the spot rate to time t.

Proof: Since $r(t+.5) > \hat{r}(t)$,

$$1 + \frac{r(t+.5)}{2} > 1 + \frac{\hat{r}(t)}{2} \tag{2.29}$$

Multiplying both sides by $(1+\hat{r}(t)/2)^{2t}$,

$$\left[1 + \frac{\hat{r}(t)}{2}\right]^{2t}\left[1 + \frac{r(t+.5)}{2}\right] > \left[1 + \frac{\hat{r}(t)}{2}\right]^{2t+1} \tag{2.30}$$

Using the relationship between spot and forward rates given in equation (2.17), the left-hand side of (2.30) can be written in terms of $\hat{r}(t+.5)$:

$$\left[1+\frac{\hat{r}(t+.5)}{2}\right]^{2t+1} > \left[1+\frac{\hat{r}(t)}{2}\right]^{2t+1} \tag{2.31}$$

But this implies, as was to be proved, that

$$\hat{r}(t+.5) > \hat{r}(t) \tag{2.32}$$

Proposition 2: If the forward rate from time t to time $t+.5$ is less than the spot rate to time t, then the spot rate to time $t+.5$ is less than the spot rate to time t.

Proof: Reverse the inequalities in the proof of proposition 1.

CHAPTER 3

Yield-to-Maturity

Chapters 1 and 2 showed that the time value of money can be described by discount factors, spot rates, or forward rates. Furthermore, these chapters showed that each cash flow of a fixed income security must be discounted at the factor or rate appropriate for the term of that cash flow.

In practice, investors and traders find it useful to refer to a bond's *yield-to-maturity*, or *yield*, the single rate that when used to discount a bond's cash flows produces the bond's market price. While indeed useful as a summary measure of bond pricing, yield-to-maturity can be misleading as well. Contrary to the beliefs of some market participants, yield is not a good measure of relative value or of realized return to maturity. In particular, if two securities with the same maturity have different yields, it is not necessarily true that the higher-yielding security represents better value. Furthermore, a bond purchased at a particular yield and held to maturity will not necessarily earn that initial yield.

Perhaps the most appealing interpretation of yield-to-maturity is not recognized as widely as it should be. If a bond's yield-to-maturity remains unchanged over a short time period, that bond's realized total rate of return equals its yield.

This chapter aims to define and interpret yield-to-maturity while highlighting its weaknesses. The presentation will show when yields are convenient and safe to use and when their use is misleading.

DEFINITION AND INTERPRETATION

Yield-to-maturity is the single rate such that discounting a security's cash flows at that rate produces the security's market price. For example, Table

1.1 reported the $6^{1}/_{4}$s of February 15, 2003, at a price of 102-18$^{1}/_{8}$ on February 15, 2001. The yield-to-maturity of the $6^{1}/_{4}$s, y, is defined such that

$$\frac{3.125}{1+y/2} + \frac{3.125}{(1+y/2)^2} + \frac{3.125}{(1+y/2)^3} + \frac{103.125}{(1+y/2)^4} = 102 + 18.125/32 \quad (3.1)$$

Solving for y by trial and error or some numerical method shows that the yield-to-maturity of this bond is about 4.8875%.[1] Note that given yield instead of price, it is easy to solve for price. As it is so easy to move from price to yield and back, yield-to-maturity is often used as an alternate way to quote price. In the example of the $6^{1}/_{4}$s, a trader could just as easily bid to buy the bonds at a yield of 4.8875% as at a price of 102-18$^{1}/_{8}$.

While calculators and computers make price and yield calculations quite painless, there is a simple and instructive formula with which to relate price and yield. The definition of yield-to-maturity implies that the price of a T-year security making semiannual payments of $c/2$ and a final principal payment of F is[2]

$$P(T) = \sum_{t=1}^{2T} \frac{c/2}{(1+y/2)^t} + \frac{F}{(1+y/2)^{2T}} \quad (3.2)$$

Note that there are $2T$ terms being added together through the summation sign since a T-year bond makes $2T$ semiannual coupon payments. This sum equals the present value of all the coupon payments, while the final term equals the present value of the principal payment. Using the case of the $6^{1}/_{4}$s of February 15, 2003, as an example of equation (3.2), $T=2$, $c=6.25$, $y=4.8875\%$, $F=100$, and $P=102.5665$.

Using the fact that[3]

$$\sum_{t=a}^{b} z^t = \frac{z^a - z^{b+1}}{1-z} \quad (3.3)$$

---

[1]Many calculators, spreadsheets, and other computer programs are available to compute yield-to-maturity given bond price and vice versa.

[2]A more general formula, valid when the next coupon is due in less than six months, is given in Chapter 5.

[3]The proof of this fact is as follows. Let $S = \sum_{t=a}^{b} z^t$. Then, $zS = \sum_{t=a+1}^{b+1} z^t$ and $S - zS = z^a - z^{b+1}$. Finally, dividing both sides of this equation by $1-z$ gives equation (3.3).

with $z=1/(1+y/2)$, $a=1$, and $b=2T$, equation (3.2) becomes

$$P(T) = \frac{c}{y}\left[1 - \left(\frac{1}{1+y/2}\right)^{2T}\right] + F\left(\frac{1}{1+y/2}\right)^{2T} \qquad (3.4)$$

Several conclusions about the price-yield relationship can be drawn from equation (3.4). First, when $c=100y$ and $F=100$, $P=100$. In words, when the coupon rate equals the yield-to-maturity, bond price equals face value, or par. Intuitively, if it is appropriate to discount all of a bond's cash flows at the rate y, then a bond paying a coupon rate of c is paying the market rate of interest. Investors will not demand to receive more than their initial investment at maturity nor will they accept less than their initial investment at maturity. Hence, the bond will sell for its face value.

Second, when $c>100y$ and $F=100$, $P>100$. If the coupon rate exceeds the yield, then the bond sells at a *premium* to par, that is, for more than face value. Intuitively, if it is appropriate to discount all cash flows at the yield, then, in exchange for an above-market coupon, investors will demand less than their initial investment at maturity. Equivalently, investors will pay more than face value for the bond.

Third, when $c<100y$, $P<100$. If the coupon rate is less than the yield, then the bond sells at a *discount* to par, that is, for less than face value. Since the coupon rate is below market, investors will demand more than their initial investment at maturity. Equivalently, investors will pay less than face value for the bond.

Figure 3.1 illustrates these first three implications of equation (3.4). Assuming that all yields are 5.50%, each curve gives the price of a bond with a particular coupon as a function of years remaining to maturity. The bond with a coupon rate of 5.50% has a price of 100 at all terms. With 30 years to maturity, the 7.50% and 6.50% coupon bonds sell at substantial premiums to par, about 129 and 115, respectively. As these bonds mature, however, the value of above-market coupons falls: receiving a coupon 1% or 2% above market for 20 years is not as valuable as receiving those above-market coupons for 30 years. Hence, the prices of these premium bonds fall over time until they are worth par at maturity. This effect of time on bond prices is known as the *pull to par*.

Conversely, the 4.50% and 3.50% coupon bonds sell at substantial discounts to par, at about 85 and 71, respectively. As these bonds mature,

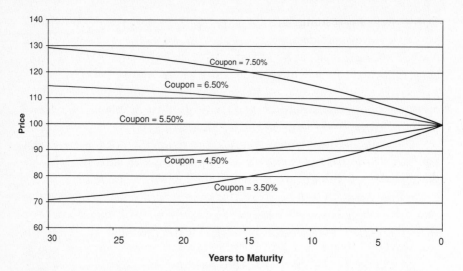

FIGURE 3.1   Prices of Bonds Yielding 5.5% with Various Coupons and Years to Maturity

the disadvantage of below-market coupons falls. Hence, the prices of these bonds rise to par as they mature.

It is important to emphasize that to illustrate simply the pull to par Figure 3.1 assumes that the bonds yield 5.50% at all times. The actual price paths of these bonds over time will differ dramatically from those in the figure depending on the realization of yields.

The fourth implication of equation (3.4) is the *annuity* formula. An annuity with semiannual payments is a security that makes a payment $c/2$ every six months for T years but never makes a final "principal" payment. In terms of equation (3.4), $F=0$, so that the price of an annuity, $A(T)$ is

$$A(T) = \frac{c}{y}\left[1 - \left(\frac{1}{1+y/2}\right)^{2T}\right] \tag{3.5}$$

For example, the value of a payment of $^{6.50}/_2$ every six months for 10 years at a yield of 5.50% is about 46.06.

The fifth implication of equation (3.4) is that as T gets very large, $P=c/y$. In words, the price of a *perpetuity*, a bond that pays coupons forever, equals the coupon divided by the yield. For example, at a yield of 5.50%, a 6.50 coupon in perpetuity will sell for $^{6.50}/_{5.50\%}$ or approximately

118.18. While perpetuities are not common, the equation $P=c/y$ provides a fast, order-of-magnitude approximation for any coupon bond with a long maturity. For example, at a yield of 5.50% the price of a 6.50% 30-year bond is about 115 while the price of a 6.50 coupon in perpetuity is about 118. Note, by the way, that an annuity paying its coupon forever is also a perpetuity. For this reason the perpetuity formula may also be derived from (3.5) with T very large.

The sixth and final implication of equation (3.4) is the following. If a bond's yield-to-maturity over a six-month period remains unchanged, then the annual total return of the bond over that period equals its yield-to-maturity. This statement can be proved as follows. Let P_0 and $P_{1/2}$ be the price of a T-year bond today and the price[4] just before the next coupon payment, respectively, assuming that the yield remains unchanged over the six-month period. By the definition of yield to maturity,

$$P_0 = \frac{c/2}{1+y/2} + \frac{c/2}{(1+y/2)^2} + \cdots + \frac{1+c/2}{(1+y/2)^{2T}} \tag{3.6}$$

and

$$P_{1/2} = \frac{c}{2} + \frac{c/2}{1+y/2} + \cdots + \frac{1+c/2}{(1+y/2)^{2T-1}} \tag{3.7}$$

Note that after six months have passed, the first coupon payment is not discounted at all since it will be paid in the next instant, the second coupon payment is discounted over one six-month period, and so forth, until the principal plus last coupon payment are discounted over $2T-1$ six-month periods. Inspection of (3.6) and (3.7) reveals that

$$P_{1/2} = (1+y/2)P_0 \tag{3.8}$$

Rearranging terms,

$$y = 2\left(\frac{P_{1/2}}{P_0} - 1\right) \tag{3.9}$$

---

[4]In this context, price is the full price. The distinction between flat and full price will be presented in Chapter 4.

The term in parentheses is the return on the bond over the six-month period, and twice that return is the bond's annual return. Therefore, if yield remains unchanged over a six-month period, the yield equals the annual return, as was to be shown.

YIELD-TO-MATURITY AND SPOT RATES

Previous chapters showed that each of a bond's cash flows must be discounted at a rate corresponding to the timing of that particular cash flow. Taking the $6^1/_4$s of February 15, 2003, as an example, the present value of the bond's cash flows can be written as a function of its yield-to-maturity, as in equation (3.1), or as a function of spot rates. Mathematically,

$$
\begin{aligned}
102 + 18.125/32 &= \frac{3.125}{1+y/2} + \frac{3.125}{\left(1+y/2\right)^2} + \frac{3.125}{\left(1+y/2\right)^3} + \frac{103.125}{\left(1+y/2\right)^4} \\
&= \frac{3.125}{1+\hat{r}_s/2} + \frac{3.125}{\left(1+\hat{r}_1/2\right)^2} + \frac{3.125}{\left(1+\hat{r}_{1.5}/2\right)^3} + \frac{103.125}{\left(1+\hat{r}_2/2\right)^4}
\end{aligned}
\tag{3.10}
$$

Equations (3.10) clearly demonstrate that yield-to-maturity is a summary of all the spot rates that enter into the bond pricing equation. Recall from Table 2.1 that the first four spot rates have values of 5.008%, 4.929%, 4.864%, and 4.886%. Thus, the bond's yield of 4.8875% is a blend of these four rates. Furthermore, this blend is closest to the two-year spot rate of 4.886% because most of this bond's value comes from its principal payment to be made in two years.

Equations (3.10) can be used to be more precise about certain relationships between the spot rate curve and the yield of coupon bonds.

First, consider the case of a flat term structure of spot rates; that is, all of the spot rates are equal. Inspection of equations (3.10) reveals that the yield must equal that one spot rate level as well.

Second, assume that the term structure of spot rates is upward-sloping; that is,

$$
\hat{r}_2 > \hat{r}_{1.5} > \hat{r}_1 > \hat{r}_s
\tag{3.11}
$$

In that case, any blend of these four rates will be below $\hat{r}_2$. Hence, the yield of the two-year bond will be below the two-year spot rate.

Third, assume that the term structure of spot rates is downward-sloping. In that case, any blend of the four spot rates will be above $\hat{r}_2$. Hence, the yield of the two-year bond will be above the two-year spot rate. To summarize,

Spot rates downward-sloping:　Two-year bond yield above two-year spot rate

Spot rates flat:　Two-year bond yield equal to two-year spot rate

Spot rates upward-sloping:　Two-year bond yield below two-year spot rate

To understand more fully the relationships among the yield of a security, its cash flow structure, and spot rates, consider three types of securities: zero coupon bonds, coupon bonds selling at par (par coupon bonds), and par nonprepayable mortgages. Mortgages will be discussed in Chapter 21. For now, suffice it to say that the cash flows of a traditional, nonprepayable mortgage are *level*; that is, the cash flow on each date is the same. Put another way, a traditional, nonprepayable mortgage is just an annuity.

Figure 3.2 graphs the yields of the three security types with varying

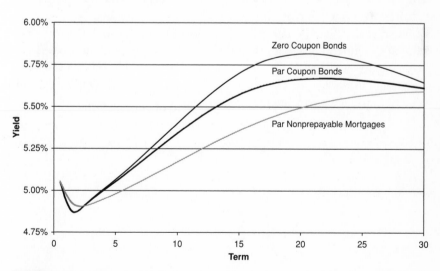

FIGURE 3.2　Yields of Fairly Priced Zero Coupon Bonds, Par Coupon Bonds, and Par Nonprepayable Mortgages

terms to maturity on February 15, 2001. Before interpreting the graph, the text will describe how each curve is generated.

The yield of a zero coupon bond of a particular maturity equals the spot rate of that maturity. Therefore, the curve labeled "Zero Coupon Bonds" is simply the spot rate curve to be derived in Chapter 4.

This chapter shows that, for a bond selling at its face value, the yield equals the coupon rate. Therefore, to generate the curve labeled "Par Coupon Bonds," the coupon rate is such that the present value of the resulting bond's cash flows equals its face value. Mathematically, given discount factors and a term to maturity of T years, this coupon rate c satisfies

$$\frac{100c}{2} \sum_{t=1}^{2T} d(t/2) + 100d(T) = 100 \tag{3.12}$$

Solving for c,

$$c = \frac{2\left[1 - d(T)\right]}{\sum_{t=1}^{2T} d(t/2)} \tag{3.13}$$

Given the discount factors to be derived in Chapter 4, equation (3.13) can be solved for each value of T to obtain the par bond yield curve.

Finally, the "Par Nonprepayable Mortgages" curve is created as follows. For comparability with the other two curves, assume that mortgage payments are made every six months instead of every month. Let X be the semiannual mortgage payment. Then, with a face value of 100, the present value of mortgage payments for T years equals par only if

$$X \sum_{t=1}^{2T} d(t/2) = 100 \tag{3.14}$$

Or, equivalently, only if

$$X = 100 \Big/ \sum_{t=1}^{2T} d(t/2) \tag{3.15}$$

Furthermore, the yield of a par nonprepayable T-year mortgage is defined such that

$$100 = X \sum_{t=1}^{2T} \frac{1}{\left(1 + y_T/2\right)^t} \tag{3.16}$$

Given a set of discount factors, equations (3.15) and (3.16) may be solved for y_T using a spreadsheet function or a financial calculator. The "Par Non-prepayable Mortgages" curve of Figure 3.2 graphs the results.

The text now turns to a discussion of Figure 3.2. At a term of .5 years, all of the securities under consideration have only one cash flow, which, of course, must be discounted at the .5-year spot rate. Hence, the yields of all the securities at .5 years are equal. At longer terms to maturity, the behavior of the various curves becomes more complex.

Consistent with the discussion following equations (3.10), the downward-sloping term structure at the short end produces par yields that exceed zero yields, but the effect is negligible. Since almost all of the value of short-term bonds comes from the principal payment, the yields of these bonds will mostly reflect the spot rate used to discount those final payments. Hence, short-term bond yields will approximately equal zero coupon yields.

As term increases, however, the number of coupon payments increases and discounting reduces the relative importance of the final principal payment. In other words, as term increases, intermediate spot rates have a larger impact on coupon bond yields. Hence, the shape of the term structure can have more of an impact on the difference between zero and par yields. Indeed, as can be seen in Figure 3.2, the upward-sloping term structure of spot rates at intermediate terms eventually leads to zero yields exceeding par yields. Note, however, that the term structure of spot rates becomes downward-sloping after about 21 years. This shape can be related to the narrowing of the difference between zero and par yields. Furthermore, extrapolating this downward-sloping structure past the 30 years recorded on the graph, the zero yield curve will cut through and find itself below the par yield curve.

The qualitative behavior of mortgage yields relative to zero yields is the same as that of par yields, but more pronounced. Since the cash flows of a mortgage are level, mortgage yields are more balanced averages of spot rates than are par yields. Put another way, mortgage yields will be more influenced than par bonds by intermediate spot rates. Consequently, if the term structure is downward-sloping everywhere, mortgage yields will be higher than par bond yields. And if the term structure is upward-sloping everywhere, mortgage yields will be lower than par bond yields. Figure 3.2 shows both these effects. At short terms, the term structure is downward-sloping and mortgage yields are above par bond yields. Mortgage yields then fall below par yields as the term structure slopes upward. As the term structure again becomes downward-sloping, however, mortgage yields are poised to rise above par yields to the right of the displayed graph.

YIELD-TO-MATURITY AND RELATIVE VALUE: THE COUPON EFFECT

All securities depicted in Figure 3.2 are fairly priced. In other words, their present values are properly computed using a single discount function or term structure of spot or forward rates. Nevertheless, as explained in the previous section, zero coupon bonds, par coupon bonds, and mortgages of the same maturity have different yields to maturity. Therefore, it is incorrect to say, for example, that a 15-year zero is a better investment than a 15-year par bond or a 15-year mortgage because the zero has the highest yield. The impact of coupon level on the yield-to-maturity of coupon bonds with the same maturity is called the *coupon effect*. More generally, yields across fairly priced securities of the same maturity vary with the cash flow structure of the securities.

The size of the coupon effect on February 15, 2001, can be seen in Figure 3.2. The difference between the zero and par rates is about 1.3 basis points[5] at a term of 5 years, 6.1 at 10 years, and 14.1 at 20 years. After that the difference falls to 10.5 basis points at 25 years and to 2.8 at 30 years. Unfortunately, these quantities cannot be easily extrapolated to other yield curves. As the discussions in this chapter reveal, the size of the coupon effect depends very much on the shape of the term structure of interest rates.

---

[5]A basis point is 1% of .01, or .0001. The difference between a rate of 5.00% and 5.01%, for example, is one basis point.

YIELD-TO-MATURITY AND REALIZED RETURN

Yield-to-maturity is sometimes described as a measure of a bond's return if held to maturity. The argument is made as follows. Repeating equation (3.1), the yield-to-maturity of the $6^1/_4$s of February 15, 2003, is defined such that

$$\frac{3.125}{1+y/2} + \frac{3.125}{\left(1+y/2\right)^2} + \frac{3.125}{\left(1+y/2\right)^3} + \frac{103.125}{\left(1+y/2\right)^4} = 102 + 18.125/32 \qquad (3.17)$$

Multiplying both sides by $(1+y/2)^4$ gives

$$3.125\left(1+\tfrac{y}{2}\right)^3 + 3.125\left(1+\tfrac{y}{2}\right)^2 + 3.125\left(1+\tfrac{y}{2}\right) + 103.125 = 102.5664\left(1+\tfrac{y}{2}\right)^4 \quad (3.18)$$

The interpretation of the left-hand side of equation (3.18) is as follows. On August 15, 2001, the bond makes its next coupon payment of 3.125. Semi-annually reinvesting that payment at rate y through the bond's maturity of February 15, 2003, will produce $3.125(1+y/2)^3$. Similarly, reinvesting the coupon payment paid on February 15, 2002, through the maturity date at the same rate will produce $3.125(1+y/2)^2$. Continuing with this reasoning, the left-hand side of equation (3.18) equals the sum one would have on February 15, 2003, assuming a semiannually compounded coupon reinvestment rate of y. Equation (3.18) says that this sum equals $102.5664(1+y/2)^4$, the purchase price of the bond invested at a semiannually compounded rate of y for two years. Hence it is claimed that yield-to-maturity is a measure of the realized return to maturity.

Unfortunately, there is a serious flaw in this argument. There is absolutely no reason to assume that coupons will be reinvested at the initial yield-to-maturity of the bond. The reinvestment rate of the coupon paid on August 15, 2001, will be the 1.5-year rate that prevails six months from the purchase date. The reinvestment rate of the following coupon will be the one-year rate that prevails one year from the purchase date, and so forth. The realized return from holding the bond and reinvesting coupons depends critically on these unknown future rates. If, for example, all of the reinvestment rates turn out to be higher than the original yield, then the realized yield-to-maturity will be higher than the original yield-to-maturity. If, at the other extreme, all of the reinvestment rates turn out to be lower than the original yield, then the realized yield will be lower than the original yield. In any case, it is extremely unlikely that the realized yield of a coupon bond held to maturity will equal its original yield-to-maturity. The uncertainty of the realized yield relative to the original yield because coupons are invested at uncertain future rates is often called *reinvestment risk*.

CHAPTER 4

Generalizations and Curve Fitting

While introducing discount factors, bond pricing, spot rates, forward rates, and yield, the first three chapters simplified matters by assuming that cash flows appear in even six-month intervals. This chapter generalizes the discussion of these chapters to accommodate the reality of cash flows paid at any time. These generalizations include accrued interest built into a bond's total transaction price, compounding conventions other than semiannual, and curve fitting techniques to estimate discount factors for any time horizon. The chapter ends with a trading case study that shows how curve fitting may lead to profitable trade ideas.

ACCRUED INTEREST

To ensure that cash flows occur every six months from a settlement date of February 15, 2001, the bonds included in the examples of Chapters 1 through 3 all matured on either August 15 or on February 15 of a given year. Consider now the $5^1/_2$s of January 31, 2003. Since this bond matures on January 31, its semiannual coupon payments all fall on July 31 or January 31. Therefore, as of February 15, 2001, the latest coupon payment of the $5^1/_2$s had been on January 31, 2001, and the next coupon payment was to be paid on July 31, 2001.

Say that investor B buys $10,000 face value of the $5^1/_2$s from investor S for settlement on February 15, 2001. It can be argued that investor B is not entitled to the full semiannual coupon payment of $10,000×^{5.50\%}/_2$ or $275 on July 31, 2001, because, as of that time, investor B will have held the bond for only about five and a half months. More precisely, since there are 166 days between February 15, 2001, and July 31, 2001, while there are 181 days between January 31, 2001, and July 31, 2001, investor B should receive only $(^{166}/_{181})\times\$275$ or $252.21 of the coupon payment. Investor S, who held the bond from the latest coupon date of January 31, 2001, to February 15, 2001, should collect the rest of the $275 coupon or $22.79. To allow investors B and S to go their separate ways after settlement, market convention dictates that investor B pay $22.79 of *accrued interest* to investor S on the settlement date of February 15, 2001. Furthermore, having paid this $22.79 of accrued interest, investor B may keep the entire $275 coupon payment of July 31, 2001. This market convention achieves the desired split of that coupon payment: $22.79 for investor S on February 15, 2001, and $275–$22.79 or $252.21 for investor B on July 31, 2001. The following diagram illustrates the working of the accrued interest convention from the point of view of the buyer.

Say that the quoted or *flat* price of the $5^1/_2$s of January 31, 2003 on February 15, 2001, is $101\text{-}4^5/_8$. Since the accrued interest is $22.79 per $10,000 face or .2279%, the *full* price of the bond is defined to be $101+^{4.625}/_{32}+.2279$ or 101.3724. Therefore, on $10,000 face amount, the *invoice* price—that is, the money paid by the buyer and received by the seller—is $10,137.24.

The bond pricing equations of the previous chapters have to be generalized to take account of accrued interest. When the accrued interest of a bond is zero—that is, when the settlement date is a coupon payment date—the flat and full prices of the bond are equal. Therefore, the previous chapters could, without ambiguity, make the statement that the price of a bond equals the present value of its cash flows. When accrued interest is not zero the statement must be generalized to say that the amount paid or received for a bond (i.e., its full price) equals the present value of its cash flows. Letting P be the bond's flat price, AI its accrued interest, and PV the present value function,

$$P + AI = PV(\text{future cash flows}) \qquad (4.1)$$

Equation (4.1) reveals an important principle about accrued interest. The particular market convention used in calculating accrued interest does not really matter. Say, for example, that everyone believes that the accrued interest convention in place is too generous to the seller because instead of being made to wait for a share of the interest until the next coupon date the seller receives that share at settlement. In that case, equation (4.1) shows that the flat price adjusts downward to mitigate this seller's advantage. Put another way, the only quantity that matters is the invoice price (i.e., the money that changes hands), and it is this quantity that the market sets equal to the present value of the future cash flows.

With an accrued interest convention, if yield does not change then the quoted price of a bond does not fall as a result of a coupon payment. To see this, let P^b and P^a be the quoted prices of a bond right before and right after a coupon payment of $c/2$, respectively. Right before a coupon date the accrued interest equals the full coupon payment and the present value of the next coupon equals that same full coupon payment. Therefore, invoking equation (4.1),

$$P^b + c/2 = c/2 + PV\left(\text{cash flows after the next coupon}\right) \qquad (4.2)$$

Simplifying,

$$P^b = PV\left(\text{cash flows after the next coupon}\right) \qquad (4.3)$$

Right after the next coupon payment, accrued interest equals zero. Therefore, invoking equation (4.1) again,

$$P^a + 0 = PV\left(\text{cash flows after the next coupon}\right) \qquad (4.4)$$

Clearly $P^a=P^b$ so that the flat price does not fall as a result of the coupon payment. By contrast, the full price does fall from $P^b+c/2$ before the coupon payment to $P^a=P^b$ after the coupon payment.[1]

COMPOUNDING CONVENTIONS

Since the previous chapters assumed that cash flows arrive every six months, the text there could focus on semiannually compounded rates. Allowing for the possibility that cash flows arrive at any time requires the consideration of other compounding conventions. After elaborating on this point, this section argues that the choice of convention does not really matter. Discount factors are traded, directly through zero coupon bonds or indirectly through coupon bonds. Therefore, it is really discount factors that summarize market prices for money on future dates while interest rates simply quote those prices with the convention deemed most convenient for the application at hand.

When cash flows occur in intervals other than six months, semiannual compounding is awkward. Say that an investment of one unit of currency at a semiannual rate of 5% grows to $1+.05/2$ after six months. What happens to an investment for three months at that semiannual rate? The answer cannot be $1+.05/4$, for then a six-month investment would grow to $(1+.05/4)^2$ and not $1+.05/2$. In other words, the answer $1+.05/4$ implies quarterly compounding. Another answer might be $(1+.05/2)^{1/2}$. While having the virtue that a six-month investment does indeed grow to $1+.05/2$, this solution essentially implies interest on interest within the six-month period. More precisely, since $(1+.05/2)^{1/2}$ equals $(1+.0497/4)$, this second solution implies quarterly compounding at a different rate. Therefore, if cash flows do arrive on a quarterly basis it is more intuitive to discard semiannual compounding and use quarterly compounding instead. More generally, it is most intuitive to use the compounding convention corresponding to the smallest cash flow frequency—monthly compounding for payments that

---

[1]Note that the behavior of quoted bond prices differs from that of stocks that do not have an accrued dividend convention. Stock prices fall by approximately the amount of the dividend on the day ownership of the dividend payment is established. The accrued convention does make more sense in bond markets than in stock markets because dividend payment amounts are generally much less certain than coupon payments.

may arrive any month, daily compounding for payments that may arrive any day, and so on. Taking this argument to the extreme and allowing cash flows to arrive at any time results in *continuous compounding*. Because of its usefulness in the last section of this chapter and in the models to be presented in Part Three, Appendix 4A describes this convention.

Having made the point that semiannual compounding does not suit every context, it must also be noted that the very notion of compounding does not suit every context. For coupon bonds, compounding seems natural because coupons are received every six months and can be reinvested over the horizon of the original bond investment to earn interest on interest. In the *money market*, however (i.e., the market to borrow and lend for usually one year or less), investors commit to a fixed term and interest is paid at the end of that term. Since there is no interest on interest in the sense of reinvestment over the life of the original security, the money market uses the more suitable choice of *simple* interest rates.[2]

One common simple interest convention in the money market is called the *actual/360* convention.[3] In that convention, lending $1 for *d* days at a rate of *r* will earn the lender an interest payment of

$$\frac{rd}{360} \qquad\qquad (4.5)$$

dollars at the end of the *d* days.

It can now be argued that compounding conventions do not really matter so long as cash flows are properly computed. Consider a loan from February 15, 2001, to August 15, 2001, at 5%. Since the number of days from February 15, 2001, to August 15, 2001, is 181, if the 5% were an actual/360 rate, the interest payment would be

---

[2]Contrary to the discussion in the text, personal, short-term time deposits often quote compound interest rates. This practice is a vestige of Regulation Q that limited the rate of interest banks could pay on deposits. When unregulated mutual funds began to offer higher rates, banks competed by increasing compounding frequency. This expedient raised interest payments while not technically violating the legal rate limits.

[3]The accrued interest convention in the Treasury market, described in the previous section, uses the *actual/actual* convention: The denominator is set to the actual number of days between coupon payments.

$$\frac{5\% \times 181}{360} = 2.5139\% \tag{4.6}$$

If the compounding convention were different, however, the interest payment would be different. Equations (4.7) through (4.9) give interest payments corresponding to 5% loans from February 15, 2001, to August 15, 2001, under semiannual, monthly, and daily compounding, respectively:

$$\frac{5\%}{2} = 2.5\% \tag{4.7}$$

$$\left(1 + \frac{5\%}{12}\right)^6 - 1 = 2.5262\% \tag{4.8}$$

$$\left(1 + \frac{5\%}{365}\right)^{181} - 1 = 2.5103\% \tag{4.9}$$

Clearly the market cannot quote a rate of 5% under each of these compounding conventions at the same time: Everyone would try to borrow using the convention that generated the lowest interest payment and try to lend using the convention that generated the highest interest payment. There can be only one market-clearing interest payment for money from February 15, 2001, to August 15, 2001.

The most straightforward way to think about this single clearing interest payment is in terms of discount factors. If today is February 15, 2001, and if August 15, 2001, is considered to be $^{181}/_{365}$ or .4959 years away, then in the notation of Chapter 1 the fair market interest payment is

$$\frac{1}{d(.4959)} - 1 \tag{4.10}$$

If, for example, $d(.4959){=}.97561$, then the market interest payment is 2.50%. Using equations (4.6) through (4.9) as a model, one can immediately solve for the simple, as well as the semiannual, monthly, and daily compounded rates that produce this market interest payment:

$$\frac{181 r_s}{360} = 2.50\% \Rightarrow r_s = 4.9724\%$$

$$\frac{r_{sa}}{2} = 2.50\% \Rightarrow r_{sa} = 5\%$$

$$\left(1 + \frac{r_m}{12}\right)^6 - 1 = 2.50\% \Rightarrow r_m = 4.9487\%$$

$$\left(1 + \frac{r_d}{365}\right)^{181} - 1 = 2.50\% \Rightarrow r_d = 4.9798\%$$

(4.11)

In summary, compounding conventions must be understood in order to determine cash flows. But with respect to valuation, compounding conventions do not matter: The market-clearing prices for cash flows on particular dates are the fundamental quantities.

YIELD AND COMPOUNDING CONVENTIONS

Consider again the $5\frac{1}{2}$s of January 31, 2003, on February 15, 2001. While the coupon payments from July 31, 2001, to maturity are six months apart, the coupon payment on July 31, 2001, is only five and a half months or, more precisely, 166 days away. How does the market calculate yield in this case?

The convention is to discount the next coupon payment by the factor

$$\frac{1}{\left(1 + y/2\right)^{166/181}}$$

(4.12)

where y is the yield of the bond and 181 is the total number of days in the current coupon period. Despite the interpretive difficulties mentioned in the previous section, this convention aims to quote yield as a semiannually compounded rate even though payments do not occur in six-month intervals. In any case, coupon payments after the first are six months apart and can be discounted by powers of $1/(1+y/2)$. In the example of the $5\frac{1}{2}$s of January 31, 2003, the price-yield formula becomes

$$P_{Full} = \frac{2.75}{\left(1 + y/2\right)^{166/181}} + \frac{2.75}{\left(1 + y/2\right)^{166/181}\left(1 + y/2\right)} + \frac{2.75}{\left(1 + y/2\right)^{166/181}\left(1 + y/2\right)^2}$$

$$+ \frac{102.75}{\left(1 + y/2\right)^{166/181}\left(1 + y/2\right)^3}$$

(4.13)

Or, simplifying slightly,

$$P_{Full} = \frac{2.75}{\left(1+y/2\right)^{166/181}} + \frac{2.75}{\left(1+y/2\right)^{166/181+1}} + \frac{2.75}{\left(1+y/2\right)^{166/181+2}} + \frac{102.75}{\left(1+y/2\right)^{166/181+3}} \quad (4.14)$$

(With the full price given earlier as 101.3724, y=4.879%.)

More generally, if a bond's first coupon payment is paid in a fraction τ of the next coupon period and if there are N semiannual coupon payments after that, then the price-yield relationship is

$$P_{Full} = \frac{c}{2}\sum_{i=0}^{N}\frac{1}{\left(1+y/2\right)^{i+\tau}} + \frac{1}{\left(1+y/2\right)^{N+\tau}} \quad (4.15)$$

BAD DAYS

The phenomenon of *bad days* is an example of how confusing yields can be when cash flows are not exactly six months apart. On August 31, 2001, the Treasury sold a new two-year note with a coupon of $3^{5}/_{8}$% and a maturity date of August 31, 2003. The price of the note for settlement on September 10, 2001, was 100-7$^{1}/_{4}$ with accrued interest of .100138 for a full price of 100.32670. According to convention, the cash flow dates of the bond are assumed to be February 28, 2002, August 31, 2002, February 28, 2003, and August 31, 2003. In actuality, August 31, 2002, is a Saturday so that cash flow is made on the next business day, September 3, 2002. Also, the maturity date August 31, 2003, is a Sunday so that cash flow is made on the next business day, September 2, 2003. Table 4.1 lists the conventional and true cash flow dates.

Reading from the conventional side of the table, the first coupon is 171 days away out of a 181-day coupon period. As discussed in the previous section, the first exponent is set to $^{171}/_{181}$ or .94475. After that, exponents are increased by one. Hence the conventional yield of the note is defined by the equation

$$100.32670 = \frac{1.8125}{\left(1+y/2\right)^{.94475}} + \frac{1.8125}{\left(1+y/2\right)^{1.94475}} + \frac{1.8125}{\left(1+y/2\right)^{2.94475}} + \frac{101.8125}{\left(1+y/2\right)^{3.94475}} \quad (4.16)$$

Solving, the conventional yield equals 3.505%.

Unfortunately, this calculation overstates yield by assuming that the cash flows arrive sooner than they actually do. To correct for this effect, the market uses a *true yield*. Reading from the true side of Table 4.1, the first cash flow date is unchanged and so is the first exponent. The cash flow date on September 3, 2002, however, is 187 days from the previous coupon payment. Defining the number of semiannual periods between these dates to be $^{187}/_{(365/2)}$ or 1.02466, the exponent for the second cash flow date is .94475+1.02466 or 1.96941. Proceeding in this way to calculate the rest of the exponents, the true yield is defined to satisfy the following equation:

$$100.32670 = \frac{1.8125}{\left(1+y/2\right)^{.94475}} + \frac{1.8125}{\left(1+y/2\right)^{1.96941}} + \frac{1.8125}{\left(1+y/2\right)^{2.94475}} + \frac{101.8125}{\left(1+y/2\right)^{3.96393}} \quad (4.17)$$

Solving, the true yield is 3.488%, or 1.7 basis points below the conventional yield.

Professional investors do care about this difference. The lesson for this section, however, is that forcing semiannual compounding onto dates that are not six months apart can cause confusion. This confusion, the coupon effect, and the other interpretive difficulties of yield might suggest avoiding yield when valuing one bond relative to another.

INTRODUCTION TO CURVE FITTING

Sensible and smooth discount functions and rate curves are useful in a variety of fixed income contexts.

TABLE 4.1 Dates for Conventional and True Yield Calculations

Conventional Dates	Days to Next Cash Flow Date	Conventional Exponents	True Dates	Days to Next Cash Flow Date	True Exponents
8/31/01	181		8/31/01	181	
9/10/01	171		9/10/01	171	
2/28/02	184	0.94475	2/28/02	187	0.94475
8/31/02	181	1.94475	9/3/02	178	1.96941
2/28/03	184	2.94475	2/28/03	186	2.94475
8/31/03		3.94475	9/2/03		3.96393

First, equipped with a discount function derived from Treasury bond prices and the techniques discussed in this section, one can value any particular Treasury bond and compare this predicted value with the bond's market price. If the market price is below the prediction, the bond might be said to be trading cheap, while if the market price exceeds the predicted price, the bond might be said to be trading rich. The trading case study at the end of this chapter describes a trade generated by this use of a discount function. Despite the U.S. Treasury market context of Part One, this kind of rich-cheap analysis may be applied to any bond market.

Second, in some markets not all market prices are known, and discount functions may be used to fill in the missing prices. In the swap market, for example (see Chapter 18), swaps of certain maturities are widely traded while swaps of other maturities hardly trade at all. As market participants need to know the values of their existing positions, and as they do occasionally trade those illiquid swaps, discount functions derived from traded swaps are commonly used to value illiquid swaps.

Third, a discount function from one market might be used to value securities in another market or to value cash flows from private transactions. Part Three, which uses discount factors to price derivatives like options, is an example of the former use. Another example, discussed in Chapter 18, is an asset swap spread, which measures the cheapness or richness of a security relative to, typically, the swap curve. An investor might have a view on the fair level of asset swap spreads or may compare the asset swap spreads of several securities as part of a rich-cheap analysis.

Chapters 1 through 3 extracted discount factors at six-month intervals from the prices of bonds that mature at six-month intervals. This procedure is of limited usefulness because discount factors of terms separated by more or less than six-month intervals are often required. In addition, on most pricing dates there may not be a single bond maturing in an exact multiple of six months, let alone enough bonds to allow for the computation of a set of discount factors. Therefore, this section introduces methods of extracting an entire discount function from the set of traded bond prices.

To illustrate the role of discount factors at intervals other than six months, consider, for example, the pricing equation for the $5\frac{1}{2}$s of July 31, 2003, as of February 15, 2001. Noting that the cash flows of this bond occur in 166, 350, 531, and 715 days, the pricing equation is

$$P_{Full} = 2.75d\left(\frac{166}{365}\right) + 2.75d\left(\frac{350}{365}\right) + 2.75d\left(\frac{531}{365}\right) + 102.75d\left(\frac{715}{365}\right) \quad (4.18)$$

Writing the arguments of the discount function in years,

$$P_{Full} = 2.75d(.45) + 2.75d(.96) + 2.75d(1.45) + 102.75d(1.96) \quad (4.19)$$

The collection of discount factors for .5 years, 1 year, 1.5 years, and so on, cannot be used directly to price this bond, nor can this bond be used directly to derive those discount factors.

A common but unsatisfactory technique of estimating an entire discount function from market data is called *linear yield interpolation*. This technique begins with a short list of bonds spanning the maturity range of interest. For reasons to become apparent shortly, bonds best suited for this purpose are those that sell near par and those liquid enough to generate accurate price quotations. Bonds selected with these criteria in mind are listed along with their yields and prices in Table 4.2. While an effort has been made to select bonds with prices near par, in some maturity ranges there simply are no bonds with prices near par. Thus, the inclusion of bonds with prices somewhat far from par is the result of a compromise among wanting liquid bonds, bonds from each maturity range, and prices close to par.

The next step is to construct a yield curve by connecting these few data points with straight lines, as illustrated in Figure 4.1. This linear interpola-

TABLE 4.2 Bonds Selected for Linear Yield Interpolation

Coupon	Maturity	Yield	Price
5.500%	07/31/01	5.001%	100.219
5.875%	11/30/01	4.964%	100.688
5.625%	11/30/02	4.885%	101.244
5.250%	08/15/03	4.887%	100.844
5.875%	11/15/04	4.988%	102.988
6.500%	10/15/06	5.107%	106.766
5.500%	02/15/08	5.157%	101.996
6.500%	02/15/10	5.251%	108.871
11.250%	02/15/15	5.483%	155.855
6.125%	08/15/29	5.592%	107.551

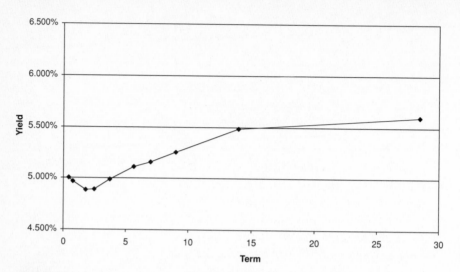

FIGURE 4.1   Linear Yield Interpolation in the Treasury Market on February 15, 2001

tion does provide an estimate of yield at any maturity, but, since yield depends on coupon (see Chapter 3), this complete yield curve still does not contain enough information from which to derive discount factors. To get around this difficulty, it is common practice to assume that the yield curve in Figure 4.1 represents yields on par bonds or a *par yield curve*. Under that assumption each point on the yield curve gives a bond's coupon, which is its yield, and that bond's price, which is par. Then, equations like (4.19) may be combined to describe the relationship between traded bond prices and discount factors. Returning to an earlier point, the necessity of assuming that the interpolated curve represents yields of par bonds is why it is best, in the first place, to select bonds that do sell near par.

Figure 4.1 looks innocuous enough, and the discount function implied by these yields, shown in Figure 4.2, also looks innocuous enough. The implications of linear yield interpolation for spot and forward rates, however, shown in Figure 4.3, are quite disappointing. The spot rate curve is a bit bumpy, but this problem tends to arise from any technique that forces a discount function to price all given bond prices exactly. This issue will be discussed further. But two other problems with the spot rate curve in Figure 4.3 are caused by linear yield interpolation itself.

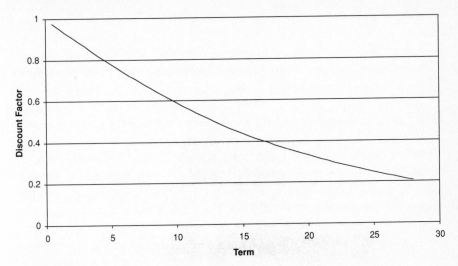

FIGURE 4.2 The Discount Function from the Linear Yield Interpolation of Figure 4.1

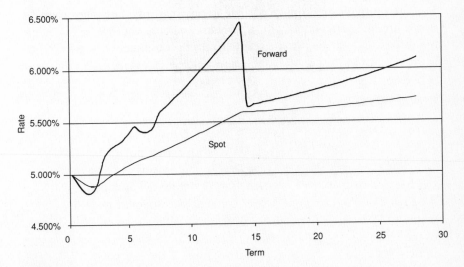

FIGURE 4.3 Spot and Forward Rates from the Linear Yield Interpolation of Figure 4.1

First, there is an unrealistic kink in the curve at all the yield data points, although the effect is most noticeable at about 14 years. This kink is caused by linear interpolation because the slope of the line drawn to the left of a given data point may be quite different from the slope of the line drawn to the right of that data point.

To describe the second problem with the spot rate curve in Figure 4.3, it is necessary to define *concave* and *convex* regions of a curve. If a line connecting two points on a curve is below the curve, the curve is said to be concave. On the other hand, if a line connecting two points on the curve is above the curve, the curve is said to be convex. See Figure 4.4.

Returning to the spot rate curve of Figure 4.3, the segments from about 5.5 years to about 14 years and from about 14 years to 30 years are convex. These convex segments are mathematical artifacts of linear yield interpolation. They are problematic because, as argued in Chapter 10, beyond a certain point, like five years, rate curves should be concave. Furthermore, simple plots of spot rates (see Figures 2.3 and 4.5) and more sophisticated smoothing techniques (see Figure 4.9) usually produce concave spot rate curves beyond five years.

The shortcomings of the spot rate curve in Figure 4.3 pale in comparison with the shortcomings of the forward rate curve in that figure. While the discussion of Chapter 10 formalizes why the bumpiness of the forward rate curve is unreasonable, particularly at longer maturities, the

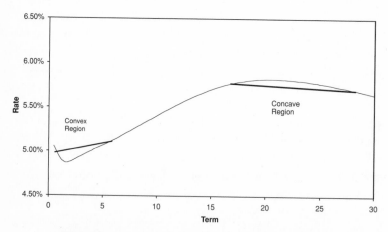

FIGURE 4.4 Convex and Concave Regions of a Curve

large jump in the forward rate at 14 years clearly defies economic sense. The graph says that investors demand 6.44% to lend money for six months, 14 years forward while they require only 5.65% to lend money for six months, 14.5 years forward. The jump in the forward rate curve is, of course, a direct consequence of the pronounced kink in the yield and spot rate curves at that point. Along the lines of the discussion in Chapter 2 relating forward rates to changes in spot rates, a rapidly rising spot rate curve implies an even more rapidly rising forward curve. Similarly, if the spot rate curve suddenly rises at a much slower rate, the forward rate curve must drop precipitously.

It is generally true that the shortcomings of a curve fitting technique are least noticeable in the discount function, more noticeable in the spot rate curve, and particularly noticeable in the forward rate curve. To illustrate why this is true, consider the following simple example. On February 15, 2001, the yields or spot rates on 9.5-year and 10-year C-STRIPS were 5.337% and 5.385%, respectively. These rates imply prices of 60.6307 and 58.7794, respectively, and a six-month rate 9.5 years forward of 6.299%. Were the yield on the 10-year C-STRIPS to be one basis point lower, at 5.375%, a change of less than .2%, the price of the 10-year C-STRIPS would rise by less than .1%. The forward rate, however, would fall by 20.1 basis points to 6.098%, a change of about 3.2%. This magnification of the change in the spot rate may be understood by recalling from Chapter 2 that a spot rate is a geometric average of all previous forwards. Therefore, it takes a relatively large move in one of the forward rates to move the average by one basis point, particularly at long maturities when many forwards make up the average. In any case, for the purposes of this section, these observations imply that any problem with the spot rate curve, due to the fitting technique or to the underlying data, will hardly be noticed in the discount function but will be magnified in the forward rate curve.

The failure of linear yield interpolation to produce smooth rate curves is caused by the technique itself. However, smooth curves are difficult to achieve with any technique that forces the discount function to price many bonds exactly. To illustrate this point and to motivate the reasons for occasionally allowing fitted discount functions to miss market data, return to the STRIPS market discussed in previous chapters.

Chapter 2 showed the spot rate curve on February 15, 2001, derived from the prices of C-STRIPS. Using the tools of Chapter 2, this spot curve, by definition, correctly prices all C-STRIPS maturing in six-month increments out to 30 years. Figure 4.5 reproduces this spot rate curve (originally shown in Figure 2.3) along with the smooth spot rate curve derived later in this chapter from coupon bond prices and presented in Figure 4.9.

The two curves are in many ways very similar. The main problem with the C-STRIPS curve is that the raw data do not produce an economically sensible, smooth curve. In other words, there are two possibilities. One, the smooth curve better represents spot rates and the price quotes making up the C-STRIPS curve are slightly unreliable or include excessively rich and cheap bonds. Two, the underlying spot rate curve is better represented by the C-STRIPS curve of Figure 4.5. The first possibility seems more likely. As the trading case study at the end of this chapter shows, however, this conclusion absolutely does not imply that deviations of data from the smooth curve should be ignored. Quite the contrary: deviations from a smooth curve might indicate trading and investing opportunities.

The shortcomings of the C-STRIPS spot curve are, as expected, magnified in the forward curve. Figure 4.6 shows the forward rate curve from the raw C-STRIPS data along with the smooth forward curve derived below and presented in Figure 4.9.

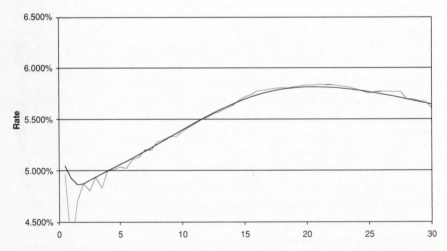

FIGURE 4.5 Spot Curves from Raw C-STRIPS Data and from a Curve Fitting Procedure

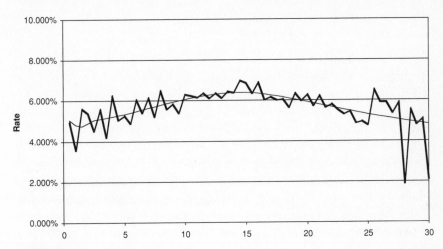

FIGURE 4.6 Forward Curves from Raw C-STRIPS Data and from a Curve Fitting Procedure

PIECEWISE CUBICS

The first step in building a smooth curve is to assume a *functional form* for the discount function, for spot rates, or for forward rates. For example, an extremely simple functional form for the discount function might be a cubic polynomial:

$$d(t) = 1 + at + bt^2 + ct^3 \qquad (4.20)$$

Given constants a, b, and c, equation (4.20) provides the discount factor for any term t. (Note that the intercept is one so that $d(0)=1$.) The goal, therefore, is to find a set of constants such that the discount function (4.20) reasonably approximates the discount function in the market, that is, such that bond values computed with (4.20) reasonably approximate market prices. Substituting (4.20) into a set of bond pricing equations like (4.19) produces a system of equations that link the constants a, b, and c to bond prices. Some optimization method can then be used to find the constants that best match market bond prices.

Alternatively, one could assume that the spot rate or forward rate function is a single cubic polynomial. In the case of the spot rate,

$$\hat{r}(t) = r_0 + at + bt^2 + ct^3 \tag{4.21}$$

As discussed in the previous section, when cash flows arrive at arbitrary dates, the continuous compounding convention is most convenient. In that case equation (4.21) describes the continuously compounded spot rate of any term, and r_0 is the *instantaneous* spot rate, that is, the spot rate appropriate for discounting over the next instant.

As it turns out, a single cubic polynomial is too simple a function to capture the complexity of many empirically observed term structures. The spot curve of Figure 2.1, for example, cannot be reproduced adequately by a single cubic. A common solution is to use a *piecewise cubic polynomial*, that is, a single function built by joining several cubic polynomials together at some set of *knot points*. For example, a spot rate curve from 0 to 30 years might be built from three cubic polynomials with knot points at 10 and 20 years. The first cubic segment would apply for terms less than 10 years, the next for terms between 10 and 20 years, and the last for terms from 20 to 30 years. Mathematically the spot function may be written as:

$$\hat{r}(t) = \begin{cases} \hat{r}_0 + a_1 t + b_1 t^2 + c_1 t^3 & t \le 10 \\ \hat{r}(10) + a_2(t-10) + b_2(t-10)^2 + c_2(t-10)^3 & 10 \le t \le 20 \\ \hat{r}(20) + a_3(t-20) + b_3(t-20)^2 + c_3(t-20)^3 & 20 \le t \le 30 \end{cases} \tag{4.22}$$

with $\hat{r}(10)$ and $\hat{r}(20)$ as shorthand for the value of the first segment at 10 years and the second segment at 20 years, respectively. This specification clearly allows for many more shapes than does a single cubic over the entire maturity range.

Note that the three cubic polynomials in (4.22) are structured so that the first two are equal at a term of 10 years while the second two are equal at a term of 20 years. This means that the resulting spot rate curve is *continuous*, that is, it doesn't jump when the function switches from one cubic to the next. But, as linear yield interpolation showed, it is also desirable to avoid places in which the slope of the spot rate curve jumps. A function that knits cubic polynomials together in a way that ensures continuity of the function, of its slope, and even of the slope of the slope, is called a *piecewise cubic spline*. While a general discussion of this method is beyond the scope of this book, Appendix 4B shows how to create a spline for the system (4.22).

APPLICATION: Fitting the Term Structure in the U.S. Treasury Market on February 15, 2001

This section fits a piecewise cubic spline to the Treasury market on February 15, 2001, and, in the process, discusses the considerations that go into fitting term structures. No claim is made that the particular fit presented here is perfect or that the particular fitting procedure used here is the best for all markets on all dates. In fact, an important theme of this section is that term structure fitting is a good part art.

The fitting process begins by gathering the sample of bonds and bond prices to be used. The objective is to collect a sample that can sensibly belong to the same term structure. In bond markets this is not as easy as it sounds. In the Treasury market there are several categories of bonds that require special attention. First, some bonds have call provisions. Second, the most recently issued bonds in each maturity range are particularly liquid and may command a liquidity premium. Third, some bonds trade *special* in the financing market (see Chapter 15) and command a premium because of their financing advantages. These bonds usually include, but are not limited to, the most recently issued bonds. Fourth, bonds issued a relatively long time ago, or very *seasoned* bonds, tend to trade differently from more recently issued bonds in the same maturity range. In February 2001, this category included the relatively high coupon bonds maturing in about five years or less (see Chapter 1).

There are three ways to handle this sample construction problem. The first and perhaps most common solution is to discard all of the bonds in the previously mentioned categories. The downside to this solution, of course, is that valuable price information is lost in the process. This cost is particularly acute in the case of the most liquid bonds since these bonds comprise the vast majority of trading in the Treasury market. The second relatively common but not particularly useful solution is to weight the noncomparable bonds less than the rest of the bonds during the fitting process. The problem with this approach is that the categories of difficult bonds tend to trade persistently rich or persistently cheap to other bonds. Therefore, while lower weights do lower the distortions that result from including these bonds, they leave the bias intact. The third solution is the most difficult and least common but potentially the best: to adjust the prices or yields of the noncomparable bonds to make them comparable. Chapter 15, for example, illustrates how to adjust the yields of bonds that trade special in the financing markets. The models of Part Three, as another example, could be used to remove the option component of callable bond yields. In any case, the benefits of this solution are proportional to the quality of the models used to make the adjustments.

In practice, the best way to deal with the sample construction problem is probably a mix of the first and third solutions. Discard the problematic bonds whose prices contain relatively little information because they are illiquid or because they trade in the same maturity range as bonds of better liquidity; discard other problematic bonds for which no sensible price adjustment can be discovered; adjust the prices of the rest.

Despite this recommendation for best practice, the fitting example of this section takes the easy path of discarding all the problematic bonds. In particular: (1) Bonds with extremely short maturities are discarded. (2) Among bonds with exactly the same maturity, only the bond with the lowest coupon is selected. Given the secular decline of interest rates in the recent past, this rule tends to discard very seasoned bonds. (3) Bonds with financing advantages are discarded. (4) For reasons to be explained more fully, of the remaining bonds the three with the longest maturities are also discarded. For expositional purposes, however, these three bonds appear in the graphs to follow.

To give an idea of the shape of the term structure, Figure 4.7 plots the yields of the selected bonds. (The gap between the 10- and 15-year maturity sectors is due to the absence of any but callable bonds in that region.) The sharp turns of the yields in the maturity region less than about 4.5 years make this region the most challenging to fit well. Therefore, the knot points of the spot rate function are placed more densely in this region than in any

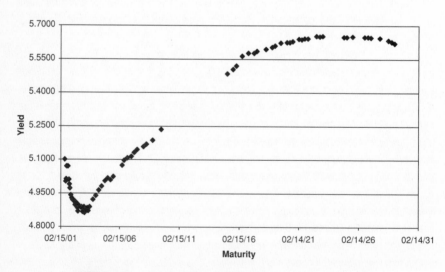

FIGURE 4.7   Treasury Coupon Bond Yields on February 15, 2001

other. For this example, the knot points are placed at .75, 1.5, 2.25, 5.18, 16.25, 25, and 30 years, making a total of seven cubic segments.

The next step is to choose the constants of the cubic segments so that the resulting spot rate function describes the data well. To describe one way to do this, let y_i be the market yield of bond i, let $\hat{y}_i$ be the predicted yield of bond i using the fitted spot rate function, and let N be the number of bonds in the sample. Then, define the *root mean square error* (RMSE) of the fit to be

$$\text{RMSE} \equiv \sqrt{\frac{1}{N}\sum_{i=1}^{N}\left(y_i - \hat{y}_i\right)^2} \tag{4.23}$$

Since $y_i - \hat{y}_i$ is the error of the assumed function in fitting the market data, RMSE may be interpreted like a standard deviation of these errors. Thus, a RMSE of 3 basis points means that ±3 basis points correspond to a 1-standard deviation error of the fit, ±6 basis points correspond to a 2-standard deviation error, and so on. In any case, choosing the parameters of the cubic segments to minimize the RMSE, which is the equivalent of the regression criterion of least squares, is one way to fit the spot rate function.

RMSE could have been defined in terms of price rather than yield error. The problem with minimizing price errors is that prices of short-term bonds are much less sensitive to yield errors than those of long-term bonds (see Chapter 6). As a result, weighting price errors equally actually weights the yield errors of short-term bonds much less than the yield errors of long-term bonds. To the extent that the goal is to produce a realistic rate function across all maturities, minimizing price errors is not so useful as minimizing yield errors.

Minimizing (4.23) in this example produces a RMSE of 1.2 basis points; more detailed results are given in the next two figures. Figure 4.8 graphs the error of each bond. The greatest errors are in the shorter-term bonds. Note that the errors of the last three bonds are shown in the figure, but, as mentioned earlier and discussed shortly, these bonds are not included in the RMSE. Finally, the greatest error of −3.5 basis points comes from the $4^3/_4$s of November 15, 2008. Since errors are defined as the market yield minus the model yield, a negative error may be interpreted to mean that the market yield is low or that the security is rich. The trading case study at the end of this chapter shows that one could have profited from the results of this fitting analysis by shorting the 11/08s and simultaneously buying neighboring bonds.

Figure 4.9, which is the same as Figure 2.2, graphs the spot and forward rates that emerge from the fit. The economic meaning of the dip and rise in the early years is described in Chapters 10 and 17. Both spot and forward rates are smooth. At the longer end of the curve, spot rates are concave. One criticism of the fit is that the longer end of the forward rate curve looks a bit convex.

Each stage of curve fitting is part art and requires a good deal of experimentation. The

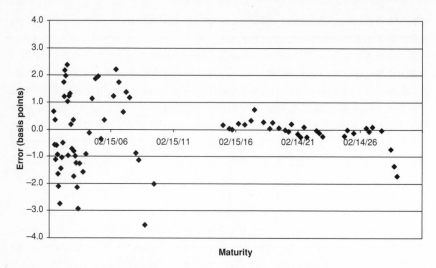

FIGURE 4.8 Pricing Errors of Chosen Curve Fit

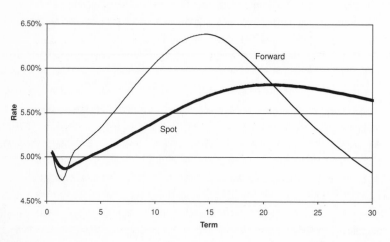

FIGURE 4.9 Fitted Spot and Forward Rate Curves in the Treasury Market on February 15, 2001

choice of bonds to be included, the number of cubic segments, and the placement of the knot points must be varied according to the contexts of time and market. A spot rate function that works well for the U.S. Treasury market will not necessarily work for the Japanese government bond market. A function that worked well for the U.S. Treasury market in 1998 will not necessarily work today. To illustrate several things that can go wrong when fitting a term structure, a poor fit of the U.S. Treasury market on February 15, 2001, is now presented.

The data selected for this purpose are the same as before except that the three longest bonds are included. The number of cubic segments is seven, as before, but the knot points are unsuitably placed at 5, 6, 7, 8, 9, 10, and 30 years. The RMSE of the resulting fit is 1.35 basis points, only .1 worse than before. But, as shown in Figures 4.10 and 4.11, this poor fit is substantially inferior to the previous, good fit.

Comparing Figure 4.10 with Figure 4.8, the errors of the poor fit are a bit worse than those of the good fit, particularly in the short end. Figure 4.11 shows that the spot and forward rate curves of the poor fit wiggle too much to be believable. Also, the forward rate curve seems to drop a bit too precipitously at the long end. What went wrong?

In the good fit, many knot points were placed in the shorter end to capture the curvature of market yields in that region. The poor fit, with only one segment out to five years, cannot capture this curvature as well. As a result, data in the shorter end are matched par-

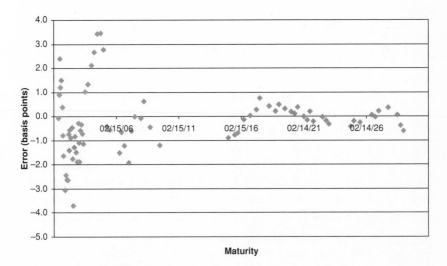

FIGURE 4.10   Pricing Errors of Alternate Curve Fit

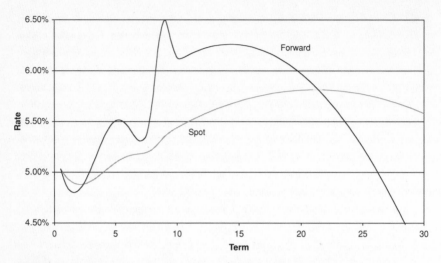

FIGURE 4.11   Alternate Fitted Spot and Forward Curves in the Treasury Market on
February 15, 2001

ticularly poorly. This illustrates the problem of *under fitting*: the functional form does not
have enough flexibility to mimic the data.

In the good fit, the knot points were not placed very densely between 5 and 10 years
because the curvature of market yields in that region did not require it. In the poor fit, five
out of seven of the cubic segments are placed there. The result is that the rate functions
have the flexibility to match the data too closely. This illustrates the problem of *over fitting*:
the wiggles fit the data well at the expense of financial realism. In fact, the 4³/₄s of November 15, 2008, with an error of .5 basis points, do not stand out in the poor fit as particularly
rich. Hence the close match to the data in this region actually performs a disservice by hid-
ing a potentially profitable trade.

The good fit recognized the existence of some curvature in the long end and therefore
used two cubic segments there, one from 16.25 to 25 years and one from 25 to 30 years.
The poor fit uses only one segment from 10 to 30 years. Some under fitting results. But,
examining the error graphs carefully, the poor fit matches the three longest-maturity bonds
better than the good fit. Since these yields slope steeply downward (see Figure 4.7), fitting
these bonds more closely results in a dramatically descending forward rate curve. The
good fit chose not to use these bonds for precisely this reason. The financial justification
for discarding these bonds is that their yields have been artificially dragged down by the liquidity advantages of even longer bonds (that had also been discarded). In other words, be-

cause these longer bonds sell at a premium justified by their liquidity advantages, and because investors are reluctant to price neighboring bonds too differently, the yields of the three bonds in question are artificially low. There is not necessarily a right answer here. The choice is between the following two stories. According to the good fit, the three bonds are slightly rich, between .7 and 1.7 basis points, and the forward curve falls 110 basis points from 20 to 30 years. According to the poor fit, the three bonds are from fair to −.6 basis points cheap, and the forward curve falls 175 basis points from 20 to 30 years.[4] One piece of evidence supporting the choice to drop the three bonds is that the C-STRIPS curve in Figure 4.5 closely corresponds to the long end of the good fit.

This section uses the U.S. Treasury market to discuss curve fitting. In principle, discount functions from other bond markets are extracted using the same set of considerations. In particular, a thorough knowledge of the market in question is required in order to obtain reasonable results.

TRADING CASE STUDY: A 7s-8s-9s Butterfly

The application of the previous section indicates that the $4^{3}/_{4}$s of November 15, 2008, are rich relative to the fitted term structure as of February 15, 2001. This application investigates whether or not one could profit from this observation.

If the 11/08s are indeed rich relative to other bonds, a trader could short them in the hope that they would cheapen, that is, in the hope that their prices would fall relative to other bonds. To be more precise, the hope would be that a repeat of the fitting exercise at some point in the future would show that the 11/08s were less rich, fair, or even cheap relative to the fitted term structure.

The trader probably wouldn't short the 11/08s *outright* (i.e., without buying some other bonds), because that would create too much market risk. If interest rates fall, an outright short position in the 11/08s would probably lose money even if the trader had been right and the 11/08s did cheapen relative to other bonds.

---

[4]Experience with the magnitude of the convexity effect on forward rates helps guide choices like these. See Chapter 10.

One way the trader might protect a short 11/08 position from market risk would be to buy a nearby issue, like the $6^1/8$s of August 15, 2007. In that case, if bond prices rise across the board the trader would lose money on the 11/08s but make money on the 8/07s. Similarly, if bond prices fall across the board the trader would make money on the 11/08s but lose money on the 8/07s. Therefore, if the 11/08s did cheapen relative to other bonds, the trader would make money regardless of the direction of the market.

The problem with buying the 8/07s against the 11/08 short position is that the yield curve might *flatten*; that is, yields of shorter maturities might rise relative to yields of longer maturities. For example, if yields in the seven-year sector rise while yields in the eight-year sector remain unchanged, the trade could lose money even if the 11/08s did cheapen relative to other bonds.

For protection against curve risk, the trader could, instead of buying only 8/07s to hedge market risk, buy some 8/07s and some 6s of 8/09. Then, assume that the yield curve flattens in that yields in the seven-year sector rise, yields in the eight-year sector stay the same, and yields in the nine-year sector fall. The 8/07 position would lose money, the 11/08 position would be flat, but the 8/09s would make money. Similarly, if the yield curve *steepens* (i.e., if yields of short maturities fall relative to yields of long maturities), the opposite would happen and the trade would probably not make or lose money. Therefore, if the 11/08s cheapen relative to other bonds, the trade will make money regardless of whether the curve flattens or steepens.

This type of three-security trade is called a *butterfly*. The security in the middle of the maturity range, in this case the 11/08s, might be called the center, middle, or body, while the outer securities are called the *wings*. In general, butterfly trades are designed to profit from a perceived mispricing while protecting against market and curve risk.

Bloomberg, an information and analytic system used widely in the financial industry, has several tools with which to analyze butterfly trades. Figure 4.12 reproduces Bloomberg's BBA or Butterfly/Barbell Arbitrage page for this trade. The dark blocks have to be filled in by the trader. The settle date is set to February 15, 2001, for all securities, the security section indicates that the trader is selling 11/08s

```
<HELP> for explanation.                                    P066 Govt   BBA

BUTTERFLY/BARBELL ARBITRAGE                              Page 1 of 6
  SETTLE DATE security 1  2/15/01                 YIELD  Cnv/Semi/Ann
             security 2  2/15/01                        M=YTM, W=YTW
             security 3  2/15/01        Future's Risk    Notional (N or C)
BUY/     SECURITY                    MOD/ADJ            PAR    RISK   DOLLAR
SELL TKR CPN MTY KEY    PRICE   YIELD  DUR    RISK     ($1M)  WEIGHT PROCEEDS

 T 4.75 11/08 Govt     97-8    5.184   6.31   6.21     1000    .621   984572

 T 6.125 8/07 Govt     105-11³₄ 5.143  5.35   5.64      551    311   580573
 T 6 8/09 Govt         105-6³₄  5.233  6.66   7.00      444    311   467137
                                                      ------ ---------
BUTTERFLY SPREAD:  .7bp GROSS, .4bp AVG               DIFF     1     63138

Market Value Weighted Ave Spread (with Cash @ 3.57  ) :   9.6 BP's

TOTAL RETURN FOR VARIOUS YIELD SHIFTS
                          PIVOTAL SHIFT (IN BP's)
                          NEG.  25        0      POS.  25
  PARALLEL SHIFT   UP  25  $   90.52  $  -21.21  $  143.67
  (IN BP's)            0   $  146.58  $    0.00  $  135.68
                 DOWN 25   $  192.20  $    9.42  $  114.67
```

FIGURE 4.12 Bloomberg's Butterfly/Barbell Arbitrage Page
Source: Copyright 2002 Bloomberg L.P.

and buying a combination of 8/07s and 8/09s, and the prices and yields are those used in the fitting exercise. The column labeled "Risk" shows the sensitivity of each bond's price to changes in its yield.[5] The 11/08s' risk of 6.21, for example, means that a one-basis point increase in yield lowers the price of $100 face value of 11/08s by 6.21 cents. Under the "Par ($1M)" column, the trader types in the face value of 11/08s in the trade, in thousands of dollars. So, in Figure 4.12, the entry of 1,000 indicates a trade with $1 million face value of 11/08s. The BBA screen calculates the face amount of the 8/07s and 8/09s the trader should hold to hedge one-half of the 11/08 risk with each wing. In this case, the short of $1 million face amount of the 11/08s requires the purchase of $551,000 8/07s and $444,000 8/09s.

---

[5]This definition of risk is identical to yield-based DV01. See Chapter 6.

The "Risk Weight" column then gives the risk of the bond position (as opposed to the risk of $100 face value of the bond). For example, since the risk of the 8/07s is 5.64 cents per $100 face value, or .0564 dollars, the risk weight of the $551,000 8/07 position is

$$\frac{.0564}{100} \times \$551,000 = \$311 \tag{4.24}$$

Using the risk weight column to summarize the trade, a position with $1 million 11/08s as the body will win $621 for every basis point increase in yield of the 11/08s and lose $311 for every basis point increase in yield of the 8/07s or 8/09s.

The "Butterfly Spread" in Figure 4.10 has two definitions. The one to the right, labeled "AVG," is here defined as the average yield of the wings minus the yield of the body. In this case,

$$\frac{5.143 + 5.233}{2} - 5.184 = .4\% \tag{4.25}$$

As it turns out, the change in the average butterfly spread over short horizons is a good approximation for the profit or loss of the butterfly trade measured in basis points of the center bond. To see this, note that the profit and loss (P&L) of this trade may be written as

$$P \& L = R W_{11/08} \Delta y_{11/08} - R W_{8/07} \Delta y_{8/07} - R W_{8/09} \Delta y_{8/09} \tag{4.26}$$

where the RWs are the risk weights and the Δy terms are the realized changes in bond yields. Notice the signs of (4.26): If the yield of the 11/08s increases and its price falls the position makes money, while if the yields of the other bonds increase and their prices fall the position loses money. Since the risk weights were set so as to allocate half of the risk to each wing,

$$R W_{11/08} = \frac{1}{2} R W_{8/07} = \frac{1}{2} R W_{8/09} \tag{4.27}$$

Substituting these equalities into (4.26),

$$P\&L = RW_{11/08}\left[\Delta y_{11/08} - \frac{\Delta y_{8/07} + \Delta y_{8/09}}{2}\right] \qquad (4.28)$$

From the definition of the average butterfly spread, illustrated by (4.25), the term in brackets of equation (4.28) is simply the negative of the change in the average butterfly spread:

$$P\&L = -RW_{11/08} \times \Delta \text{AVG Butterfly Spread} \qquad (4.29)$$

To summarize, if the average butterfly spread falls by one basis point, the trade will make the risk weight of the 11/08s or $621.

How much should the trader expect to make on this butterfly? According to the fitting exercise, the 11/08s are 3.5 basis points rich, the 8/07s are 1.2 basis points cheap, and the 8/09s are 2 basis points rich. If these deviations from fair value all disappear, the average butterfly spread will fall by $3.5 + \frac{1}{2} \times 1.2 - \frac{1}{2} \times 2$ or 3.1 basis points. Note that the trade is expected to make money by being short the rich 11/08s, make money by being long[6] the cheap 8/07s, but lose money by being long the rich 8/09s. If there were a cheap issue of slightly longer maturity than the 11/08s, the trader would prefer to buy that to hedge curve risk. But in this case the 8/09s are the only possibility. In any case, if the average butterfly spread can be expected to fall 3.1 basis points, the trade might be expected to make 621×3.1 or $1,925 for each $1 million of 11/08s. A not unreasonable position size of $100 million might be expected to make about $192,500.

Bloomberg allows for the tracking of an average butterfly spread over time. Defining the index N08 to be the average butterfly spread of this trade, Figure 4.13 shows the path of the spread from February 1, 2001, to August 15, 2001. Over this sample period, the spread did happen to fall between 3.5 and 4.5 basis points, depending on when exactly the trade was initiated and unwound and on the costs of exe-

---

[6]Being long a security is trader jargon for owning a security or, more generally, for having an exposure to a particular security, interest rate, or other market factor. The term "long" is used to distinguish such a position from a short position.

cuting the trade. (The y-axis labels −0.01, −0.02, etc. mean that the spread fell one basis point, two basis points, etc.)

The calculations so far have not included the financing frictions of putting on a butterfly trade. The costs of these frictions will be discussed in Chapter 15. For now, suffice it to say that none of the bonds in this butterfly had any particular financing advantages over the relevant time period. Assuming that the trader times things relatively well and exits the trade sometime in April, a financing friction of 10 to 20 basis points for four months on a $100 million position would cost from about $33,000 to $67,000. This cost is small relative to the 3.5 to 4.5 basis points of profit amounting to between $217,350 and $279,450.

Before concluding this case study, it should be mentioned that equal risk weights on each wing are not necessarily the best weights for immunizing against curve shifts. The empirical determination of optimal weights will be discussed in Chapter 8. The theoretical issues surrounding the determination of optimal weights are discussed throughout Parts Two and Three.

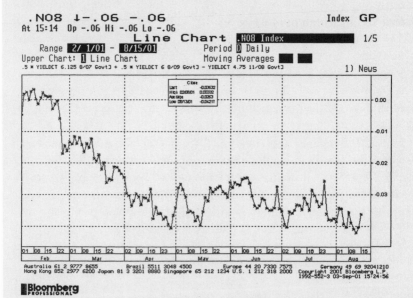

FIGURE 4.13   Butterfly Spread from February 1, 2001 to August 15, 2001
Source: Copyright 2002 Bloomberg L.P.

APPENDIX 4A
CONTINUOUS COMPOUNDING

Under annual, semiannual, monthly, and daily compounding, one unit of currency invested at the rate r for t years grows to, respectively,

$$(1+r)^T$$
$$(1+r/2)^{2T}$$
$$(1+r/12)^{12T} \qquad (4.30)$$
$$(1+r/365)^{365T}$$

More generally, if interest is paid n times per year the investment will grow to

$$(1+r/n)^{nT} \qquad (4.31)$$

Taking the logarithm of (4.31) gives

$$nT\log(1+r/n) = \frac{T\log(1+r/n)}{1/n} \qquad (4.32)$$

By l'Hôpital's rule the limit of the right-hand side of (4.32) as n gets very large is rT. But since the right-hand side of (4.32) is the logarithm of (4.31), it must be the case that the limit of (4.31) as n gets very large is e^{rT} where $e=2.71828\ldots$ is the base of the natural logarithm. Therefore, if n gets very large so that interest is paid every instant (i.e., if the rate is continuously compounded), an investment of one unit of currency will grow to

$$e^{rT} \qquad (4.33)$$

Equivalently, the present value of \$1 to be received in T years is e^{-rT} dollars. Therefore, under continuous compounding the spot rate is defined such that

$$d(t) = e^{-\hat{r}(t)t} \tag{4.34}$$

Defining the forward rate requires a bit of development. In the case of semiannual compounding, spot and forward rates are related by the following equation:

$$\left(1+\hat{r}(t)/2\right)^{2t}\left(1+r(t+.5)/2\right) = \left(1+\hat{r}(t+.5)/2\right)^{2t+1} \tag{4.35}$$

Using the relationship between spot rates and discount factors, equation (4.35) becomes

$$\frac{1}{d(t)}\left(1+r(t+.5)/2\right) = \frac{1}{d(t+.5)} \tag{4.36}$$

Analogously, in the case of compounding n times per year,

$$\frac{1}{d(t)}\left(1+r(t+1/n)/n\right) = \frac{1}{d(t+1/n)} \tag{4.37}$$

Solving (4.37) for the forward rate,

$$r(t+1/n) = -\frac{d(t+1/n)-d(t)}{1/n}\frac{1}{d(t+1/n)} \tag{4.38}$$

In the case of continuous compounding, n gets very large and the first fraction of equation (4.38) is recognized as the derivative of the discount function. Taking limits of all the terms of (4.38) as n gets very large,

$$r(t) = -\frac{d'(t)}{d(t)} \tag{4.39}$$

Finally, to derive the relationship between forward rates and spot rates under continuous compounding, take the derivative of (4.34) and substitute the result into (4.39):

$$r(t) = \hat{r}(t) + t\hat{r}'(t) \tag{4.40}$$

(Inspection of equation (4.40) proves the relationship between spot and forward curves described in Chapter 2: $r(t) \geq \hat{r}(t) \Leftrightarrow \hat{r}'(t) \geq 0$ and $r(t) \leq \hat{r}(t) \Leftrightarrow \hat{r}'(t) \leq 0$. In words, the forward rate exceeds the spot rate if and only if spot rates are increasing. Also, the forward rate is less than the spot rate if and only if spot rates are decreasing.)

The text of this chapter points out that continuous compounding allows for a mathematically consistent way of defining spot and forward rates when cash flows may occur at any term. This appendix shows the relationships among discount factors, continuously compounded spot rates, and continuously compounded forward rates. With these relationships the family of continuously compounded spot rate functions discussed in this chapter can be converted into discount functions. These functions can, in turn, be used to price cash flows maturing at any set of terms. In addition, using the values of these discount functions at evenly spaced intervals allows the underlying term structure to be quoted in terms of rates of any compounding frequency.

APPENDIX 4B
A SIMPLE CUBIC SPLINE

The system (4.22) is written to ensure that the spot rate curve does not jump at the knot points. To ensure that the slope does not jump, either, begin by writing the derivative of the spot rate function:

$$\hat{r}'(t) = \begin{cases} a_1 + 2b_1 t + 3c_1 t^2 & t \leq 10 \\ a_2 + 2b_2(t-10) + 3c_2(t-10)^2 & 10 \leq t \leq 20 \\ a_3 + 2b_3(t-20) + 3c_3(t-20)^2 & 20 \leq t \leq 30 \end{cases} \quad (4.41)$$

For the derivatives at a term of 10 years to be the same for the first and second cubic segments, it must be the case that

$$a_2 = a_1 + 20b_1 + 300c_1 \quad (4.42)$$

Similarly, for the derivatives at 20 years to be equal for the second and third segments, it must be the case that

$$a_3 = a_2 + 20b_2 + 300c_2 \quad (4.43)$$

To ensure that the second derivative does not jump, either, write down the second derivative of the spot rate function:

$$\hat{r}''(t) = \begin{cases} 2b_1 + 6c_1 t & t \leq 10 \\ 2b_2 + 6c_2(t-10) & 10 \leq t \leq 20 \\ 2b_3 + 6c_3(t-20) & 20 \leq t \leq 30 \end{cases} \qquad (4.44)$$

From (4.44), the conditions for continuity of the second derivative are:

$$b_2 = b_1 + 30c_1$$
$$b_3 = b_2 + 30c_2 \qquad (4.45)$$

There are 10 unknown constants in the system (4.33), four for the first segment and three for each of the other two. (In the first segment $\hat{r}_0$ has a special interpretation but is nevertheless an unknown constant.) Equations (4.42), (4.43), and (4.45) give four constraints on these parameters. Thus, in this relatively simple piecewise cubic, six degrees of freedom are left to obtain a reasonable fit of market data.

TWO

Measures of Price Sensitivity and Hedging

CHAPTER **5**

One-Factor Measures of Price Sensitivity

The interest rate risk of a security may be measured by how much its price changes as interest rates change. Measures of price sensitivity are used in many ways, four of which will be listed here. First, traders hedging a position in one bond with another bond or with a portfolio of other bonds must be able to compute how each of the bond prices responds to changes in rates. Second, investors with a view about future changes in interest rates work to determine which securities will perform best if their view does, in fact, obtain. Third, investors and risk managers need to know the volatility of fixed income portfolios. If, for example, a risk manager concludes that the volatility of interest rates is 100 basis points per year and computes that the value of a portfolio changes by $10,000 dollars per basis point, then the annual volatility of the portfolio is $1 million. Fourth, asset-liability managers compare the interest rate risk of their assets with the interest rate risk of their liabilities. Banks, for example, raise money through deposits and other short-term borrowings to lend to corporations. Insurance companies incur liabilities in exchange for premiums that they then invest in a broad range of fixed income securities. And, as a final example, defined benefit plans invest funds in financial markets to meet obligations to retirees.

Computing the price change of a security given a change in interest rates is straightforward. Given an initial and a shifted spot rate curve, for example, the tools of Part One can be used to calculate the price change of any security with fixed cash flows. Similarly, given two spot rate curves the models in Part Three can be used to calculate the price change of any *derivative* security whose cash flows depend on the level of rates. Therefore, the challenge of measuring price sensitivity comes not so much from the computation of price changes given changes in interest rates but in defining what is meant by changes in interest rates.

One commonly used measure of price sensitivity assumes that all bond yields shift in *parallel*; that is, they move up or down by the same number of basis points. Other assumptions are a parallel shift in spot rates or a parallel shift in forward rates. Yet another reasonable assumption is that each spot rate moves in some proportion to its maturity. This last assumption is supported by the observation that short-term rates are more volatile than long-term rates.[1] In any case, there are very many possible definitions of changes in interest rates.

An *interest rate factor* is a random variable that impacts interest rates in some way. The simplest formulations assume that there is only one factor driving all interest rates and that the factor is itself an interest rate. For example, in some applications it might be convenient to assume that the 10-year par rate is that single factor. If parallel shifts are assumed as well, then the change in every other par rate is assumed to equal the change in the factor, that is, in the 10-year par rate.

In more complex formulations there are two or more factors driving changes in interest rates. It might be assumed, for example, that the change in any spot rate is the linearly interpolated change in the two-year and 10-year spot rates. In that case, knowing the change in the two-year spot rate alone, or knowing the change in the 10-year spot rate alone, would not allow for the determination of changes in other spot rates. But if, for example, the two-year spot rate were known to increase by three basis points and the 10-year spot rate by one basis point, then the six-year rate, just between the two- and 10-year rates, would be assumed to increase by two basis points.

There are yet other complex formulations in which the factors are not themselves interest rates. These models, however, are deferred to Part Three.

This chapter describes one-factor measures of price sensitivity in full generality, in particular, without reference to any definition of a change in rates. Chapter 6 presents the commonly invoked special case of parallel

---

[1] In countries with a central bank that targets the overnight interest rate, like the United States, this observation does not apply to the very short end of the curve.

yield shifts. Chapter 7 discusses multi-factor formulations. Chapter 8 shows how to model interest rate changes empirically.

The assumptions about interest rate changes and the resulting measures of price sensitivity appearing in Part Two have the advantage of simplicity but the disadvantage of not being connected to any particular pricing model. This means, for example, that the hedging rules developed here are independent of the pricing or valuation rules used to determine the quality of the investment or trade that necessitated hedging in the first place. At the cost of some complexity, the assumptions invoked in Part Three consistently price securities and measure their price sensitivities.

DV01

Denote the price-rate function of a fixed income security by $P(y)$, where y is an interest rate factor. Despite the usual use of y to denote a yield, this factor might be a yield, a spot rate, a forward rate, or a factor in one of the models of Part Three. In any case, since this chapter describes one-factor measures of price sensitivity, the single number y completely describes the term structure of interest rates and, holding everything but interest rates constant, allows for the unique determination of the price of any fixed income security.

As mentioned above, the concepts and derivations in this chapter apply to any term structure shape and to any one-factor description of term structure movements. But, to simplify the presentation, the numerical examples assume that the term structure of interest rates is flat at 5% and that rates move up and down in parallel. Under these assumptions, all yields, spot rates, and forward rates are equal to 5%. Therefore, with respect to the numerical examples, the precise definition of y does not matter.

This chapter uses two securities to illustrate price sensitivity. The first is the U.S. Treasury 5s of February 15, 2011. As of February 15, 2001, Figure 5.1 graphs the price-rate function of this bond. The shape of the graph is typical of coupon bonds: Price falls as rate increases, and the curve is very slightly convex.[2]

The other security used as an example in this chapter is a one-year *European call option* struck at par on the 5s of February 15, 2011. This

---

[2]The discussion of Figure 4.4 defines a convex curve.

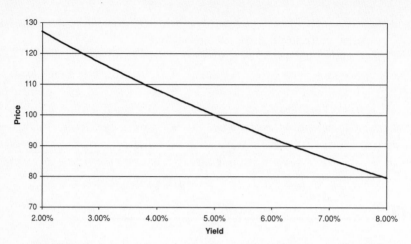

FIGURE 5.1   The Price-Rate Function of the 5s of February 15, 2011

option gives its owner the right to purchase some face amount of the bond after exactly one year at par. (Options and option pricing will be discussed further in Part Three and in Chapter 19.) If the call gives the right to purchase $10 million face amount of the bond then the option is said to have a face amount of $10 million as well. Figure 5.2 graphs the price-rate function. As in the case of bonds, option price is expressed as a percent of face value.

In Figure 5.2, if rates rise 100 basis points from 3.50% to 4.50%, the price of the option falls from 11.61 to 5.26. Expressed differently, the change in the value of the option is (5.26–11.61)/100 or –.0635 per basis point. At higher rate levels, option price does not fall as much for the same increase in rate. Changing rates from 5.50% to 6.50%, for example, lowers the option price from 1.56 to .26 or by only .013 per basis point.

More generally, letting ΔP and Δy denote the changes in price and rate and noting that the change measured in basis points is $10,000 \times \Delta y$, define the following measure of price sensitivity:

$$DV01 \equiv -\frac{\Delta P}{10,000 \times \Delta y} \qquad (5.1)$$

DV01 is an acronym for *dollar value of an '01* (i.e., .01%) and gives the change in the value of a fixed income security for a one-basis point decline

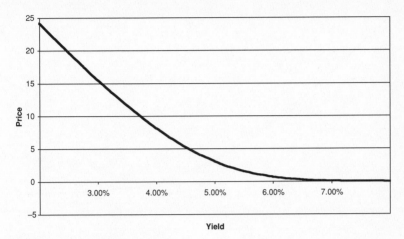

FIGURE 5.2 The Price-Rate Function of a One-Year European Call Option Struck at Par on the 5s of February 15, 2011

in rates. The negative sign defines DV01 to be positive if price increases when rates decline and negative if price decreases when rates decline. This convention has been adopted so that DV01 is positive most of the time: All fixed coupon bonds and most other fixed income securities do rise in price when rates decline.

The quantity $^{\Delta P}/_{\Delta y}$ is simply the slope of the line connecting the two points used to measure that change.[3] Continuing with the option example, $^{\Delta P}/_{\Delta y}$ for the call at 4% might be graphically illustrated by the slope of a line connecting the points (3.50%, 11.61) and (4.50%, 5.26) in Figure 5.2. It follows from equation (5.1) that DV01 at 4% is proportional to that slope.

Since the price sensitivity of the option can change dramatically with the level of rates, DV01 should be measured using points relatively close to the rate level in question. Rather than using prices at 3.50% and 4.50% to measure DV01 at 4%, for example, one might use prices at 3.90% and 4.10% or even prices at 3.99% and 4.01%. In the limit, one would use the slope of the line *tangent* to the price-rate curve at the desired rate level. Figure 5.3 graphs the tangent lines at 4% and 6%. That the line AA in this fig-

---

[3]The slope of a line equals the change in the vertical coordinate divided by the change in the horizontal coordinate. In the price-rate context, the slope of the line is the change in price divided by the change in rate.

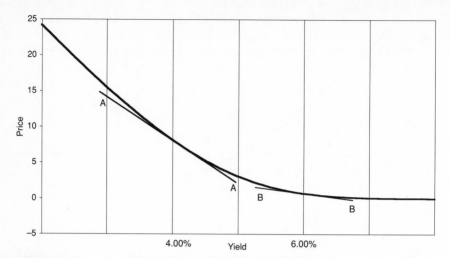

FIGURE 5.3 A Graphical Representation of DV01 for the One-Year Call on the 5s of February 15, 2011

ure is steeper than the line BB indicates that the option is more sensitive to rates at 4% than it is at 6%.

The slope of a tangent line at a particular rate level is equal to the *derivative* of the price-rate function at that rate level. The derivative is written $dP(y)/dy$ or simply dP/dy. (The first notation of the derivative emphasizes its dependence on the level of rates, while the second assumes awareness of this dependence.) For readers not familiar with the calculus, "d" may be taken as indicating a small change and the derivative may be thought of as the change in price divided by the change in rate. More precisely, the derivative is the limit of this ratio as the change in rate approaches zero.

In some special cases to be discussed later, dP/dy can be calculated explicitly. In these cases, DV01 is defined using this derivative and

$$\text{DV01} = -\frac{1}{10,000}\frac{dP(y)}{dy} \tag{5.2}$$

In other cases DV01 must be estimated by choosing two rate levels, computing prices at each of the rates, and applying equation (5.1).

As mentioned, since DV01 can change dramatically with the level of rates it should be measured over relatively narrow ranges of rate.[4] The first three columns of Table 5.1 list selected rate levels, option prices, and DV01 estimates from Figure 5.2. Given the values of the option at rates of 4.01% and 3.99%, for example, DV01 equals

$$-\frac{\Delta P}{10,000 \times \Delta y} = -\frac{8.0866 - 8.2148}{10,000 \times \left(4.01\% - 3.99\%\right)} = .0641 \qquad (5.3)$$

In words, with rates at 4% the price of the option falls by about 6.41 cents for a one-basis point rise in rate. Notice that the DV01 estimate at 4% does not make use of the option price at 4%: The most stable numerical estimate chooses rates that are equally spaced above and below 4%.

Before closing this section, a note on terminology is in order. Most market participants use DV01 to mean yield-based DV01, discussed in Chapter 6. Yield-based DV01 assumes that the yield-to-maturity changes by one basis point while the general definition of DV01 in this chapter allows for any measure of rates to change by one basis point. To avoid confusion, some market participants have different names for DV01 measures according to the assumed measure of changes in rates. For example, the change in price after a parallel shift in forward rates might be called DVDF or DPDF while the change in price after a parallel shift in spot or zero rates might be called DVDZ or DPDZ.

A HEDGING EXAMPLE, PART I: HEDGING A CALL OPTION

Since it is usual to regard a call option as depending on the price of a bond, rather than the reverse, the call is referred to as the derivative security and the bond as the underlying security. The rightmost columns of Table 5.1

---

[4]Were prices available without error, it would be desirable to choose a very small difference between the two rates and estimate DV01 at a particular rate as accurately as possible. Unfortunately, however, prices are usually not available without error. The models developed in Part Three, for example, perform so many calculations that the resulting prices are subject to numerical error. In these situations it is not a good idea to magnify these price errors by dividing by too small a rate difference. In short, the greater the pricing accuracy, the smaller the optimal rate difference for computing DV01.

TABLE 5.1 Selected Option Prices, Underlying Bond Prices, and DV01s at Various Rate Levels

Rate Level	Option Price	Option DV01	Bond Price	Bond DV01
3.99%	8.2148		108.2615	
4.00%	8.1506	0.0641	108.1757	0.0857
4.01%	8.0866		108.0901	
4.99%	3.0871		100.0780	
5.00%	3.0501	0.0369	100.0000	0.0779
5.01%	3.0134		99.9221	
5.99%	0.7003		92.6322	
6.00%	0.6879	0.0124	92.5613	0.0709
6.01%	0.6756		92.4903	

list the prices and DV01 values of the underlying bond, namely the 5s of February 15, 2011, at various rates.

If, in the course of business, a market maker sells $100 million face value of the call option and rates are at 5%, how might the market maker hedge interest rate exposure by trading in the underlying bond? Since the market maker has sold the option and stands to lose money if rates fall, bonds must be purchased as a hedge. The DV01 of the two securities may be used to figure out exactly how many bonds should be bought against the short option position.

According to Table 5.1, the DV01 of the option with rates at 5% is .0369, while the DV01 of the bond is .0779. Letting F be the face amount of bonds the market maker purchases as a hedge, F should be set such that the price change of the hedge position as a result of a one-basis point change in rates equals the price change of the option position as a result of the same one-basis point change. Mathematically,

$$F \times \frac{.0779}{100} = 100,000,000 \times \frac{.0369}{100}$$

$$F = 100,000,000 \times \frac{.0369}{.0779} \tag{5.4}$$

(Note that the DV01 values, quoted per 100 face value, must be divided by 100 before being multiplied by the face amount of the option or of the bond.) Solving for F, the market maker should purchase approximately $47.37 million face amount of the underlying bonds. To summarize this hedging strategy, the sale of $100 million face value of options risks

$$\$100,000,000 \times \frac{.0369}{100} = \$36,900 \qquad (5.5)$$

for each basis point decline in rates, while the purchase of $47.37 million bonds gains

$$\$47,370,000 \times \frac{.0779}{100} = \$36,901 \qquad (5.6)$$

per basis point decline in rates.

Generally, if DV01 is expressed in terms of a fixed face amount, hedging a position of F_A face amount of security A requires a position of F_B face amount of security B where

$$F_B = \frac{-F_A \times \mathrm{DV01}_A}{\mathrm{DV01}_B} \qquad (5.7)$$

To avoid careless trading mistakes, it is worth emphasizing the simple implications of equation (5.7), assuming that, as usually is the case, each DV01 is positive. First, hedging a long position in security A requires a short position in security B and hedging a short position in security A requires a long position in security B. In the example, the market maker sells options and buys bonds. Mathematically, if $F_A>0$ then $F_B<0$ and vice versa. Second, the security with the higher DV01 is traded in smaller quantity than the security with the lower DV01. In the example, the market maker buys only $47.37 million bonds against the sale of $100 million options. Mathematically, if $\mathrm{DV01}_A>\mathrm{DV01}_B$ then $F_B>-F_A$, while if $\mathrm{DV01}_A<\mathrm{DV01}_B$ then $-F_A>F_B$.

(There are occasions in which one DV01 is negative.[5] In these cases equation (5.7) shows that a hedged position consists of simultaneous longs or shorts in both securities. Also, the security with the higher DV01 in absolute value is traded in smaller quantity.)

Assume that the market maker does sell $100 million options and does buy $47.37 million bonds when rates are 5%. Using the prices in Table

---

[5]For an example in the mortgage context see Chapter 21.

5.1, the cost of establishing this position and, equivalently, the value of the position after the trades is

$$-\$100,000,000 \times \frac{3.0501}{100} + \$47,370,000 \times \frac{100}{100} = \$44,319,900 \quad (5.8)$$

Now say that rates fall by one basis point to 4.99%. Using the prices in Table 5.1 for the new rate level, the value of the position becomes

$$-\$100,000,000 \times \frac{3.0871}{100} + \$47,370,000 \times \frac{100.0780}{100} = \$44,319,849 \quad (5.9)$$

The hedge has succeeded in that the value of the position has hardly changed even though rates have changed.

To avoid misconceptions about market making, note that the market maker in this example makes no money. In reality, the market maker would purchase the option at its midmarket price minus some spread. Taking half a tick, for example, the market maker would pay half of $1/_{32}$ or .015625 less than the market price of 3.0501 on the $100 million for a total of $15,625. This spread compensates the market maker for effort expended in the original trade and for hedging the option over its life. Some of the work involved in hedging after the initial trade will become clear in the sections continuing this hedging example.

DURATION

DV01 measures the dollar change in the value of a security for a basis point change in interest rates. Another measure of interest rate sensitivity, *duration*, measures the percentage change in the value of a security for a unit change in rates.[6] Mathematically, letting D denote duration,

$$D \equiv -\frac{1}{P}\frac{\Delta P}{\Delta y} \quad (5.10)$$

---

[6]A unit change means a change of one. In the rate context, a change of one is a change of 10,000 basis points.

As in the case of DV01, when an explicit formula for the price-rate function is available, the derivative of the price-rate function may be used for the change in price divided by the change in rate:

$$D \equiv -\frac{1}{P}\frac{dP}{dy} \qquad (5.11)$$

Otherwise, prices at various rates must be substituted into (5.10) to estimate duration.

Table 5.2 gives the same rate levels, option prices, and bond prices as Table 5.1 but computes duration instead of DV01. Once again, rates a basis point above and a basis point below the rate level in question are used to compute changes. For example, the duration of the underlying bond at a rate of 4% is given by

$$D = -\frac{(108.0901 - 108.2615)/108.1757}{4.01\% - 3.99\%} = 7.92 \qquad (5.12)$$

One way to interpret the duration number of 7.92 is to multiply both sides of equation (5.10) by Δy:

$$\frac{\Delta P}{P} = -D\Delta y \qquad (5.13)$$

TABLE 5.2 Selected Option Prices, Underlying Bond Prices, and Durations at Various Rate Levels

Rate Level	Option Price	Option Duration	Bond Price	Bond Duration
3.99%	8.2148		108.2615	
4.00%	8.1506	78.60	108.1757	7.92
4.01%	8.0866		108.0901	
4.99%	3.0871		100.0780	
5.00%	3.0501	120.82	100.0000	7.79
5.01%	3.0134		99.9221	
5.99%	0.7003		92.6322	
6.00%	0.6879	179.70	92.5613	7.67
6.01%	0.6756		92.4903	

In the case of the underlying bond, equation (5.13) says that the percentage change in price equals minus 7.92 times the change in rate. Therefore, a one-basis point increase in rate will result in a percentage price change of $-7.92\times.0001$ or $-.0792\%$. Since the price of the bond at a rate of 4% is 108.1757, this percentage change translates into an absolute change of $-.0792\%\times108.1757$ or $-.0857$. In words, a one-basis point increase in rate lowers the bond price by .0857. Noting that the DV01 of the bond at a rate of 4% is .0857 highlights the point that duration and DV01 express the same interest rate sensitivity of a security in different ways.

Duration tends to be more convenient than DV01 in the investing context. If an institutional investor has $10 million to invest when rates are 5%, the fact that the duration of the option vastly exceeds that of the bond alerts the investor to the far greater risk of investing money in options. With a duration of 7.79, a $10 million investment in the bonds will change by about .78% for a 10-basis point change in rates. However, with a duration of 120.82, the same $10 million investment will change by about 12.1% for the same 10-basis point change in rates!

In contrast to the investing context, in a hedging problem the dollar amounts of the two securities involved are not the same. In the example of the previous section, for instance, the market maker sells options worth about $3.05 million and buys bonds worth $47.37 million.[7] The fact that the DV01 of an option is so much less than the DV01 of a bond tells the market maker that a hedged position must be long much less face amount of bonds than it is short face amount of options. In the hedging context, therefore, the dollar sensitivity to a change in rates (i.e., DV01) is more convenient a measure than the percentage change in price (i.e., duration).

Tables 5.1 and 5.2 illustrate the difference in emphasis of DV01 and duration in another way. Table 5.1 shows that the DV01 of the option declines with rates, while Table 5.2 shows that the duration of the option increases with rates. The DV01 numbers show that for a fixed face amount of option the dollar sensitivity declines with rates. Since, however, declining rates also lower the price of the option, percentage price sensitivity, or duration, actually increases.

---

[7]To finance this position the market maker will borrow the difference between these dollar amounts. See Chapter 15 for a discussion about financing positions.

Like the section on DV01, this section closes with a note on terminology. As defined in this chapter, duration may be computed for any assumed change in the term structure of interest rates. This general definition is also called *effective duration*. Many market participants, however, use the term duration to mean Macaulay duration or modified duration, discussed in Chapter 6. These measures of interest rate sensitivity explicitly assume a change in yield-to-maturity.

CONVEXITY

As mentioned in the discussion of Figure 5.3 and as seen in Tables 5.1 and 5.2, interest rate sensitivity changes with the level of rates. To illustrate this point more clearly, Figure 5.4 graphs the DV01 of the option and underlying bond as a function of the level of rates. The DV01 of the bond declines relatively gently as rates rise, while the DV01 of the option declines sometimes gently and sometimes violently depending on the level of rates. *Convexity* measures how interest rate sensitivity changes with rates.

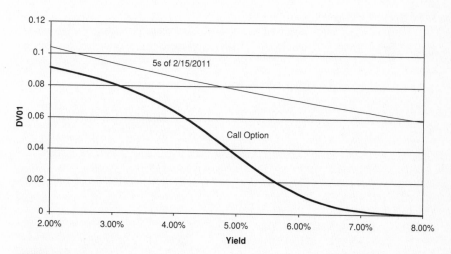

FIGURE 5.4 DV01 of the 5s of February 15, 2011, and of the Call Option as a Function of Rates

Mathematically, convexity is defined as

$$C = \frac{1}{P}\frac{d^2P}{dy^2} \tag{5.14}$$

where d^2P/dy^2 is the *second derivative* of the price-rate function. Just as the first derivative measures how price changes with rates, the second derivative measures how the first derivative changes with rates. As with DV01 and duration, if there is an explicit formula for the price-rate function then (5.14) may be used to compute convexity. Without such a formula, convexity must be estimated numerically.

Table 5.3 shows how to estimate the convexity of the bond and the option at various rate levels. The convexity of the bond at 5%, for example, is estimated as follows. Estimate the first derivative between 4.99% and 5% (i.e., at 4.995%) by dividing the change in price by the change in rate:

$$\frac{100 - 100.0780}{5\% - 4.99\%} = -780 \tag{5.15}$$

Table 5.3 displays price to four digits but more precision is used to calculate the derivative estimate of −779.8264. This extra precision is often necessary when calculating second derivatives.

Similarly, estimate the first derivative between 5% and 5.01% (i.e., at 5.005%) by dividing the change in the corresponding prices by the change

TABLE 5.3 Convexity Calculations for the Bond and Option at Various Rates

Rate Level	Bond Price	First Derivative	Convexity	Option Price	First Derivative	Convexity
3.99%	108.2615			8.2148		
4.00%	108.1757	−857.4290	75.4725	8.1506	−641.8096	2,800.9970
4.01%	108.0901	−856.6126		8.0866	−639.5266	
4.99%	100.0780			3.0871		
5.00%	100.0000	−779.8264	73.6287	3.0501	−369.9550	9,503.3302
5.01%	99.9221	−779.0901		3.0134	−367.0564	
5.99%	92.6322			0.7003		
6.00%	92.5613	−709.8187	71.7854	0.6879	−124.4984	25,627.6335
6.01%	92.4903	−709.1542		0.6756	−122.7355	

in rate to get −779.0901. Then estimate the second derivative at 5% by dividing the change in the first derivative by the change in rate:

$$\frac{\Delta^2 P}{\Delta y^2} = \frac{-779.0901 + 779.8264}{5.005\% - 4.995\%} = 7,363 \qquad (5.16)$$

Finally, to estimate convexity, divide the estimate of the second derivative by the bond price:

$$C = \frac{1}{P}\frac{\Delta^2 P}{\Delta y^2} = \frac{7,363}{100} = 73.63 \qquad (5.17)$$

Both the bond and the option exhibit positive convexity. Mathematically positive convexity simply means that the second derivative is positive and, therefore, that $C>0$. Graphically this means that the price-rate curve is convex. Figures 5.1 and 5.2 do show that the price-rate curves of both bond and option are, indeed, convex. Finally, the property of positive convexity may also be thought of as the property that DV01 falls as rates increase (see Figure 5.4).

Fixed income securities need not be positively convex at all rate levels. Some important examples of negative convexity are callable bonds (see the last section of this chapter and Chapter 19) and mortgage-backed securities (see Chapter 21).

Understanding the convexity properties of securities is useful for both hedging and investing. This is the topic of the next few sections.

A HEDGING EXAMPLE, PART II: A SHORT CONVEXITY POSITION

In the first section of this hedging example the market maker buys $47.37 million of the 5s of February 15, 2011, against a short of $100 million options. Figure 5.5 shows the profit and loss, or P&L, of a long position of $47.37 million bonds and of a long position of $100 million options as rates change. Since the market maker is actually short the options, the P&L of the position at any rate level is the P&L of the long bond position minus the P&L of the long option position.

By construction, the DV01 of the long bond and option positions are the same at a rate level of 5%. In other words, for small rate changes, the

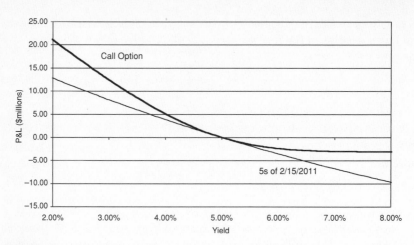

FIGURE 5.5 P&L of Long Positions in the 5s of February 15, 2011, and in the Call Option

change in the value of one position equals the change in the value of the other. Graphically, the P&L curves are tangent at 5%.

The previous section of this example shows that the hedge performs well in that the market maker neither makes nor loses money after a one-basis point change in rates. At first glance it may appear from Figure 5.5 that the hedge works well even after moves of 50 basis points. The values on the vertical axis, however, are measured in millions. After a move of only 25 basis points, the hedge is off by about $80,000. This is a very large number in light of the approximately $15,625 the market maker collected in spread. Worse yet, since the P&L of the long option position is always above that of the long bond position, the market maker loses this $80,000 whether rates rise or fall by 25 basis points.

The hedged position loses whether rates rise or fall because the option is more convex than the bond. In market jargon, the hedged position is *short convexity*. For small rate changes away from 5% the values of the bond and option positions change by the same amount. Due to its greater convexity, however, the sensitivity of the option changes by more than the sensitivity of the bond. When rates increase, the DV01 of both the bond and the option fall but the DV01 of the option falls by more. Hence, after further rate increases, the option falls in value less than the bond, and the P&L of the option position stays above that of the bond position. Similarly, when rates decline below 5%, the DV01 of both the bond and option rise but the DV01 of the option rises by more. Hence, after further rate declines the option rises in value more than the bond, and the P&L of the option position again stays above that of the bond position.

This discussion reveals that DV01 hedging is *local*, that is, valid in a particular neighborhood of rates. As rates move, the quality of the hedge deteriorates. As a result, the market maker will need to *rehedge* the position. If rates rise above 5% so that the DV01 of the option position falls by more than the DV01 of the bond position, the market maker will have to sell bonds to reequate DV01 at the higher level of rates. If, on the other hand, rates fall below 5% so that the DV01 of the option position rises by more than the DV01 of the bond position, the market maker will have to buy bonds to reequate DV01 at the lower level of rates.

An erroneous conclusion might be drawn at this point. Figure 5.5 shows that the value of the option position exceeds the value of the bond position at any rate level. Nevertheless, it is not correct to conclude that the option position is a superior holding to the bond position. In brief, if market prices are correct, the price of the option is high enough relative to the price of the bond to reflect its convexity advantages. In particular, holding rates constant, the bond will perform better than the option over time, a disadvantage of a long option position not captured in Figure 5.5. In summary, the long option position will outperform the long bond position if rates move a lot, while the long bond position will outperform if rates stay about the same. It is in this sense, by the way, that a long convexity position is long volatility while a short convexity position is short volatility. In any case, Chapter 10 explains the pricing of convexity in greater detail.

ESTIMATING PRICE CHANGES AND RETURNS WITH DV01, DURATION, AND CONVEXITY

Price changes and returns as a result of changes in rates can be estimated with the measures of price sensitivity used in previous sections. Despite the abundance of calculating machines that, strictly speaking, makes these approximations unnecessary, an understanding of these estimation techniques builds intuition about the behavior of fixed income securities and, with practice, allows for some rapid mental calculations.

A *second-order Taylor approximation* of the price-rate function with respect to rate gives the following approximation for the price of a security after a small change in rate:

$$P(y + \Delta y) \approx P(y) + \frac{dP}{dy} \Delta y + \frac{1}{2} \frac{d^2 P}{dy^2} \Delta y^2 \qquad (5.18)$$

Subtracting P from both sides and then dividing both sides by P gives

$$\frac{\Delta P}{P} \approx \frac{1}{P} \frac{dP}{dy} \Delta y + \frac{1}{2} \times \frac{1}{P} \frac{d^2 P}{dy^2} \Delta y^2 \qquad (5.19)$$

Then, using the definitions of duration and convexity in equations (5.11) and (5.14),

$$\frac{\Delta P}{P} \approx -D \Delta y + \frac{1}{2} C \Delta y^2 \qquad (5.20)$$

In words, equation (5.20) says that the percentage change in the price of a security (i.e., its return) is approximately equal to minus the duration multiplied by the change in rate plus half the convexity multiplied by the change in rate squared. As an example, take the price, duration, and convexity of the call option on the 5s of February 15, 2011, from Tables 5.2 and 5.3. Equation (5.20) then says that for a 25-basis point increase in rates

$$\%\Delta P = -120.82 \times .0025 + (1/2)9503.3302 \times .0025^2$$
$$= -.30205 + .02970 \qquad (5.21)$$
$$= -27.235\%$$

At a starting price of 3.0501, the approximation to the new price is 3.0501 minus .27235×3.0501 or .83070, leaving 2.2194. Since the option price when rates are 5.25% is 2.2185, the approximation of equation (5.20) is relatively accurate.

In the example applying (5.20), namely equation (5.21), the duration term of about 30% is much larger than the convexity term of about 3%. This is generally true. While convexity is usually a larger number than duration, for relatively small changes in rate the change in rate is so much larger than the change in rate squared that the duration effect dominates. This fact suggests that it may sometimes be safe to drop the convexity term completely and to use the *first-order approximation* for the change in price:

$$\frac{\Delta P}{P} \approx -D\Delta y \qquad (5.22)$$

This approximation follows directly from the definition of duration and, therefore, basically repeats equation (5.13).

Figure 5.6 graphs the option price, the first-order approximation of (5.22), and the second-order approximation of (5.20). Both approximations work well for very small changes in rate. For larger changes the second-order approximation still works well, but for very large changes it, too, fails. In any case, the figure makes clear that approximating price changes with duration ignores the curvature or convexity of the price-rate function. Adding a convexity term captures a good deal of this curvature.

In the case of the bond price, both approximations work so well that displaying a price graph over the same range of rates as Figure 5.6 would make it difficult to distinguish the three curves. Figure 5.7, therefore, graphs the bond price and the two approximations for rates greater than 5%. Since the option is much more convex than the bond, it is harder to

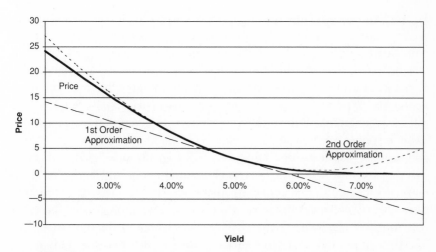

FIGURE 5.6 First and Second Order Approximations to Call Option Price

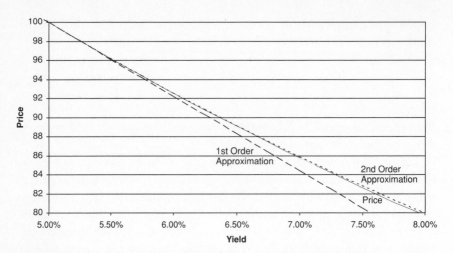

FIGURE 5.7   First and Second Order Approximations to Price of 5s of
February 15, 2011

capture its curvature with the one-term approximation (5.22) or even with
the two-term approximation (5.20).

CONVEXITY IN THE INVESTMENT AND
ASSET-LIABILITY MANAGEMENT CONTEXTS

For very convex securities duration may not be a safe measure of return. In
the example of approximating the return on the option after a 25-basis
point increase in rates, duration used alone overstated the loss by about
3%. Similarly, since the duration of very convex securities can change dramatically as rate changes, an investor needs to monitor the duration of investments. Setting up an investment with a particular exposure to interest
rates may, unattended, turn into a portfolio with a very different exposure
to interest rates.

Another implication of equation (5.20), mentioned briefly earlier, is
that an exposure to convexity is an exposure to volatility. Since Δy^2 is always positive, positive convexity increases return so long as interest
rates move. The bigger the move in either direction, the greater the gains
from positive convexity. Negative convexity works in the reverse. If C is
negative, then rate moves in either direction reduce returns. This is another way to understand why a short option position DV01-hedged with

bonds loses money whether rates gap up or down (see Figure 5.5). In the investment context, choosing among securities with the same duration expresses a view on interest rate volatility. Choosing a very positively convex security would essentially be choosing to be long volatility, while choosing a negatively convex security would essentially be choosing to be short volatility.

Figures 5.6 and 5.7 suggest that asset-liability managers (and hedgers, where possible) can achieve greater protection against interest rate changes by hedging duration and convexity instead of duration alone. Consider an asset-liability manager who sets both the duration and convexity of assets equal to those of liabilities. For any interest rate change, the change in the value of assets will more closely resemble the change in the value of liabilities than had duration alone been matched. Furthermore, since matching convexity sets the change in interest rate sensitivity of the assets equal to that of the liabilities, after a small change in rates the sensitivity of the assets will still be very close to the sensitivity of the liabilities. In other words, the asset-liability manager need not rebalance as often as in the case of matching duration alone.

MEASURING THE PRICE SENSITIVITY OF PORTFOLIOS

This section shows how measures of portfolio price sensitivity are related to the measures of its component securities. Computing price sensitivities can be a time-consuming process, especially when using the term structure models of Part Three. Since a typical investor or trader focuses on a particular set of securities at one time and constantly searches for desirable portfolios from that set, it is often inefficient to compute the sensitivity of every portfolio from scratch. A better solution is to compute sensitivity measures for all the individual securities and then to use the rules of this section to compute portfolio sensitivity measures.

A price or measure of sensitivity for security i is indicated by the subscript i, while quantities without subscripts denote portfolio quantities. By definition, the value of a portfolio equals the sum of the value of the individual securities in the portfolio:

$$P = \sum_i P_i \tag{5.23}$$

Recall from the introduction to this chapter that y is a single rate or factor sufficient to determine the prices of all securities. Therefore, one can compute the derivative of price with respect to this rate or factor for all securities in the portfolio and, from (5.23),

$$\frac{dP}{dy} = \sum \frac{dP_i}{dy} \qquad (5.24)$$

Dividing both sides of by 10,000,

$$\frac{1}{10,000} \frac{dP}{dy} = \sum \frac{1}{10,000} \frac{dP_i}{dy} \qquad (5.25)$$

Finally, using the definition of DV01 in equation (5.2),

$$DV01 = \sum DV01_i \qquad (5.26)$$

In words, the DV01 of a portfolio is the sum of the individual DV01 values.

The rule for duration is only a bit more complex. Starting from equation (5.24), divide both sides by $-P$.

$$-\frac{1}{P} \frac{dP}{dy} = \sum -\frac{1}{P} \frac{dP_i}{dy} \qquad (5.27)$$

Multiplying each term in the summation by one in the form P_i/P_i,

$$-\frac{1}{P} \frac{dP}{dy} = \sum -\frac{P_i}{P} \frac{1}{P_i} \frac{dP_i}{dy} \qquad (5.28)$$

Finally, using the definition of duration from (5.11),

$$D = \sum \frac{P_i}{P} D_i \qquad (5.29)$$

In words, the duration of a portfolio equals a weighted sum of individual durations where each security's weight is its value as a percentage of portfolio value.

The formula for the convexity of a portfolio can be derived along the same lines as the duration of a portfolio, so the convexity result is given without proof:

$$C = \sum \frac{P_i}{P} C_i \qquad (5.30)$$

The next section applies these portfolio results to the case of a callable bond.

A HEDGING EXAMPLE, PART III: THE NEGATIVE CONVEXITY OF CALLABLE BONDS

A *callable bond* is a bond that the issuer may repurchase or *call* at some fixed set of prices on some fixed set of dates. Chapter 19 will discuss callable bonds in detail and will demonstrate that the value of a callable bond to an investor equals the value of the underlying noncallable bond minus the value of the issuer's embedded option. Continuing with the example of this chapter, assume for pedagogical reasons that there exists a 5% Treasury bond maturing on February 15, 2011, and callable in one year by the U.S. Treasury at par. Then the underlying noncallable bond is the 5s of February 15, 2011, and the embedded option is the option introduced in this chapter, namely the right to buy the 5s of February 15, 2011, at par in one year. Furthermore, the value of this callable bond equals the difference between the value of the underlying bond and the value of the option.

Figure 5.8 graphs the price of the callable bond and, for comparison, the price of the 5s of February 15, 2011. Chapter 19 will discuss why the callable bond price curve has the shape that it does. For the purposes of this chapter, however, notice that for all but the highest rates in the graph the callable bond price curve is concave. This implies that the callable bond is *negatively convex* in these rate environments.

Table 5.4 uses the portfolio results of the previous section and the results of Tables 5.1 through 5.3 to compute the DV01, duration, and convexity of the callable bond at three rate levels. At 5%, for example, the callable bond price is the difference between the bond price and the option price: 100–3.0501 or 96.9499. The DV01 of the callable bond price is the difference between the DV01 values listed in Table 5.1: .0779–.0369 or

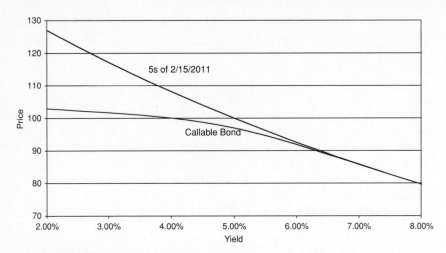

FIGURE 5.8 Price of Callable Bond and of 5s of February 15, 2011

.0410. The convexity of the callable bond is the weighted sum of the individual convexities listed in Table 5.3:

$$103.15\% \times 73.63 - 3.15\% \times 9,503.33 = -223 \qquad (5.31)$$

A market maker wanting to hedge the sale of $100 million callable bonds with the 5s of February 15, 2011, would have to buy $100 million times the ratio of the DV01 measures or, in millions of dollars, $100 \times {}^{.0411}\!/_{.0779}$ or 52.76. Figure 5.9 graphs the P&L from a long position in the callable bonds and from a long position in this hedge.

The striking aspect of Figure 5.9 is that the positive convexity of the bond and the negative convexity of the callable bond combine to make the

TABLE 5.4 Price, DV01, Duration, and Convexity of Callable Bond

Rate Level	Callable Price	Bond Price	Fraction of Value	Option Price	Fraction of Value	Callable DV01	Callable Duration	Callable Convexity
4.00%	100.0251	108.1757	108.15%	8.1506	−8.15%	0.0216	2.162983	−146.618
5.00%	96.9499	100.0000	103.15%	3.0501	−3.15%	0.0411	4.238815	−223.039
6.00%	91.8734	92.5613	100.75%	0.6879	−0.75%	0.0586	6.376924	−119.563

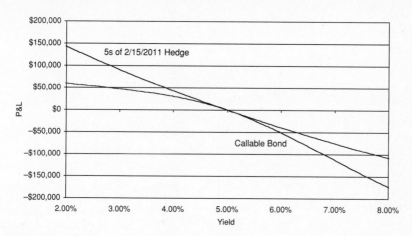

FIGURE 5.9　P&L from Callable Bond and from 5s of February 15, 2011, Hedge

DV01 hedge quite unstable away from 5%. Not only do the values of the two securities increase or decrease away from 5% at different rates, as is also the case in Figure 5.5, but in Figure 5.9 the values are driven even further apart by opposite curvatures. In summary, care must be exercised when mixing securities of positive and negative convexity because the resulting hedges or comparative return estimates are inherently unstable.

CHAPTER 6

Measures of Price Sensitivity Based on Parallel Yield Shifts

Chapter 5 defined various measures of price sensitivity in a general, one-factor framework. This chapter defines measures of price sensitivity in a more restricted setting, namely, that of parallel shifts in yield. These measures have two important weaknesses. First, they can be reasonably used only for securities with fixed cash flows. Second, the assumption of parallel yield shifts is not a particularly good one and, at times, is internally inconsistent. Despite these weaknesses, however, there are several reasons fixed income professionals must understand these measures. First, these measures of price sensitivity are simple to compute, easy to understand, and, in many situations, perfectly reasonable to use. Second, these measures are widely used in the financial industry. Third, much of the intuition gained from a full understanding of these measures carries over to more general measures of price sensitivity.

YIELD-BASED DV01

Yield-based DV01 is a special case of DV01 introduced in Chapter 5. In particular, yield-based DV01 assumes that the yield of a security is the interest rate factor and that the pricing function $P(y)$ is the price-yield relationship introduced in Chapter 3 as equation (3.2) or equation (3.4).[1] For convenience, these equations are reproduced here[2] with the face value set at 100:

---

[1]For expositional ease, the derivations in this chapter assume that coupon flows are in six-month intervals from the settlement date. The derivations in the more general case are very similar.
[2]In Chapter 3 the pricing function was written as a function of years to maturity. Since the emphasis of this chapter is price sensitivity to rate changes, the pricing function is written as a function of yield.

$$P(y) = \sum_{t=1}^{2T} \frac{c/2}{(1+y/2)^t} + \frac{100}{(1+y/2)^{2T}} \tag{6.1}$$

$$P(y) = \frac{c}{y}\left[1 - \frac{1}{(1+y/2)^{2T}}\right] + \frac{100}{(1+y/2)^{2T}} \tag{6.2}$$

Both these equations give the price of a bond with annual coupon payment c per 100 face value, yield to maturity y, and years to maturity T.

DV01, as defined in equation (5.2), equals the derivative of the price function with respect to the rate factor divided by 10,000. In the special case of this chapter, the rate factor is the yield of the bond under consideration. Hence,

$$DV01 = -\frac{1}{10,000}\frac{dP}{dy} \tag{6.3}$$

It is important to emphasize that while equation (6.3) looks very much like equation (5.2), the derivative means something different here from what it meant there. Here the derivative is the change in the price given by equation (6.1) or (6.2) with respect to yield: The one rate that discounts all cash flows is perturbed. In Chapter 5 the derivative is the change in the price, as determined by some pricing model, with respect to any specified interest rate shift (e.g., a parallel shift in forward rates, a volatility-weighted shift in spot rates, etc.).

Yield-based DV01 is one of the special cases mentioned in Chapter 5 for which the derivative of the price-rate function can be computed explicitly. Differentiating equation (6.1),

$$\frac{dP}{dy} = -\frac{1}{1+y/2}\left[\sum_{t=1}^{2T}\frac{t}{2}\frac{c/2}{(1+y/2)^t} + T\frac{100}{(1+y/2)^{2T}}\right] \tag{6.4}$$

Then, according to equation (6.3), dividing both sides of (6.4) by $-10,000$ gives yield-based DV01. For expositional simplicity, the rest of this chapter usually refers to yield-based DV01 simply as DV01.

$$DV01 = \frac{1}{10,000}\times\frac{1}{1+y/2}\left[\sum_{t=1}^{2T}\frac{t}{2}\frac{c/2}{(1+y/2)^t} + T\frac{100}{(1+y/2)^{2T}}\right] \tag{6.5}$$

Equation (6.5) may look messy, but its terms can be interpreted for easy memorization. The first term inside the summation, namely,

$$\frac{t}{2}\frac{c/2}{\left(1+y/2\right)^{t}} \tag{6.6}$$

may be described as follows. The first factor, $t/2$, is the number of years to the receipt of a particular cash flow. For example, the first coupon is indexed by $t=1$ so the cash flow arrives in $t/2=.5$ years, while the last coupon is indexed by $t=2T$ so the cash flow arrives in T years. The second factor denotes the present value of the coupon payment paid in $t/2$ years. Hence, in words, the term recorded in (6.6) is the time-weighted present value of the tth coupon payment. Similarly, the second term in the brackets of equation (6.5), namely

$$T\frac{100}{\left(1+y/2\right)^{2T}} \tag{6.7}$$

is the time-weighted present value of the principal payment. To summarize, then, equation (6.5) says the following: DV01 is the sum of the time-weighted present values of a bond's cash flows divided by 10,000 multiplied by one plus half the yield.

Table 6.1 illustrates the computation of DV01 for the U.S. Treasury 5.625s of February 15, 2006, as of February 15, 2001. The cash flow on August 15, 2003, for example, equals half the coupon or 2.8125 and is paid in 2.5 years. Since the yield of the bond is 5.0441%, the time-weighted present value of this cash flow is

$$2.5\times\frac{2.8125}{\left(1+.050441/2\right)^{5}}=6.2079 \tag{6.8}$$

Finally, since the sum of all the time-weighted present values is 454.8511, the DV01 is

$$\frac{1}{10,000}\times\frac{1}{1+.050441/2}\times454.8511=.044366 \tag{6.9}$$

The DV01 of the 5.625s of February 15, 2006, says that a one-basis point decline in the bond's yield increases its price by about 4.4 cents per $100 face value.

TABLE 6.1   Calculating the DV01 of the 5.625s of
2/15/2006

Yield: 5.0441%

Date	Term	Cash Flow	Present Value	Time-Weighted PV
8/15/01	0.5	2.8125	2.7433	1.3717
2/15/02	1	2.8125	2.6758	2.6758
8/15/02	1.5	2.8125	2.6100	3.9150
2/15/03	2	2.8125	2.5458	5.0916
8/15/03	2.5	2.8125	2.4832	6.2079
2/15/04	3	2.8125	2.4221	7.2662
8/15/04	3.5	2.8125	2.3625	8.2687
2/15/05	4	2.8125	2.3044	9.2175
8/15/05	4.5	2.8125	2.2477	10.1146
2/15/06	5	102.8125	80.1444	400.7219
		Sums:	102.5391	454.8511
		DV01:		0.044366

An equation for DV01 more compact than (6.5) may be derived by differentiating equation (6.2) instead of (6.1). Doing this shows that

$$\frac{dP}{dy} = -\frac{c}{y^2}\left(1 - \frac{1}{\left(1+y/2\right)^{2T}}\right) - \left(100 - \frac{c}{y}\right)\frac{T}{\left(1+y/2\right)^{2T+1}} \qquad (6.10)$$

Dividing by −10,000, it follows immediately that

$$\text{DV01} = \frac{1}{10,000}\left[\frac{c}{y^2}\left(1 - \frac{1}{\left(1+y/2\right)^{2T}}\right) + \left(100 - \frac{c}{y}\right)\frac{T}{\left(1+y/2\right)^{2T+1}}\right] \qquad (6.11)$$

Substituting $c=5.625$, $y=5.0441\%$, and $T=5$ into (6.11) gives .044366, as before. Equation (6.10) will prove particularly useful in deriving simple expressions for several special cases.

Having defined yield-based DV01, its most important limitation becomes clear. A market maker might buy $1 million face amount of a security with a DV01 of .05 and hedge it by selling $1 million times .05/.044366 of the 5.625s of February 15, 2006, or about $1.127 million face amount. Given the assumptions in computing DV01, however, this hedge will work as intended only if the yield of the bond bought changes by the same amount as the yield of the 5.625s of February 15, 2006. It is in this sense that DV01 (along with the other measures of price sensitivity in this chapter) requires parallel yield shifts.

MODIFIED AND MACAULAY DURATION

Chapter 5 defined duration as

$$D = -\frac{1}{P}\frac{dP}{dy} \tag{6.12}$$

Modified duration, written D_{Mod}, is the special case of duration when a bond is priced using its yield, that is, when the pricing function is given by (6.1) or (6.2) and the derivative is given by (6.4) or (6.10). Substituting (6.4) into (6.12),

$$D_{Mod} = \frac{1}{P}\frac{1}{1+y/2}\left[\sum_{t=1}^{2T}\frac{t}{2}\frac{c/2}{\left(1+y/2\right)^{t}} + T\frac{100}{\left(1+y/2\right)^{2T}}\right] \tag{6.13}$$

In words, modified duration equals the time-weighted present value of the cash flows divided by price[3] times one plus half the yield. Since the price of a bond is just the sum of the present values of its cash flows, Table 6.1 contains all the required data to compute the modified duration of the 5.625s of February 15, 2006:

$$D_{Mod} = \frac{1}{102.5391} \times \frac{1}{1+.050441/2}\,454.8511 = 4.3268 \tag{6.14}$$

Substituting (6.10) into (6.12) gives a more compact expression for D_{Mod}:

$$D_{Mod} = \frac{1}{P}\left[\frac{c}{y^{2}}\left(1 - \frac{1}{\left(1+y/2\right)^{2T}}\right) + \left(100 - \frac{c}{y}\right)\frac{T}{\left(1+y/2\right)^{2T+1}}\right] \tag{6.15}$$

---

[3]For the pricing dates and bonds used in the examples of this chapter, accrued interest is zero. When this is not the case, the price appearing in the duration definitions is the full or invoice price.

Macaulay duration, denoted by D_{Mac}, is not very popular today but has one useful interpretation that is described in the next section. This measure of price sensitivity is a simple transformation of modified duration:

$$D_{Mac} = \left(1 + \frac{y}{2}\right) D_{Mod} \qquad (6.16)$$

Using the definitions of D_{Mod} in (6.13) and (6.15) gives two expressions for D_{Mac}:

$$D_{Mac} = \frac{1}{P}\left[\sum_{t=1}^{2T} \frac{t}{2} \frac{c/2}{\left(1+y/2\right)^t} + T \frac{100}{\left(1+y/2\right)^{2T}}\right] \qquad (6.17)$$

$$D_{Mac} = \frac{1+y/2}{P}\left[\frac{c}{y^2}\left(1 - \frac{1}{\left(1+y/2\right)^{2T}}\right) + \left(100 - \frac{c}{y}\right)\frac{T}{\left(1+y/2\right)^{2T+1}}\right] \qquad (6.18)$$

Equation (6.17) says that Macaulay duration equals the time-weighted present value of cash flows divided by price. From the numbers in Table 6.1, the Macaulay duration of the 5.625s of February 15, 2006, is 454.8511/102.5391 or 4.4359.

Despite the fact that modified and Macaulay duration are very special cases of duration as defined in Chapter 5, in this chapter, for ease of exposition, these measures are sometimes referred to simply as duration.

ZERO COUPON BONDS AND A REINTERPRETATION OF DURATION

A convenient property of Macaulay duration is that the Macaulay duration of a T-year zero coupon bond equals T. This relationship is written as follows, where the vertical line and subscript indicate that D_{Mac} is evaluated for the case $c=0$:

$$D_{Mac}\big|_{c=0} = T \qquad (6.19)$$

Hence the Macaulay duration of a six-month zero is simply .5 while that of a 10-year zero is simply 10. To derive this property, set the coupon to zero in equation (6.17) or (6.18) and note that the price of a zero coupon bond equals $100/(1+y/2)^{2T}$.

Longer-maturity zeros have larger durations and, therefore, greater price sensitivity than shorter-maturity zeros. This makes intuitive sense. A change in yield will affect the price of a six-month zero through one period of discounting. The same change in yield, however, affects the price of a 10-year zero through 20 periods of discounting.

The fact that the Macaulay duration of zeros equals years to maturity allows for a convenient interpretation of the Macaulay duration of any other bond. The previous section calculates that the Macaulay duration of the 5.625s due February 15, 2006, is 4.4359. But the D_{Mac} of a zero coupon bond maturing in 4.4359 years is also 4.4359. Therefore, the first order price sensitivity of the 5.625s of February 15, 2006, equals that of a zero maturing in 4.4359 years. In other words, the price sensitivity of zeros can be taken as a benchmark against which to judge the sensitivity of other bonds. Furthermore, the equivalence between Macaulay duration and zero coupon maturity helps explain the industry practice of quoting duration in years, that is, saying that the duration of the 5.625s of February 15, 2006, is 4.4359 years.

The special case of the Macaulay duration of zeros can also be used to reinterpret the mathematical expression for the Macaulay duration of any bond. In particular, the special case of zeros is useful for understanding why the present value of each cash flow in (6.17) is multiplied by the years to the receipt of that cash flow. To explain, rewrite equation (6.17) slightly:

$$D_{Mac} = \left[\sum_{t=1}^{2T} \frac{t}{2} \frac{1}{P} \frac{c/2}{\left(1+y/2\right)^t} + T \frac{1}{P} \frac{100}{\left(1+y/2\right)^{2T}} \right] \tag{6.20}$$

Recall from Part One that a coupon bond may be viewed as a portfolio of zero coupon bonds, in particular a portfolio with $c/2$ face value of zeros that mature on each coupon payment date and an additional 100 face value of zeros maturing on the principal payment date. Continuing with this perspective, the term

$$\frac{1}{P} \frac{c/2}{\left(1+y/2\right)^t} \tag{6.21}$$

in (6.20) denotes the value of the zeros in the portfolio that replicate the tth coupon payment as a fraction of total portfolio value (i.e., of bond price). Similarly, the term

$$\frac{1}{P}\frac{100}{\left(1+y/2\right)^{2T}} \tag{6.22}$$

denotes the value of the zeros in the portfolio that replicate the principal payment as a fraction of total portfolio value. But since the Macaulay duration of a zero equals its years to maturity, the right-hand side of (6.20) is the weighted sum of durations of the replicating zeros where the weights are the value of each zero as a fraction of total portfolio value, that is, of the coupon bond price. This means that (6.20) may be interpreted as saying that the Macaulay duration of a coupon bond equals the duration of its replicating portfolio of zeros. Therefore, in conclusion, the present value of each cash flow in the calculation of Macaulay duration is weighted by its years to receipt because years to receipt is the duration of the corresponding zero in the replicating portfolio.

While the special case of a zero coupon bond is cleanest for Macaulay duration, it may also be derived for DV01 and modified duration. In particular,

$$DV01\Big|_{c=0} = \frac{T}{100\left(1+y/2\right)^{2T+1}} \tag{6.23}$$

$$D_{Mod}\Big|_{c=0} = \frac{T}{1+y/2} \tag{6.24}$$

PAR BONDS AND PERPETUITIES

Two other special cases of DV01 and duration prove useful. As discussed in Chapter 3, for bonds selling at par $P=100$ and $c=100y$. Substituting these values into (6.11), (6.15), and (6.18) gives the following expressions:

$$DV01\Big|_{P=100} = \frac{1}{100y}\left(1-\frac{1}{\left(1+y/2\right)^{2T}}\right) \tag{6.25}$$

$$D_{Mod}\Big|_{P=100} = \frac{1}{y}\left(1 - \frac{1}{\left(1+y/2\right)^{2T}}\right) \tag{6.26}$$

$$D_{Mac}\Big|_{P=100} = \frac{1+y/2}{y}\left(1 - \frac{1}{\left(1+y/2\right)^{2T}}\right) \tag{6.27}$$

Perpetuities make coupon payments forever. Mathematically, $T=\infty$, where ∞ is the symbol for infinity. Taking the limit as maturity approaches infinity in equations (6.2), (6.11), (6.15), and (6.18) gives the following expressions[4]:

$$P\Big|_{T=\infty} = \frac{c}{y} \tag{6.28}$$

$$DV01\Big|_{T=\infty} = \frac{c}{10,000y^2} \tag{6.29}$$

$$D_{Mod}\Big|_{T=\infty} = \frac{1}{y} \tag{6.30}$$

$$D_{Mac}\Big|_{T=\infty} = \frac{1+y/2}{y} \tag{6.31}$$

Note that the derivation of the perpetuity values did not have to assume that the perpetuity never makes its principal payment. Letting maturity extend to infinity lowers the value of any principal to zero; There is no difference in value between a bond that pays only coupons forever and a bond that pays coupons forever and then pays principal. This observation implies that the DV01 and duration expressions given earlier provide a limiting case for any coupon bond. In other words, if the maturity of a coupon bond is extended long enough, its DV01 and duration will approximately equal the DV01 and duration of a perpetuity with the same coupon.

---

[4]When taking the limit of a term like $T/(1+{}^y/_2)^{2T}$, note that the numerator increases linearly in T while the denominator increases exponentially. Consequently, the limit of this term is 0.

DURATION, DV01, MATURITY, AND COUPON: A GRAPHICAL ANALYSIS

Figure 6.1 uses the equations of this chapter to show how Macaulay duration varies across bonds. For the purposes of this figure all yields are fixed at 5%. At this yield, the Macaulay duration of a perpetuity is 20.5. Since a perpetuity has no maturity, this duration is shown in Figure 6.1 as a horizontal line. Also, since, by equation (6.31), the Macaulay duration of a perpetuity does not depend on coupon, this line is a benchmark for the duration of any coupon bond with a sufficiently long maturity.

Since the Macaulay duration of a zero coupon bond equals its years to maturity, the 45° line in the figure gives zero coupon duration.

From equations (6.26) and (6.27) it is clear that the duration of a par bond always increases with maturity. As in the context of zeros, the longer the term, the greater impact changes in yield have on value. The duration of par bonds rises from zero at a maturity of zero and steadily approaches the duration of a perpetuity.

The premium curve in Figure 6.1 is constructed assuming a coupon of 9%, while the discount curve is constructed assuming a coupon of 1%. According to the figure, for any given maturity, duration falls as coupon increases: Zeros have the highest duration and premium bonds the lowest.

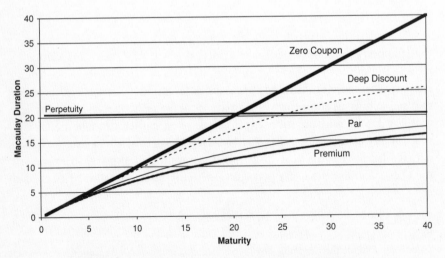

FIGURE 6.1   Macaulay Duration across Bonds Yielding 5%

The intuition behind this fact is that higher-coupon bonds have a greater fraction of their value paid earlier. The higher the coupon, the larger the weights on the duration terms of early years relative to those of later years. Alternatively, the portfolio of zeros replicating relatively high coupon bonds contains a relatively large fraction of its value in shorter-term zeros. From either of these perspectives, higher-coupon bonds are effectively shorter-term bonds and therefore have lower duration.

A little-known fact about duration can be extracted from Figure 6.1. If the discount is deep enough—that is, if the coupon is low enough relative to yield, as it is in this figure—the duration of a discount bond rises above the duration of a perpetuity. But since at some large maturity the duration of a discount bond must approach the duration of a perpetuity, the duration of the discount bond must eventually fall as maturity increases. This phenomenon is not common, but relatively recently bonds have been issued with 50 and 100 years to maturity. Should these sell at a substantial discount at some time in their lives, portfolio managers may find themselves holding bonds that become more sensitive to rates as they mature.

The major difference between DV01 and duration is that DV01 measures an absolute change in price while duration measures a percentage change. To understand how this difference impacts the behavior of DV01 with maturity, rewrite equations (6.3), (6.12), and (6.16) to express DV01 in terms of duration:

$$DV01 = \frac{P \times D_{Mod}}{10,000}$$

$$= \frac{P \times D_{Mac}}{10,000\left(1 + y/2\right)} \tag{6.32}$$

Not surprisingly, for a given duration, bonds with higher prices tend to have higher absolute price sensitivities. So while duration almost always increases with maturity, (6.32) shows that the behavior of DV01 with maturity also depends on how price changes with maturity. What will be called the *duration effect* tends to increase DV01 with maturity while what will be called the *price effect* can either increase or decrease DV01 with maturity.

Figure 6.2 graphs DV01 as a function of maturity under the same assumptions used in Figure 6.1. Since the DV01 of a perpetuity, unlike its Macaulay or modified duration, depends on the coupon rate, the perpetuity line is removed.

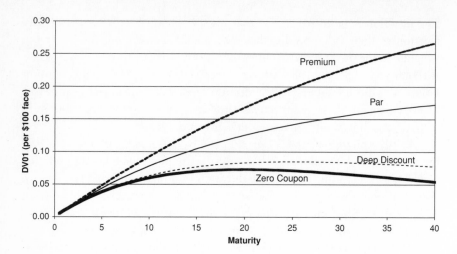

FIGURE 6.2 DV01 across Bonds Yielding 5%

Inspection of equation (6.25) reveals that the DV01 of par bonds always increases with maturity. Since the price of par bonds is always 100, the price effect does not come into play, and, as in the case of duration, longer par bonds have greater price sensitivity. The curve approaches .2, the DV01 of a par perpetuity at a yield of 5%.

As discussed in Chapter 3, extending the maturity of a premium bond increases its price. As a result, the price and duration effects combine so that the DV01 of a premium bond increases with maturity faster than the DV01 of a par bond. Of course, at some maturity beyond the graph, the price of the bond increases very slowly and the price effect becomes less important. The DV01 eventually approaches that of a perpetuity with a coupon of 9% (i.e., .36).

As discussed in Chapter 3, extending the maturity of a discount bond lowers its price. For a relatively short-maturity discount bond, the duration effect dominates and the DV01 of the discount bond increases with maturity. Then the price effect catches up and the DV01 of the discount bond declines with maturity. At some maturity the DV01 approaches .04, that of a perpetuity with a 1% coupon.

The DV01 of a zero behaves like that of a discount bond except that it eventually falls to zero. With no coupon payments, the present value of a zero with a longer and longer maturity approaches zero, and so does its DV01.

Figure 6.2 also shows that, unlike duration, DV01 rises with coupon. This fact is immediately evident from equation (6.5). For a given yield and maturity, higher coupons imply higher dollar prices and higher absolute price sensitivity.

DURATION, DV01, AND YIELD

Inspection of equation (6.5) reveals that increasing yield lowers DV01. This fact has already been introduced: Chapter 5 discussed how bonds with fixed coupons display positive convexity, another way of saying that the derivative and DV01 fall as yield increases. As it turns out, increasing yield also lowers duration. The intuition behind this fact is that increasing yield lowers the present value of all payments but lowers the present value of the longer payments most. This implies that the value of the longer payments falls relative to the value of the whole bond. But since the duration of these longer payments is greatest, lowering their corresponding weights in the duration equation must lower the duration of the whole bond. Conversely, decreasing yield increases DV01 and duration.

Table 6.2 illustrates the effect of yield on modified duration for the 5.625s of February 15, 2006. The longest payment constitutes 77.3% of the bond price at a yield of 7% but 79% at a yield of 3%. By contrast, the shortest payment constitutes only 2.9% of price at a yield of 7% but 2.5% at a yield of 3%. This increase in percentage value of the longer payments relative to the shorter payments as yields fall raises modified duration in this example from 4.26 to 4.40.

YIELD-BASED CONVEXITY

Chapter 5 defined convexity as

$$C = \frac{1}{P} \frac{d^2 P}{dy^2} \tag{6.33}$$

In the special case of the pricing function taken in this chapter, yield-based convexity may be derived by taking the second derivative of the price-yield function or by differentiating equation (6.4):

TABLE 6.2 The Modified Duration of the 5.625s of 2/15/2006 at Different Yields

Term	Cash Flow	Yield: 7% Present Value	PV/Price	Yield: 3% Present Value	PV/Price
0.5	2.8125	2.7174	2.9%	2.7709	2.5%
1	2.8125	2.6255	2.8%	2.7300	2.4%
1.5	2.8125	2.5367	2.7%	2.6896	2.4%
2	2.8125	2.4509	2.6%	2.6499	2.4%
2.5	2.8125	2.3680	2.5%	2.6107	2.3%
3	2.8125	2.2880	2.4%	2.5721	2.3%
3.5	2.8125	2.2106	2.3%	2.5341	2.3%
4	2.8125	2.1358	2.3%	2.4967	2.2%
4.5	2.8125	2.0636	2.2%	2.4598	2.2%
5	102.8125	72.8857	77.3%	88.5902	79.0%
Price		94.2823		112.1041	
Modified Duration		4.2576		4.3992	

$$\frac{d^2P}{dy^2} = \frac{1}{\left(1+y/2\right)^2}\left[\sum_{t=1}^{2T}\frac{t}{2}\frac{t+1}{2}\frac{c/2}{\left(1+y/2\right)^t} + T\left(T+.5\right)\frac{100}{\left(1+y/2\right)^{2T}}\right] \quad (6.34)$$

So yield-based convexity, sometimes referred to as simply convexity, is defined as

$$C = \frac{1}{P\left(1+y/2\right)^2}\left[\sum_{t=1}^{2T}\frac{t}{2}\frac{t+1}{2}\frac{c/2}{\left(1+y/2\right)^t} + T\left(T+.5\right)\frac{100}{\left(1+y/2\right)^{2T}}\right] \quad (6.35)$$

In words, the present values of the cash flows are weighted by time multiplied by time plus one half, summed up, and divided by price multiplied by one plus half the yield squared. For the 5.625s of February 15, 2006, Table 6.3 gives the weights for the calculation of convexity along with the other necessary information to compute the convexity value of 22.2599.

YIELD-BASED CONVEXITY OF ZERO COUPON BONDS

Setting $c=0$ and $P=100/(1+y/2)^{2T}$ in equation (6.35) gives the convexity of a zero coupon bond:

TABLE 6.3 Calculating the Convexity of the 5.625s of 2/15/2006

Yield: 5.0441%

Date	Term	Cash Flow	Present Value	Weighted PV
8/15/01	0.5	2.8125	2.7433	1.3717
2/15/02	1	2.8125	2.6758	4.0137
8/15/02	1.5	2.8125	2.6100	7.8300
2/15/03	2	2.8125	2.5458	12.7290
8/15/03	2.5	2.8125	2.4832	18.6238
2/15/04	3	2.8125	2.4221	25.4319
8/15/04	3.5	2.8125	2.3625	33.0750
2/15/05	4	2.8125	2.3044	41.4789
8/15/05	4.5	2.8125	2.2477	50.5731
2/15/06	5	102.8125	80.1444	2,203.9706
		Sums:	102.5391	2,399.0975
		Convexity:		22.2599

$$C\Big|_{c=0} = \frac{T(T+.5)}{(1+y/2)^2} \qquad (6.36)$$

From (6.36) it is clear that longer-maturity zeros have greater convexity. In fact, convexity increases with the square of maturity. In any case, the price-yield curve of a longer-maturity zero will be more curved than that of a shorter-maturity zero. Furthermore, since a coupon bond is a portfolio of zeros, longer-maturity coupon bonds usually have greater convexity than shorter-maturity coupon bonds.

Just as in the cases of DV01 and duration, equation (6.36) may be used to reinterpret the convexity formula in (6.35). Given the convexity of a zero coupon bond and the fact that the convexity of a portfolio equals the weighted convexity of its components, the convexity formula may be viewed as the convexity of the portfolio of zeros making up the coupon bond.

THE BARBELL VERSUS THE BULLET

In the asset-liability context, *barbelling* refers to the use of a portfolio of short- and long-maturity bonds rather than intermediate-maturity bonds.

An asset-liability manager might have liabilities each with duration equal to nine years and, as a result, with portfolio duration equal to nine years. The proceeds gained from incurring those liabilities could be used to purchase several assets with duration equal to nine years, or alternatively, to purchase 2- and 30-year securities that, as a portfolio, have a duration equal to nine years. The former set of assets is called a *bullet portfolio* and the latter a *barbell portfolio*.

The simple expressions for the Macaulay duration and convexity of zeros derived in the previous sections may be used to begin an analysis of *barbelling*. For this simple example, assume that the yield curve is flat at 5%. A nine-year zero coupon bond has a Macaulay duration of nine years and a convexity of $9 \times 9.5/(1+^{.05}/_2)^2$ or 81.38. A barbell portfolio with 75% of its value in two-year zeros and 25% in 30-year zeros will have Macaulay duration equal to $.75 \times 2 + .25 \times 30$ or 9, matching the duration of the liabilities. The convexity of the barbell portfolio, however, is

$$.75\frac{2 \times 2.5}{\left(1+.05/2\right)^2} + .25\frac{30 \times 30.5}{\left(1+.05/2\right)^2} = 221.30 \qquad (6.37)$$

which is substantially greater than the convexity of the liabilities.

A barbell has greater convexity than a bullet because duration increases linearly with maturity while convexity increases with the square of maturity. If a combination of short and long durations, essentially maturities, equals the duration of the bullet, that same combination of the two convexities, essentially maturities squared, must be greater than the convexity of the bullet. In the example, the particularly high convexity of the 30-year zero, on the order of the square of 30, more than compensates for the lower convexity of the two-year zero. As a result, the convexity of the portfolio exceeds the convexity of the nine-year zero.

Figure 6.3 graphs the price-yield curve of the barbell and bullet portfolios in this example. Note that the values of the two portfolios are assumed to be equal at 5%. This corresponds to the problem of an asset-liability manager who needs to invest a fixed sum with duration equal to 9 at a yield of 5%. As Chapter 5 discussed in the example of hedging an option, the portfolio of greater convexity does better whether rates rise or fall. As noted there, however, this does not imply that the barbell portfolio is superior to the bullet. Chapter 10 will show how bonds are priced to reflect

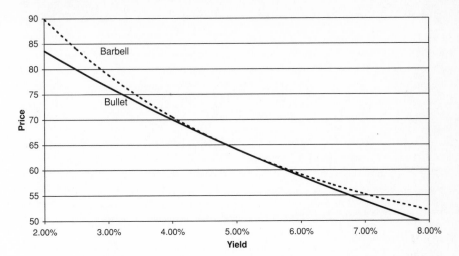

FIGURE 6.3   Price-Yield Curves of Barbell and Bullet

their convexity advantage. In fact, the bullet outperforms if rates move by a relatively small amount, up or down, while the barbell outperforms if rates move by a relatively large amount.

The intuition gained from the barbell-bullet example can be used to understand the convexity properties of other portfolios. In general, spreading out the cash flows of a portfolio (without changing its duration) raises its convexity.

CHAPTER 7

Key Rate and Bucket Exposures

A major weakness of the approach taken in Chapters 5 and 6, as well as in some of the term structure models in Part Three, is the assumption that movements in the entire term structure can be described by one interest rate factor. To put it bluntly, the change in the six-month rate is assumed to predict perfectly the change in the 10-year and 30-year rates. So, for example, a (naive) DV01 analysis would allow for the hedging of a position in 10- or 30-year bonds with six-month securities.

One-factor approaches, particularly when used carelessly, present a danger for hedging and asset-liability management. Consider the case of an asset-liability manager who hedges the yield-based duration of a nine-year liability with a barbell of two- and 30-year assets. If two-, nine-, and 30-year yields change in parallel by some small amount, then, by the definition of duration matching, the total value of the portfolio will be approximately unchanged. But what if the 30-year rate increases and the rest of the curve stays the same? Or what if the nine-year rate decreases and the rest of the curve stays the same? In these cases the value of assets will fall below the value of liabilities. In short, hedging with a model that assumes parallel shifts or any other strong relationship between yields of different maturities will fail to protect against changes in the shape of the yield curve, whether against flattening, steepening, or some other twist.

One approach toward solving this problem is to construct a model with more than one factor. Say, for example, a short-term rate and a long-term rate were taken as factors. One would then compute a sensitivity or duration with respect to each of the two factors. Hedging and asset-liability management would be implemented with respect to both durations. In other words, total portfolio duration with respect to each factor would be set to zero. The procedure in this particular example would protect a portfolio against movements in either end of the curve whether or not these movements occur simultaneously. Of course, the portfolio would be subject to gains or losses from changes in intermediate rates that are not perfectly predicted by changes in the short- and long-term rates selected as factors.

Chapter 13 will discuss two-factor models for the purpose of simultaneous pricing and hedging. This chapter presents two commonly used techniques for the purpose of multi-factor hedging, that is, for measuring exposures to several regions of the yield curve and for protecting against a relatively wide variety of yield curve movements.

KEY RATE SHIFTS

In this technique a set of *key rates* is assumed to describe the movements of the entire term structure. Put another way, the technique assumes that given the key rates any other rate may be determined. The following choices must be made to apply the technique: the number of key rates, the type of rate to be used (usually spot rates or par yields), the terms of the key rates, and the rule for computing all other rates given the key rates. These choices are examined in the next several sections.

Assume for now that there are four key rates, the two-, five-, 10-, and 30-year par yields. The change in the term structure of par yields accompanying a one-basis point change in each of the key rates is assumed to be as shown in Figure 7.1. Each of these shapes is called a *key rate shift*. Each key rate affects par yields from the term of the previous key rate (or zero) to the term of the next key rate (or the last term). Specifically, the two-year

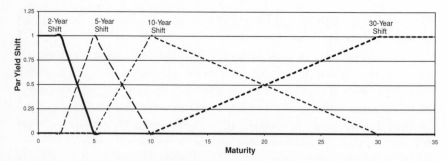

FIGURE 7.1 Key Rate Shifts

key rate affects all par yields of term zero to five, the five-year affects par yields of term two to 10, the 10-year affects par yields of term five to 30, and the 30-year affects par yields from 10 on. The impact of each key rate is one basis point at its own maturity and declines linearly to zero at the term of the adjacent key rate. To the left of the two-year key rate and to the right of the 30-year key rate, the effect remains at one basis point.

There are several appealing features about the impacts of the key rates described in Figure 7.1. First, consistent with the spirit of key rate exposures, each region of the par yield curve is affected by a combination of the key rates closest to it. The seven-year rate, for example, is affected by changes in the five-year and 10-year rates while the 15-year rate is affected by changes in the 10-year and 30-year rates. Second, each rate is most affected by the key rate closest to it. The nine-year rate is strongly impacted by the 10-year rate and slightly impacted by the five-year rate. Third, the impacts of the key rates change smoothly. The five-year key rate affects the seven-year rate only a bit more than it affects the eight-year rate, while the 10-year key rate affects the seven-year rate only a bit less than it affects the eight-year rate. Fourth, the sum of the key rate shifts equals a parallel shift in the par yield curve. The appeal of this property will be discussed in the next section.

The fact that the shifts are linear between key rates is not essential. Quite the contrary: The arbitrary shape of the shifts is a theoretical weakness of the key rate approach. One might easily argue, for example, that the shifts should at least be smooth curves rather than piecewise linear segments. However, in practice, the advantage of extra smoothness may not justify the increased complexity caused by abandoning the simplicity of straight lines.

KEY RATE 01s AND KEY RATE DURATIONS

Table 7.1 summarizes the calculation of *key rate 01s*, the key rate equivalent of DV01, and of *key rate durations*, the key rate equivalent of duration. The security used in the example is a nonprepayable mortgage requiring a payment of $3,250 every six months for 30 years. So that the the numbers are easily reproduced, it is assumed that the par yield curve is flat at 5%, but no such restrictive assumption is necessary. Like DV01 and duration, key rate exposures can be calculated assuming any initial term structure so long as the security can be priced at that term structure and at

TABLE 7.1   Key Rate Exposures of a 30-Year Nonprepayable Mortgage

	($)	Key Rate 01($)	Key Rate Duration	Percent of Total
Monthly payment:	$3,250			
Par yields flat at:	5%			
Initial value	100,453.13			
After 2-year shift	100,452.15	0.98	0.10	0.9%
After 5-year shift	100,449.36	3.77	0.38	3.3%
After 10-year shift	100,410.77	42.37	4.22	37.0%
After 30-year shift	100,385.88	67.26	6.70	58.8%
Total:		114.38	11.39	

the term structure after applying the required shift. In this simple case, pricing is done by discounting,[1] but for more complicated securities, like real mortgages that are prepayable, the models of Part Three must be used.

Table 7.1 reports that the value of the mortgage at the initial term structure is $100,453.13 and that the value after a five-year key rate shift of 1 basis point is $100,449.36. Therefore, the five-year key rate 01 is

$$-\left(\$100,449.36 - \$100,453.13\right) = \$3.77 \qquad (7.1)$$

and, multiplying by 10,000 and dividing by price, the five-year key rate duration is

$$10,000 \times \$3.77 / \$100,453.13 = .38 \qquad (7.2)$$

The last row of the table adds the key rate 01s and durations. Since the sum of the key rate shifts is a parallel shift in the par yield curve, the sums of the key rate 01s and durations closely match the DV01 and duration, respectively, under the assumption of a parallel shift in the par yield curve.

---

[1]More specifically, given the original par yield curve or any shifted par yield curve, the definitions of Part One may be used to compute discount factors. These, in turn, can be used to price any set of fixed cash flows.

Therefore, key rate exposures essentially decompose a sensitivity measure like DV01 or duration into component sensitivities. The last column of Table 7.1 gives the percent of the total sensitivity attributable to movement in different segments of the term structure.

The pattern of key rate sensitivities across key rate depends on several factors. First, this pattern reflects the distribution of cash flows. A 10-year par bond, on the one hand, has no exposure to the two-, five-, and 30-year key rates but 100% exposure to the 10-year key rate. (The next section elaborates on this point.) The nonprepayable mortgage, on the other hand, with cash flows spread evenly over the entire maturity spectrum, will have exposure to all the key rates. Second, the sensitivity to short-term key rates is likely to be relatively low since the DV01 or duration of short-term cash flows is relatively low. Third, the sensitivity to longer-term key rates is depressed by the fact that longer-term cash flows are worth less than shorter-term cash flows. The duration of a cash flow due in 30 years is relatively high, but the value of that cash flow as a percentage of the value of the security is relatively small. As a result, the change in value of that cash flow has a smaller effect on the value of the security than its duration might indicate. Fourth, the pattern of key rate exposures is affected by the choice of key rates. If key rates were oddly chosen to be nine-, 10-, 11-, and 30-year par yields, the 10-year key rate would affect only cash flows between nine and 11 years to maturity. In that case, except for coupon bonds maturing in about 10 years, key rate exposures would not show much sensitivity to the 10-year rate. By contrast, with the common choice of two-, five-, 10-, and 30-year par yields, the 10-year key rate has the largest span of all the key rates, covering 25 years of the term structure.

HEDGING WITH KEY RATE EXPOSURES

As discussed in the next section, the choice of two-, five-, 10-, and 30-year par yields as key rates indicates a desire to hedge with two-, five-, 10-, and 30-year par bonds. In that case, hedging the nonprepayable mortgage analyzed in the previous section is accomplished by selling the portfolio of these hedging securities that matches each key rate exposure computed in Table 7.1. Table 7.2 begins computing the composition of this portfolio by computing the key rate 01s of the hedging securities. To make the example realistic without complicating it too much, it is assumed that the liquid

TABLE 7.2   Key Rate Exposures of Four Hedging Securities

Par yields flat at: 5%

		Key Rate 01s (100 Face)			
Coupon	Term	2-Year	5-Year	10-Year	30-Year
5%	2	0.01881	0	0	0
5%	5	0	0.04375	0	0
8%	10	0.00122	0.00468	0.08308	0
5%	30	0	0	0	0.15444
Nonprepayable mortage:		0.98129	3.77314	42.36832	67.25637

two-, five-, and 30-year bonds sell for par but that the liquid 10-year security has a coupon of 8% and sells at a premium.

Since the two-year par yield is a key rate, changing any other key rate does not, by definition, change the two-year par rate. Consequently, two-year par bonds have no exposure to any key rate except the two-year key rate. Similarly, five-, 10-, and 30-year par bonds have no exposure to any key rate but that of the corresponding maturity. Since three of the hedging securities in Table 7.2 are par bonds at maturities corresponding to key rates, they have sensitivities to one key rate each. By contrast, since the 10-year hedging bond is not a par bond, its price is not completely determined by the 10-year par yield.[2] In particular, its price is sensitive to changes in the two- and five-year key rates.

Let F_2, F_5, F_{10}, and F_{30} be the face amounts of the bonds in the hedging portfolio to be sold against the nonprepayable mortgage. Only two of the bonds, namely the two-year and 10-year, have an exposure to the two-year key rate. Therefore, for the two-year key rate exposure of the hedging portfolio to equal that of the mortgage it must be the case that

$$\frac{.01881}{100} F_2 + \frac{.00122}{100} F_{10} = .98129 \qquad (7.3)$$

---

[2]Consider the following simple example. One par yield curve slopes upward everywhere and one slopes downward everywhere, but both have 10-year par yields equal to 5%. A 10-year bond with an 8% coupon certainly does not have the same price under both yield curves.

Note that since the key rate 01s of the bonds are reported per 100 face, they need to be divided by 100 in equation (7.3). The key rate 01 of the mortgage is reported for the face amount to be hedged, so it stands as is.

Two bonds have exposures to the five-year key rate, namely the five-year and 10-year bonds. To hedge against changes in the five-year key rate, it must be the case that

$$\frac{.04375}{100} F_5 + \frac{.00468}{100} F_{10} = 3.77314 \qquad (7.4)$$

Only one bond has an exposure to each of the 10- and 30-year key rates, namely the 10- and 30-year bonds, respectively. Hedging against changes in these key rates requires that

$$\frac{.08308}{100} F_{10} = 42.36832 \qquad (7.5)$$

and

$$\frac{.15444}{100} F_{30} = 67.25637 \qquad (7.6)$$

Solving equations (7.3) through (7.6) simultaneously gives the following solution for the face value of the hedging bonds in the hedging portfolio:

$$
\begin{aligned}
F_2 &= 1{,}920 \\
F_5 &= 3{,}173 \\
F_{10} &= 50{,}998 \\
F_{30} &= 43{,}549
\end{aligned}
\qquad (7.7)
$$

A portfolio of the nonprepayable mortgage and a short position in these quantities of hedging bonds has no exposure to any of the four key rates. In other words, this hedged portfolio will be approximately immune to any combination of key rate movements. Possible combinations include the 10-year key rate moving up by five basis points and all other key rates staying the same, the two- and 30-year key rates moving down by three basis points and other key rates staying the same, and so forth. The hedged portfolio is only approximately immune for two reasons. First, as usual with derivative-based hedging, the quality of hedge deteriorates as the size of the interest rate change increases. Second and more important, the hedge will work as intended only if the par yields between key rates move as assumed. If the 20-year rate does something very different from what was assumed in Figure 7.1, the supposedly hedged portfolio will suffer losses or experience gains.

The hedging method described in this section makes full use of a security's key rate profile. But key rate analysis may be used in a less formal way. If a hedger wanted to use only one bond to hedge the mortgage (and was willing to assume any accompanying curve risk), the key rate profile in Table 7.1 indicates that a par security maturing between 10 and 30 years might be the best choice. If the hedger were willing to purchase two of the hedging securities listed, Table 7.1 certainly points to the 10- and 30-year securities. More generally, if a hedger chooses to hedge with a relatively small number of securities, a key rate profile can guide the selection of those securities. In fact, since many practitioners rely on DV01 hedging, particularly to mange risk over a short time, they might use key rates to select their single hedging security. The extreme example in the chapter introduction, of hedging a position in 10- and 30-year bonds with six-month securities, would be avoided by a key rate analysis (if not by common sense).

CHOOSING KEY RATES

The greater the number of key rates, the better the quality of the resulting hedge. Using four key rates and, therefore, four securities to hedge a portfolio can protect against a wider variety of yield curve changes than DV01-hedging. Then why not use very many key rates? Using 20 key rates and 20 securities to hedge a portfolio might very well be feasible if the portfolio's composition were relatively constant over time and if the portfolio's key rate durations were relatively stable. A portfolio with these characteristics would also benefit from *bucket exposures* and perhaps even *immunization*, described in the next sections. On the other hand, for a portfolio with a changing composition or with key rate durations that change significantly with the level of rates, trading 20 securities every time the portfolio or its sensitivities change would probably prove too costly and onerous.

Key rates are usually defined as par yields or spot rates. If par bonds are used as hedging securities, par yields are a particularly convenient choice. First, as mentioned previously, each hedging security has an exposure to one and only one key rate. Second, computing the sensitivity of a par bond of a given maturity with respect to the par yield of the same maturity is the same as computing DV01. In other words, the key rate exposures of the hedging securities equal their DV01s. To illustrate the convenience of par yield key rates with par hedging bonds, suppose in the example of the previous section that the 10-year bond sold at par like the other three hedging bonds. In that case, the hedging equations (7.3) through (7.6) reduce to the following simpler form:

$$\frac{.01881}{100} F_2 = .98129 \tag{7.8}$$

$$\frac{.04375}{100} F_5 = 3.77314 \tag{7.9}$$

$$\frac{.08308}{100} F_{10} = 42.36832 \tag{7.10}$$

$$\frac{.15444}{100} F_{30} = 67.25637 \tag{7.11}$$

To compute the hedge amount in this case, simply divide each key rate exposure by the DV01 (per unit face value) of the hedging bond of corresponding maturity.

The disadvantage of using par yields, particularly when combined with the assumption that intermediate yields are found by the lines drawn in Figure 7.1, is that the changes in the forward rate curve implied by these yields changes have a bizarre shape. The problem is similar to that of the forward curve emerging from linear yield interpolation in Figure 4.3: Kinks in the yield curve translate into sizable jumps in the forward curve. Changing key rates to spot rates has the same disadvantage.

Setting key rates to forward rates naturally solves this problem: The shifted forward curve is only as odd as the shapes in Figure 7.1. The problem with shifting forward rates is that spot rate changes are no longer local. Changing the forward rates from two to five years while keeping all other forward rates constant, for example, changes all the spot rates from two years and beyond. True, the effect on a 30-year rate is much less than the effect on a five-year rate, but the key rate interpretation of shocking one part of the term structure at a time is lost. Forward shifts will, however, be the more natural set of shifts in bucket analysis, described in the next section.

With respect to the terms of the key rates, it is clearly desirable to spread them out over the maturity range of interest. More subtly, well-chosen terms make it possible to hedge the resulting exposures with securities that are traded and, even better, with liquid securities. As an example, consider a swap market in an emerging market currency. A dealer might make markets in long-term swaps of any maturity but might observe prices and hedge easily only in, for example, 10- and 30-year swaps. In that case there would not be much point in using 10-, 20-, and 30-year par swap yields as key rates. If all maturities between 10 and 30 years were of extremely limited liquidity, it would be virtually impossible to hedge against changes in those three ill-chosen key rates. If a 20-year security did trade with limited liquidity the decision would be more difficult. Including a 20-year key rate would allow for better hedging of privately transacted, intermediate-maturity swaps but would substantially raise the cost of hedging.

BUCKET SHIFTS AND EXPOSURES

A *bucket* is jargon for a region of some curve, like a term structure of interest rates. Bucket shifts are similar to key rate shifts but differ in two respects. First, bucket analysis usually uses very many buckets while key rate analysis tends to use a relatively small number of key rates. Second, each bucket shift is a parallel shift of forward rates as opposed to the shapes of the key rate shifts described previously. The reasons for these differences can be explained in the context for which bucket analysis is particularly well suited, namely, managing the interest rate risk of a large swap portfolio.

Swaps are treated in detail in Chapter 18, but a few notes are necessary for the discussion here. Since this section focuses on the risk of the fixed side of swaps, the reader may, for now, think of swap cash flows as if they come from coupon bonds. Given the characteristics of the swap market, agreements to receive or pay those fixed cash flows for a particular set of terms (e.g., 2, 5, and 10 years) may be executed at very low bid-ask spreads. Unwinding those agreements after some time, however, or entering into new agreements for different terms to maturity, can be costly. As a result, market making desks and other types of trading accounts tend to remain in swap agreements until maturity. A common problem in the industry, therefore, is how to hedge extremely large books of swaps.

The practice of accumulating swaps leads to large portfolios that change in composition only slowly. As mentioned, this characteristic makes it reasonable to hedge against possible changes in many small segments of the term structure. While hedging against these many possible shifts requires many initial trades, the stability of the underlying portfolio composition assures that these hedges need not be adjusted very frequently. Therefore, in this context, risk can be reduced at little expense relative to the holding period of the underlying portfolio.

As discussed in previous sections, liquid coupon bonds are the most convenient securities with which to hedge portfolios of U.S. Treasury bonds. While, analogously, liquid swaps are convenient for hedging portfolios of less liquid swaps, it turns out that *Eurodollar futures* contracts play an important role as well. These futures will be treated in detail in Chapter 17, but the important point for this section is that Eurodollar futures may be used to hedge directly the risk of changes in forward rates. Furthermore, they are relatively liquid, particularly in the shorter terms. The relative ease of hedging forward rates makes it worthwhile to compute exposures of portfolios to changes in forward rates.

Figure 7.2 graphs the bucket exposures of receiving the fixed side of $100 million of a 6% par swap assuming, for simplicity, that swap rates are flat at 6%. (It should be emphasized, and it should become clear shortly, that the assumption of a flat term structure is not at all necessary for the computation of bucket exposures.) The graph shows, for example, that the exposure to the six-month rate 2.5 years forward is about $4,200.

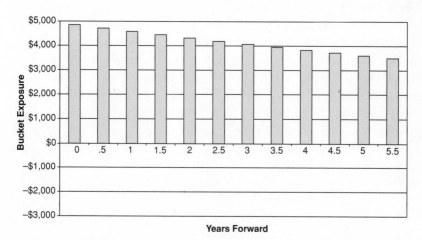

FIGURE 7.2 Bucket Exposures of a Six-Year Par Swap

In other words, a one-basis point increase in the six-month rate 2.5 years forward lowers the value of a $100 million swap by $4,200. The sum of the bucket exposures, in this case $49,768, is the exposure of the swap to a simultaneous one-basis point change to all the forwards. If the swap rate curve is flat, as in this simple example, this sum exactly equals the DV01 of the fixed side of the swap. In more general cases, when the swap rate curve is not flat, the sum of the forward exposures is usually close to the DV01. In any case, Figure 7.2 and this discussion reveal that this swap can be hedged by paying fixed cash flows in a swap agreement of similar coupon and maturity or by hedging exposures to the forward rates directly with Eurodollar futures.

Table 7.3 shows the computation of the particular bucket exposure mentioned in the previous paragraph. The original forward rate curve is flat at 6%, and the par swap, by definition, is priced at 100% of face amount. For the perturbed forward curve, the six-month rate 2.5 years forward is raised to 6.01%, and all other forwards are kept the same. The new spot rate curve and discount factors are then computed using the rela-

TABLE 7.3 Exposure of a $100 million 6% Par Swap to the Six-Month Rate 2.5 Years Forward

Initial forward curve flat at 6%

Bucket exposure: $4,187

Years Forward	Cash Flow ($millions)	Perturbed Forward	Perturbed Spot	Discount Factor
0	3	6.00%	6.0000%	0.970874
0.5	3	6.00%	6.0000%	0.942596
1	3	6.00%	6.0000%	0.915142
1.5	3	6.00%	6.0000%	0.888487
2	3	6.00%	6.0000%	0.862609
2.5	3	6.01%	6.0017%	0.837444
3	3	6.00%	6.0014%	0.813052
3.5	3	6.00%	6.0012%	0.789371
4	3	6.00%	6.0011%	0.766380
4.5	3	6.00%	6.0010%	0.744058
5	3	6.00%	6.0009%	0.722386
5.5	103	6.00%	6.0008%	0.701346
	Perturbed value ($millions):			99.995813

tionships of Part One. Next, the fixed side of the swap is valued at 99.995813% of face value by discounting its cash flows. Finally, the bucket exposure for $100 million of the swap is

$$-\$100,000,000 \times \left(99.995813\% - 100\%\right) = \$4,187 \qquad (7.12)$$

Say that a market maker receives fixed cash flows from a customer in a $100 million, six-year par swap and pays fixed cash flows to another customer in a $141.8 million, four-year par swap. The cash flows of the resulting portfolio and the bucket exposures are given in Table 7.4. A negative exposure means that an increase in that particular forward rate raises the value of the portfolio. The bucket exposures sum to zero so that the portfolio is neutral with respect to parallel shifts of the forward rate curve. This discussion, therefore, is a very simple example of a growing swap book that is managed so as to have, in some sense, no outright interest rate exposure.

TABLE 7.4 Bucket Exposures for a Position Hedged for Parallel Shifts

Initial forward curve flat at 6%

Coupon	6.00%	6.00%
Maturity	6.0	4.0
Face ($mm)	100.000	−141.801

Years Forward	Cash Flow ($millions)		Portfolio Flows ($millions)	Bucket Exposure ($)
0.00	3.000	−4.254	−1.254	−2,029
0.50	3.000	−4.254	−1.254	−1,970
1.00	3.000	−4.254	−1.254	−1,913
1.50	3.000	−4.254	−1.254	−1,857
2.00	3.000	−4.254	−1.254	−1,803
2.50	3.000	−4.254	−1.254	−1,750
3.00	3.000	−4.254	−1.254	−1,699
3.50	3.000	−146.055	−143.055	−1,650
4.00	3.000	0.000	3.000	3,832
4.50	3.000	0.000	3.000	3,720
5.00	3.000	0.000	3.000	3,612
5.50	103.000	0.000	103.000	3,507
Total:				0

Figure 7.3 graphs the bucket exposures of this simple portfolio. Since a six-year swap has been hedged by a four-year swap, interest rate risk remains from six-month rates 4 to 5.5 years forward. The total of this risk is exactly offset by negative exposures to six-month rates from 0 to 3.5 years forward. So while the portfolio has no risk with respect to parallel shifts of the forward curve, it can hardly be said that the portfolio has no interest rate risk. The portfolio will make money in a flattening of the forward curve, that is, when rates 0 to 3.5 years forward rise relative to rates 4 to 5.5 years forward. Conversely, the portfolio will lose money in a steepening of the forward curve, that is, when rates 0 to 3.5 years forward fall relative to rates 4 to 5.5 years forward.

A market maker with a portfolio characterized by Figure 7.3 may very well decide to eliminate this curve exposure by trading the relevant forward rates through Eurodollar futures. The market maker could certainly reduce this curve exposure by trading par swaps and could neutralize this exposure completely by entering into a sufficient number of swap agreements. But hedging directly with Eurodollar futures has the advantages of simplicity and, often, of liquidity. Also, should the forward exposure profile change with the level of rates and the shape of the curve, adjustments to a portfolio of Eurodollar futures are preferable to adding even more swaps to the market maker's growing book.

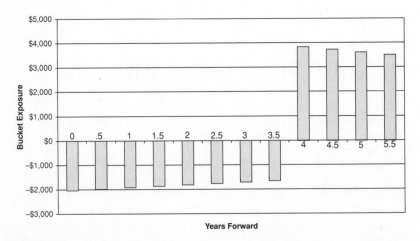

FIGURE 7.3   Bucket Exposures of a Six-Year Swap Hedged with a Four-Year Swap

As each Eurodollar futures contract is related to a particular three-month forward rate and as 10 years of these futures trade at all times,[3] it is common to divide the first 10 years of exposure into three-month buckets. In this way any bucket exposure may, if desired, be hedged directly with Eurodollar futures. Beyond 10 years the exposures are divided according to the same considerations as when choosing the terms of key rates.

IMMUNIZATION

The principles underlying hedging with key rate or bucket exposures can be extrapolated to a process known as *immunization*. No matter how many sources of interest rate risk are hedged, some interest rate risk remains unless the exposure to each and every cash flow has been perfectly hedged. For example, an insurance company may, by using actuarial tables, be able to predict its future liabilities relatively accurately. It can then immunize itself to interest rate risk by holding a portfolio of assets with cash flows that exactly offset the company's future expected liabilities.

The feasibility of immunization depends on the circumstances, but it is worth pointing out the spectrum of tolerances for interest rate risk as revealed by hedging techniques. On the one extreme are hedges that protect against parallel shifts and other single-factor specifications described in Part Three. Away from that extreme are models with relatively few factors like the two- and multi-factor models of Chapter 13, like the empirical approach discussed in Chapter 8, and like most practical applications of key rates. Toward the other extreme are bucket exposures and, at that other extreme, immunization.

MULTI-FACTOR EXPOSURES AND RISK MANAGEMENT

While this chapter focuses on how to quantify the risk of particular changes in the term structure and on how to hedge that risk, key rate and bucket exposures may also be applied to problems in the realm of risk management.

The introduction to Chapter 5 mentioned that a risk manager could combine an assumption that the annual volatility of interest rates is 100 basis points with a computed DV01 of $10,000 per basis point to conclude

---

[3]The longer-maturity Eurodollar futures are not nearly so liquid as the earlier ones.

that the annual volatility of a portfolio is $1 million. But this measure of portfolio volatility has the same drawback as one-factor measures of price sensitivity: The volatility of the entire term structure cannot be adequately summarized with just one number. As to be discussed in Part Three, just as there is a term structure of interest rates, there is a term structure of volatility. The 10-year par rate, for example, is usually more volatile than the 30-year par rate.

Key rate and bucket analysis may be used to generalize a one-factor estimation of portfolio volatility. In the case of key rates, the steps are as follows: (1) Estimate a volatility for each of the key rates and estimate a correlation for each pair of key rates. (2) Compute the key rate 01s of the portfolio. (3) Compute the variance and volatility of the portfolio. The computation of variance is quite straightforward given the required inputs. For example, if there are only two key rates, R_1 and R_2, if the key rate 01s of the portfolio are $KR01_1$ and $KR01_2$, and if the portfolio value is P, then the change in the value of the portfolio is

$$\Delta P = KR01_1 \Delta R_1 + KR01_2 \Delta R_2 \tag{7.13}$$

where Δ denotes a change. Furthermore, letting σ^2 with the appropriate subscript denote a particular variance and letting ρ denote the correlation between changes in the two key rates, the variance of the portfolio is simply

$$\sigma_P^2 = KR01_1^2 \sigma_1^2 + KR01_2^2 \sigma_2^2 + 2 \times KR01_1 \times KR01_2 \times \rho \sigma_1 \sigma_2 \tag{7.14}$$

The standard deviation or volatility of the portfolio is simply, of course, the square root of this variance. Bucket analysis may be used in the same way, but a volatility must be assigned to each forward rate and many more correlation pairs must be estimated.

CHAPTER 8

Regression-Based Hedging

DV01 and duration measure price sensitivity under any given assumptions about term structure movement. Yield-based DV01 and modified duration assume parallel yield shifts, key rates assume the particular local perturbations described in Chapter 7, and the models of Part Three make more complex assumptions. The goal of all these choices is to approximate the empirical reality of how interest rates behave. When practitioners hedge with DV01, for example, they express the view that a large part of the variation of nearby yields may be explained by parallel shifts. The general approach may be summarized as empirically analyzing term structure behavior, capturing the important features of that behavior in a relatively simple model, and then calculating price sensitivities based on that model.

An alternative approach is to use empirical analysis directly as the model of interest rate behavior. This chapter shows how regression analysis is used for hedging. The first section, on volatility-weighted hedges, maintains the assumption of a single driving interest rate factor and, therefore, of perfect correlation across bond yields, but allows changes to be other than parallel. The second section, on single-variable regression hedging, continues to assume that only one bond is used to hedge any other bond, but allows bond yields to be less than perfectly correlated. The third section, on two-variable regression hedging, assumes that two bonds are used to hedge any other bond, implicitly recognizing that even two bonds cannot perfectly hedge a given bond. To conclude the chapter, the fourth section presents a trading case study about how 20-year Treasury bonds might be hedged and, at the same time, asks if those bonds were fairly priced in the third quarter of 2001.

VOLATILITY-WEIGHTED HEDGING

Consider the following fairly typical market maker problem. A client sells the market maker a 20-year bond. In the best of circumstances the market maker would immediately sell that same bond to another client and pocket the bid-ask spread. More likely, the market maker will immediately sell the most correlated liquid security, in this case a 30-year bond,[1] to hedge interest rate risk. When another client does appear to buy the 20-year bond, the market maker will sell that bond and lift the hedge—that is, buy back the 30-year bond sold as the hedge.

A market maker who believes that the 20- and 30-year yields move in parallel would hedge with DV01, as described in Chapter 6. But what if a 1.1-basis point increase in the 20-year yield is expected to accompany a one-basis point increase in the 30-year yield? In that case the market maker would trade F_{30} face amount of the 30-year bond to hedge F_{20} face amount of the 20-year bond such that the P&L of the resulting position is zero. Mathematically,

$$-F_{20} \times 1.1 \times \frac{DV01_{20}}{100} - F_{30} \times \frac{DV01_{30}}{100} = 0 \qquad (8.1)$$

where $DV01_{20}$ and $DV01_{30}$ are, as usual, per 100 face value. Note the role of the negative signs in the P&L on the left-hand side of equation (8.1). If the 20-year yield increases by 1.1 basis points then a position of F_{20} face amount of 20-year bonds experiences a P&L of $-F_{20} \times 1.1 \times DV01_{20}/100$. This number is negative for a long position in 20-year bonds (i.e., $F_{20}>0$) and positive for a short position in 20-year bonds (i.e., $F_{20}<0$).

The hedge described in equation (8.1) is called a *volatility-weighted* hedge because, unlike simple DV01 hedging, it recognizes that the 20-year yield tends to fluctuate more than the 30-year yield. The effectiveness of this hedge is, of course, completely dependent on the predictive power of the volatility ratio. To illustrate, say that both yields are 5.70% and that the 20- and 30-year bonds in question sell for par. In that case, using the

---

[1]The text purposely ignores bond futures contracts, discussed in Chapter 20. Since the *cheapest-to-deliver* security of the bond futures contract may very well have a maturity of approximately 20 years, a market maker might very well choose to sell the bond futures contract to hedge the purchase of a 20-year bond.

equations of Chapter 6, the DV01s are .118428 and .142940, respectively. With a volatility ratio equal to 1.1, solving equation (8.1) for F_{30} shows that the purchase of $10 million face amount 20-year bonds should be hedged with a position of

$$F_{30} = -F_{20} \times 1.1 \times DV01_{20}/DV01_{30}$$

$$= -\$10,000,000 \times 1.1 \times \frac{.118428}{.142940} \qquad (8.2)$$

$$= -\$9,113,670$$

or a short of about $9.1 million face amount of 30-year bonds. (Note that a strict DV01 hedge would entail selling only about $8.3 million 30-year bonds. Since, however, the 20-year yield is now assumed more volatile than the 30-year yield, more 30-year bonds must be sold to hedge anticipated price changes in the 20-year bonds.)

The number 1.1 in equations (8.1) and (8.2) is called the *risk weight*[2] of the hedging security, in this case of the 30-year bond. To understand this usage, rearrange the terms of equation (8.1) as follows:

$$1.1 = \frac{-F_{30} \times DV01_{30}}{F_{20} \times DV01_{20}} \qquad (8.3)$$

In words, the quantity 1.1 gives the total DV01 risk of the hedging position as a fraction of the DV01 risk of the underlying position.

If a long position of $10 million 20-year bonds is hedged according to equation (8.2) and it turns out that the 20-year yield increases not by 1.1 but by 1.3 basis points when the 30-year yield increases by 1 basis point, the position will change in value by

$$-\$10,000,000 \times 1.3 \frac{.118428}{100} + \$9,113,670 \frac{.142940}{100} = -\$2,369 \qquad (8.4)$$

Similarly, if the ratio turns out to be 1.3 and the 30-year rate increases by 5 basis points, the supposedly hedged position will lose five times the amount indicated by equation (8.4) or about $12,000.

The simplest way to estimate the volatility ratio is to compute the two volatilities from recent data. Collect a time series on 20-year yields and on

---

[2]The definition of the term risk weight here is not the same as that used by Bloomberg in the trading case study of Chapter 4.

30-year yields, compute changes of these yields from one day to the next or from one week to the next, and then calculate the standard deviation of these changes. This procedure requires a bit of work and a few important decisions. First, in bond markets, data usually exist for particular issues and not for particular maturities. So, to obtain a time series on 20- or 30-year yields requires some splicing of data from different bond issues. Of course, if an investigator is content to use a relatively short history, yields of individual issues may be used. In swap markets this problem does not arise because data series are usually for new par swaps of fixed maturities. Second, in bond markets, it is important to avoid estimating the volatility of a particular bond over a period in which it sometimes had, and sometimes did not have, particular liquidity or financing advantages. (See Chapter 15.) Third, choosing a time period to analyze is crucial to the applicability of the results. Since the goal is to predict the volatility ratio in the future as accurately as possible, it is enormously important to perform a study using relevant observations. Sometimes these relevant observations are exclusively from the recent past and sometimes they are from disjoint, past periods that were characterized by economic and market conditions similar to those of the present. The thinking behind these choices, rather than the technicalities of computing hedge ratios, is what makes hedging a challenge. Fourth, yield changes may be computed over each day, each week, each month, and so on. It can be shown that the smaller the time interval, the more accurate the estimate of volatility. If, however, the data series has many small errors, it may be better to use changes over longer time intervals. For example, a series that repeats the same yield observation for two or three consecutive days probably suffers from *stale data*. Using daily changes on such a series will clearly underestimate volatility. Hence, in that case, computing weekly changes would probably produce more accurate results.

Using data from January 1995 to September 2001 on one-day changes in 20- and *double-old* 30-year yields[3] in the U.S. Treasury market produces

---

[3]A double-old bond is not the most recently issued bond in a particular maturity range, nor the second most recently issued bond in that maturity range, but the third most recently issued. Double-old bonds tend to be relatively liquid but tend not to have the financing advantages and liquidity premium associated with more recently issued bonds. Therefore, double-old bonds are particularly suitable for empirical study. Chapter 15 will discuss the impact of the issuance cycle on bond pricing in more detail.

volatilities of 5.27 and 4.94 basis points per day, respectively. The ratio of these volatilities is about 1.066. If it were felt that this time period were applicable to the present, 1.066 might be used instead of 1.1 as the risk weight of 30-year bonds for hedging 20-year bonds.

One way to assess the safety or danger of using an estimate like that described in the previous paragraph is to see how the volatility ratio changes over time. Figure 8.1 graphs the volatility ratio over the time period mentioned. The volatility on a particular day is computed from yield changes over the previous 30 days. The volatility ratio over these many smaller time periods ranges from .95 to 1.2. Perhaps more troubling is that the ratio fluctuates dramatically over relatively short periods of time. Furthermore, the most recent time period displays the greatest fluctuations. In practice, volatility-weighted hedging works well for securities that are similar in cash flow (e.g., coupon bonds with comparable terms). As this example shows, 20- and 30-year coupon bonds may not be similar enough for this kind of hedging.

ONE-VARIABLE REGRESSION-BASED HEDGING

Another popular hedge is based on a *regression* of changes in one yield on changes in the other yield. Let Δy_t^{20} and Δy_t^{30} be the changes in the 20- and

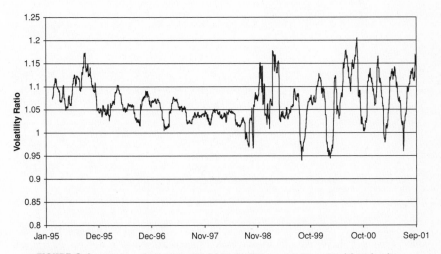

FIGURE 8.1   Ratio of 20-Year Yield Volatility to 30-Year Yield Volatility

30-year yields from dates $t{-}\Delta t$ to date t. Regression analysis often begins with the following model of the behavior of these changes[4]:

$$\Delta y_t^{20} = \alpha + \beta \times \Delta y_t^{30} + \varepsilon_t \qquad (8.5)$$

Changes in the 30-year yield, called the *independent variable*, are used to predict changes in the 20-year yield, called the *dependent variable*. The intercept, α, and slope, β, need to be estimated from the data. The error term, ε_t, reflects how much the actual 20-year yield change on a particular day differs from the change predicted by the constants α and β and by the change in the 30-year yield. The regression model assumes that the error, on average, equals zero and that it is uncorrelated with changes in the independent variable.

In words, equation (8.5) says that changes in the 20-year yield are linearly related to changes in the 30-year yield. Assume, for example, that the data give estimates of $\alpha{=}0$ and $\beta{=}1.06$. If on a particular day $\Delta y_t^{30}{=}3$ basis points, then the predicted change in the 20-year yield, written $\Delta \hat{y}_t^{20}$, is

$$\begin{aligned} \Delta \hat{y}_t^{20} &= \alpha + \beta \times \Delta \hat{y}_t^{30} \\ &= 0 + 1.06 \times 3 = 3.18 \end{aligned} \qquad (8.6)$$

If $\Delta y_t^{20}{=}4$ basis points, then the error that day, according to equation (8.5) is

$$\begin{aligned} \varepsilon_t &= \Delta y_t^{20} - \alpha - \beta \Delta y_t^{30} \\ &\equiv \Delta y_t^{20} - \Delta \hat{y}_t^{20} \\ &= 4 - 3.18 = .82 \end{aligned} \qquad (8.7)$$

The estimates of α and β are usually obtained by minimizing the sum of the squares of the error terms over the observation period—that is, by minimizing

$$\sum_t \Delta \varepsilon_t^2 \qquad (8.8)$$

This estimation criterion is also known as *least squares*.

---

[4]Sometimes the percentage changes in yields are used instead of changes. It is a separate empirical question to determine which specification better describes empirical reality.

Figure 8.2 graphs the changes in the 20-year yield against changes in the 30-year yield over the sample period mentioned in the previous section. The data do for the most part fall along a line, supporting the empirical model specified in equation (8.5).

Estimating the constants of the equation by least squares can be done in many computer programs, statistical packages, and spreadsheets. A typical regression output for this application is summarized in Table 8.1. According to the table, α, the constant of the regression, is estimated at .0007. It is typically the case in regressions of changes in yields on other changes in yields that this constant is close to zero. In this case, for example, the 20-year yield does not tend to drift consistently up or down when the 30-year yield is not moving. This intuition is supported not only by the very small estimate of α but by its *t-statistic* as well. The t-statistic measures the statistical significance of the estimated coefficient. With enough data, a common rule of thumb regards a t-statistic less than two as indicating that the data cannot distinguish between the estimated coefficient and a coefficient of zero. In this example, the estimate of .0007 is not statistically distinguishable from zero.

According to Table 8.1 the estimated value of β is about 1.057, indicating that this value should be used as the risk weight for computing the quantity of 30-year bonds to hedge 20-year bonds. Applying equation (8.3) with this risk weight calls for a sale of about $8.76 million face

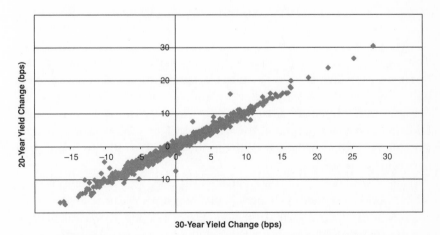

30-Year Yield Change (bps)

FIGURE 8.2 20-Year Yield Changes versus 30-Year Yield Changes

TABLE 8.1 Regression Analysis of Changes in 20-Year Yields on 30-Year Yields

Number of observations	1,680	
R-squared	98.25%	
Standard error	0.6973	
Regression Coefficients	**Value**	**t-Statistic**
Constant	0.0007	0.0438
Change in 30-year yield	1.0570	306.9951

amount of 30-year bonds to hedge a $10 million long face amount position of 20-year bonds. The t-statistic of the risk weight is, not surprisingly, vastly greater than 2: It would be inconceivable for changes in the 20-year yield to be uncorrelated with changes in the 30-year yield.

The *standard error* of the regression equals the standard deviation of the error terms. In this example, a standard error of .6973 means that a one-standard-deviation error in the prediction of the change in 20-year yields based on 30-year yields is about .7 basis points per day. At a 20-year DV01 of .118428, the hedged $10 million face position in 20-year bonds hedged would be subject to a daily one-standard-deviation profit or loss of

$$.6973 \times \frac{.118428}{100} \times \$10,000,000 = \$8,258 \qquad (8.9)$$

This hedging risk is large relative to a market maker's bid-ask spread. If a market maker is able to collect a spread of .25 or even .5 basis points, equation (8.9) shows that this spread can easily be wiped out by the unpredictable behavior of 20-year yields relative to 30-year yields. Like the conclusion about the volatility-weighted approach, the one-variable regression hedge of a 20-year bond with a 30-year bond does not seem adequate.

The "R-squared" of the regression is 98.25%. This means that 98.25% of the variance of changes in the 20-year yield can be explained by changes in the 30-year yield. In the one-factor case, the R-squared is actually the square of the correlation between the two changes. Here, the correlation between changes in the 20- and 30-year yields is $\sqrt{.9825}$=.9912.

Some additional insight into regression hedging can be gained by focusing on the following fact about the regression-based risk weight:

$$\beta = \frac{\rho \sigma_{20}}{\sigma_{30}} \qquad (8.10)$$

The symbols σ_{20} and σ_{30} denote the volatilities of the dependent and independent variables, respectively, and ρ denotes the correlation between them. In the case of the 20- and 30-year yields, the previous section reported that σ_{20}=5.27 and σ_{30}=4.94. The R-squared of the regression gives ρ=.9912. Substituting these values into equation (8.10) produces β=1.057 as reported in Table 8.1.

According to equation (8.10), the higher the volatility ratio of 20-year yield changes to 30-year yield changes, the larger the 30-year risk weight. (A similar result is discussed in the previous section.) Also, the larger the correlation between the yield changes, the larger the 30-year risk weight. Intuitively, the greater this correlation, the greater the usefulness of the 30-year bond in hedging the 20-year bond. At the opposite extreme, for example, when ρ=0, the 30-year bond is not helpful at all in hedging the 20-year bond. In that (unlikely) case, the regression-based risk weight is zero for any volatility ratio.

Equation (8.10) also reveals the difference between the volatility-weighted hedge and the regression-based hedge. The risk weight of the former equals the ratio of volatilities while the risk weight of the latter is the correlation times this ratio. In this sense, a volatility-weighted hedge assumes that changes in the two bond yields are perfectly correlated (i.e., that ρ=1.0), while the regression approach recognizes the imperfect correlation between changes in the two yields.

This section concludes by revisiting least squares as a criterion for estimating equation (8.5). Since β is used as the risk weight on the 30-year bond,

$$\beta = \frac{-F_{30} DV01_{30}}{F_{20} DV01_{20}} \qquad (8.11)$$

Substituting this expression into the error term of the regression, given in the first line of (8.7),

$$\varepsilon_t = \Delta y_t^{20} - \alpha + \frac{F_{30} DV01_{30}}{F_{20} DV01_{20}} \Delta y_t^{30} \qquad (8.12)$$

Rearranging terms and dropping α, since it is usually quite small,

$$\varepsilon_t = \frac{1}{F_{20}\mathrm{DV01}_{20}}\left[F_{20}\mathrm{DV01}_{20}\,\Delta y_t^{20} + F_{30}\mathrm{DV01}_{30}\,\Delta y_t^{30}\right] \qquad (8.13)$$

The term in brackets is the P&L of a short position in 20-year bonds hedged with a long position in 30-year bonds, so ε_t equals this P&L per unit of risk in 20-year bonds. Similarly, the standard deviation and variance of ε_t equals the standard deviation and variance of this P&L per unit of risk in 20-year bonds. Since, in this context, minimizing the sum of the squared errors is equivalent to minimizing the variance or standard deviation of the errors,[5] the least squares criterion is equivalent to minimizing the standard deviation of the P&L of a regression-based hedged position.

TWO-VARIABLE REGRESSION-BASED HEDGING

The change in the 20-year yield is probably better predicted by changes in both 10- and 30-year yields than by changes in 30-year yields alone. Consequently, a market maker hedging a long position in 20-year bonds may very well consider selling a combination of 10- and 30-year bonds rather than 30-year bonds alone. Appropriate risk weights for the 10- and 30-year bonds may be found by estimating the following regression model:

$$\Delta y_t^{20} = \alpha + \beta_{10} \times \Delta y_t^{10} + \beta_{30} \times \Delta y_t^{30} + \varepsilon_t \qquad (8.14)$$

The coefficients β_{10} and β_{30} give the risk weights of the two-variable regression hedge. More precisely, the face amount of the 10-year and 30-year bonds used to hedge a particular face amount of 20-year bonds is determined by the following equations:

$$\beta_{10} = \frac{-F_{10}\mathrm{DV01}_{10}}{F_{20}\mathrm{DV01}_{20}} \qquad (8.15)$$

---

[5]When a constant is included in the regression equation, it is a property of least squares that the average error equals zero.

and

$$\beta_{30} = \frac{-F_{30}\text{DV01}_{30}}{F_{20}\text{DV01}_{20}} \tag{8.16}$$

Once again, these regression coefficients are called risk weights because they give the DV01 risk in each hedging bond as a fraction of the DV01 of the security or portfolio being hedged. To understand why this hedge works, note that the P&L of the hedged position is

$$P \& L = -F_{10}\text{DV01}_{10}\Delta y_t^{10} - F_{30}\text{DV01}_{30}\Delta y_t^{30} - F_{20}\text{DV01}_{20}\Delta y_t^{20} \tag{8.17}$$

Rearranging slightly and using equations (8.15) and (8.16),

$$P \& L = F_{20}\text{DV01}_{20}\left[\beta_{10}\Delta y_t^{10} + \beta_{30}\Delta y_t^{30} - \Delta y_t^{20}\right] \tag{8.18}$$

But, according to the regression model (8.14), the term in brackets, on average, equals $-\alpha$. Usually α is approximately equal to zero, but, in any case, according to the regression model, the term in brackets does not depend on changes in yields. In other words, so long as the regression model may be relied on to describe changes in yields, the hedge described by equations (8.15) and (8.16) does create a portfolio that is, on average, immune to interest rate changes.

Table 8.2 gives the results of estimating the regression model in (8.14). For the same reasons that double-old 30-year bonds are used in the one-variable regression, double-old 10-year and double-old 30-year bonds are used here. The value of the constant and its associated t-statistic show that α may be taken as approximately equal to zero. The coefficients on the 10- and 30-year yield changes indicate that about 16.1% of the DV01 of the 20-year holding should be offset with 10-year DV01, and about 87.7% should be offset with 30-year DV01. The t-statistics on both these coefficients confirm that both risk weights are statistically distinguishable from zero.

In the one-variable regression of the previous section the 30-year risk weight is 1.057 or 105.7%. In the two-factor regression the risk weight on the 30-year falls to 87.7% because some of the DV01 risk is transferred to

TABLE 8.2 Regression Analysis of Changes in
20-Year Yields on 10- and 30-Year Yields

Number of observations	1,680	
R-squared	98.63%	
Standard error	0.6170	
Regression Coefficients	**Value**	**t-Statistic**
Constant	0.0067	0.4441
Change in 10-year yield	0.1613	21.5978
Change in 30-year yield	0.8774	99.0826

the 10-year. So long as changes in the 10-year yield are positively correlated with changes in the 20-year yield, it is to be expected that the hedge
will allocate some risk to the 10-year. Since the 30-year had all the risk in
the one-variable case, it follows that the 30-year should lose some risk allocation when the 10-year is added to the analysis.

In the one-variable case the risk weight of the 30-year is greater than
one because the correlation between the yields is quite close to one and because the volatility of the 20-year yield exceeds that of the 30-year. See
equation (8.10). In the two-variable case, since most of the hedging risk is
still allocated to the 30-year, the sum of the two risk weights still exceeds
one. If it had happened that the two-variable analysis gave a much higher
risk weight on the 10-year than on the 30-year, the sum of the two risk
weights might have been less than one. The correlation between each of the
independent variables and the dependent variable is quite close to one and
the volatility of changes in the 10-year yield in the sample, at about 5.9 basis points per day, is greater than the volatility of the 30-year yield in the
sample, at about 4.9 basis points per day.

While the regression results of Table 8.2 strongly support the inclusion
of a 10-year security in the hedge portfolio, the overall quality of the hedge
has not improved dramatically from the one-variable case. The R-squared
increased by only about .4%, and the standard error is still relatively high
at about .62 basis points.

This and the previous section presented the science of regression hedging. The following section shows that a proper hedging program requires
an understanding of the relevant markets in addition to the ability to run
and understand regression analysis.

TRADING CASE STUDY: The Pricing of the 20-Year U.S. Treasury Sector

In September 2001 many market participants claimed that the 20-year sector was cheap. These claims were backed up by a wide variety of analyses and arguments. The one common thread across these claims, however, was the recommendation that the purchase of 20-year bonds should be hedged with a 10-year risk weight of over 40% and a 30-year risk below 70%.[6] These weights differ qualitatively from the regression-based weights derived in the previous section: approximately 16% for the 10-year and 88% for the 30-year.

For any given risk weights β_{10} and β_{30}, whether they derive from a regression model or not, an index of the relative value of the 20-year sector, I, may be defined as follows:

$$I = \beta_{10} y_t^{10} + \beta_{30} y_t^{30} - y_t^{20} \tag{8.19}$$

Equation (8.18) reveals that the change in I is proportional to the P&L from a long position in the 20-year bond hedged with the given risk weights. It follows that I is an index of the cumulative profit from this hedged position. High values of I, with the 20-year yield low relative to 10- and 30-year yields, indicate that the 20-year bond is relatively rich. Low values of I, with the 20-year yield high relative to the others, indicate that the 20-year bond is relatively cheap.

Figure 8.3 graphs the index I over the sample period studied in this chapter for the case of equal risk weights, that is, $\beta_{10}=.5$ and $\beta_{30}=.5$. While these weights do not necessarily match those suggested by market participants who advocated buying the 20-year sector, they do capture the common thread of having a much greater 10-year risk weight and a much lower 30-year risk weight than the weights estimated in the previous section.

According to the figure, the index fluctuated between approximately −.1 and −.24 from the beginning of the sample until August

---

[6]Several of the more sophisticated approaches included an additional risk weight on bonds of shorter maturity (e.g., two- or five-year bonds).

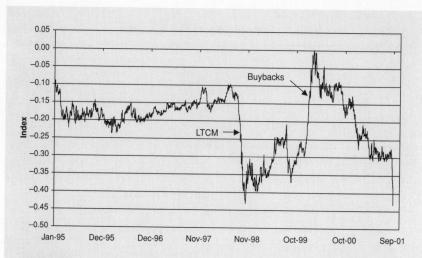

FIGURE 8.3   Index of 20-Year Bonds versus 10- and 30-Year Bonds; Equal Risk Weights

1998. Then, Long Term Capital Management (LTCM) suffered its losses, and, in the ensuing market action, many traders were forced to liquidate *basis* positions in the futures market (see Chapter 20) by covering short futures positions and selling longs in the 20-year sector. These forced sales of 20-year bonds cheapened the sector dramatically, as shown in the figure. After that episode the sector fitfully recovered and fell again. A dramatic recovery took place, however, when in early 2000 the U.S. Treasury announced that it would begin to buy back its bonds in this and nearby sectors to deal with the new reality of budget surpluses. The market soon came to believe that this buyback program would not, in the end, be sufficient to prop up values in the sector. Despite that disillusionment, the dramatic cheapening of the 20-year sector starting in March 2000 is remarkable. Falling from a value of about 0 at the height of buyback optimism to a value of about –.43 at the end of the sample implies an enormous cheapening of 43 basis points.

When examining indexes of value it is often a good idea to determine whether a risk factor has been omitted. In other words, is there a variable other than the cheapness of the 20-year sector that can explain Figure 8.3? Figure 8.4 shows that there is.

Figure 8.4 superimposes the slope of the 10s–30s curve (i.e., $y_t^{30} - y_t^{10}$) on Figure 8.3. The explanatory power of the curve variable is remarkable: Whenever the curve steepens the 20-year bond cheapens, at least as measured by the index I. As might be expected, the magnitude of the curve change does not seem to explain the full magnitude of the reaction of I to the idiosyncratic effects of the fall of LTCM or of the buyback announcement. The magnitude of the curve change does, however, seem to explain the magnitude of the apparent cheapening of the 20-year bond from the height of buyback optimism to the end of the sample period.

The evidence of Figure 8.4 does not necessarily mean that the 20-year sector is not cheap. It does strongly imply, however, that whatever cheapness characterizes the 20-year sector is highly correlated with the slope of the yield curve from 10 to 30 years. Put another way, purchasing the allegedly cheap 20-year bond and selling 10- and 30-year bonds with equal risk weights will exhibit a P&L

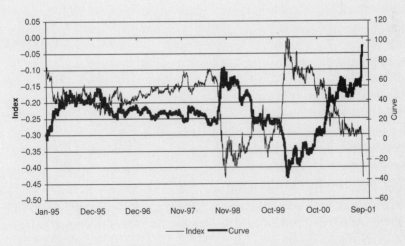

FIGURE 8.4   Evenly Weighted 20-Year Index and 10s–30s Curve

profile similar to that of a simple curve trade that has nothing to do with the 20-year bond, namely, selling 10-year bonds and buying 30-year bonds. Both positions make money when the yield curve between 10 and 30 years flattens.

The regression hedge presented in the previous section does not suffer from this problem. Define an index, $\tilde{I}$, based on the risk weights from the two-variable regression. Specifically,

$$\tilde{I} = .161 \times y_{10} + .877 \times y_{30} - y_{20} \qquad (8.20)$$

Figure 8.5 graphs this index over the sample period.

The LTCM dislocation and the buyback program are evident in this figure as they were in Figures 8.3 and 8.4. However, unlike those figures, Figure 8.5 shows an index that has not cheapened at all since March 2000. It seems that the risk weights used to $\tilde{I}$ construct adequately hedge against curve risk.

It is no surprise that the regression methodology outlined in the previous section does control for curve risk. The estimated regression relationship can be written as a function of the change in the 10- and 30-year yields:

$$\Delta y_t^{20} \approx .1613 \Delta y_t^{10} + .8774 \Delta y_t^{30} \qquad (8.21)$$

But this relationship can also be written as a function of the 10-year yield and of the curve:

$$\Delta y_t^{20} \approx 1.0387 \Delta y_t^{10} + .8774 \left(\Delta y_t^{30} - \Delta y_t^{10} \right) \qquad (8.22)$$

Equation (8.22) says that the 20-year yield will change by about 1.04 basis points for every basis point change in the 10-year with a fixed curve. Also, the 20-year yield will change by about .88 basis points

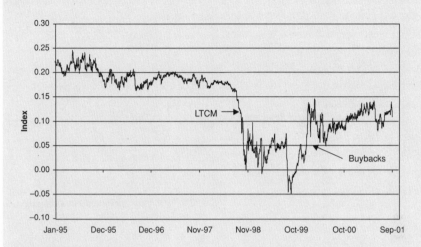

FIGURE 8.5   Index of 20-Year Bonds versus 10- and 30-Year Bonds; Regression Risk Weights

for every basis point change in the curve with a fixed 10-year yield. In short, the regression-based hedge can be thought of as hedging against changes in 10- and 30-year yields or as hedging against changes in the level of yield and the curve.

To complete the discussion, Figure 8.6 tests the index $\tilde{I}$ as Figure 8.4 tests the index I, namely by superimposing the curve on the index. Figure 8.6 shows that, LTCM and buybacks aside, $\tilde{I}$ is not very much related to the curve. As a result, a trade based on $\tilde{I}$ is a pure play on the 20-year sector relative to the 10- and 30-year sectors. Unfortunately for the trade's prospects, however, the 20-year sector does not appear particularly rich or cheap by recent historical experience as measured by the index $\tilde{I}$.

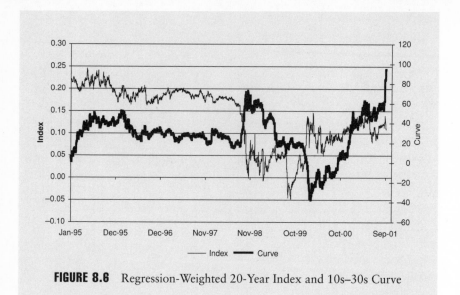

FIGURE 8.6 Regression-Weighted 20-Year Index and 10s–30s Curve

A COMMENT ON LEVEL REGRESSIONS

When computing risk weights for hedging, some practitioners regress yields on yields instead of changes in yields on changes in yields. Mathematically, in the one-variable case, instead of using equation (8.5), repeated here for easy reference,

$$\Delta y_t^{20} = \alpha + \beta \times \Delta y_t^{30} + \varepsilon_t \qquad (8.23)$$

they use the following empirical model:

$$y_t^{20} = \alpha + \beta \times y_t^{30} + \varepsilon_t \qquad (8.24)$$

The interest rate behavior implied by equation (8.24) is odd in the following way. Say that $\alpha=0$ and $\beta=1$ so that if the 30-year yield is 5%, then (8.24) predicts that the 20-year yield is 5%. This prediction is implied by (8.24) whether the 20-year yield is currently 5%, 10%, or 3%. But if the 20-year yield is mispriced at 10% on a particular day, surely it is likely that it will be somewhat mispriced on the next day. In other words, surely 5% cannot be the best guess for the 20-year yield on the next day.[7]

Continuing with the assumption that $\alpha=0$ and $\beta=1$, the regression of changes assumes that the 20- and 30-year yields change by the same amount. If the 30-year yield is 5% and the 20-year yield is 10% on a particular day, the change model predicts that the spread between the yields on the next day will remain at 5%. If it is believed that the 20-year bond is mispriced relative to the 30-year bond and that the market will correct this mispricing, then this change model is not precisely the right model, either. But predicting that the spread will be 5% the next day is probably better than predicting that it will immediately drop to zero.

---

[7]Technically, the error terms of equation (8.24) are most probably *serially correlated*, that is, correlated across time. This is a violation of one of the assumptions of least squares that impairs the efficiency of that estimation procedure.

Term Structure Models

The Science of Term Structure Models

Part One described how to price fixed income securities with fixed cash flows relative to other securities with fixed cash flows. While many such securities do trade in fixed income markets, there are also many securities whose cash flows are not fixed. Consider a European call option on $1,000 face value of a particular bond with a strike at par. This security gives the holder the right to buy $1,000 face value of the bond for $1,000 on the maturity date of the option. If the price of the bond on that maturity date turns out to be $1,050, the holder will choose to exercise the call by paying $1,000 for a security worth $1,050. In that case the cash flow from the option is $50. But if the price of the bond on that maturity date turns out to be $950, the holder will choose not to exercise the call and the cash flow from the option is $0. Thus, the cash flow from an option depends on the value of an underlying security or, equivalently, on the level of interest rates.

Any security whose cash flows depend on the level of bond prices is called an *interest rate derivative* or an *interest rate contingent claim*. This chapter uses a very simple setting to show how to price derivative securities relative to a set of underlying securities by arbitrage arguments. Unlike the arbitrage pricing of securities with fixed cash flows introduced in Part One, the techniques of this chapter require strong assumptions about how interest rates may evolve in the future.

RATE AND PRICE TREES

Assume that the market six-month and one-year spot rates are 5% and 5.15%, respectively. Taking these market rates as given is equivalent to taking the prices of a six-month bond and a one-year bond as given. Securities with assumed prices are called underlying securities to distinguish them from the derivative securities priced by arbitrage arguments.

Next, assume that six months from now the six-month rate will be either 4.50% or 5.50% with equal probability. This very strong assumption is depicted by means of a *binomial tree*, where "binomial" means that only two future values are possible:

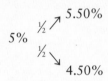

$$
5\% \quad
\begin{array}{c}
\nearrow^{\frac{1}{2}} \; 5.50\% \\[6pt]
\searrow_{\frac{1}{2}} \; 4.50\%
\end{array}
$$

Note that the columns in the tree represent dates. The six-month rate is 5% today, which will be called date 0. On the next date six months from now, which will be called date 1, there are two possible outcomes or *states of the world*. The 5.50% state will be called the *up state* while the 4.50% state will be called the *down state*.

Given the current term structure of spot rates (i.e., the current six-month and one-year rates), trees for the prices of six-month and one-year zero-coupon bonds may be computed. The price tree for $1,000 face value of the six-month zero is

$$
975.61 \quad
\begin{array}{c}
\nearrow^{\frac{1}{2}} \; 1{,}000 \\[6pt]
\searrow_{\frac{1}{2}} \; 1{,}000
\end{array}
$$

since $1,000/(1+.05/2)=$975.61. (For easy readability, dollar signs are not included in price trees.)

Note that in a tree for the value of a particular security, the maturity of the security falls with the date. On date 0 of the preceding tree the security is a six-month zero, while on date 1 the security is a maturing zero.

The price tree for $1,000 face value of a one-year zero is the following:

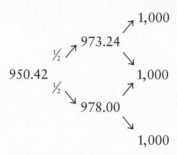

The three date 2 prices of $1,000 are, of course, the maturity values of the one-year zero. The two date 1 prices come from discounting this certain $1,000 at the then-prevailing six-month rate. Hence, the date 1 up state price is $1,000/(1+^{.055}/_2)$ or $973.2360, and the date 1 down state price is $1,000/(1+^{.045}/_2)$ or 977.9951. Finally, the date 0 price is computed using the given date 0 one-year rate of 5.15%: $1,000/(1+^{.0515}/_2)^2$ or 950.4230.

The probabilities of moving up or down the tree may be used to compute average or *expected* values. The expected value of the one-year zero's price on date 1 is

$$\frac{1}{2}\$973.24 + \frac{1}{2}\$978.00 = \$975.62 \qquad (9.1)$$

Discounting this expected value to date 0 at the date 0 six-month rate gives an *expected discounted value*[1] of

$$\left[\frac{1}{2}\$973.24 + \frac{1}{2}\$978.00\right]\Big/\left(1 + .05/2\right) = \$951.82 \qquad (9.2)$$

Note that the one-year zero's expected discounted value of $951.82 does not equal its given market price of $950.42. These two numbers need not be equal because investors do not price securities by expected discounted value. Over the next six months the one-year zero is a risky security, worth

---

[1]Over one period, discounting the expected value and taking the expectation of discounted values are the same. But, as shown in Chapter 17, over many periods the two are different and, with the approach taken throughout Part Three, taking the expectation of discounted values is correct—hence the choice of the term expected discounted value.

$973.24 half the time and $978.00 the other half of the time for an average or expected value of $975.62. If investors do not like this price uncertainty they would prefer a security worth $975.62 on date 1 with certainty. More specifically, a security worth $975.62 with certainty after six months would, by the arguments of Part One, sell for $975.62/(1+$^{.05}$/$_2$) or 951.82 as of date 0. By contrast, investors penalize the risky one-year zero coupon bond with an average price of $975.62 after six months by pricing it at $950.42. The next chapter elaborates further on investor *risk aversion* and how large an impact it might be expected to have on bond prices.

ARBITRAGE PRICING OF DERIVATIVES

The text now turns to the pricing of a derivative security. What is the price of a call option, maturing in six months, to purchase $1,000 face value of a then six-month zero at $975? Begin with the price tree for this call option.

$$??? \quad {}^{\frac{1}{2}} \nearrow {}^{0}_{} \\ {}^{\frac{1}{2}} \searrow {}_{3}$$

If on date 1 the six-month rate is 5.50% and a six-month zero sells for $973.23, the right to buy that zero at $975 is worthless. On the other hand, if the six-month rate turns out to be 4.50% and the price of a six-month zero is $978, then the right to buy the zero at $975 is worth $978–$975 or $3. This description of the option's terminal payoffs empha-sizes the derivative nature of the option: Its value depends on the values of some underlying set of securities.

As discussed in Chapter 1, a security is priced by arbitrage by finding and pricing its replicating portfolio. When, as in that context, cash flows do not depend on the levels of rates, the construction of the replicating portfolio is relatively simple. The derivative context is more difficult be-cause cash flows do depend on the levels of rates, and the replicating portfolio must replicate the derivative security for any possible interest rate scenario.

To price the option by arbitrage, construct a portfolio on date 0 of un-derlying securities, namely six-month and one-year zero coupon bonds, that will be worth $0 in the up state on date 1 and $3 in the down state. To solve this problem, let $F_{.5}$ and F_1 be the face values of six-month and one-year zeros in the replicating portfolio, respectively. Then, these values must satisfy the following two equations:

$$F_s + .97324F_1 = \$0 \qquad (9.3)$$

$$F_s + .97800F_1 = \$3 \qquad (9.4)$$

Equation (9.3) may be interpreted as follows. In the up state, the value of the replicating portfolio's now maturing six-month zero is its face value. The value of the once one-year zeros, now six-month zeros, is .97324 per dollar face value. Hence, the left-hand side of equation (9.3) denotes the value of the replicating portfolio in the up state. This value must equal $0, the value of the option in the up state. Similarly, equation (9.4) requires that the value of the replicating portfolio in the down state equal the value of the option in the down state.

Solving equations (9.3) and (9.4), $F_s = -\$613.3866$ and $F_1 = \$630.2521$. In words, on date 0 the option can be replicated by buying about $630.25 face value of one-year zeros and simultaneously shorting about $613.39 face amount of six-month zeros. Since this is the case, the law of one price requires that the price of the option equal the price of the replicating portfolio. But this portfolio's price is known and is equal to

$$.97561F_s + .95042F_1 = -.97561 \times \$613.3866 + .95042 \times \$630.2521$$
$$= \$.58 \qquad (9.5)$$

Therefore, the price of the option must be $.58.

Recall that pricing based on the law of one price may be enforced by arbitrage. If the price of the option were less than $.58, arbitrageurs could buy the option, short the replicating portfolio, keep the difference, and have no future liabilities. Similarly, if the price of the option were greater than $.58, arbitrageurs could short the option, buy the replicating portfolio, keep the difference, and, once again, have no future liabilities. Thus, ruling out profits from riskless arbitrage implies an option price of $.58.

It is important to emphasize that the option cannot be priced by expected discounted value. Under that method, the option price would appear to be

$$\frac{.5 \times \$0 + .5 \times \$3}{1 + .05/2} = \$1.46 \qquad (9.6)$$

The true option price is less than this value because investors dislike the risk of the call option and, as a result, will not pay as much as its expected discounted value. Put another way, the risk penalty implicit in the call option price is inherited from the risk penalty of the one-year zero, that is, from the property that the price of the one-year zero is less than its expected discounted value. Once again, the magnitude of this effect is discussed in Chapter 10.

This section illustrates arbitrage pricing with a call option, but it should be clear that arbitrage can be used to price any security with cash flows that depend on the six-month rate. Consider, for example, a security that, in six months, requires a payment of $200 in the up state but generates a payment of $1,000 in the down state. Proceeding as in the option example, find the portfolio of six-month and one-year zeros that replicates these two terminal payoffs, price this replicating portfolio as of date 0, and conclude that the price of the hypothetical security equals the price of the replicating portfolio.

A remarkable feature of arbitrage pricing is that the probabilities of up and down moves never enter into the calculation of the arbitrage price. See equations (9.3) through (9.5). The explanation for this somewhat surprising observation follows from the principles of arbitrage. Arbitrage pricing requires that the value of the replicating portfolio match the value of the option in both the up and the down states. Therefore, the composition of the replicating portfolio is the same whether the probability of the up state is 20%, 50%, or 80%. But if the composition of the portfolio does not depend directly on the probabilities, and if the prices of the securities in the portfolio are given, then the price of the replicating portfolio and hence the price of the option cannot depend directly on the probabilities, either.

Despite the fact that the option price does not depend directly on the probabilities, these probabilities must have some impact on the option price. After all, as it becomes more and more likely that rates will rise to 5.50% and that bond prices will be low, the value of options to purchase bonds must fall. The resolution of this apparent paradox is that the option price depends indirectly on the probabilities through the price of the one-year zero. Were the probability of an up move to increase suddenly, the current value of a one-year zero would decline. And since the replicating portfolio is long one-year zeros, the value of the option would decline as well. In summary, a derivative like an option depends on the probabilities only through current bond prices. Given bond prices, however, probabilities are not needed to derive arbitrage-free prices.

RISK-NEUTRAL PRICING

Risk-neutral pricing is a technique that modifies an assumed interest rate process, like the one assumed at the start of this chapter, so that any contingent claim can be priced without having to construct and price its replicating portfolio. Since the original interest rate process has to be modified only once, and since this modification requires no more effort than pricing a single contingent claim by arbitrage, risk-neutral pricing is an extremely efficient way to price many contingent claims under the same assumed rate process.

In the example of this chapter, the price of a one-year zero does not equal its expected discounted value. The price of the one-year zero is $950.42, computed from the given one-year spot rate of 5.15%. At the same time, the expected discounted value of the one-year zero is $951.82, as derived in equation (9.2) and reproduced here:

$$\left[\frac{1}{2}\$973.24 + \frac{1}{2}\$978.00\right]\Big/\left(1 + .05/2\right) = \$951.82 \tag{9.7}$$

The probabilities of $1/2$ for the up and down states are the assumed true or real-world probabilities. But there are some other probabilities, called *risk-neutral* probabilities, that do cause the expected discounted value to equal the market price. To find these probabilities, let the risk-neutral probability in the up and down states be p and $1-p$, respectively. Then, solve the following equation:

$$\left[\$973.24p + \$978.00(1 - p)\right]\Big/\left(1 + .05/2\right) = \$950.42 \tag{9.8}$$

The solution is $p=.8024$. In words, under the risk-neutral probabilities of .8024 and .1976 the expected discounted value equals the market price.

In later chapters the difference between true and risk-neutral probabilities is described in terms of the *drift* in interest rates. Under the true probabilities there is a 50% chance that the six-month rate rises from 5% to 5.50% and a 50% chance that it falls from 5% to 4.50%. Hence the expected change in the six-month rate, or the drift of the six-month rate, is zero. Under the risk-neutral probabilities there is an 80.24% chance of a 50 basis point increase in the six-month rate and a 19.76% chance of a 50 basis point decline. Hence the drift of the six-month rate under these probabilities is 30.24 basis points.

As pointed out in the previous section, the expected discounted value of the option payoffs is $1.46, while the arbitrage price is $.58. But what if expected discounted value is computed using the risk-neutral probabilities? The resulting option value would be

$$\frac{.8024 \times \$0 + .1976 \times \$3}{1 + .05/2} = \$.58 \tag{9.9}$$

The fact that the arbitrage price of the option equals its expected discounted value under the risk-neutral probabilities is not a coincidence. In general, to value contingent claims by risk-neutral pricing, proceed as follows. First, find the risk-neutral probabilities that equate the prices of the underlying securities with their expected discounted values. (In the simple example of this chapter the only risky, underlying security is the one-year zero.) Second, price the contingent claim by expected discounted value under these risk-neutral probabilities. The remainder of this section will describe intuitively why risk-neutral pricing works. Since the argument is a bit complex, it is broken up into four steps.

Step 1: Given trees for the underlying securities, the price of a security that is priced by arbitrage does not depend on investors' risk preferences. This assertion can be supported as follows.

A security is priced by arbitrage if one can construct a portfolio that replicates its cash flows. Under the assumed process for interest rates in this chapter, for example, the sample bond option is priced by arbitrage. By contrast, it is unlikely that a specific common stock can be priced by arbitrage because no portfolio of underlying securities can mimic the idiosyncratic fluctuations in a single common stock's market value.

If a security is priced by arbitrage and everyone agrees on the price evolution of the underlying securities, then everyone will agree on the replicating portfolio. In the option example, both an extremely risk-averse, re-tired investor and a professional gambler would agree that a portfolio of about $630.25 face of one-year zeros and –$613.39 face of six-month zeros replicates the option. And since they agree on the composition of the replicating portfolio and on the prices of the underlying securities, they must also agree on the price of the derivative.

Step 2: Imagine an economy identical to the true economy with respect to current bond prices and the possible values of the six-month rate over time but different in that the investors in the imaginary economy are risk neutral. Unlike investors in the true economy, investors in the imaginary economy do not penalize securities for risk and, therefore, price securities by expected discounted value. It follows that, under the probability of the up state in the imaginary economy, the expected discounted value of the one-year zero equals its market price. But this is the probability that satisfies equation (9.8), namely the risk-neutral probability of .8024.

Step 3: The price of the option in the imaginary economy, like any other security in that economy, is computed by expected discounted value. Since the probability of the up state in that economy is .8024, the price of the option in that economy is given by equation (9.9) and is, therefore, $.58.

Step 4: Step 1 implies that given the prices of the six-month and one-year zeros, as well as possible values of the six-month rate, the price of an option does not depend on investor risk preferences. It follows that since the real and imaginary economies have the same bond prices and the same possible values for the six-month rate, the option price must be the same in both economies. In particular, the option price in the real economy must equal $.58, the option price in the imaginary economy. More generally, the price of a derivative in the real economy may be computed by expected discounted value under the risk-neutral probabilities.

ARBITRAGE PRICING IN A MULTI-PERIOD SETTING

Maintaining the binomial assumption, the tree of the previous chapter might be extended for another six months as follows:

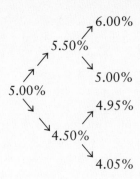

When, as in this tree, an up move followed by a down move does not give the same rate as a down move followed by an up move, the tree is said to be *nonrecombining*. From an economic perspective, there is nothing wrong with this kind of tree. To justify this particular tree, for example, one might argue that when short rates are 5% or higher they tend to change in increments of 50 basis points. But when rates fall below 5%, the size of the change starts to decrease. In particular, at a rate of 4.50% the short rate may change by only 45 basis points. A volatility process that depends on the level of rates exhibits *state-dependent* volatility.

Despite the economic reasonableness of nonrecombining trees, practitioners tend to avoid them because such trees are difficult or even impossible to implement. After six months there are two possible rates, after one year there are four, and after N semiannual periods there are 2^N possibilities. So, for example, a tree with semiannual steps large enough to price 10-year securities will, in its rightmost column alone, have over 500,000 nodes, while a tree used to price 20-year securities will in its rightmost column have over 500 billion nodes. Furthermore, as discussed later in the chapter, it is often desirable to reduce substantially the time interval between dates. In short, even with modern computers, trees that grow this quickly are computationally unwieldy. This doesn't mean, by the way, that the effects that give rise to nonrecombining trees, like state-dependent volatility, have to be abandoned. It simply means that these effects must be implemented in a more efficient way.

Trees in which the up-down and down-up states have the same value are called *recombining* trees. An example of this type of tree that builds on the two-date tree of the previous sections is

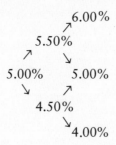

Note that there are two nodes after six months, three after one year, and so on. A tree with weekly rather than semiannual steps capable of pricing a 30-year security would have only 52×30+1 or 1,561 nodes in its rightmost column. Evidently, recombining trees are much more manageable than nonrecombining trees from a computational viewpoint.

As trees grow it becomes convenient to develop a notation with which to refer to particular nodes. One convention is as follows. The dates, represented by columns of the tree, are numbered from left to right starting with 0. The states, represented by rows of the tree, are numbered from bottom to top, starting from 0 as well. For example, in the preceding tree the six-month rate on date 2, state 0 is 4%. The six-month rate on state 1 of date 1 is 5.50%.

Continuing where the option example left off, having derived the risk-neutral tree for the pricing of a one-year zero, the goal is to extend the tree for the pricing of a 1.5-year zero assuming that the 1.5-year spot rate is 5.25%. Ignoring the probabilities for a moment, several nodes of the 1.5-year zero price tree can be written down immediately:

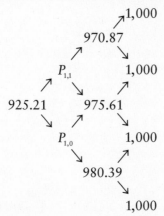

On date 3 the zero with an original term of 1.5 years matures and is worth its face value of $1,000. On date 2 the value of the then six-month zero equals its face value discounted for six months at the then-prevailing spot rates of 6%, 5%, and 4% in states 2, 1, and 0, respectively:

$$\frac{\$1,000}{1+.06/2} = \$970.87$$

$$\frac{\$1,000}{1+.05/2} = \$975.61 \tag{9.10}$$

$$\frac{\$1,000}{1+.04/2} = \$980.39$$

Finally, on date 0 the 1.5-year zero equals its face value discounted at the given 1.5-year spot rate: $\$1,000/(1+{}^{.0525}/_2)^3$ or $\$925.21$.

The prices of the zero on date 1 in states 1 and 0 are denoted $P_{1,1}$ and $P_{1,0}$, respectively. The then one-year zero prices are not known because, at this point in the development, possible values of the one-year rate in six months are not available.

The previous section showed that the risk-neutral probability of an up move on date 0 is .8024. Letting q be the risk-neutral probability of an up move on date 1,[2] the tree becomes

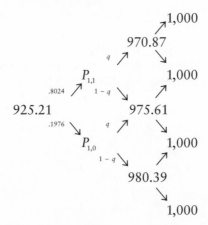

By the definition of risk-neutral probabilities, expected discounted value under these probabilities must produce market prices. With respect to the 1.5-year zero price on date 0, this requires that

$$\frac{.8024P_{1,1} + .1976P_{1,0}}{1 + .05/2} = \$925.21 \tag{9.11}$$

With respect to the prices of a then one-year zero on date 1,

$$P_{1,1} = \frac{\$970.87q + \$975.61(1-q)}{1 + .055/2}$$

$$P_{1,0} = \frac{\$975.61q + \$980.39(1-q)}{1 + .045/2} \tag{9.12}$$

While equations (9.11) and (9.12) may appear complicated, substituting (9.12) into (9.11) results in a linear equation in the one unknown, q. Solving this resulting equation reveals that $q=.6489$. Therefore, the risk-neutral interest rate process may be summarized by the following tree:

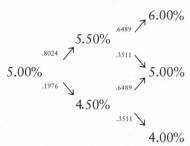

Furthermore, any derivative security that depends on the six-month rate in 6 months and in one year may be priced by computing its discounted expected value along this tree. An example appears in the next section.

The difference between the true and the risk-neutral probabilities may once again be described in terms of drift. From dates 1 to 2, the drift under the true probabilities is zero. Under the risk-neutral probabilities the drift is computed from a 64.89% chance of a 50-basis point increase in the six-month rate and a 35.11% chance of a 50-basis point decline in the rate. These numbers give a drift or expected change of 14.89 basis points.

Substituting q=.6489 back into equations (9.12) completes the tree for the price of the 1.5-year zero:

$$
\begin{array}{ccccccc}
 & & & & & & 1{,}000 \\
 & & & & & \nearrow & \\
 & & & & 970.87 & & \\
 & & & {}_{.6489}\nearrow & & \searrow & \\
 & & 946.51 & & & & 1{,}000 \\
 & {}_{.8024}\nearrow & & {}_{.3511}\searrow & & \nearrow & \\
925.21 & & & & 975.61 & & \\
 & {}_{.1976}\searrow & & {}_{.6489}\nearrow & & \searrow & \\
 & & 955.78 & & & & 1{,}000 \\
 & & & {}_{.3511}\searrow & & \nearrow & \\
 & & & & 980.39 & & \\
 & & & & & \searrow & \\
 & & & & & & 1{,}000
\end{array}
$$

It follows immediately from this tree that the one-year spot rate six months from now may be either 5.5736% or 4.5743% since

$$\$946.51 = \frac{\$1{,}000}{\left(1+5.5736\%/2\right)^2}$$

$$\$955.78 = \frac{\$1{,}000}{\left(1+4.5743\%/2\right)^2}$$

(9.13)

The fact that the possible values of the one-year spot rate can be extracted from the tree is, at first, surprising. The starting point of the example is the date 0 values of the .5-, 1-, and 1.5-year spot rates as well as an assumption about the evolution of the six-month rate over the next year. But since this information in combination with arbitrage or risk-neutral arguments is sufficient to determine the price tree for the 1.5-year zero, it is sufficient to determine the possible values of the one-year spot rate in six months. Considering this fact from another point of view, having specified initial spot rates and the evolution of the six-month rate, a modeler may not make any further assumptions about the behavior of the one-year rate.

The six-month rate process completely determines the one-year rate process because the model presented here has only one factor. Writing down a tree for the evolution of the six-month rate alone implicitly assumes that prices of all fixed income securities can be determined by the evolution of that rate. Multi-factor models for which this is not the case will be introduced in Chapter 13.

Just as some replicating portfolio can reproduce the cash flows of a security from date 0 to date 1, some other replicating portfolios can reproduce the cash flows of a security from date 1 to date 2. The composition of these replicating portfolios depends on the date and state. More specifically, the replicating portfolios held on date 0, on state 0 of date 1, and on state 1 of date 1 are usually different. From the trading perspective, the replicating portfolio must be adjusted as time passes and as interest rates change. This process is known as *dynamic replication*, in contrast to the *static replication* strategies of Part One. As an example of static replication, the portfolio of zero coupon bonds that replicates a coupon bond does not change over time nor with the level of rates.

Having built a tree out to date 2 it should be clear how to extend the tree to any number of dates. Assumptions about the future possible values of the short-term rate have to be extrapolated even further into the future and risk-neutral probabilities have to be calculated to produce a given set of bond prices.

EXAMPLE: PRICING A CMT SWAP

Equipped with the tree built in the previous section, this section prices a particular derivative security, namely $1,000,000 face value of a stylized *constant maturity Treasury (CMT) swap*. This swap pays

$$\frac{\$1,000,000}{2}\left(y_{CMT} - 5\%\right) \tag{9.14}$$

every six months until it matures, where y_{CMT} is a semiannually compounded yield, of a predetermined maturity, at the time of payment. The text prices a one-year CMT swap on the six-month yield.

Since six-month semiannually compounded yields equal six-month spot rates, rates in the tree of the previous section can be substituted into (9.14) to calculate the payoffs of the CMT swap. On date 1, the state 1 and state 0 payoffs are, respectively,

$$\frac{\$1,000,000}{2}\left(5.50\% - 5\%\right) = \$2,500$$
$$\frac{\$1,000,000}{2}\left(4.50\% - 5\%\right) = -\$2,500 \tag{9.15}$$

Similarly on date 2, the state 2, 1, and 0 payoffs are, respectively,

$$\frac{\$1,000,000}{2}\left(6\%-5\%\right)=\$5,000$$

$$\frac{\$1,000,000}{2}\left(5\%-5\%\right)=\$0 \qquad (9.16)$$

$$\frac{\$1,000,000}{2}\left(4\%-5\%\right)=-\$5,000$$

The possible values of the CMT swap at maturity, on date 2, are given by (9.16). The possible values on date 1 are given by the expected discounted value of the date 2 payoffs under the risk-neutral probabilities plus the date 1 payoffs given by (9.15). The resulting date 1 values in states 1 and 0, respectively, are

$$\frac{.6489\times\$5,000+.3511\times\$0}{1+.055/2}+\$2,500=\$5,657.66$$

$$\frac{.6489\times\$0+.3511\times\left(-\$5,000\right)}{1+.045/2}-\$2,500=-\$4,216.87 \qquad (9.17)$$

Finally, the value of the swap on date 0 is the expected discounted value of the date 1 payoffs, given by (9.17), under the risk neutral probabilities:

$$\frac{.8024\times\$5,657.66+.1976\times\left(-\$4,216.87\right)}{1+.05/2}=\$3,616.05 \qquad (9.18)$$

The following tree summarizes the value of the stylized CMT swap over dates and states:

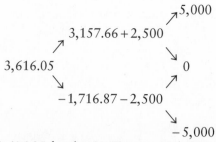

A value of $3,616.05 for the CMT swap might seem surprising at first. After all, the cash flows of the CMT swap are zero at a rate of 5%, and 5% is, under the real probabilities, the average rate on each date. The explanation, of course, is that the risk-neutral probabilities, not the real probabilities, determine the arbitrage price of the swap. The expected discounted value of the swap can be computed by following the steps leading to (9.17) and (9.18) but using the real probabilities of .5 for all up and down moves. The result of these calculations does give a value close to zero, namely –$5.80.

The expected cash flow of the CMT swap on both dates 1 and 2, under the real probabilities, is zero. It follows immediately that the discounted value of these expected cash flows is zero. At the same time, the expected discounted value of the CMT swap is –$5.80. Why are these values different? The answer to this question is deferred to Chapter 17.

REDUCING THE TIME STEP

To this point this chapter has assumed that the time elapsed between dates of the tree is six months. The methodology outlined previously, however, can be easily adapted to any time step of Δt years. For monthly time steps, for example, $\Delta t = \frac{1}{12}$ or .0833, and one-month rather than six-month interest rates appear on the tree. Furthermore, discounting must be done over the appropriate time interval. If the rate of term Δt is r, then discounting means dividing by $1 + r\Delta t$. In the case of monthly time steps, discounting with a one-month rate of 5% means dividing by $1 + \frac{.05}{12}$.

In practice there are two reasons to choose time steps smaller than six months. First, securities rarely make all of their payments in even six-month intervals from the starting date. Reducing the time step to a month, a week, or even a day can ensure that all of a security's cash flows are sufficiently close in time to some date in the tree. Second, assuming that the six-month rate can take on only two values in six months, three values in one year, and so on, produces a tree that is too coarse for many practical pricing problems. Reducing the step size can fill the tree with enough rates to price contingent claims with sufficient accuracy.

Figures 9.1 through 9.4 illustrate the effect of step size on the assumed distribution of the six-month rate in six months. The horizontal axes show the interest rate and the vertical axes the probability that corresponding rates are realized. The binomial trees underlying each figure assume that the initial rate is 5% and that the standard deviation of the six-month rate in six months is 65 basis points. Finally, each graph restricts the range of rates to between 3% and 7% so as to cover a bit more than three standard

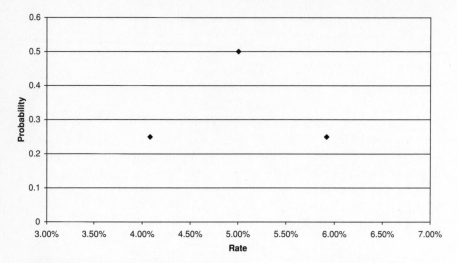

FIGURE 9.1   Probability Distribution of the Six-Month Rate in Six Months; Quarterly Time Steps

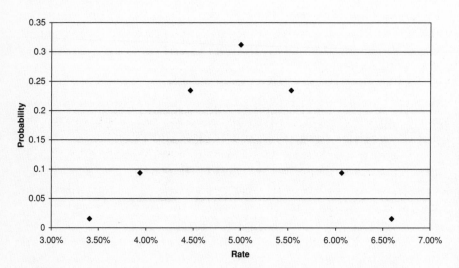

FIGURE 9.2   Probability Distribution of the Six-Month Rate in Six Months; Monthly Time Steps

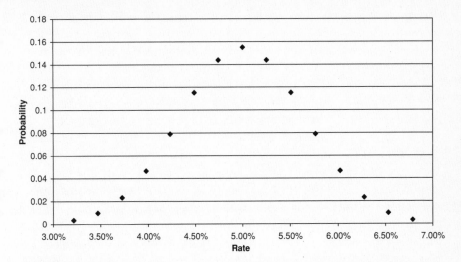

FIGURE 9.3 Probability Distribution of the Six-Month Rate in Six Months; Weekly Time Steps

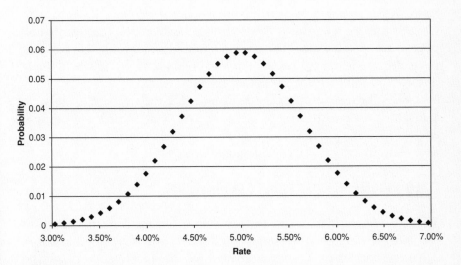

FIGURE 9.4 Probability Distribution of the Six-Month Rate in Six Months; Daily Time Steps

deviations of possible rates. With quarterly steps (Figure 9.1) the probability distribution is quite unrealistic because there are only three possible values for the six-month rate at the end of six months. Decreasing the time step to monthly (Figure 9.2), weekly (Figure 9.3), and daily (Figure 9.4) increases the number of possible values for the six-month rate in six months. The distributions resulting from weekly and daily time steps are clearly much more realistic than the first example introduced in this chapter.

While smaller time steps generate more realistic interest rate distributions, it is not the case that smaller time steps are always desirable. First, the greater the number of computations in pricing a security, the more attention must be paid to numerical issues like round-off error. Second, since decreasing the time step increases computation time, practitioners requiring quick answers cannot make the time step arbitrarily small. Customers calling market makers in options on swaps, or *swaptions*, for example, expect price quotations within minutes if not sooner. Time step in a model used to price swaptions must be consistent with the market maker's required response time.

The best choice of step size ultimately depends on the problem at hand. When pricing a 30-year callable bond, for example, a model with monthly time steps may provide a realistic enough interest rate distribution to generate reliable prices. The same monthly steps, however, will certainly be inadequate to price a one-month bond option: That tree would imply only two possible rates on the option expiration date.

While the trees in this chapter assume that the step size is the same throughout the tree, this need not be the case. Sophisticated implementations of trees allow step size to vary across dates in order to achieve a balance between realism and computational concerns.

FIXED INCOME VERSUS EQUITY DERIVATIVES

While the ideas behind pricing fixed income and equity derivatives are similar in many ways, there are important differences as well. In particular, it is worth describing why models created for the stock market cannot be adopted without modification for use in fixed income markets.

The famous Black-Scholes pricing analysis of stock options can be summarized as follows. Under the assumption that the stock price evolves according to a particular random process and that the short-term interest rate is constant, it is possible to form a portfolio of stocks and short-term bonds that replicates the payoffs of an option. Therefore, by arbitrage arguments, the price of the option must equal the known price of the replicating portfolio.

Say that an investor wants to price an option on a five-year bond by a direct application of the Black-Scholes logic. The investor would have to begin by making an assumption about how the price of the five-year bond evolves over time. But this is considerably more complicated than making assumptions about how the price of a stock evolves over time. First, the price of a bond must converge to its face value at maturity while the random process describing the stock price need not be constrained in any similar way. Second, because of the maturity constraint, the volatility of a bond's price must eventually get smaller as the bond approaches maturity. The Black-Scholes stock analysis, making the simpler assumption that the stock volatility is constant, is not as appropriate for bonds. Third, in the stock option context, where stock volatility is very large relative to short-term rate volatility, it may be relatively harmless to assume that the short-term rate is constant. However, simultaneously assuming that the bond price follows some random process and that the short-term interest rate is constant makes little economic sense.[3]

These objections led researchers to make assumptions about the random evolution of the interest rate rather than of the bond price. In that way bond prices would naturally approach par, price volatilities would naturally approach zero, and the interest rate would no longer be assumed constant. But this approach raises another set of questions. Which interest rate is assumed to evolve in a certain way? Making assumptions about the five-year rate over time is not particularly helpful for two reasons. First, five-year coupon bond prices depend on shorter rates as well. Second, pricing an option on a five-year bond requires assumptions about the bond's future possible prices. But, knowing how the five-year rate evolves over

---

[3]These three objections are less important in the case of short-term options on long-term bonds. In that case, since the underlying security is far from maturity, the pull of price to par and volatility to zero are relatively small effects. Also, since short-term rates (especially when a central bank pegs the overnight rate) are not very volatile and are substantially less than perfectly correlated with long-term rates, the assumption of a constant short-term rate is comparable to the parallel assumption in the case of stock options. In light of these considerations, some practitioners do apply the Black-Scholes analysis in this particular fixed income context.

time does not meet this requirement because, in a very short time, the option's underlying security will no longer be a five-year bond. Therefore, one must make assumptions about the evolution of the entire term structure of interest rates to price bond options and other derivatives. In the one-factor case described in this chapter it has been shown that modeling the evolution of the short-term rate is sufficient, combined with arbitrage arguments, to build a model of the entire term structure. In short, despite the enormous importance of the Black-Scholes analysis, the fixed income context demands special attention.

CHAPTER 10

The Short-Rate Process and the Shape of the Term Structure

Given the initial term structure and assumptions about the true interest rate process for the short-term rate, Chapter 9 showed how to derive the risk-neutral process used to determine arbitrage prices for all fixed income securities. Models that follow this approach and take the initial term structure as given are called *arbitrage-free* models of the term structure. Another approach, to be described in this and subsequent chapters, is to derive the risk-neutral process from assumptions about the true interest rate process and about the risk premium demanded by the market for bearing interest rate risk. Models that follow this approach do not necessarily match the initial term structure and are called *equilibrium* models. The benefits and weaknesses of each class of models are discussed throughout Chapters 11 to 13.

This chapter describes how assumptions about the true interest rate process and about the risk premium determine the level and shape of the term structure. For equilibrium models an understanding of the relationships between the model assumptions and the shape of the term structure is important in order to make reasonable assumptions in the first place. For arbitrage-free models an understanding of these relationships reveals the assumptions implied by the market through the observed term structure.

Many economists might find this chapter remarkably narrow. An economist asked about the shape of the term structure would undoubtedly make reference to macroeconomic factors such as the marginal productivity of capital, the propensity to save, and expected inflation. The more modest goal of this chapter is to connect the dynamics of the short-term rate of interest and the risk premium with the shape of the term structure. While this goal does fall short of answers that an economist might provide, it is more ambitious than the derivation of arbitrage restrictions on bond and derivative prices given the prices of a set of underlying bonds.

The first sections of this chapter present simple examples to illustrate the roles of interest rate expectations, volatility and convexity, and risk premium in the determination of the term structure. A more general, mathematical description of these effects follows. Finally, an application illustrates the concepts and describes the magnitudes of the various effects in the context of the U.S. Treasury market.

EXPECTATIONS

The word expectations implies uncertainty. Investors might expect the one-year rate to be 10%, but know there is a good chance it will turn out to be 8% or 12%. For the purposes of this section alone the text assumes away uncertainty so that the statement that investors expect or forecast a rate of 10% means that investors assume that the rate will be 10%. The sections following this one reintroduce uncertainty.

To highlight the role of interest rate forecasts in determining the shape of the term structure, consider the following simple example. The one-year interest rate is currently 10%, and all investors forecast that the one-year interest rate next year and the year after will also be 10%. In that case, investors will discount cash flows using forward rates of 10%. In particular, the price of one-, two-, and three-year zero coupon bonds per dollar face value (using annual compounding) will be

$$P(1) = \frac{1}{1.10} \tag{10.1}$$

$$P(2) = \frac{1}{(1.10)(1.10)} = \frac{1}{1.10^2} \tag{10.2}$$

$$P(3) = \frac{1}{(1.10)(1.10)(1.10)} = \frac{1}{1.10^3} \tag{10.3}$$

From inspection of equations (10.1) through (10.3), the term structure of spot rates in this example is flat at 10%. Very simply, investors are willing to lock in 10% for two or three years because they assume that the one-year rate will always be 10%.

Now assume that the one-year rate is still 10%, but that all investors forecast the one-year rate next year to be 12% and the one-year rate in two years to be 14%. In that case, the one-year spot rate is still 10%. The two-year spot rate, $\hat{r}(2)$, is such that

$$P(2) = \frac{1}{(1.10)(1.12)} = \frac{1}{(1+\hat{r}(2))^2} \qquad (10.4)$$

Solving, $\hat{r}(2)$=10.995%. Similarly, the three-year spot rate, $\hat{r}(3)$, is such that

$$P(3) = \frac{1}{(1.10)(1.12)(1.14)} = \frac{1}{(1+\hat{r}(3))^3} \qquad (10.5)$$

Solving, $\hat{r}(3)$=11.998%. Hence, the evolution of the one-year rate from 10% to 12% to 14% generates an upward-sloping term structure of spot rates: 10%, 10.995%, and 11.988%. In this case investors require rates above 10% when locking up their money for two or three years because they assume one-year rates will be higher than 10%. No investor, for example, would buy a two-year zero at a yield of 10% when it is possible to buy a one-year zero at 10% and, when it matures, buy another one-year zero at 12%.

Finally, assume that the one-year rate is 10%, but that investors forecast it to fall to 8% in one year and to 6% in two years. In that case, it is easy to show that the term structure of spot rates will be downward-sloping. In particular, $\hat{r}(1)$=10%, $\hat{r}(2)$=8.995%, and $\hat{r}(3)$=7.988%.

These simple examples reveal that expectations can cause the term structure to take on any of a myriad of shapes. Over short horizons, one can imagine that the financial community would have specific views about the future of the short-term rate. The term structure in the U.S. Treasury market on February 15, 2001, analyzed later in this chapter, implies that the short-term rate would fall for about two years and then rise again.[1] At the time this was known as the "V-shaped" recovery. At first, the economy would continue to weaken and the Federal Reserve would continue to reduce the federal funds target rate in an attempt to spur growth. Then the

---

[1]Strangely enough, Eurodollar futures at the same time implied that rates would fall for less than one year before rising again. (Chapter 17 will describe Eurodollar futures.)

economy would rebound sharply and the Federal Reserve would be forced to increase the target rate to keep inflation in check.[2]

Over long horizons the path of expectations cannot be as specific as those mentioned in the previous paragraph. For example, it would be difficult to defend the position that the one-year rate 29 years from now will be substantially different from the one-year rate 30 years from now. On the other hand, one might make an argument that the long-run expectation of the short-term rate is, for example, 5% (2.50% due to the long-run real rate of interest and 2.50% due to long-run inflation). Hence, forecasts can be very useful in describing the level and shape of the term structure over short time horizons and the level of rates over very long horizons. This conclusion has important implications for extracting expectations from observed interest rates (see the application at the end of this chapter), for curve fitting techniques not based on term structure models (see Chapter 4), and for the use of arbitrage-free models of the term structure (see Chapters 11 to 13).

VOLATILITY AND CONVEXITY

This section drops the assumption that investors believe their forecasts are realized and assumes instead that investors understand the volatility around their expectations. To isolate the implications of volatility on the shape of the term structure, this section assumes that investors are risk neutral so that they price securities by expected discounted value. The next section drops this assumption.

Assume that the following tree gives the true process for the one-year rate:

$$
\begin{array}{ccccc}
 & & & & \overset{\frac{1}{2}\,\nearrow}{}14\% \\
 & & \overset{\frac{1}{2}\,\nearrow}{}12\% & & \\
 \overset{\frac{1}{2}\,\nearrow}{}& & & \overset{\frac{1}{2}\,\searrow}{}& \\
10\% & & & & 10\% \\
 \overset{\frac{1}{2}\,\searrow}{}& & & \overset{\frac{1}{2}\,\nearrow}{}& \\
 & & 8\% & & \\
 & & & \overset{\frac{1}{2}\,\searrow}{}& \\
 & & & & 6\%
\end{array}
$$

---

[2]Those who thought the economy would take some time to recover predicted a "U-shaped" recovery. Those even more pessimistic expected an "L-shaped" recovery.

Note that the expected interest rate on date 1 is .5×8%+.5×12% or 10% and that the expected rate on date 2 is .25×14%+.5×10%+.25×6% or 10%. In the previous section, with no volatility around expectations, flat expectations of 10% imply a flat term structure of spot rates. That is not the case in the presence of volatility.

The price of a one-year zero is, by definition, $^1/_{1.10}$ or .909091, implying a one-year spot rate of 10%. Under the assumption of risk neutrality, the price of a two-year zero may be calculated by discounting the terminal cash flow using the preceding interest rate tree:

$$
\begin{array}{ccccc}
 & & & & 1 \\
 & & .892857 & \nearrow^{\;\frac{1}{2}} & \\
 & \nearrow^{\;\frac{1}{2}} & & \searrow^{\;\frac{1}{2}} & \\
.826720 & & & & 1 \\
 & \searrow_{\;\frac{1}{2}} & & \nearrow^{\;\frac{1}{2}} & \\
 & & .925926 & & \\
 & & & \searrow_{\;\frac{1}{2}} & \\
 & & & & 1
\end{array}
$$

Hence, the two-year spot rate is such that $.82672=1/(1+\hat{r}(2))^2$, implying that $\hat{r}(2)=9.982\%$.

Even though the one-year rate is 10% and the expected one-year rate in one year is 10%, the two-year spot rate is 9.982%. The 1.8-basis point difference between the spot rate that would obtain in the absence of uncertainty, 10%, and the spot rate in the presence of volatility, 9.982%, is the effect of convexity on that spot rate. This convexity effect arises from the mathematical fact, a special case of *Jensen's Inequality*, that

$$
E\left[\frac{1}{1+r}\right] > \frac{1}{E\left[1+r\right]} = \frac{1}{1+E\left[r\right]} \tag{10.6}
$$

Figure 10.1 graphically illustrates this equation. The figure assumes that there are two possible values for r, r_{Low} and r_{High}. The curve gives values of $1/(1+r)$ for the various values of r. The midpoint of the straight line connecting $1/(1+r_{Low})$ to $1/(1+r_{High})$ equals the average of those two values. Under the assumption that the two rates occur with equal probability, this average equals the point labeled $E[1/(1+r)]$ in the figure. Under the same assumption, the point on the abscissa labeled $E[1+r]$ equals the expected value of $1+r$ and the corresponding point on the curve equals $1/E[1+r]$. Clearly, $E[1/(1+r)]$ is

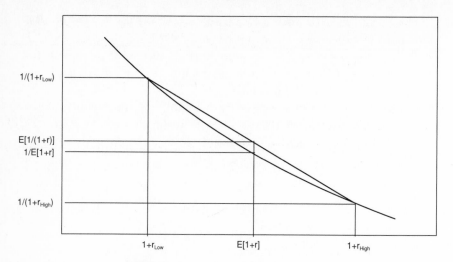

FIGURE 10.1 An Illustration of Convexity

greater than $1/E(1+r)$. To summarize, equation (10.6) is true because the pricing function of a zero, $1/(1+r)$, is convex rather than concave.

Returning to the example of this section, equation (10.6) may be used to show why the one-year spot rate is less than 10%. The spot rate one year from now may be 12% or 8%. According to (10.6),

$$.5 \times \frac{1}{1.12} + .5 \times \frac{1}{1.08} > \frac{1}{.5 \times 1.12 + .5 \times 1.08} = \frac{1}{1 + .10} \qquad (10.7)$$

Dividing both sides by 1.10,

$$\frac{1}{1.10} \left(.5 \times \frac{1}{1.12} + .5 \times \frac{1}{1.08} \right) > \frac{1}{1.10^2} \qquad (10.8)$$

The left-hand side of (10.8) is the price of the two-year zero coupon bond today. In words, then, equation (10.8) says that the price of the two-year zero is greater than the result of discounting the terminal cash flow by 10% over the first period and by the expected rate of 10% over the second period. It follows immediately that the yield of the two-year zero, or the two-year spot rate, is less than 10%.

The tree presented at the start of this section may also be used to price a three-year zero. The resulting price tree is

$$
\begin{array}{c}
& & & & 1 \\
& & & {}^{1\!/_2}\nearrow & \\
& & \nearrow .877193 & & \\
& {}^{1\!/_2}\nearrow & & {}^{1\!/_2}\searrow & \\
& .797448 & & & 1 \\
{}^{1\!/_2}\nearrow & & {}^{1\!/_2}\searrow & & {}^{1\!/_2}\nearrow \\
.752309 & & & .909091 & \\
& {}^{1\!/_2}\searrow & & {}^{1\!/_2}\nearrow & {}^{1\!/_2}\searrow \\
& .857633 & & & 1 \\
& & {}^{1\!/_2}\searrow & & {}^{1\!/_2}\nearrow \\
& & .943396 & & \\
& & & {}^{1\!/_2}\searrow & \\
& & & & 1
\end{array}
$$

The three-year spot rate, such that $.752309 = 1/(1+\hat{r}(3))^3$, is 9.952%. Therefore, the value of convexity in this spot rate is 10%–9.952% or 4.8 basis points, whereas the value of convexity in the two-year spot rate was only 1.8 basis points.

It is generally true that, all else equal, the value of convexity increases with maturity. This will be proved shortly. For now, suffice it to say that the convexity of the price of a zero maturing in N years, $1/(1+r)^N$, increases with N. In other words, if Figure 10.1 were redrawn for the function $1/(1+r)^3$, for example, instead of $1/(1+r)$, the resulting curve would be more convex.

Chapters 5 and 6 show that bonds with greater convexity perform better when yields change a lot but mentioned that this greater convexity is paid for at times that yields do not change very much. The discussion in this section shows that convexity does, in fact, lower bond yields. The mathematical development in a later section ties these observations together by showing exactly how the advantages of convexity are offset by lower yields.

The previous section assumes no interest rate volatility and, consequently, yields are completely determined by forecasts. In this section, with the introduction of volatility, yield is reduced by the value of convexity. So it may be said that the value of convexity arises from volatility. Furthermore, the value of convexity increases with volatility. In the tree introduced at the start of the section, the standard deviation of rates is 200 basis points a year.[3] Now consider a tree with a standard deviation of 400 basis points a year:

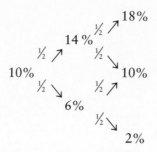

The expected one-year rate in one year and in two years is still 10%. Spot rates and convexity values for this case may be derived along the same lines as before. Figure 10.2 graphs three term structures of spot rates: one with no volatility around the expectation of 10%, one with a volatility of 200 basis points a year (the tree of the first example), and one with a volatility of 400 basis points per year (the tree preceding this paragraph). Note that

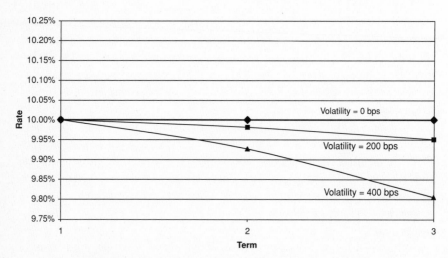

FIGURE 10.2   Volatility and the Shape of the Term Structure

---

[3]Chapter 11 describes the computation of the standard deviation of rates implied by an interest rate tree.

the value of convexity, measured by the distance between the rates assuming no volatility and the rates assuming volatility, increases with volatility. Figure 10.2 also shows that the value of convexity increases with maturity.

For very short terms and realistic volatility, the value of convexity is quite small. Simple examples, however, must use short terms, so convexity effects would hardly be discernible without raising volatility to unrealistic levels. Therefore, this section is forced to choose unrealistically large volatility values. The application at the end of this chapter uses realistic volatility to present typical convexity values.

RISK PREMIUM

To illustrate the effect of risk premium on the term structure, consider again the second interest rate tree presented in the preceding section, with a volatility of 400 basis point per year. Risk-neutral investors would price a two-year zero by the following calculation:

$$
\begin{aligned}
.827541 &= .5\big[1/1.14 + 1/1.06\big]/1.1 \\
&= .5\big[.877193 + .943396\big]/1.1
\end{aligned}
\tag{10.9}
$$

By discounting the expected future price by 10%, equation (10.9) implies that the expected return from owning the two-year zero over the next year is 10%. To verify this statement, calculate this expected return directly:

$$
.5 \times \frac{.877193 - .827541}{.827541} + .5 \times \frac{.943396 - .827541}{.827541} = .5 \times 6\% + .5 \times 14\%
$$
$$
= 10\%
\tag{10.10}
$$

Would investors really invest in this two-year zero offering an expected return of 10% over the next year? The return will, in fact, be either 6% or 14%. While these two returns do average to 10%, an investor could, instead, buy a one-year zero with a certain return of 10%. Presented with this choice, any risk-averse investor will prefer an investment with a certain return of 10% to an investment with a risky return that averages 10%. In other words, investors require compensation for bearing interest rate risk.[4]

---

[4]This is a bit of an oversimplification. See the discussion at the end of the section.

Risk-averse investors demand a return higher than 10% for the two-year zero over the next year. This return can be effected by pricing the zero coupon bond one year from now at less than the prices of $1/1.14$ or .877193 and $1/1.06$ or .943396. Equivalently, future cash flows could be discounted at rates higher than the possible rates of 14% and 6%. The next section shows that adding, for example, 20 basis points to each of these rates is equivalent to assuming that investors demand an extra 20 basis points for each year of modified duration risk. Assuming this is indeed the fair market *risk premium*, the price of the two-year zero would be computed as follows:

$$.826035 = .5\left[1/1.142 + 1/1.062\right]/1.1 \qquad (10.11)$$

First, this is below the price of .827541 obtained in equation (10.9) by assuming that investors are risk-neutral. Second, the increase in the discounting rates has increased the expected return of the two-year zero. In one year, if the interest rate is 14% then the price of a one-year zero will be $1/1.14$ or .877193. If the interest is 6%, then the price of a one-year zero will be $1/1.06$ or .943396. Therefore, the expected return of the two-year zero priced at .826035 is

$$\frac{.5\left[.877193 + .943396\right] - .826035}{.826035} = 10.20\% \qquad (10.12)$$

Hence, recalling that the one-year zero has a certain return of 10%, the risk-averse investors in this example demand 20 basis points in expected return to compensate them for the one year of modified duration risk inherent in the two-year zero.[5]

Continuing with the assumption that investors require 20 basis points for each year of modified duration risk, the three-year zero, with its approximately two years of modified duration risk,[6] needs to offer an expected return of 40 basis points. The next section shows that this return

---

[5]The reader should keep in mind that a two-year zero has one year of interest rate risk only in this stylized example: It has been assumed that rates can move only once a year. In reality rates can move at any time, so a two-year zero has two years of interest rate risk.

[6]See the previous footnote.

can be effected by pricing the three-year zero as if rates next year are 20 basis points above their true values and as if rates the year after next are 40 basis points above their true values. To summarize, consider the following two trees. If the tree to the left depicts the actual or true interest rate process, then pricing with the tree to the right provides investors with a risk premium of 20 basis points for each year of modified duration risk. If this risk premium is, in fact, embedded in market prices, then by definition, the tree to the right is the risk-neutral interest rate process.

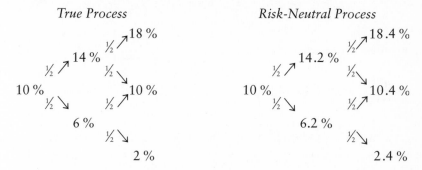

| | | *True Process* | | | | *Risk-Neutral Process* |
| | | | | | | |

The text now verifies that pricing the three-year zero with the risk-neutral process does offer an expected return of 10.4%, assuming that rates actually move according to the true process.

The price of the three-year zero can be computed by discounting using the risk-neutral tree:

To find the expected return of the three-year zero over the next year, proceed as follows. Two years from now the three-year zero will be a one-year zero with no interest rate risk.[7] Therefore, its price will be determined by discounting at the actual interest rate at that time: $1/1.18$ or .847458, $1/1.10$ or .909091, and $1/1.02$ or .980392. One year from now, however, the three-year zero will be a two-year zero with one year of modified duration risk. Therefore, its price at that time will be determined by using the risk-neutral rates of 14.20% and 6.20%. In particular, the two possible prices of the three-year zero in one year are

$$.769067 = .5(.847458 + .909091)/1.142 \qquad (10.13)$$

and

$$.889587 = .5(.909091 + .980392)/1.062 \qquad (10.14)$$

Finally, then, the expected return of the three-year zero over the next year is

$$\frac{.5(.769067 + .889587) - .751184}{.751184} = 10.40\% \qquad (10.15)$$

To summarize, in order to compensate investors for about two years of modified duration risk, the return on the three-year zero is about 40 basis points above the 10% certain return of a one-year zero.

Continuing with the assumption of 400 basis point volatility, Figure 10.3 graphs the term structure of spot rates for three cases: no risk premium, a risk premium of 20 basis points per year of modified duration risk, and a risk premium of 40 basis points. In the case of no risk premium, the term structure of spot rates is downward-sloping due to convexity. A risk premium of 20 basis points pushes up spot rates of longer maturity while convexity pulls them down. In the short end the risk premium effect dominates and the term structure is mildly upward-sloping. In the long end the convexity effect dominates and the term structure is mildly downward-sloping. The next section clarifies why risk premium tends to dominate in

---

[7]This is an artifact of this example in which rates change only once a year.

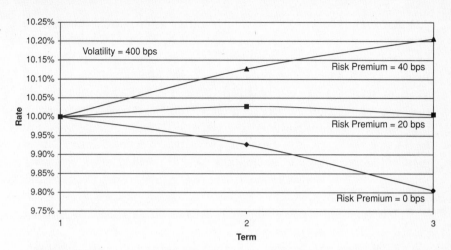

FIGURE 10.3 Volatility, Risk Premium, and the Shape of the Term Structure

the short end while convexity tends to dominate in the long end. Finally, a risk premium as large as 40 basis points dominates the convexity effect, and the term structure of spot rates is upward-sloping. The convexity effect is still evident, however, from the fact that the curve increases more rapidly from one to two years than from two to three years.

Just as the section on volatility uses unrealistically high levels of volatility to illustrate its effects, this section uses unrealistically high levels of the risk premium to illustrate its effects. The application at the end of this section focuses on reasonable magnitudes for the various effects in the context of the U.S. Treasury market.

Before closing this section, a few remarks on the sources of an interest rate risk premium are in order. Asset pricing theory (e.g., the Capital Asset Pricing Model, or CAPM) teaches that assets whose returns are positively correlated with aggregate wealth or consumption will earn a risk premium. Consider, for example, a traded stock index. That asset will almost certainly do well if the economy is doing well and poorly if the economy is doing poorly. But investors, as a group, already have a lot of exposure to the economy. To entice them to hold a little more of the economy in the form of a traded stock index requires the payment of a risk premium; that is, the index must offer an expected return greater than the risk-free rate of return. On the other hand, say that there exists an asset that is negatively correlated with the economy. Holdings in that asset allow investors to reduce their exposure to the economy. As a result, investors would accept an expected return on that asset below the risk-free rate of return. That asset, in other words, would have a negative risk premium.

This section assumes that bonds with interest rate risk earn a risk premium. In terms of asset pricing theory, this is equivalent to assuming that bond returns are positively correlated with the economy or, equivalently, that falling interest rates are associated with good times. One argument supporting this assumption is that interest rates fall when inflation and expected inflation fall and that low inflation is correlated with good times.

The concept of a risk premium in fixed income markets has probably gained favor more for its empirical usefulness than for its theoretical solidity. On average, over the past 70 years, the term structure of interest rates has sloped upward.[8] While the market may from time to time expect that interest rates will rise, it is hard to believe that the market expects interest rates to rise on average. Therefore, expectations cannot explain a term structure of interest rates that, on average, slopes upward. Convexity, of course, leads to a downward-sloping term structure. Hence, of the three effects described in this chapter, only a positive risk premium can explain a term structure that, on average, slopes upward.

An uncomfortable fact, however, is that over earlier time periods the term structure has, on average, been flat.[9] Whether this means that an interest rate risk premium is a relatively recent phenomenon that is here to stay or that the experience of persistently upward-sloping curves is only partially due to a risk premium is a question beyond the scope of this book. In short, the theoretical and empirical questions with respect to the existence of an interest rate risk premium have not been settled.

A MATHEMATICAL DESCRIPTION OF EXPECTATIONS, CONVEXITY, AND RISK PREMIUM

This section presents an approach to understanding the components of return in fixed income markets. While the treatment is mathematical, the aim is intuition rather than mathematical rigor.

---

[8]See, for example, Homer and Sylla (1996), pp. 394–409.
[9]See, for example, Homer and Sylla (1996), pp. 394–409.

Let $P(y, t; c)$ be the price of a bond at time t with a yield y and a continuously paid coupon rate of c. A continuously paid coupon means that over a small time interval, dt, the bond makes a coupon payment of cdt. No real bonds pay continuous coupons, but the assumption will make the mathematical development of this section simpler without any loss of intuition. Note, by the way, that the coupon rate is written after the semicolon to indicate that the coupon rate is fixed.

By *Ito's Lemma* (a discussion of which is beyond the mathematical scope of this book),

$$dP = \frac{\partial P}{\partial y}dy + \frac{\partial P}{\partial t}dt + \frac{1}{2}\frac{\partial^2 P}{\partial y^2}\sigma^2 dt \tag{10.16}$$

where dP, dy, and dt are the changes in price, yield, and time, respectively over the next instant and σ is the volatility of yield measured in basis point per year. The two first-order partial derivatives, $\partial P/\partial y$ and $\partial P/\partial t$, denote the change in the bond price for a unit change in yield (with time unchanged) and the change in the bond price for a unit change in time (with yield unchanged), respectively, over the next instant. Finally, the second-order partial derivative, $\partial^2 P/\partial y^2$, gives the change in $\partial P/\partial y$ for a unit change in yield (with time unchanged) over the next instant. Dividing both sides of (10.16) by price,

$$\frac{dP}{P} = \frac{1}{P}\frac{\partial P}{\partial y}dy + \frac{1}{P}\frac{\partial P}{\partial t}dt + \frac{1}{2}\frac{1}{P}\frac{\partial^2 P}{\partial y^2}\sigma^2 dt \tag{10.17}$$

Thus, equation (10.17) breaks down the return from bond price changes over the next instant, dP/P, into three components. This equation can be written in a more intuitive form by invoking several facts from throughout this book.

First, recall from Chapter 3 that, with an unchanged yield, the total return of a bond over a coupon interval equals its yield multiplied by the time interval. Appendix 10A proves the continuous time equivalent of that statement:

$$y = \frac{1}{P}\frac{\partial P}{\partial t} + \frac{c}{P} \tag{10.18}$$

In words, the yield equals the return of the bond in the form of price appreciation plus the return in the form of coupon income. Rearranging (10.18) slightly,

$$\frac{1}{P}\frac{\partial P}{\partial t} = y - \frac{c}{P} \tag{10.19}$$

Second, Chapter 6 shows that modified duration and yield-based convexity, written here as D and C, respectively, may be written as

$$D = -\frac{1}{P}\frac{\partial P}{\partial y} \tag{10.20}$$

$$C = \frac{1}{P}\frac{\partial^2 P}{\partial y^2} \tag{10.21}$$

Substituting equations (10.19), (10.20), and (10.21) into (10.17),

$$\frac{dP + cdt}{P} \approx ydt - Ddy + \frac{1}{2}C\sigma^2 dt \tag{10.22}$$

The left-hand side of this equation is the total return of the bond—that is, its capital gain, dP, plus its coupon payment, cdt, divided by the initial price. The right-hand side of (10.22) gives the three components of total return. The first component equals the return due to the passage of time—that is, the return to the bondholder over some short time horizon if yields remain unchanged. The second and third components equal the return due to change in yield. The second term says that increases in yield reduce bond return and that the greater the duration of the bond, the greater this effect. This term is perfectly consistent with the discussion of interest rate sensitivity in Part Two of the book.

The third term on the right-hand side of equation (10.22) is consistent with the related discussions in Chapters 5 and 6. Equation (5.20) showed that bond return increases with convexity multiplied by the change in yield squared. Here, in equation (10.22), C is multiplied by the volatility of yield instead of the yield squared. By the definition of volatility and variance, of course, these quantities are very closely related: Variance equals the expected value of the yield squared minus the square of the expected yield.

Equation (5.20) implied that positive convexity increases return whether rates rise or fall. Equation (10.22) implies the same thing. Also, Chapters 5 and 6 concluded that the greater the change in yield, the greater the performance of bonds with high convexity relative to bonds with low convexity. Similarly, equation (10.22) shows that the greater the volatility of yield, the greater this convexity-induced advantage. The text soon discusses the cost of this increased return.

To draw conclusions about the expected returns of bonds with different duration and convexity characteristics, it will prove useful to take the expectation of each side of (10.22), obtaining

$$E\left[\frac{dP}{P}\right] + \frac{cdt}{P} = ydt - DE[dy] + \frac{1}{2}C\sigma^2 dt \qquad (10.23)$$

Equation (10.23) divides expected return into its mathematical components. These components are analogous to those in equation (10.22): a return due to the passage of time, a return due to expected changes in yield, and a return due to volatility and convexity. To develop equation (10.23) further, the analysis must incorporate the economics of expected return.

Risk-neutral investors demand that each bond offer an expected return equal to the short-term rate of interest. The interest rate risk of one bond relative to another would not affect the required expected returns. Mathematically,

$$E\left[\frac{dP}{P}\right] + \frac{cdt}{P} = rdt \qquad (10.24)$$

Risk-averse investors demand higher expected returns for bonds with more interest rate risk. Appendix 10A shows that the interest rate risk of a bond over the next instant may be measured by its duration and that risk-averse investors demand a risk premium proportional to duration. In the context of this section, where yield is the interest rate factor, risk may be measured by modified duration. Letting the risk premium parameter be λ, the expected return equation becomes

$$E\left[\frac{dP}{P}\right] + \frac{cdt}{P} = rdt + \lambda D dt \qquad (10.25)$$

Say, for example, that the short-term interest rate is 4%, that the modified duration of a particular bond is five years, and that the risk premium is 10 basis points per year of duration risk. Then, according to equation (10.25), the total expected return of that bond equals 4%+5×.1% or 4.5% per year.

Another useful way to think of the risk premium is in terms of the *Sharpe ratio* of a security, defined as its expected excess return (i.e., its expected return above the short-term interest rate), divided by the standard deviation of the return. Since the random part of a bond's return comes from its duration times the change in yield, the standard deviation of the return equals the duration times the standard deviation of the yield. Therefore, the Sharpe ratio of a bond, S, may be written as

$$S = \frac{E[dP/P] + cdt/P - rdt}{\sigma D dt} \qquad (10.26)$$

Comparing equations (10.26) and (10.25), one can see that $S = \lambda/\sigma$. So, continuing with the numerical example, if the risk premium is 10 basis points per year and if the standard deviation of yield is assumed to be 100 basis points per year, then the Sharpe ratio of a bond investment is $^{10}/_{100}$ or 10%.

Equipped with an economic description of expected returns, the text can now draw conclusions about the determination of yield. Substitute the expected return equation (10.25) into the breakdown of expected return given by equation (10.23) to see that

$$y = r + D\left[E[dy]\big/dt + \lambda\right] - \frac{1}{2}C\sigma^2 \qquad (10.27)$$

Equation (10.27) mathematically describes the determinants of yield presented in this section. The effect of expectations is given by the terms of r and $E[dy]$. For intuition, let y' denote the yield of the bond one instant from now, let $\Delta y \equiv y' - y$, and let Δt denote the time interval. Then, the expectations terms of (10.27) alone say that

$$y = r + D\left[E[y'] - y\right]\big/\Delta t \qquad (10.28)$$

Solving for y,

$$y = \frac{r\Delta t + DE[y']}{\Delta t + D} \qquad (10.29)$$

In words, due to expectations alone, the yield of a bond is a weighted average of the current short-term rate and the expected yield of the bond an instant from now. The greater the short-term rate and the greater the expected yield, the greater is the current bond yield. Furthermore, extrapolating this reasoning, the expected yield, in turn, is determined by expectations about the short-term rate of interest from the next instant to the maturity of the bond. Finally, the greater a bond's duration, the more its yield is determined by expected future rates relative to the current short-term rate.

The risk premium term of equation (10.27) shows an effect on yield of $D\lambda$. As illustrated by the examples of this chapter, yield increases with the size of the required risk premium and with the interest rate risk (i.e., duration) of the bond.

The discussion of the risk premium in the previous section and the construction of the risk-neutral trees in Chapter 9 show that pricing bonds as if the short-term rate drifted up by a certain amount each year has the same effect as a risk premium. Inspection of equation (10.27) more formally reveals this equivalence. As mentioned in the context of equation (10.29), the expected change in yield is driven by expected changes in the short-term rate. Increasing the expected yield by 10 basis points per year implies increasing the expected short-term rate by 10 basis points per year. Hence, equation (10.27) says that increasing the risk premium, λ, by a fixed number of basis points is empirically indistinguishable from increasing the expected short-term rate by the same number of basis points per year. From a data perspective this means that the term structure at any given time cannot be used to distinguish between market expectations of rate changes and risk premium. From a modeling perspective this means that only the risk-neutral process is relevant for pricing. Dividing the drift into expectations and risk premium might be very useful in determining whether the model seems reasonable from an economic point of view, but this division has no pricing implications.

The term $-(\frac{1}{2})C\sigma^2$ in equation (10.27) gives the effect of convexity on yield. Recalling from Chapter 6 that a bond's convexity increases with maturity, this term shows that the convexity effect on yield increases with maturity and with interest rate volatility, as illustrated in the simple examples given earlier.

Recall from Part Two that duration increases more or less linearly with maturity while convexity increases more or less with maturity squared. This observation, combined with equation (10.27), implies that, holding everything else equal, as maturity increases, the convexity effect eventually dominates the risk premium effect. However, as will be discussed in the next section and in next few chapters, the volatility of yields tends to decline with maturity. The 10-year yield, for example, is more volatile than the 30-year yield. Therefore, as maturity increases, the increase in the convexity effect in (10.27) may be muted by falling volatility.

Equation (10.23) shows that the expected return of a bond is enhanced by its convexity in the quantity $(1/2)C\sigma^2$ per unit time. But the convexity term in equation (10.27) shows that the yield and, therefore, the return due to the passage of time are reduced by exactly that amount. Hence, as claimed in Chapters 5 and 6 and as mentioned earlier in this chapter, a bond priced by arbitrage offers no advantage in expected return due to its convexity. In fact, the expected return condition (10.25) ensured that this had to be so. None of this means, of course, that the return profile of bonds with different convexity measures will be the same. Bonds with higher convexity will perform better when yields change a lot, while bonds with lower convexity will perform better when yields do not change by much.

APPLICATION: Expectations, Convexity, and Risk Premium in the U.S. Treasury Market on February 15, 2001

Figure 10.4 shows four curves. The uppermost curve is the par yield curve on February 15, 2001. These par yields are computed from the spot rates constructed in Chapter 4. The other three curves break down the par yields into the components discussed in this section: expectations, risk premium, and convexity.

As shown in the previous section, convexity impacts the yield of a bond by $-(1/2)C\sigma^2$. The convexity of a particular par bond may be computed using the formulas given in Chapter 6.

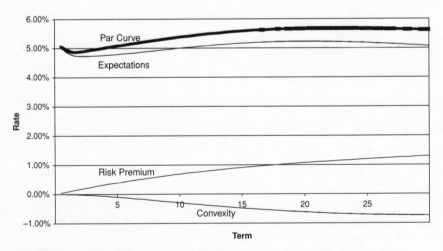

FIGURE 10.4 Expectations, Convexity, and Risk Premium Estimates in the Treasury Market, February 15, 2001

Choosing the level of volatility to input into the convexity effect, however, requires some comment. The desired quantity, the volatility of the yield in question, is unknown. The most common substitute choices are one's best guess, recent historical volatility, or implied volatility. The relative merits of these choices will be discussed in Chapter 12, but Figure 10.4 uses implied volatilities from the relatively liquid short-term options on 2-, 5-, 10-, and 30-year Treasury securities. Table 10.1 lists these implied volatilities as of February 15, 2001.

Notice that the term structure of volatilities slopes upward and then downward. For the purposes of Figure 10.4, implied volatilities on bonds of intermediate maturities were assumed to be linear in the given volatilities. For maturities less than two years, the two-year volatility was used. So, for example, the convexity effect on a 20-year security is computed as follows. The convexity of a 20-year par bond at a yield of 5.67% is about 194.5. Interpolating 91.5 basis points per year for a 10-year yield and 68.6 basis points per year for a 30-year yield gives an approximation for 20-year volatility of about 80 basis points per year. Therefore, the magnitude of the convexity effect is estimated at about 62 basis points:

$$\frac{1}{2} \times 194.5 \times (.80\%)^2 = .62\% \qquad (10.30)$$

Figure 10.4 illustrates that the magnitude of the convexity effect increases with maturity. When increasing maturity, the increase in bond convexity offsets the decrease in volatility.

Adding the convexity effect to the par yields leaves expectations and risk premium. Given the observational equivalence of these two effects (see the previous section and Chapter 11), there is no scientific way to separate them by observing a given term structure of yields. Therefore, for the purposes of drawing Figure 10.4, several strong assumptions were made.[10] First, the long-run expectation of the short-term rate is about

TABLE 10.1 Volatilities Implied from Short-Dated Bond Options

Term	Basis Point Volatility
2	92.6
5	95.4
10	91.5
30	68.6

---

[10]The reader is very much encouraged to critique these assumptions and postulate a different decomposition of yields.

5%, corresponding to a long-run real rate of 2.50% and a long-run inflation rate of 2.50%. Second, the expectation curve is relatively linear at longer maturities. As mentioned in the discussion of expectations in this chapter, while the market might expect the short-term rate to move toward some long-term level, it is hard to defend any expected fluctuations in the short-term rate 20 or 30 years in the future. Third, the risk premium is a constant. While the risk premium may, in theory, depend on calendar time and on the level of rates, very little theoretical work has been done to justify these relatively complex specifications. Fourth, the Sharpe ratio of bonds is not too far from historical norms.

As it turns out, a risk premium of 9 basis points per year satisfies these objectives relatively well, although not perfectly well. The resulting expectations curve exhibits a dip and then a gradual increase to a long-run level. The dip is perfectly acceptable, corresponding to beliefs about near-term economic activity and the Federal Reserve's likely responses to that activity. On the other hand, that the expectation curve rises above 5%, to a maximum of about 5.23%, before falling back to 5% violates, at least to some extent, the second objective of the previous paragraph. Lastly, using the volatilities given in Table 10.1, the magnitude of the risk premium gives Sharpe ratios ranging from 9.4% for 5-year bonds to 13.1% for 30-year bonds. These values are in the range of historical plausibility.

Decompositions of the sort described here are useful in forming opinions about which sectors of a bond market are rich or cheap. Say, for example, that one accepts the decomposition presented here but does not accept that the expected short-term rate 20 years from now can be so far above the expected short rate 10 and 30 years from now. In that case, one must conclude that 20-year yields are too high relative to 10-year and 30-year yields, or, equivalently, that the 20-year sector is cheap. This conclusion suggests purchasing 20-year Treasury bonds rather than 10- and 30-year bonds or, more aggressively, buying 20-year bonds and shorting 10- and 30-year bonds. This, in fact, is the trade suggested in the trading case study in Chapter 8. (The trade is rejected there because the 20-year sector did not seem cheap relative to recent history.)

APPENDIX 10A
PROOFS OF EQUATIONS (10.19) AND (10.25)

Proof of Equation (10.19)

Under continuous compounding, the present value of the continuously paid coupon payments from time t to the maturity of the bond at time T is

$$\int_{t=s}^{T} ce^{-y(s-t)}ds = \frac{c}{y}\left[1 - e^{-y(T-t)}\right]$$ (10.31)

Adding the present value of the final principal payment to the value of the coupon flow, the price of the bond is

$$P = \frac{c}{y}\left[1 - e^{-y(T-t)}\right] + e^{-y(T-t)}$$ (10.32)

Note that this is the continuous time equivalent of equation (3.4).

Taking the derivative of (10.32) with respect to t,

$$\frac{\partial P}{\partial t} = \left(y - c\right)e^{-y(T-t)}$$ (10.33)

But, rearranging (10.32) shows that

$$\left(y - c\right)e^{-y(T-t)} = yP - c$$ (10.34)

Finally, combining equations (10.33) and (10.34),

$$\frac{\partial P}{\partial t} = yP - c$$ (10.35)

or

$$\frac{1}{P}\frac{\partial P}{\partial t} = y - \frac{c}{P}$$ (10.36)

as was to be proved.

Proof of Equation (10.25)

This proof follows that of Ingersoll (1987) and assumes some knowledge of stochastic processes and their associated notation. The notation will be described in Chapter 11.

Let x be some interest rate factor that follows the process

$$dx = \mu dt + \sigma dw$$ (10.37)

Let P be the full price of some security that depends on x and time. Then, by Ito's Lemma,

$$dP = P_x dx + P_t dt + \frac{1}{2} P_{xx} \sigma^2 dt \qquad (10.38)$$

Dividing both sides by P, taking expectations, and defining α_p to be the expected return of the security,

$$\alpha_p dt \equiv E\left[\frac{dP}{P}\right] = \frac{P_x}{P} \mu dt + \frac{P_t}{P} dt + \frac{1}{2} P_{xx} \sigma^2 dt \qquad (10.39)$$

Combining (10.38) and (10.39),

$$\frac{dP}{P} - \alpha_p dt = \frac{P_x}{P} \sigma dw \qquad (10.40)$$

Since equation (10.40) is valid for any security, it is also valid for security Q:

$$\frac{dQ}{Q} - \alpha_Q dt = \frac{Q_x}{Q} \sigma dw \qquad (10.41)$$

Now consider the strategy of investing \$1 in security P and

$$-\frac{P_x Q}{PQ_x} \qquad (10.42)$$

dollars in security Q. Using equations (10.40) and (10.41), the return on this portfolio is

$$\frac{dP}{P} - \frac{P_x Q}{PQ_x} \frac{dQ}{Q} = \alpha_p dt - \frac{P_x Q}{PQ_x} \alpha_Q dt \qquad (10.43)$$

Notice that there is no random variable on the right-hand side of (10.43). This particular portfolio was, in fact, chosen so as to hedge completely the risk of P with Q. In any case, since the portfolio has no risk it must earn the short-term rate r:

$$\alpha_p dt - \frac{P_x Q}{PQ_x} \alpha_Q dt = \left(1 - \frac{P_x Q}{PQ_x}\right) r dt \qquad (10.44)$$

Rearranging (10.44),

$$\frac{\alpha_P - r}{-P_x/P} = \frac{\alpha_Q - r}{-Q_x/Q} \equiv \lambda(x,t)$$

(10.45)

Equation (10.45) says that the expected return of any security above the short-term rate divided by its duration with respect to the factor x must equal some function λ. This function cannot depend on any characteristic of the security because (10.45) is true for all securities. The function may depend on the factor and time, although this book, for simplicity, assumes that λ is a constant. Rewriting (10.45), for each security it must be true that

$$E\left[\frac{dP}{P}\right] \equiv \alpha_P dt = r dt + \lambda D_x dt$$

(10.46)

The derivation here assumes there are no coupon payments, while the discussion in the text accounts for a coupon payment. Also, the derivation here uses an arbitrary interest rate factor, while the discussion in the text takes the yield of a particular bond as the factor. This is somewhat inconsistent since this derivation requires every security to have the same factor while the text implies a result simultaneously valid for every bond at its own yield.

CHAPTER 11

The Art of Term Structure Models: Drift

Chapters 9 and 10 show that assumptions about the true and risk-neutral short-term rate processes determine the term structure of interest rates and the prices of fixed income derivatives. The goal of this chapter and Chapter 12 is to describe the most common building blocks of term structure models. Selecting and rearranging these building blocks to create suitable models for the purpose at hand is the art of term structure modeling.

This chapter begins with an extremely simple model and then discusses the implications of adding a constant drift, a time-deterministic drift, and a mean-reverting drift. Chapter 12 discusses the implications of varying the assumptions about the volatility of the short rate and about its probability distribution.

NORMALLY DISTRIBUTED RATES, ZERO DRIFT: MODEL 1

The discussion begins with a particularly simple model to be called Model 1. The continuously compounded, instantaneous rate $r(t)$ is assumed to evolve in the following way:

$$dr = \sigma dw \qquad (11.1)$$

The quantity dr denotes the change in the rate over a small time interval, dt, measured in years; σ denotes the annual *basis point volatility* of rate changes; and *dw* denotes a normally distributed random variable with a mean of zero and a standard deviation of $\sqrt{dt}$.[1]

Say, for example, that the current value of the short-term rate is 6.18%, that volatility equals 113 basis points per year, and that the time interval under consideration is one month or $^1/_{12}$ years. Mathematically, $r(0)\equiv r_0=6.18\%$, $\sigma=.0113$, and $dt=^1/_{12}$. A month passes and the random variable *dw*, with a mean of zero and a standard deviation of $\sqrt{^1/_{12}}$ or .2887, happens to take on a value of .15. With these values the change in the short-term rate given by (11.1) is

$$dr = .0113 \times .15 = .17\% \qquad (11.2)$$

or 17 basis points. Since the short-term rate started at 6.18%, the short-term rate after a month is 6.35%.

Since the expected value of *dw* is zero, (11.1) says that the expected change in the rate or the drift is zero. Since the standard deviation of *dw* is $\sqrt{dt}$, so that the standard deviation of σdw is $\sigma\sqrt{dt}$, the standard deviation of the change in the rate is also $\sigma\sqrt{dt}$. For the sake of brevity the standard deviation of the change in the rate will be referred to as simply the standard deviation of the rate. Continuing with the numerical example, the process (11.1) says that the drift is zero and that the standard deviation of the rate is $\sigma\sqrt{dt}=.0113\times\sqrt{^1/_{12}}=.326\%$ or 32.6 basis points per month.

A rate tree may be used to approximate the process (11.1). Dates 0 to 2 take the following form:

$$
\begin{array}{ccccc}
 & & & & r_0 + 2\sigma\sqrt{dt} \\
 & & & {\scriptstyle\frac{1}{2}}\nearrow & \\
 & & r_0 + \sigma\sqrt{dt} & & \\
 & {\scriptstyle\frac{1}{2}}\nearrow & & {\scriptstyle\frac{1}{2}}\searrow & \\
r_0 & & & & r_0 \\
 & {\scriptstyle\frac{1}{2}}\searrow & & {\scriptstyle\frac{1}{2}}\nearrow & \\
 & & r_0 - \sigma\sqrt{dt} & & \\
 & & & {\scriptstyle\frac{1}{2}}\searrow & \\
 & & & & r_0 - 2\sigma\sqrt{dt}
\end{array}
$$

---

[1]It is beyond the mathematical scope of the text to explain why the random variable is denoted like a change, namely *dw*. But the text uses this notation since it is the convention in the field.

In the case of the numerical example, substituting the sample values into this tree gives the following:

$$
\begin{array}{c}
 6.832\ \% \\
 {\scriptstyle \frac{1}{2}}\nearrow \\
 6.506\ \% \\
 {\scriptstyle \frac{1}{2}}\nearrow \qquad {\scriptstyle \frac{1}{2}}\searrow \\
6.180\ \% \qquad\qquad 6.180\ \% \\
 {\scriptstyle \frac{1}{2}}\searrow \qquad {\scriptstyle \frac{1}{2}}\nearrow \\
 5.854\ \% \\
 {\scriptstyle \frac{1}{2}}\searrow \\
 5.528\ \%
\end{array}
$$

To understand why these trees are representations of the process (11.1), consider the transition from date 0 to date 1. The change in the interest rate in the up state is $\sigma\sqrt{dt}$ and the change in the down state is $-\sigma\sqrt{dt}$. Therefore, with the probabilities given in the tree, the expected change in the rate, often denoted $E[dr]$, is

$$
E\left[dr\right] = .5 \times \sigma\sqrt{dt} + .5 \times \left(-\sigma\sqrt{dt}\right) = 0 \tag{11.3}
$$

The variance of the rate, often denoted $V[dr]$, from date 0 to date 1 is computed as follows:

$$
\begin{aligned}
V\left[dr\right] &= E\left[dr^2\right] - \left\{E\left[dr\right]\right\}^2 \\
&= .5 \times \left(\sigma\sqrt{dt}\right)^2 + .5 \times \left(-\sigma\sqrt{dt}\right)^2 - 0 \\
&= \sigma^2 dt
\end{aligned} \tag{11.4}
$$

(The first equation follows from the definition of variance.) Since the variance is $\sigma^2 dt$, the standard deviation, which is the square root of the variance, is $\sigma\sqrt{dt}$.

Equations (11.3) and (11.4) show that the drift and volatility implied by the tree match the drift and volatility of the interest rate process (11.1). The process and the tree are not identical because the random variable in the process, having a normal distribution, can take on any value while a single step in the tree leads to only two possible values. In the example, when dw takes on a value of .15, the short rate changes from 6.18% to 6.35%. In the tree, however, the only two possible rates are 6.506% and

5.854%. Nevertheless, as shown in Chapter 9, after a sufficient number of time steps the branches of the tree used to approximate the process (11.1) will be numerous enough to approximate a normal distribution. Figure 11.1 shows the distribution of short rates after one year, or the *terminal distribution* after one year, as implied by the numerical example of the process. The tick marks on the x-axis are one standard deviation apart from one another.

Models in which the terminal distribution of interest rates has a normal distribution, like Model 1, are called *normal models*. One problem with these models is that the short-term rate can become negative. A negative short-term rate does not make much economic sense because people would never lend money at a negative rate when they could hold cash and earn a zero rate instead.[2] The distribution in Figure 11.1, drawn to encompass three standard deviations above and below the mean, shows that over a horizon of one year the interest rate process will almost certainly not exhibit negative interest rates. The probability that the short-term rate in process (11.1) becomes negative, however, increases with the horizon.

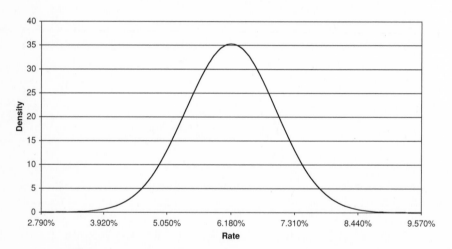

FIGURE 11.1   Distribution of Short Rates after One Year, Model 1

---

[2]Actually, the interest rate could be slightly negative if a security or bank account were safer than holding cash and provided some transactional advantages relative to cash.

Over 10 years, for example, the standard deviation of the terminal distribution in the numerical example is $.0113 \times \sqrt{10}$ or 3.573%. Starting with a short-term rate of 6.18%, reaching a rate of zero requires a random shock of only $^{6.18\%}/_{3.575\%}$ or 1.73 standard deviations.

The extent to which the possibility of negative rates makes a model unusable depends on the application. For securities whose value depends mostly on the average path of the interest rate, like coupon bonds, the possibility of negative rates typically does not rule out an otherwise desirable model. For securities that are asymmetrically sensitive to the probability of low interest rates, however, using a normal model could be dangerous. Consider the extreme example of a 10-year option to buy a long-term coupon bond at a yield of 0%. The model of this section would assign that option much too high a value because the model assigns too much probability to negative rates.

The techniques of Chapter 9 may be used to price fixed coupon bonds under Model 1. Figure 11.2 graphs the semiannually compounded par, spot, and forward rate curves for the numerical example along with data from U.S. dollar swap par rates as of February 16, 2001.[3] The initial value

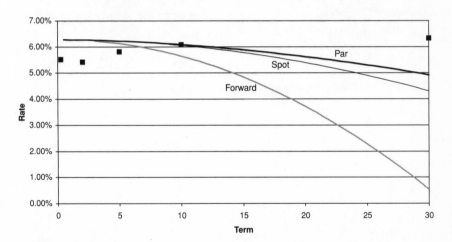

FIGURE 11.2 Rate Curves from Model 1 and Selected Market Swap Rates, February 16, 2001

---

[3]Swaps will be discussed in Chapter 18. For now, the reader may think of swap rates as par rates on fixed coupon bonds.

of the short-term rate in the example, 6.18%, is set so that the model and market 10-year, semiannually compounded par rates are equal at 6.086%. All of the other data points shown are quite different from their model values. The desirability of fitting market data exactly is discussed in its own section, but Figure 11.2 clearly demonstrates that the simple model of this section does not have enough flexibility to capture the shape of even relatively simple term structures.

The model term structure is downward-sloping. As the model has no drift, rates decline with term solely because of convexity. Table 11.1 shows the magnitudes of convexity effects on par rates of selected terms.[4] The numbers are realistic in the sense that a volatility of 113 basis points a year is reasonable. In fact, the volatility of the 10-year swap rate on February 16, 2001, as implied by options markets,[5] was 113 basis points. The convexity numbers are not necessarily realistic, however, because, as this chapter demonstrates, the magnitude of the convexity effect depends on the model, and Model 1 is almost certainly not the best model of interest rate behavior.

The term structure of volatility in Model 1 is constant at 113 basis points per year. In other words, the standard deviation of changes in the par rate of any maturity is 113 basis points per year. As shown in Figure 11.3, this implication of the model fails to capture the implied volatility

TABLE 11.1   Convexity
Effects on Par Rates,
Model 1

Term	Convexity Effect
2	−0.8
5	−5.1
10	−18.8
30	−135.3

---

[4]The convexity effect is the difference between the par yield in the model with the assumed volatility and the par yield in the same structural model but with volatility set to zero.
[5]Chapter 19 will discuss implied volatility.

structure in the market. The volatility data in Figure 11.3 show that the term structure of volatility is *humped*—that is, that volatility initially rises with term but eventually declines. As this shape is quite common it will be revisited in Chapter 13, in the context of a model that attempts to capture this feature.

The last aspect of this model to be analyzed is its factor structure. The model's only factor is the short-term rate. If this rate increases by 10 semi-annually compounded basis points, how would the term structure change? In this simple model the answer is that all rates would increase by 10 basis points. While not a particularly interesting-looking graph, for comparison with other models Figure 11.4 graphs the effect of a 10-basis point shift of the factor on spot rates of all terms. Clearly, the model of this section is a model of parallel shifts.

DRIFT AND RISK PREMIUM: MODEL 2

The term structures implied by Model 1 always look like Figure 11.2: relatively flat for early terms and then downward sloping. Chapter 10 pointed out that the term structure tends to slope upward and that this behavior might be explained by the existence of a risk premium. The model of this section, to be called Model 2, adds a drift to Model 1, interpreted

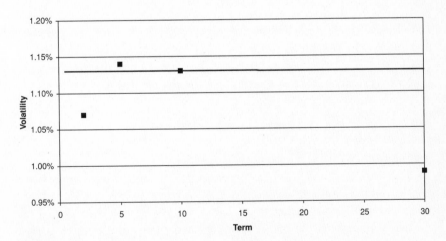

FIGURE 11.3 Par Rate Volatility from Model 1 and Selected Implied Volatilities, February 16, 2001

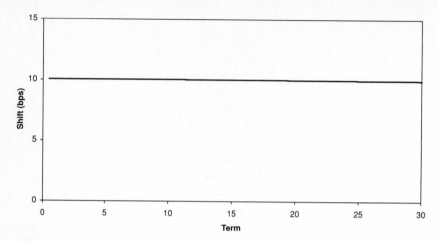

FIGURE 11.4 Sensitivity of Spot Rates to a 10 Basis Point Change in the Factor, Model 1

as a risk premium, in order to obtain a richer model in an economically coherent way.

The dynamics of the risk-neutral process in Model 2 are written as

$$dr = \lambda dt + \sigma dw \tag{11.5}$$

The process (11.5) differs from that of Model 1 by adding a drift to the short-term rate equal to λdt. For this section, consider the values $r_0=5.138\%$, $\lambda=.229\%$, and $\sigma=1.10\%$. If the realization of the random variable, dw, is again .15 over a month, then the change in rate is

$$dr = .229\% \times \left(1/12\right) + 1.10\% \times .15 = .1841\% \tag{11.6}$$

Starting from 5.138%, the new rate is 5.322%.

The drift of the rate is $.229\% \times (1/12) = .019\%$, or 1.9 basis points per month, and the standard deviation is $1.10\% \times \sqrt{1/12} = .3175\%$, or 31.75 basis points per month. As discussed in Chapter 10, the drift in the risk-neutral process is a combination of the true expected change in the interest rate and of a risk premium. A drift of 1.9 basis points per month may arise because the market expects the short-term rate to increase by 1.9 basis points a month. The same drift might also arise because the short-term rate is expected to increase by one basis point with a risk premium of .9 basis points or because the short-term rate is expected to fall by .1 basis points with a risk premium of two basis points.

The tree approximating this model is

$$
\begin{array}{c}
r_0 + 2\lambda dt + 2\sigma\sqrt{dt} \\
\nearrow^{\frac{1}{2}} \\
r_0 + \lambda dt + \sigma\sqrt{dt} \\
\nearrow^{\frac{1}{2}} \qquad \searrow_{\frac{1}{2}} \\
r_0 \qquad\qquad\qquad r_0 + 2\lambda dt \\
\searrow_{\frac{1}{2}} \qquad \nearrow^{\frac{1}{2}} \\
r_0 + \lambda dt - \sigma\sqrt{dt} \\
\searrow_{\frac{1}{2}} \\
r_0 + 2\lambda dt - 2\sigma\sqrt{dt}
\end{array}
$$

It is easy to verify that the drift and standard deviation of the tree match those of the process (11.6).

The terminal distribution of the numerical example of this process after one year is normal with a mean of 5.138%+1×.229% or 5.367% and a standard deviation of 110 basis points. After 10 years, the terminal distribution is normal with a mean of 5.138%+10×.229% or 7.428% and a standard deviation of 1.10%×$\sqrt{10}$=3.479% or 347.9 basis points. Note that the constant drift, by raising the mean of the terminal distribution, makes it less likely that the risk-neutral process will exhibit negative rates.

Figure 11.5 shows the rate curves in this example along with the par swap rate data. The values of r_0 and λ are calibrated to match the two- and 10-year par swap rates, while the value of σ is chosen to be the average implied volatility of the two- and 10-year par rates. The results are satisfying in that the resulting curve can match the data much more closely than did the curve of Model 1 shown in Figure 11.2. Slightly unsatisfying is the relatively high value of λ required. Interpreted as a risk premium alone, a value of .229% with a volatility of 110 basis points implies a relatively high Sharpe ratio of about .21. On the other hand, interpreting λ as a combination of true drift and risk premium is difficult in the long end where, as argued in Chapter 10, it is difficult to make a case for rising expected rates. These interpretive difficulties arise because Model 2 is still not flexible enough to explain the shape of the term structure in an economically

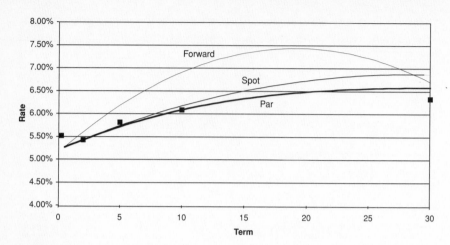

FIGURE 11.5   Rate Curves from Model 2 and Selected Market Swap Rates, February 16, 2001

meaningful way. In fact, the use of r_0 and λ to match the two- and 10-year rates in this relatively inflexible model may be the reason that the model curve overshoots the 30-year par yield by about 25 basis points.

Moving from Model 1 with zero drift to Model 2 with a constant drift does not qualitatively change the term structure of volatility, the magnitude of convexity effects, or the parallel shift nature of the model.

Model 2 is an equilibrium model because no effort has been made to match the observed term structure closely. The next section presents an arbitrage-free version of Model 2.

TIME-DEPENDENT DRIFT: THE HO-LEE MODEL

The dynamics of the risk-neutral process in the Ho-Lee model are written as

$$dr = \lambda(t)dt + \sigma dw \tag{11.7}$$

In contrast to Model 2, the drift here depends on time. In other words, the drift of the process may change from date to date. It might be an annualized drift of –20 basis points over the first month, of 10 basis points over the second month, of 20 basis points over the third month, and so on. A drift that varies with time is called a *time-dependent* drift. Just as with a constant drift, the time-dependent drift over each time period represents some combination of the risk premium and of expected changes in the short-term rate.

The flexibility of the Ho-Lee model is easily seen from its corresponding tree:

$$
\begin{array}{c}
r_0 + \lambda_1 dt + \sigma\sqrt{dt} \quad
\begin{array}{c}
\nearrow^{\frac{1}{2}} r_0 + (\lambda_1 + \lambda_2) dt + 2\sigma\sqrt{dt} \\
\end{array} \\
\searrow_{\frac{1}{2}} \\
r_0 + (\lambda_1 + \lambda_2) dt \\
r_0 + \lambda_1 dt - \sigma\sqrt{dt} \\
\searrow_{\frac{1}{2}} r_0 + (\lambda_1 + \lambda_2) dt - 2\sigma\sqrt{dt}
\end{array}
$$

The free parameters λ_1 and λ_2 may be used to match the prices of bonds with fixed cash flows. The procedure may be described as follows. With $dt = {}^1/_{12}$, set r_0 equal to the one-month rate. Next, obtain a monthly spot rate curve from traded bond prices using the techniques of Chapter 4. Then find λ_1 such that the model produces a two-month spot rate equal to that of the initial spot rate curve. Then find λ_2 such that the model produces a three-month spot rate equal to that of the initial spot rate curve. Continue in this fashion until the tree ends. The procedure is very much like that used to construct the trees in Chapter 9. The only difference is that Chapter 9 adjusts the probabilities to match the spot rate curve while this section adjusts the rates. As it turns out, the two procedures are equivalent so long as the step size is small enough.

The rate curves resulting from this model match all the rates that are input into the model. Just as adding a constant drift to Model 1 to obtain Model 2 does not affect the shape of the term structure of volatility nor the parallel shift characteristic of the model, making the drift time-dependent also does not change these features.

DESIRABILITY OF FITTING TO THE TERM STRUCTURE

The desirability of matching market prices is the central issue in deciding between arbitrage-free and equilibrium models. Not surprisingly, the choice depends on the purpose of building the model in the first place.

One important use of arbitrage-free models is for quoting the prices of securities not actively traded based on the prices of more liquid securities. A customer might ask a swap desk to quote a rate on a swap to a particular date, say three years and four months away, while liquid market prices may be observed only for three- and four-year swaps, or sometimes only for two- and five-year swaps. In this situation the swap desk may price the odd-maturity swap using an arbitrage-free model essentially as a means of interpolating between observed market prices.

Interpolating by means of arbitrage-free models may very well be superior to other curve fitting methods, from linear interpolation to more sophisticated approaches like piecewise cubic splines (see Chapter 4). The potential superiority of arbitrage-free models arises from their being based on economic and financial reasoning. In an arbitrage-free model the expectations and risk premium built into neighboring swap rates and the convexity implied by the model's volatility assumptions are used to compute, for example, the three-year and four-month swap rate. In a purely mathematical curve fitting technique, by contrast, the chosen functional form heavily determines the intermediate swap rate. Selecting linear, quadratic, or cubic interpolation results in different intermediate swap rates for no obvious economic or financial reason. This potential superiority of arbitrage-free models depends crucially on the validity of the assumptions built into the models. A poor volatility assumption, for example, resulting in a poor estimate of the convexity effect, might make an arbitrage-free model perform worse than a less financially sophisticated technique.

Another important use of arbitrage-free models is to value and hedge derivative securities for the purpose of making markets or for proprietary trading. For these purposes many practitioners wish to assume that some set of underlying securities is priced fairly. For example, when trading an option on a 10-year Treasury, many practitioners assume that the 10-year Treasury is itself priced fairly. (An analysis of the fairness of the 10-year Treasury can always be done separately.) Since arbitrage-free models match the prices of many traded securities by construction, these models are ideal for the purpose of pricing derivatives given the prices of underlying securities.

That a model matches market prices does not necessarily imply that it provides fair values and accurate hedges for derivative securities. The argument for fitting models to market prices is that a good deal of information about the future behavior of interest rates is incorporated into market prices, and, therefore, a model fitted to those prices captures that interest rate behavior. While this is a perfectly reasonable argument, two warnings are appropriate. First, a mediocre or bad model cannot be rescued by calibrating it to match market prices. If, for example, the parallel shift assumption is not a good enough description of reality for the application at hand, adding a time-dependent drift to a parallel shift model so as to match a set of bond prices will not make the model suitable for that application. Second, the argument for fitting to market prices assumes that those market prices are fair in the context of the model. There are, however, many situations in which particular securities, particular classes of securities, or particular maturity ranges of securities have been distorted due to supply and demand imbalances, taxes, liquidity differences, and other factors unrelated to interest rate models. In these cases fitting to market prices will make a model worse by attributing these outside factors to the interest rate process. If, for example, a large bank liquidates its portfolio of bonds or swaps with approximately seven years to maturity and, in the process, depresses prices and raises rates around that maturity, it would be incorrect to assume that expectations of rates seven years in the future have risen. Being careful about the word fair, the seven-year securities in this example are fair in the sense that liquidity considerations at a particular time require their prices to be relatively low. The seven-year securities are not fair, however, with respect to the expected evolution of interest rates and the market risk premium. For this reason, in fact, investors and traders might buy these relatively cheap bonds or swaps and hold them past the liquidity event in the hope of selling at a profit.

Another way to express the problem of fitting the drift to the term structure is to recognize that the drift of a risk-neutral process arises only from expectations and risk premium. A model that assumes one drift from years 15 to 16 and another drift from years 16 to 17 implicitly assumes one of two things. First, the expectation today of the one-year rate in 15 years differs from the expectation today of the one-year rate in 16 years. Second, the risk premium in 15 years differs in a particular way from the risk premium in 16 years. Since neither of these assumptions is particularly palatable, a fitted drift that changes dramatically from one year to the next is likely to be erroneously attributing non-interest rate effects to the interest rate process.

If the purpose of a model is to value bonds or swaps relative to one another, then taking a large number of bond or swap prices as given is clearly inappropriate: Arbitrage-free models, by construction, conclude that all of these bond or swap prices are fair relative to one another. Investors wanting to choose among securities, market makers looking to pick up value by strategically selecting hedging securities, or traders looking to profit from temporary mispricings must, therefore, rely on equilibrium models.

Having starkly contrasted arbitrage-free and equilibrium models, it should be noted that, in practice, there need not be a clear line between the two approaches. A model might posit a deterministic drift for a few years to reflect relatively short-term interest rate forecasts and posit a constant drift from then on. Another model might take the prices of two-, five-, 10-, and 30-year bond or swap rates as given so as to assume that the most liquid securities are fair while allowing the model to value other securities. The proper blending of the arbitrage-free and equilibrium approaches is an important part of the art of term structure modeling.

MEAN REVERSION: THE VASICEK (1977) MODEL

Assuming that the economy tends toward some equilibrium based on such fundamental factors as the productivity of capital, long-term monetary policy, and so on, short-term rates will be characterized by *mean reversion*. When the short-term rate is above its long-run equilibrium value, the drift is negative, driving the rate down toward this long-run value. When the rate is below its equilibrium value, the drift is positive, driving the rate up toward this value. In addition to being a reasonable assumption about short rates,[6] mean reversion enables a model to capture features of term structure behavior in an economically intuitive way.

The risk-neutral dynamics of the Vasicek model are written as

$$dr = k(\theta - r)dt + \sigma dw \qquad (11.8)$$

---

[6]While reasonable, mean reversion is a strong assumption. Long time series of interest rates from relatively stable markets might display mean reversion because there happened to be no catastrophe over the time period, that is, precisely because a long time series exists. Hyperinflation, for example, is not consistent with mean reversion and results in the destruction of a currency and its associated interest rates. When mean reversion ends, the time series ends. In short, the most severe critics of mean reversion would say that interest rates mean revert until they don't.

The constant θ denotes the long-run value or central tendency of the short-term rate in the risk-neutral process and the positive constant k denotes the speed of mean reversion. Note that in this specification the greater the difference between r and θ the greater the expected change in the short-term rate toward θ.

Because the process (11.8) is the risk-neutral process, the drift combines both interest rate expectations and risk premium. Furthermore, market prices do not depend on how the risk-neutral drift is divided across its two sources. Nevertheless, in order to understand whether or not the parameters of a model make sense, it is useful to make assumptions sufficient to separate the drift and the risk premium. Assuming, for example, that the true interest rate process exhibits mean reversion to a long-term value r_∞ and, as assumed previously, that the risk premium enters into the risk-neutral process as a constant drift, the Vasicek model takes the following form:

$$dr = k\left(r_\infty - r\right)dt + \lambda dt + \sigma dw$$
$$= k\left(\left[r_\infty + \lambda/k\right] - r\right)dt + \sigma dw \tag{11.9}$$

The process in (11.8) is identical to that in (11.9) so long as

$$\theta \equiv r_\infty + \lambda/k \tag{11.10}$$

Note that very many combinations of r_∞ and λ produce the same θ and, through the risk-neutral process (11.8), the same market prices.

For the purposes of this section, let k=.025, σ=126 basis points per year, r_0=5.121%, r_∞=6.179%, and λ=.229%. According to (11.10), then, θ=15.339%. With these parameters, the process (11.8) says that over the next month the expected change in the short rate is

$$.025 \times \left(15.339\% - 5.121\%\right)/12 = .0213\% \tag{11.11}$$

or 2.13 basis points. The volatility over the next month is $126 \times \sqrt{1/12}$ or 36.4 basis points.

Representing this process with a tree is not quite so straightforward as the simpler processes described previously because the most obvious representation leads to a nonrecombining tree. Over the first time step,

$$5.121\% + .025\ \left(15.339\%\text{--}5.121\%\right)\big/12 + .0126\big/\sqrt{12} = 5.5060\%$$

5.121%
$\tfrac{1}{2}$
$\tfrac{1}{2}$

$$5.121\% + .025\ \left(15.339\%\text{--}5\ 121\%\right)\big/12 - .0126\big/\sqrt{12} = 4.7786\%$$

To extend the tree from date 1 to date 2, start from the up state of 5.5060%. The tree branching from there is

$$5.506\% + .025\ \left(15.339\% - 5.5060\%\right)\big/12 + .0126\big/\sqrt{12} = 5.8902\%$$

5.5060%
$\tfrac{1}{2}$
$\tfrac{1}{2}$

$$5.506\% + .025\ \left(15.339\% - 5.5060\%\right)\big/12 - .0126\big/\sqrt{12} = 5.1628\%$$

while the tree branching from the date 1 down state of 4.7786% is

$$4.7786\% + .025\ \left(15.339\% - 4.7786\%\right)\big/12 + .0126\ \big/\sqrt{12} = 5.1643\%$$

4.7786%
$\tfrac{1}{2}$
$\tfrac{1}{2}$

$$4.7786\% + .025\ \left(15.339\% - 4.7786\%\right)\big/12 - .0126\ \big/\sqrt{12} = 4.4369\%$$

To summarize, the most straightforward tree representation of (11.8) takes the following form:

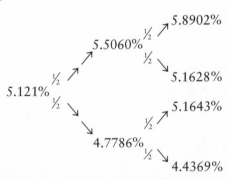

This tree does not recombine since the drift increases with the difference between the short rate and θ. Since 4.7786% is further from θ than

5.5060%, the drift from 4.7786% is greater than the drift from 5.5060%. In this model, the volatility component of an up move followed by a down move does perfectly cancel the volatility component of a down move followed by an up move. But since the drift from 4.7786% is greater, the move up from 4.7786% produces a larger short-term rate than a move down from 5.5060%.

There are many ways to represent the Vasicek model with a recombining tree. One method is presented here, but it is beyond the scope of this book to discuss the numerical efficiency of the various possibilities.[7]

The first time step of the tree may be taken as shown previously:

$$
5.121\% \quad
\begin{array}{c}
\overset{\tfrac{1}{2}}{\nearrow} \; 5.5060\% \\[6pt]
\underset{\tfrac{1}{2}}{\searrow} \; 4.7786\%
\end{array}
$$

Next, fix the center node of the tree on date 2. Since the expected perturbation due to volatility over each time step is zero, the drift alone determines the expected value of the process after each time step. After the first time step the expected value is

$$5.121\% + .025(15.339\% - 5.121\%)/12 = 5.1423\% \qquad (11.12)$$

After the second time step the expected value is

$$5.1423\% + .025(15.339\% - 5.1423\%)/12 = 5.1635\% \qquad (11.13)$$

Take this value as the center node on date 2 of the recombining tree:

---

[7]For discussions on numerical implementations see, for example, Brigo and Mercurio (2001), Heston and Zhou (2000), and Hull (2000).

$$5.121\% \overset{\tfrac{1}{2}\nearrow}{\underset{\tfrac{1}{2}\searrow}{}} \begin{array}{c} 5.5060\,\% \overset{p}{\underset{1-p}{}} \overset{\nearrow}{\searrow} r^{uu} \\ \\ 4.7786\,\% \overset{q}{\underset{1-q}{}} \overset{\nearrow}{\searrow} 5.1635\% \\ r^{dd} \end{array}$$

The parts of the tree to be solved for, namely, the missing probabilities and interest rate values, are given variable names.

According to the process (11.8) and the parameters set in this section, the expected rate and standard deviation of the rate from 5.5060% are, respectively,

$$5.5060\% + .025\big(15.339\% - 5.5060\%\big)/12 = 5.5265\% \qquad (11.14)$$

and

$$.0126\sqrt{1/12} = .3637\% \qquad (11.15)$$

For the recombining tree to match this expectation and standard deviation, it must be the case that

$$p \times r^{uu} + \big(1-p\big) \times 5.1635\% = 5.5265\% \qquad (11.16)$$

and, by the definition of standard deviation,

$$\sqrt{p \times \big(r^{uu} - 5.5265\%\big)^2 + \big(1-p\big) \times \big(5.1635\% - 5.5265\%\big)^2} = .3637\% \quad (11.17)$$

Solving equations (11.16) and (11.17), $r^{uu}=5.8909\%$ and $p=.4990$.

The same procedure may be followed to compute r^{dd} and q. The expected rate from 4.7786% is

$$4.7786\% + .025\left(15.339\% - 4.7786\%\right)/12 = 4.8006\% \qquad (11.18)$$

and the standard deviation is again 36.37 basis points. From 4.7786%, then, it must be the case that

$$q \times 5.1635\% + \left(1-q\right) \times r^{dd} = 4.8006\% \qquad (11.19)$$

and

$$\sqrt{q \times \left(5.1635\% - 4.8006\%\right)^2 + \left(1-q\right) \times \left(r^{dd} - 4.8006\%\right)^2} = .3637\% \quad (11.20)$$

Solving equations (11.19) and (11.20), r^{dd}=4.4361% and q=.5011.

Putting the results from the up and down states together, a recombining tree approximating the process (11.8) for the parameters of this section is

To extend the tree to the next date, begin again at the center. From the center node of date 2, the expected rate of the process is

$$5.1635\% + .025 \times \left(15.339\% - 5.1635\%\right)\big/12 = 5.1847\% \qquad (11.21)$$

As in constructing the tree for date 1, adding and subtracting the standard deviation of .3637% to the average value 5.1847% (obtaining 5.5484% and 4.8210%) and using probabilities of 50% for up and down movements satisfy the requirements of the process at the center of the tree:

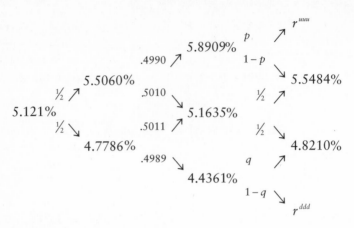

The unknown parameters can be solved for in the same manner as described in building the tree on date 2.

The text now turns to the effects of mean reversion on the term structure. Figure 11.6 illustrates the impact of mean reversion on the terminal, risk-neutral distributions of the short rate at different horizons. The expectation of the short-term rate as a function of horizon gradually rises from its current value of 5.121% toward its limiting value of θ=15.339%. Because the mean reverting parameter k=.025 is relatively small, the horizon expectation rises very slowly toward 15.339%. While mathematically be-

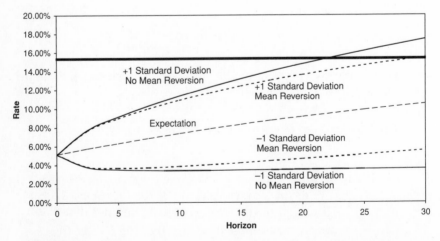

FIGURE 11.6   Mean Reversion and the Terminal Distributions of Short Rates

yond the scope of this book, it can be shown that the distance between the current value of a factor and its goal decays exponentially at the mean reverting rate. Since the interest rate is currently 15.339%–5.121% or 10.218% away from its goal, the distance between the expected rate at a 10-year horizon and the goal is

$$10.2180\% \times e^{-.025 \times 10} = 7.9578\% \tag{11.22}$$

Therefore, the expectation of the rate in 10 years is 15.3390%–7.9578% or 7.3812%.

For completeness, the expectation of the rate in the Vasicek model after T years is

$$r_0 e^{-kT} + \theta\left(1 - e^{-kT}\right) \tag{11.23}$$

In words, the expectation is a weighted average of the current short rate and its long-run value, where the weight on the current short rate decays exponentially at a speed determined by the mean reverting parameter.

The mean reverting parameter is not a particularly intuitive way of describing how long it takes a factor to revert to its long-term goal. A more intuitive quantity is the factor's *half-life*, defined as the time it takes the factor to progress half the distance toward its goal. In the example of this section, the half-life of the interest rate, HL, is given by the following equation:

$$\left(15.339\% - 5.121\%\right)e^{-.025 \times HL} = \frac{1}{2}\left(15.339\% - 5.121\%\right) \tag{11.24}$$

Solving,

$$e^{-.025 \times HL} = 1/2$$
$$HL = \ln(2)/.025 \tag{11.25}$$
$$HL = 27.73$$

where ln is the natural logarithm function. In words, the interest rate factor takes 27.73 years to cover half the distance between its starting value and its goal. This can be seen visually in Figure 11.6 where the expected rate 30 years from now is about halfway between the current value and θ. Larger mean reverting parameters produce shorter half-lives.

Figure 11.6 also shows one-standard deviation intervals around expectations both for the mean reverting process of this section and for a process with the same expectation and the same σ but without mean reversion. The standard deviation of the terminal distribution of the short rate after T years in the Vasicek model is

$$\sqrt{\frac{\sigma^2}{2k}\left(1-e^{-2kT}\right)} \tag{11.26}$$

In the numerical example, with a mean reverting parameter of .025 and a volatility of 126 basis point, the short rate in 10 years is normally distributed with an expected value of 7.3812%, derived earlier, and a standard deviation of

$$\sqrt{\frac{.0126^2}{2\times.025}\left(1-e^{-2\times.025\times10}\right)} \tag{11.27}$$

or 353 basis points. Using the same expected value and σ but no mean reversion, the standard deviation is $\sigma\sqrt{T}=.0126\sqrt{10}$ or 398 basis points. Pulling the interest rate toward a long-term goal dampens volatility relative to processes without mean reversion, particularly at long horizons.

To avoid confusion in terminology, note that the mean reverting model in this section set volatility equal to 126 basis points "per year." Because of mean reversion, however, this does not mean that the standard deviation of the terminal distribution after T years increases with the square root of time. Without mean reversion, this is the case, as reported in the previous paragraph. With mean reversion, the standard deviation increases with horizon more slowly than that, producing a standard deviation of only 353 basis points after 10 years.

Figure 11.7 graphs the rate curves in this parameterization of the Vasicek model. The values of r_0 and θ were calibrated to match the two- and 10-year par rates in the market. As a result, Figure 11.7 qualitatively resembles Figure 11.5. The mean reversion parameter might have been used to make the model fit the observed term structure more closely, but, as discussed in the next paragraph, this parameter was used to produce a particular term structure of volatility. In conclusion, Figure 11.7 shows that the model as calibrated in this section is probably not flexible enough to produce the range of term structures observed in practice.

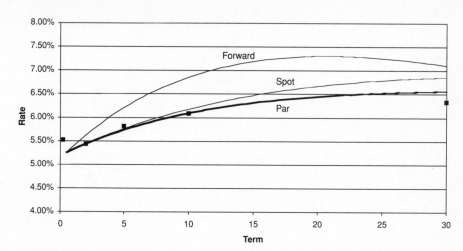

FIGURE 11.7 Rate Curves from the Vasicek Model and Selected Market Swap Rates, February 16, 2001

The term structure of volatility in a model with mean reversion differs dramatically from that in a model without mean reversion. Figure 11.8 shows that the volatility of par rates declines with term in the Vasicek model. In this example the mean reversion and volatility parameters are chosen to fit the implied 10- and 30-year volatilities. As a result, the model matches the market at those two terms but overstates the volatility for shorter terms. While Figure 11.8 certainly shows an improvement relative to the flat term structure of volatility shown in Figure 11.3, mean reversion in this model generates a term structure of volatility that slopes downward everywhere. Chapter 13 shows that a second factor can produce the humped volatility structure evident in the market.

Since mean reversion lowers the volatility of longer-term par rates, it must also lower the impact of convexity on these rates. Table 11.2 reports the convexity effect at several terms. Recall that the convexity effects listed in Table 11.1 are generated from a model with no mean reversion and a volatility of 113 basis points per year. Since this section set volatility equal to 126 basis points per year and since the mean reversion parameter is relatively slow, the convexity effects for terms up to 10 years are slightly larger in Table 11.2 than in Table 11.1. But by a term of 30 years the dampening effect of mean reversion on volatility manifests

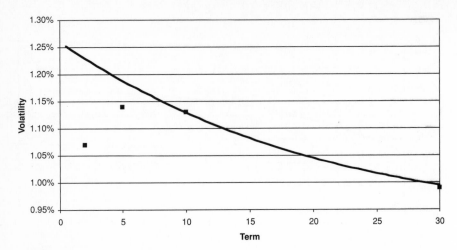

FIGURE 11.8 Par Rate Volatility from the Vasicek Model and Selected Implied Volatilities, February 16, 2001

TABLE 11.2 Convexity Effects on Par Rates, the Vasicek Model

Term	Convexity Effect
2	–1.0
5	–5.8
10	–19.1
30	–74.7

itself, and the convexity effect in the Vasicek model of about 75 basis points is substantially below the 135 basis-point effect in the model without mean reversion.

Figure 11.9 shows the shape of the interest rate factor in a mean reverting model, that is, how the spot rate curve is affected by a 10-basis point increase in the short-term rate. Short-term rates rise by about 10 basis points but longer-term rates are impacted less. The 30-year spot rate, for example, falls by only seven basis points. Hence a model with mean reversion is not a parallel shift model.

The implications of mean reversion for the term structure of volatility

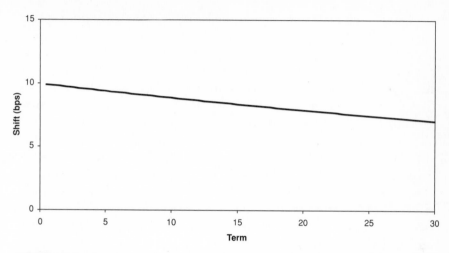

FIGURE 11.9 Sensitivity of Spot Rates to a 10 Basis Point Change in the Factor, the Vasicek Model

and factor shape may be better understood by reinterpreting the assumption that short rates tend toward a long-term goal. Assuming that short rates move as a result of some news or *shock* to the economic system, mean reversion implies that the effect of this shock eventually dissipates. After all, regardless of the shock, the short rate is assumed to arrive ultimately at the same long-term goal.

Economic news is said to be *long-lived* if it changes the market's view of the economy many years in the future. For example, news of a technological innovation that raises productivity would be a relatively long-lived shock to the system. Economic news is said to be *short-lived* if it changes the market's view of the economy in the near but not far future. An example of this kind of shock might be news that retail sales were lower than expected due to excessively cold weather over the holiday season. In this interpretation, mean reversion measures the length of economic news in a term structure model. A very low mean reversion parameter—that is, a very long half-life—implies that news is long-lived and that it will affect the short rate for many years to come. On the other hand, a very high mean reversion parameter—that is, a very short half-life—implies that news is short-lived and that it affects the short rate for a relatively short period of time.

Interpreting mean reversion as the length of economic news explains the factor structure and the downward-sloping term structure of volatility in the Vasicek model. Rates of every term are combinations of current economic conditions, as measured by the short-term rate, and of long-term economic conditions, as measured by the long-term value of the short rate (i.e., θ). In a model with no mean reversion, rates are determined exclusively by current economic conditions. Shocks to the short-term rate affect all rates equally, giving rise to parallel shifts and a flat term structure of volatility. In a model with mean reversion, shorter-term rates are determined mostly by current economic conditions while longer-term rates are determined mostly by long-term economic conditions. As a result, shocks to the short rate affect shorter-term rates more than longer-term rates and give rise to a downward-sloping term structure of volatility and a downward-sloping factor structure.

CHAPTER 12

The Art of Term Structure Models: Volatility and Distribution

This chapter continues the presentation of the building blocks of term structure models by introducing different specifications of volatility and different interest rate distributions. The chapter concludes with a list of commonly used interest rate models to show the many ways in which the building blocks of Chapters 11 and 12 have been assembled in practice.

TIME-DEPENDENT VOLATILITY: MODEL 3

Just as a time-dependent drift may be used to fit very many bond or swap rates, a time-dependent volatility function may be used to fit very many option prices. A particularly simple model with a time-dependent volatility function might be written as follows:

$$dr = \lambda(t)dt + \sigma(t)dw \qquad (12.1)$$

Unlike the Ho-Lee model presented in Chapter 11, the volatility of the short rate in equation (12.1) depends on time. If, for example, the function $\sigma(t)$ were such that $\sigma(1)=.0126$ and $\sigma(2)=.0120$, then the volatility of the short rate in one year is 126 basis points per year while the volatility of the short rate in two years is 120 basis points per year.

To illustrate the features of time-dependent volatility, consider the following special case of (12.1) that will be called Model 3:

$$dr = \lambda(t)dt + \sigma e^{-\alpha t}dw \qquad (12.2)$$

In (12.2) the volatility of the short rate starts at the constant σ and then exponentially declines to zero. (Volatility could have easily been designed to decline to another constant instead of zero, but Model 3 serves its pedagogical purpose well enough.)

Setting σ=126 basis points and α=.025, Figure 12.1 graphs the standard deviation of the terminal distribution of the short rate at various horizons.[1] Note that the standard deviation rises rapidly with horizon at first but then rises more slowly. The particular shape of the curve depends, of course, on the volatility function chosen for (12.2), but very many shapes are possible with the more general volatility specification in (12.1).

Deterministic volatility functions are popular, particularly among market makers in interest rate options. Consider the example of *caplets*. At expiration, a caplet pays the difference between the short rate and a strike, if positive, on some notional amount. Furthermore, the value of a

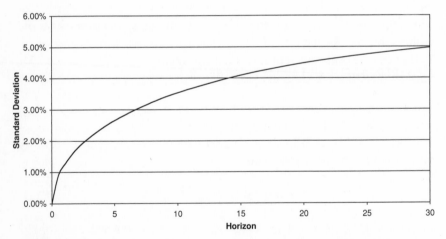

FIGURE 12.1   Standard Deviation of Terminal Distributions of Short Rates, Model 3

---

[1]The mathematics necessary for these computations are beyond the scope of this book. Furthermore, since Model 3 is invoked more to make a point about time-dependent volatility than to present a popular term structure model, the corresponding tree has also been omitted.

caplet depends on the distribution of the short rate at the caplet's expiration. Therefore, the flexibility of the deterministic functions $\lambda(t)$ and $\sigma(t)$ may be used to match the market prices of caplets expiring on many different dates.

The behavior of standard deviation as a function of horizon in Figure 12.1 resembles the impact of mean reversion on horizon standard deviation in Figure 11.6. In fact, setting the initial volatility and decay rate in Model 3 equal to the volatility and mean reversion rate of the numerical example of the Vasicek model, the standard deviations of the terminal distributions from the two models turn out to be identical. Furthermore, if the time-dependent drift in Model 3 matches the average path of rates in the numerical example of the Vasicek model, then the two models produce exactly the same terminal distributions.

While the two models are equivalent with respect to terminal distributions, they are very different in other ways. Just as the models in Chapter 11 without mean reversion are parallel shift models, Model 3 is a parallel shift model. Also, the term structure of volatility in Model 3 (i.e., the volatility of rates of different terms) is flat. Since the volatility in Model 3 changes over time, the term structure of volatility is flat at levels of volatility that change over time, but it is still always flat.

The arguments for and against using time-dependent volatility resemble those for and against using a time-dependent drift. If the purpose of the model is to quote fixed income option prices that are not easily observable, then a model with time-dependent volatility provides a means of interpolating from known to unknown option prices. If, however, the purpose of the model is to value and hedge fixed income securities, including options, then a model with mean reversion might be preferred. First, while mean reversion is based on the economic intuitions outlined in Chapter 11, time-dependent volatility relies on the difficult argument that the market has a forecast of short-rate volatility in, for example, 10 years that differs from its forecast of volatility in 11 years. Second, the downward-sloping factor structure and term structure of volatility in the mean reverting models capture the behavior of interest rate movements better than parallel shifts and a flat term structure of volatility. (See Chapter 13.) It may very well be that the Vasicek model does not capture the behavior of interest rates sufficiently well to be used for a particular valuation or hedging purpose. But in that case it is unlikely that a parallel shift model calibrated to match caplet prices will be better suited for that purpose.

VOLATILITY AS A FUNCTION OF THE SHORT RATE: THE COX-INGERSOLL-ROSS AND LOGNORMAL MODELS

The models in Chapter 11 along with Model 3 assume that the basis point volatility of the short rate is independent of the level of the short rate. This is almost certainly not true at extreme levels of the short rate. Periods of high inflation and high short-term interest rates are inherently unstable and, as a result, the basis point volatility of the short rate tends to be high. Also, when the short-term rate is very low, its basis point volatility is limited by the fact that interest rates cannot decline much below zero.

Economic arguments of this sort have led to specifying the volatility of the short rate as an increasing function of the short rate. The risk-neutral dynamics of the Cox-Ingersoll-Ross (CIR) model are

$$dr = k(\theta - r)dt + \sigma\sqrt{r}\,dw \qquad (12.3)$$

Since the first term on the right-hand side of (12.3) is not a random variable and since the standard deviation of dw equals $\sqrt{dt}$ by definition, the annualized standard deviation of dr (i.e., the basis point volatility) is proportional to the square root of the rate. Put another way, in the CIR model the parameter σ is constant, but basis point volatility is not: annualized basis point volatility equals $\sigma\sqrt{r}$ and, therefore, increases with the level of the short rate.

Another popular specification is that the basis point volatility is proportional to rate. In this case the parameter σ is often called *yield volatility*. Two examples of this volatility specification are the Courtadon model:

$$dr = k(\theta - r)dt + \sigma r\,dw \qquad (12.4)$$

and the simplest *lognormal* model,[2] to be called Model 4:

$$dr = ar\,dt + \sigma r\,dw \qquad (12.5)$$

---

[2]There are some technical problems with the lognormal model. See Brigo and Mercurio (2001).

(The next section explains why this is called a lognormal model.) In these two specifications the yield volatility is constant but the basis point volatility equals σr and, therefore, increases with the level of the rate.

Figure 12.2 graphs the basis point volatility as a function of rate for the cases of the constant, square root, and proportional specifications. For comparison purposes, the values of σ in the three cases are set so that basis point volatility equals 100 at a short rate of 8% in all cases. Mathematically,

$$\sigma_{bp} = .01$$
$$\sigma_{CIR} \times \sqrt{.08} = .01 \Rightarrow \sigma_{CIR} = .0354 \qquad (12.6)$$
$$\sigma_y \times .08 = .01 \Rightarrow \sigma_y = 12.5\%$$

Note that the units of these volatility measures are somewhat different. Basis point volatility is in the units of an interest rate (e.g., 100 basis points), while yield volatility is expressed as a percentage of the short rate (e.g., 12.5%).

As shown in Figure 12.2, the CIR and proportional volatility specifications have basis point volatility increasing with rate but at different speeds. Both models have the basis point volatility equal to zero at a rate of zero.

The property that basis point volatility equals zero when the short rate is zero, combined with the condition that the drift is positive when the rate

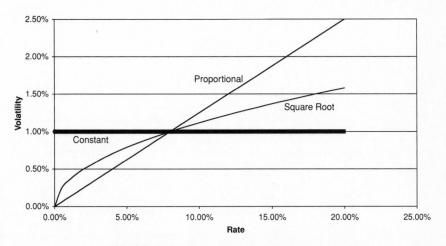

FIGURE 12.2 Three Volatility Specifications

is zero, guarantees that the short rate cannot become negative. This is certainly an improvement over models with constant basis point volatility that allow interest rates to become negative. It should be noted, however, that choosing a model depends on the purpose at hand. Say, for example, that a trader believes the following: One, the assumption of constant volatility is best in the current economic environment. Two, the possibility of negative rates has a small impact on the pricing of the securities under consideration. And three, the computational simplicity of constant volatility models has great value. In that case the trader might very well prefer a model that allows some probability of negative rates.

Figure 12.3 graphs terminal distributions of the short rate after 10 years under the CIR, normal, and lognormal volatility specifications. In order to emphasize the difference in the shape of the three distributions, the parameters have been chosen so that all of the distributions have an expected value of 5% and a standard deviation of 2.32%. The figure illustrates the advantage of the CIR and lognormal models in not allowing negative rates. The figure also indicates that out-of-the-money option prices could differ significantly under the three models. Even if, as in this case, the central tendency and volatility of the three distributions are the same, the probability of outcomes away from the means are different

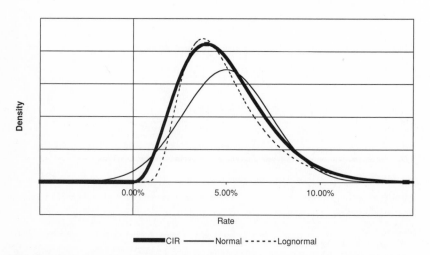

FIGURE 12.3   Terminal Distributions of the Short Rate after 10 Years in Cox-Ingersoll-Ross, Normal, and Lognormal Models

enough to generate significantly different option prices. (See Chapter 19.) More generally, the shape of the distribution used in an interest rate model can be an important determinant of that model's performance.

TREE FOR THE ORIGINAL SALOMON BROTHERS MODEL[3]

This section shows how to construct a binomial tree to approximate the dynamics for a lognormal model with a deterministic drift. Describe the model as follows:

$$dr = \tilde{a}(t)rdt + \sigma rdw \tag{12.7}$$

By Ito's Lemma (which is beyond the mathematical scope of this book),

$$d\big[\ln(r)\big] = \frac{dr}{r} - \frac{1}{2}\sigma^2 dt \tag{12.8}$$

Substituting (12.7) into (12.8),

$$d\big[\ln(r)\big] = \big\{\tilde{a}(t) - \sigma^2/2\big\}dt + \sigma dw \tag{12.9}$$

Redefining the notation of the time-dependent drift so that $a(t) \equiv \tilde{a}(t) - \sigma^2/2$, equation (12.9) becomes

$$d\big[\ln(r)\big] = a(t)dt + \sigma dw \tag{12.10}$$

Recalling the models of Chapter 11, equation (12.10) says that the natural logarithm of the short rate is normally distributed. Furthermore, by definition, a random variable has a lognormal distribution if its natural logarithm has a normal distribution. Therefore, (12.10) implies that the short rate has a lognormal distribution.

Equation (12.10) may be described as the Ho-Lee model (see Chapter 11) based on the natural logarithm of the short rate instead of on the short

---

[3]A description of this model appeared in a Salomon Brothers publication in 1987. It is not to be inferred that this model is presently in use by any particular entity.

rate itself. Adapting the tree for the Ho-Lee model accordingly easily gives the tree for the first three dates:

$$
\ln r_0
\;\nearrow^{\frac{1}{2}}\;
\ln r_0 + a_1 dt + \sigma\sqrt{dt}
\;\nearrow^{\frac{1}{2}}\;
\ln r_0 + \left(a_1 + a_2\right)dt + 2\sigma\sqrt{dt}
$$

$$
\ln r_0
\;\searrow_{\frac{1}{2}}\;
\ln r_0 + a_1 dt - \sigma\sqrt{dt}
$$

$$
\ln r_0 + a_1 dt + \sigma\sqrt{dt}
\;\searrow_{\frac{1}{2}}\;
\ln r_0 + \left(a_1 + a_2\right)dt
$$

$$
\ln r_0 + a_1 dt - \sigma\sqrt{dt}
\;\nearrow^{\frac{1}{2}}\;
\ln r_0 + \left(a_1 + a_2\right)dt
\;\searrow_{\frac{1}{2}}\;
\ln r_0 + \left(a_1 + a_2\right)dt - 2\sigma\sqrt{dt}
$$

To express this tree in rate, as opposed to the natural logarithm of the rate, exponentiate each node:

$$
r_0
\;\nearrow^{\frac{1}{2}}\;
r_0 e^{a_1 dt + \sigma\sqrt{dt}}
\;\nearrow^{\frac{1}{2}}\;
r_0 e^{\left(a_1 + a_2\right)dt + 2\sigma\sqrt{dt}}
$$

$$
\;\searrow_{\frac{1}{2}}\;
r_0 e^{a_1 dt - \sigma\sqrt{dt}}
\;\nearrow^{\frac{1}{2}}\;
r_0 e^{\left(a_1 + a_2\right)dt}
\;\searrow_{\frac{1}{2}}\;
r_0 e^{\left(a_1 + a_2\right)dt - 2\sigma\sqrt{dt}}
$$

This tree shows that the perturbations to the short rate in a lognormal model are multiplicative as opposed to the additive perturbations in normal models. This observation, in turn, reveals why the short rate in this model cannot become negative. Since e^x is positive for any value of x, so long as r_0 is positive every node of the lognormal tree produces a positive rate.

The tree also reveals why volatility in a lognormal model is expressed as a percentage of the rate. Recall the mathematical fact that, for small values of x,

$$
e^x \approx 1 + x \tag{12.11}
$$

Setting $a_1=0$ and $dt=1$, for example, the top node of date 1 may be approximated as

$$r_0 e^\sigma \approx r_0 \left(1 + \sigma\right) \tag{12.12}$$

Volatility is clearly a percentage of the rate in equation (12.12). If, for example, $\sigma=12.5\%$, then the short rate in the up state is 12.5% above the initial short rate.

As in the Ho-Lee model, the constants that determine the drift (i.e., a_1 and a_2) may be used to match market bond prices.

A LOGNORMAL MODEL WITH MEAN REVERSION: THE BLACK-KARASINSKI MODEL

The Vasicek model, a normal model with mean reversion, was the last model presented in Chapter 11. The last model presented in this chapter is a lognormal model with mean reversion called the Black-Karasinski model. The model allows the mean reverting parameter, the central tendency of the short rate, and volatility to depend on time, firmly placing the model in the arbitrage-free class. A user may, of course, use or remove as much time dependence as desired.

The dynamics of the model are written as

$$dr = k(t)\left(\ln \tilde\theta(t) - \ln r\right)r dt + \sigma(t)r dt \tag{12.13}$$

or, equivalently,[4] as

$$d\left[\ln r\right] = k(t)\left(\ln \theta(t) - \ln r\right)dt + \sigma(t)dt \tag{12.14}$$

In words, equation (12.14) says that the natural logarithm of the short rate is normally distributed. It reverts to $\ln\theta(t)$ at a speed of $k(t)$ with a volatility of $\sigma(t)$. Viewed another way, the natural logarithm of the short rate follows a time-dependent version of the Vasicek model.

---

[4]Note that the drift function has been redefined from (12.13) to (12.14), analogous to the drift transformation from (12.7) to (12.10).

As in the previous section, the corresponding tree may be written in terms of the rate or the natural logarithm of the rate. Choosing the former, the process over the first date is

$$
r_0 \quad
\begin{array}{l}
\nearrow^{1/2} \quad r_0 e^{k(1)\left(\ln\theta(1)-\ln r_0\right)dt+\sigma(1)\sqrt{dt}} \equiv r_1 e^{\sigma(1)\sqrt{dt}} \\[2em]
\searrow_{1/2} \quad r_0 e^{k(1)\left(\ln\theta(1)-\ln r_0\right)dt-\sigma(1)\sqrt{dt}} \equiv r_1 e^{-\sigma(1)\sqrt{dt}}
\end{array}
$$

The variable r_1 is introduced for readability. The natural logarithms of the rates in the up and down states are

$$
\ln r_1 + \sigma(1)\sqrt{dt} \tag{12.15}
$$

and

$$
\ln r_1 - \sigma(1)\sqrt{dt} \tag{12.16}
$$

respectively. It follows that the step down from the up state requires a rate of

$$
r_1 e^{\sigma(1)\sqrt{dt}} e^{k(2)\left[\ln\theta(2)-\left\{\ln r_1+\sigma(1)\sqrt{dt}\right\}\right]dt-\sigma(2)\sqrt{dt}} \tag{12.17}
$$

while the step up from the down state requires a rate of

$$
r_1 e^{-\sigma(1)\sqrt{dt}} e^{k(2)\left[\ln\theta(2)-\left\{\ln r_1-\sigma(1)\sqrt{dt}\right\}\right]dt+\sigma(2)\sqrt{dt}} \tag{12.18}
$$

A little algebra shows that the tree recombines only if

$$
k(2) = \frac{\sigma(1)-\sigma(2)}{\sigma(1)dt} \tag{12.19}
$$

Imposing the restriction (12.19) would require that the mean reversion speed be completely determined by the time-dependent volatility function. But these parts of a term structure model serve two distinct purposes. Chapter 11 showed that the mean reversion function controls the term structure of volatility, that is, the current volatility of rates of different terms. The first section of this chapter discusses how time-dependent volatility controls the future volatility of the short-term rate, that is, the prices of options that expire at different times. To create a model flexible enough to control mean reversion and time-dependent volatility separately, Black and Karasinski had to construct a recombining tree without imposing (12.19). To do so they allow the time step, *dt*, to change over time.

Rewriting equations (12.17) and (12.18) with the time steps labeled dt_1 and dt_2 gives the following values for the up-down and down-up rates:

$$r_1 e^{\sigma(1)\sqrt{dt_1}} e^{k(2)\left[\ln\theta(2)-\left\{\ln r_1+\sigma(1)\sqrt{dt_1}\right\}\right]dt_2-\sigma(2)\sqrt{dt_2}} \tag{12.20}$$

$$r_1 e^{-\sigma(1)\sqrt{dt_1}} e^{k(2)\left[\ln\theta(2)-\left\{\ln r_1-\sigma(1)\sqrt{dt_1}\right\}\right]dt_2+\sigma(2)\sqrt{dt_2}} \tag{12.21}$$

A little algebra now shows that the tree recombines if

$$k(2) = \frac{1 - \dfrac{\sigma(2)\sqrt{dt_2}}{\sigma(1)\sqrt{dt_1}}}{dt_2} \tag{12.22}$$

The length of the first time step can be set arbitrarily. The length of the second time step is set to satisfy (12.22), allowing the user freedom in choosing the mean reversion and volatility functions independently.

SELECTED LIST OF ONE-FACTOR TERM STRUCTURE MODELS

Several models, some discussed in the text and others not, are listed together in this section for easy reference. For a more detailed discussion of individual models see Brigo and Mercurio (2001), Chan, Karolyi, Longstaff, and Sanders (1992), Hull (2000), Rebonato (1996), and Vasicek (1977).

Normal Models

Ho-Lee:

$$dr = \lambda(t)dt + \sigma dw$$

Hull and White:

$$dr = k\big(\theta(t) - r\big)dt + \sigma(t)dw$$

Vasicek:

$$dr = k\big(\theta - r\big)dt + \sigma dw$$

Lognormal Models

Black-Derman-Toy[5]:

$$dr = -\frac{d\big[\ln\sigma(t)\big]}{dt}\big(\ln\theta(t) - \ln r\big)rdt + \sigma(t)rdw$$

Black-Karasinski:

$$dr = k(t)\big(\ln\theta(t) - \ln r\big)rdt + \sigma(t)rdw$$

Dothan/Rendleman and Bartter:

$$dr = ardt + \sigma rdw$$

Original Salomon Brothers:

$$dr = a(t)rdt + \sigma rdw$$

Other Distributions

Chan, Karolyi, Longstaff, and Sanders:

$$dr = k\big(\theta - r\big)dt + \sigma r^\gamma dw$$

---

[5]Note that the speed of mean reversion depends entirely on the volatility function. The Black-Karasinski model avoids this by allowing the length of the time step to change.

Courtadon:

$$dr = k(\theta - r)dt + \sigma r dw$$

Cox-Ingersoll-Ross:

$$dr = k(\theta - r)dt + \sigma \sqrt{r} dw$$

APPENDIX 12A
CLOSED-FORM SOLUTIONS FOR SPOT RATES

This appendix lists formulas for spot rates in various models mentioned in Chapters 11 and 12. These allow one to understand and experiment with the relationships between the parameters of a model and the resulting term structure. The spot rates of term T, $\hat{r}(T)$, are continuously compounded rates. The discount factors of term T are, therefore, given by $d(t)=e^{-\hat{r}(T)T}$.

Model 1

$$\hat{r}(T) = r_0 - \frac{\sigma^2 T^2}{6} \qquad (12.23)$$

Model 2

$$\hat{r}(T) = r_0 + \frac{\lambda T}{2} - \frac{\sigma^2 T^2}{6} \qquad (12.24)$$

Vasicek

$$\hat{r}(T) = \theta + \frac{1 - e^{-kT}}{kT}(r_0 - \theta) - \frac{\sigma^2}{2k^2}\left(1 + \frac{1 - e^{-2kT}}{2kT} - 2\frac{1 - e^{-kT}}{kT}\right) \qquad (12.25)$$

Model 3 with $\lambda(t)=\lambda$

$$\hat{r}(T) = r_0 + \frac{\lambda T}{2} - \sigma^2 \frac{2\alpha^2 T^2 - 2\alpha T + 1 - e^{-2\alpha T}}{8\alpha^3 T} \qquad (12.26)$$

Cox-Ingersoll-Ross

Let $P(T)$ be the price of a zero coupon bond maturing at time T. In the CIR model,

$$P(T) = A(T)e^{-B(T)r_0} \tag{12.27}$$

where

$$A(T) = \left[\frac{2he^{(k+h)T/2}}{2h + (k+h)(e^{hT} - 1)} \right]^{2k\theta/\sigma^2} \tag{12.28}$$

$$B(T) = \frac{2(e^{hT} - 1)}{2h + (k+h)(e^{hT} - 1)} \tag{12.29}$$

and

$$h = \sqrt{k^2 + 2\sigma^2} \tag{12.30}$$

The spot rate then, by definition, is

$$\hat{r}(T) = -\frac{1}{T}\ln P(T) \tag{12.31}$$

CHAPTER 13

Multi-Factor Term Structure Models

The models of Chapters 9 through 12 assume that changes in the entire term structure of interest rates can be explained by changes in a single rate. The models differ in how that single rate impacts the term structure, whether through a parallel shift or through a shorter-lived shock, but in all of the models, rates of all terms are perfectly correlated. According to these models, knowing the change in any rate is sufficient to predict perfectly the change in any other rate.

For some purposes a one-factor analysis might be appropriate. Corporations planning to issue long-term debt, for example, might not find it worthwhile to study how the two-year rate moves relative to the 30-year rate. But for fixed income professionals exposed to the risk of the term structure reshaping, one-factor models usually prove inadequate.

The first section of this chapter motivates the need for multi-factor models through an empirical analysis of the behavior of the swap curve.[1] As an introduction to multi-factor models, the next sections present a two-factor model, its properties, and its tree implementation. The concluding section briefly surveys other two-factor and multi-factor approaches.

MOTIVATION FROM PRINCIPAL COMPONENTS

Applied to a term structure of interest rates, *principal components* are a mathematical expression of typical changes in term structure shape as ex-

---

[1]Interest rate swaps are discussed in Chapter 18. For now the reader should think of swaps as fixed coupon bonds selling at par.

tracted from data on changes in rates. A full explanation of the technique is beyond the scope of this text,[2] but much can be learned by studying the results of such an analysis. Figure 13.1 graphs the first three principal components of term structure changes using data on the three-month London Interbank Offer Rate (LIBOR)[3] and on two-, five-, 10-, and 30-year U.S. dollar swap rates from the early 1990s through 2001.

The first component is, by industry convention, labeled parallel. The interpretation of this component is as follows. When par yields move approximately in parallel, the three-month rate rises by .9 basis points, the two-year rate by 9.6 basis points, the five-year rate by 10.4 basis points, the 10-year rate by 10 basis points, and the 30-year rate by 8.1 basis points. Furthermore, principal component analysis reveals that this first component explains about 85.6% of the total variance of term structure changes.

The magnitude and sign of all the principal components are arbitrary. For Figure 13.1 the first component is scaled so that the 10-year rate increases by 10 basis points. The figure could just as well have been drawn

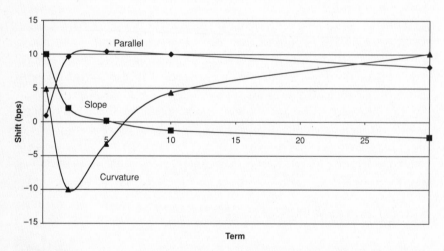

FIGURE 13.1   The First Three Principal Components from Changes in U.S. Dollar Swap Rates

---

[2]For a detailed, applied treatment, see Baygun, Showers, and Cherpelis (2000).
[3]See Chapter 17.

with the 10-year rate decreasing by one basis point. The only information to be extracted from the figure is the shape of the components (i.e., how a change in each component affects par rates of different terms).

The first component is not exactly a parallel shift, but it is close enough, particularly if the three-month point is ignored, to justify the convention of calling the first component a parallel shift. Furthermore, this empirical analysis supports the contention that a one-factor parallel shift model might be perfectly suitable for some purposes: The first component is pretty close to parallel, and it explains 85.6% of the variance of term structure changes. The empirical analysis also supports the contention that a one-factor mean-reverting model, with its downward-sloping factor structure (see Figure 11.9), would be even better at capturing the 85.6% of the variance described by the first component.

The shape of the first principal component is very much related to the humped term structure of volatility mentioned in Chapter 11. Since this first component explains most of the variation in term structure changes, the overall term structure of volatility is likely to have a similar shape. And, indeed, this is the case. Using the same data sample, the annualized basis point volatilities[4] of the rates are 55.9 for the three-month rate, 94.2 for the two-year rate, 97.4 for the five-year rate, 94.5 for the 10-year rate, and 81.3 for the 30-year rate.

The second component is usually called slope and accounts for about 8.7% of the total variance of term structure changes. By construction, each component is not correlated with any other. According to the data then, a parallel shift shaped like the first component and a slope shift shaped like the second component are not correlated. The second component does not exactly describe the slope of the term structure as that word is commonly used: This term structure shift is not a straight line from one term to the next. Rather, this second component seems to be dominated by the movement of the very short end of the curve relative to the longer terms. In Fig-

---

[4]The annualized volatility is computed by multiplying the standard deviation of daily changes by the square root of the number of days in a year. Since there is less information and, therefore, less of a source of volatility on nonbusiness days, it is probably a good idea to weight business days more than nonbusiness days when annualizing volatility. A common convention is to use $\sqrt{260}$ or about 16.12 as an annualizing factor since there are approximately 260 business days in a year.

ure 13.1 this component is normalized so that the three-month rate increases by 10 basis points.

The third component is typically called curvature and accounts for about 4.5% of the total variance. Again, by construction, a shift of this shape is not correlated with the other components. Curvature is not a bad name for the third component. The described move is a bowing of the two- and five-year rates relative to a close-to-parallel move of the three-month and 10-year rates. The 30-year rate moves in the opposite direction of the bowing of the two- and five-year rates. In Figure 13.1 this component is normalized so that the two-year rate decreases by 10 basis points.

In principal component analysis there are as many components as data series, in this case five. The fourth and fifth components are omitted from Figure 13.1 as they account for less than 1% each of the total variance. Conversely, the focus is on the first three components that together contribute 98.8% of the total variance.

The decision to focus exclusively on the first three components expresses the following view: changes in the three-month and two-, five-, 10-, and 30-year rates can be very well described by linear combinations of the first three components. Linear combinations of the components are obtained by scaling each component up or down and then adding them together. For example, a term structure move on a particular day might be best described as one unit of the first component plus one-half unit of the second component minus one-quarter unit of the third component.

These empirical results show that while one factor might be sufficient for some purposes, fixed income professionals are likely to require models with more than one factor. More precisely, the percentage of total variance explained by each factor may be considered when choosing the number of factors. In addition, the shape of the principal components provides some guidance with respect to desirable factor structures in term structure models.

Before concluding this section it should be noted that principal component analysis paints an overall picture of typical term structure movements. While the analysis may be a good starting point for model building, it need not accurately describe rate changes for any particular day or for any particular trade. First, the current economic environment might not resemble that over which the principal components were derived. A period in which the Federal Reserve is very active, for example, might produce very different principal components than one over which the Fed is not active. (If particularly relevant historical periods do exist, possibly including the very recent past, then this problem might be at least partially avoided by estimating principal components over these relevant periods.) Second, shape changes from one day to the next might differ considerably from a typical move over a sample period. Third, idiosyncratic moves of particular bond or swap rates (i.e., moves due to non-interest-rate-related factors) cannot typically be captured by principal component analysis. Since these moves are idiosyncratic, an analysis of average behavior discards them as noise.

A TWO-FACTOR MODEL

To balance usefulness, tractability, pedagogical value, and industry practice, a model with two normally distributed mean reverting factors is presented in this section. For convenience, the model will be called the V2 or two-factor Vasicek model. Mathematically, the risk-neutral dynamics of the model are written as

$$dx = k_x(\theta_x - x)dt + \sigma_x dw_x \qquad (13.1)$$

$$dy = k_y(\theta_y - y)dt + \sigma_y dw_y \qquad (13.2)$$

$$E[dxdy] = \rho\sigma_x\sigma_y dt \qquad (13.3)$$

$$r = x + y \qquad (13.4)$$

Equations (13.1) and (13.2) are recognizable from the discussions in Chapters 11 and 12 as mean reverting processes. But here x and y are factors; neither is an interest rate by itself. As stated in equation (13.4), the short-term rate in the model is the sum of these two factors.

For the model to have explanatory power above and beyond that of the Vasicek model, the two factors have to be materially different from one another. Typically the first factor is assigned a relatively low mean reversion speed, making it a long-lived factor, and the second factor is assigned a relatively high mean reversion speed, making it a short-lived factor. This framework is motivated by intuition about different kinds of economic news, outlined in Chapter 11. Furthermore, ignoring the very short end for a moment, the first principal component has the appearance of a long-lived factor, while the second has the appearance of a short-lived factor.

As posited in Chapter 11, the random variables dw_x and dw_y each have a normal distribution with a mean of zero and a standard deviation of $\sqrt{dt}$. Now that there are two such random variables in the model, the correlation between them has to be specified. Equation (13.3) says that the effect of this correlation is to make the covariance between the change in x and the change in y equal to $\rho \sigma_x \sigma_y dt$.[5] Since correlation equals covariance divided by the product of standard deviations, (13.3) implies that the correlation between the factor changes is ρ.

As discussed in Chapter 11, the economic reasonableness of a model may be checked by determining whether drift can sensibly be broken down into expectations and risk premium. Somewhat arbitrarily assigning the entire risk premium to the long-lived factor, θ_x may be divided along the lines of Chapter 11 as follows:

$$\theta_x = x_\infty + \lambda/k_x \tag{13.5}$$

For the purposes of this chapter, the following parameter values will be used:

$$
\begin{aligned}
k_x &= .028 \\
k_y &= 2 \\
x_\infty &= 6.50\% \\
\lambda &= .17\% \\
\theta_x &= x_\infty + \lambda/k_x = .1257 \\
\theta_y &= 0 \\
\sigma_x &= 1.34\% \\
\sigma_y &= 1.12\% \\
\rho &= -.85 \\
x_0 &= 5.413\% \\
y_0 &= -.869\% \\
r_0 &= 4.544\%
\end{aligned}
\tag{13.6}
$$

Furthermore, for building trees, $dt = 1/12$.

---

[5]Since the time step is small, $E[dx] \times E[dy]$ is assumed to be negligible. This means that the covariance of dx and dy equals $E[dxdy]$.

In words, this parameterization may be described as follows. Changes in the short-term interest rate are generated by the sum of a long-lived factor, with a half-life of about 25 years, and a short-lived factor, with a half-life of about four months. The long factor has a current value of 5.413% and is expected to rise gradually to 6.50%. The short-term interest rate is well below 5.413%, however, because the short factor has a value of about −87 basis points. This factor is expected to rise relatively rapidly to zero. With respect to pricing, there is a risk premium of about 17 basis points per year on the long factor that corresponds to a Sharpe ratio of $^{17}/_{134}$ or 12.7%. The role of the volatility and correlation values requires a more detailed treatment and is discussed later in the chapter.

TREE IMPLEMENTATION

The first step in constructing the two-dimensional tree is to construct the one-dimensional tree for each factor. The method is explained in Chapter 11, in the context of the Vasicek model. Therefore, only the results are presented here. For the x factor,

$$
\begin{array}{c}
& & & \nearrow^{.4992} & 6.219\% \\
& & 5.817\% & & \\
& \nearrow^{½} & & \searrow_{.5008} & \\
5.413\% & & & & 5.446\% \\
& \searrow_{½} & & \nearrow^{.5006} & \\
& & 5.043\% & & \\
& & & \searrow_{.4994} & 4.674\%
\end{array}
$$

And, for the y factor,

$$
\begin{array}{c}
& & & \nearrow^{.4204} & -.037\% \\
& & -.401\% & & \\
& \nearrow^{½} & & \searrow_{.5796} & \\
-.869\% & & & & -.604\% \\
& \searrow_{½} & & \nearrow^{.5050} & \\
& & -1.048\% & & \\
& & & \searrow_{.4950} & -1.148\%
\end{array}
$$

Assume for the moment that the drift of both factors is zero. In that case the following two-dimensional tree or grid depicts the process from dates 0 to 2. The starting point of the process is the center, (x_0, y_0). On date 1 there are four possible outcomes since each of the two factors might rise or fall. These outcomes are enclosed in square brackets. On date 2 each of the two factors might rise or fall again. This process leads to one of eight new states of the world, enclosed in curly brackets, or a return to the original state in the center.

$$\left\{x^{dd}, y^{uu}\right\} \qquad\qquad \left\{x_0, y^{uu}\right\} \qquad\qquad \left\{x^{uu}, y^{uu}\right\}$$
$$\qquad \left[x^{d}, y^{u}\right] \qquad\qquad\qquad \left[x^{u}, y^{u}\right]$$
$$\left\{x^{dd}, y_0\right\} \qquad\qquad \left(x_0, y_0\right) \qquad\qquad \left\{x^{uu}, y_0\right\}$$
$$\qquad \left[x^{d}, y^{d}\right] \qquad\qquad\qquad \left[x^{u}, y^{d}\right]$$
$$\left\{x^{dd}, y^{dd}\right\} \qquad\qquad \left\{x_0, y^{dd}\right\} \qquad\qquad \left\{x^{uu}, y^{dd}\right\}$$

To avoid clutter, the probabilities of moving from one state of the world to another are not shown in this diagram but will, of course, appear in the discussion to follow.

The diagram assumes that the factors have zero drift. Since the factors do drift, the diagram must be adjusted in the following sense. An up move followed by a down move does not return to the original factor value but to that original value plus two dates of drift. So, for example, a return on date 2 to (x_0, y_0) should be thought of as a return of each factor to its center node as of date 2 rather than a return of each factor to its original value.

As mentioned, over the first date the two-dimensional tree has four possible outcomes. Using the values from the one-factor trees, these four outcomes are enumerated as follows, with the variables denoting their probabilities of occurrence:

$$\left(5.413\%, -.869\%\right) \rightarrow \begin{cases} \left[5.817\%, -.401\%\right] & ; \pi^{uu} \\ \left[5.817\%, -1.048\%\right] & ; \pi^{ud} \\ \left[5.043\%, -.401\%\right] & ; \pi^{du} \\ \left[5.043\%, -1.048\%\right] & ; \pi^{dd} \end{cases}$$

The unknown probabilities must satisfy the following conditions. First, the tree for x has the probability of moving up to 5.817% equal to $1/2$. Therefore, the probability of moving to either the "uu" or "ud" states of the two-dimensional tree must also be $1/2$. Mathematically,

$$\pi^{uu} + \pi^{ud} = \tfrac{1}{2} \tag{13.7}$$

Second, since the probability of y moving up to $-.401\%$ is $\tfrac{1}{2}$, the probability of moving to either the "uu" or "du" states must also be $\tfrac{1}{2}$:

$$\pi^{uu} + \pi^{du} = \tfrac{1}{2} \tag{13.8}$$

Third, the sum of the four probabilities must equal 1:

$$\pi^{uu} + \pi^{ud} + \pi^{du} + \pi^{dd} = 1 \tag{13.9}$$

Fourth, the probabilities must impose the covariance condition (13.3). To calculate the left-hand side of (13.3), compute the product of the change in x and the change in y for each of the four possible outcomes, multiply each product by its probability of occurrence, and then sum across outcomes. The covariance condition, therefore, is

$$
\begin{aligned}
&\pi^{uu}\left(5.8165\% - 5.413\%\right)\left(-.401\% + .869\%\right) \\
&+\pi^{ud}\left(5.8165\% - 5.413\%\right)\left(-1.048\% + .869\%\right) \\
&+\pi^{du}\left(5.043\% - 5.413\%\right)\left(-.401\% + .869\%\right) \\
&+\pi^{dd}\left(5.043\% - 5.413\%\right)\left(-1.048\% + .869\%\right) \\
&= -.85 \times 1.34\% \times 1.12\%/12
\end{aligned}
\tag{13.10}
$$

Despite its appearance, the system of equations (13.7) through (13.10) is quite easy to solve:

$$
\begin{aligned}
\pi^{uu} &= .03748\% \\
\pi^{ud} &= .46252\% \\
\pi^{du} &= .46252\% \\
\pi^{dd} &= .03748\%
\end{aligned}
\tag{13.11}
$$

Having solved for the probabilities, the final step is to sum the two factors in each node to obtain the short-term interest rate. The following two-dimensional tree summarizes the process from date 0 to date 1:

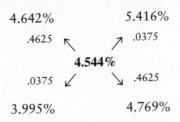

Note that the high negative correlation between the factors manifests itself as a very low probability that both factors rise and a very low probability that both factors fall.

To complete the two-dimensional tree from date 1 to date 2, a set of four probabilities must be computed from each of the four states of the world on date 1, that is, from each state enclosed in square brackets in the original diagram. Solving for these probabilities is done the same way as solving for the probabilities from date 0 to date 1. The solution for the transition from the four states on date 1 to the nine possible states on date 2 is as follows:

```
   4.637%              5.409%              6.182%
      .4195 ↖ ↗ .0009     .4201 ↖ ↗ .0003
           4.642%              5.416%
      .0798 ↙ ↘ .4998     .0807 ↙ ↘ .4989
   4.070%              4.842%              5.615%
      .4988 ↖ ↗ .0062     .4966 ↖ ↗ .0084
           3.995%              4.769%
      .0005 ↙ ↘ .4945     .0043 ↙ ↘ .4907
   3.526%              4.298%              5.071%
```

The tree-building procedure described here does not guarantee that the probabilities will always be between 0 and 1. In this example, in fact, a strict application of the method does give some slightly negative probabilities for the "uu" and "dd" states. The problem has been patched here by reducing the correlation slightly, from −.85 to about −.83. An alternative solution is to reduce the step size until all the probabilities are in the allowable range.

PROPERTIES OF THE TWO-FACTOR MODEL

Figure 13.2 graphs the rate curves generated by the V2 model along with the swap rate data on February 16, 2001. Apart from the three-month rate, the model is flexible enough to fit the shape of the term structure. The long-lived factor's true process and the risk premium give enough flexibility to capture the intermediate terms and long end of the curves while the short-lived factor process gives enough flexibility to capture the shorter to intermediate terms.

As mentioned in Part One, the shape of the very short end of the curve in early 2001 was dictated by specific expectations about how the Fed would lower short-term rates and then, as the economy regained strength, how it would be forced to raise short-term rates. The model of this chapter clearly does not have enough flexibility to capture these detailed short-end views. If a particular application requires a model to reflect the very short end accurately, several solutions are possible. One, allow the model to miss the very long end of the curve and use all of the model's flexibility to capture the very short end to 10 years. Two, add a time-dependent drift to capture the detailed short-end rate expectations that prevail at the time. After a relatively short time this drift function should turn into the

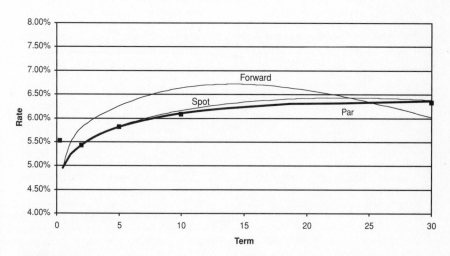

FIGURE 13.2   Rate Curves from the Two-Factor Model and Selected Market Swap Rates, February 16, 2001

constant drift parameters of the model. This compromise between time-dependent and constant drifts is consistent with the view that the market can have detailed expectations about rates for only the very near future. Three, an additional factor may be added to capture the very short end more accurately.

Figure 13.3 graphs the decomposition of the par rate curve implied by the model into expectations, risk premium, and convexity. Graphs of this sort are useful to check the reasonableness of the economic assumptions underlying a term structure model.

One-factor models without time-dependent parameters cannot generate a humped term structure of volatility. Time-dependent parameters can generate such shapes at the cost of making detailed assumptions about the behavior of mean reversion and volatility in the distant future. By contrast, the two-factor model of this section generates a humped term structure of volatility that closely corresponds to market data through the negative correlation of the short- and long-lived factors. Figure 13.4 graphs the term structure of volatility implied by the model of this chapter along with market data of implied par rate volatility.

The negative correlation between the factors causes the humped shape in the following manner. Negative correlation means that shocks to the long-lived factor (or long-factor) are partially offset by shocks of the oppo-

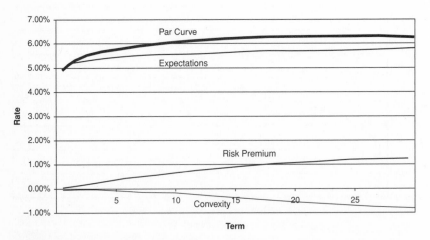

FIGURE 13.3   Expectations, Convexity, and Risk Premium Estimates in the Two-Factor Model, February 16, 2001

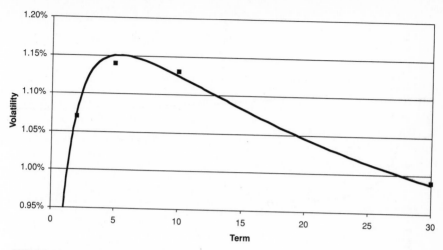

FIGURE 13.4 Par Rate Volatility from the Two-Factor Model and Selected Implied Volatilities, February 16, 2001

site sign to the short-lived factor (or short-factor). This behavior dampens the volatility of short-term rates. But, since the long-factor is, by definition, longer-lived than the short-factor, the dampening effect of the opposing short-factor shocks has little impact on longer-term rates. In other words, the long-factor shock impacts rates of all terms while the offsetting short-factor shock primarily affects shorter-term rates.

Negative correlation may seem like a mathematical trick to create the desired term structure of volatility, but there is an economic rationale behind the assumption. Particularly low short-end rate volatility is a result of central banks pegging the short-term rate for policy reasons. As a result, economic news or shocks affect short-term rates only after policy makers allow the shocks to pass into the short-term rate. In this light, part of the shock to the short-factor may be viewed as the Federal Reserve's canceling out the shock to the long-factor (i.e., pegging the short-term rate). In the model, this part of the shock to the short-factor must be very negatively correlated with the long-factor. The rest of the shock to the short-factor, however, may reflect short-lived economic news and need not be correlated with the long-factor.

Figure 13.5 graphs the factor structure of the two-factor model. Each line shows the effect of a 10 basis point increase in the value of a factor on

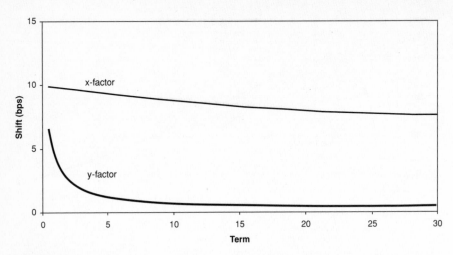

FIGURE 13.5   Sensitivity of Spot Rates to a 10 Basis Point Change in the Factors, the Two-Factor Model

par rates of different terms. Both factors are clearly characterized by mean reversion, and the x factor is clearly more long-lived than the y factor. Figure 13.5 is slightly misleading because the factors are negatively correlated. The graph visually implies that the factors move independently, whereas, in the model, a shift of one factor is likely to accompany an opposite shift of the other factor. Figure 13.6 graphs a combination shift: a shift down of the y factor combined with the expected accompanying shift up of the x factor.[6] The combination shift has the same shape as the first principal component shown in Figure 13.1. The negative correlation allowing the model to capture the observed term structure of volatility also generates a shift resembling the primary principal component.

A major weakness of the parameterization of the two-factor model presented in this chapter is that the correlation of any pair of the two-, five-, 10-, and 30-year rates is about 99%. Because the half-life of the y factor is assumed to be only four months, the model does act like a two-factor model for relatively short-term rates. In fact, the correlation of the three-month rate with each of these longer rates is between 79% and 86%. But

---

[6]For a given dy, the expected dx is $(\rho \sigma_x / \sigma_y) dy$.

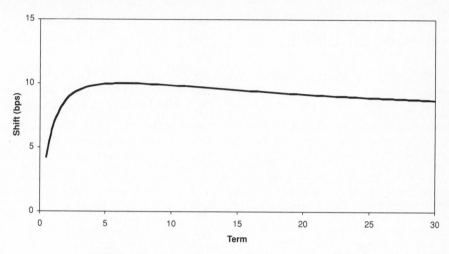

FIGURE 13.6 A Combination of x- and y-Factor Shifts

since shocks to the y factor dissipate very rapidly (see Figure 13.5), they contribute very little to the total volatility of longer-term rates. As a result, changes in longer-term rates are driven almost exclusively by changes in the long-lived factor. This in turn implies that these longer-term rates are very highly correlated or, equivalently, that with respect to these rates the model is essentially a one-factor model.

The parameters given in (13.6) might be adjusted in several ways to lower the correlation between pairs of the short-, intermediate-, and long-term rates. Possibilities include increasing the half-life of the short-lived factor and increasing the volatility of the short-lived factor relative to that of the long-term factor. The user of the model must, of course, check the impact of these changes on other model properties and determine whether the new parameters are more or less suitable for the purpose at hand.

While parameterizations of two-factor models can be adjusted to reduce the correlation between particular rates, these models cannot typically achieve levels of correlation across the curve that are as low as implied by market data. This is not very surprising because only two random variables generate changes for the entire yield curve. If the application at hand depends crucially on the correlation structure, models with a greater number of factors might be required.

OTHER TWO-FACTOR AND MULTI-FACTOR MODELING APPROACHES

The building blocks of drift and volatility described in Chapters 11 and 12 may be assembled in many permutations to model individual factors. In full generality, the drift and volatility of each factor may depend on the level of that factor as well as on the level of the other factors. Then, setting the short-term rate equal to the sum of the factors completes the model specification. Since the possibilities are limitless, many such models have been suggested. The most appropriate choice depends, as usual, on the needs of the application.

Some two- and multi-factor models have particularly interesting motivations. Longstaff and Schwartz (1992) suggested a model in which the factors are the short-term rate and the volatility of the short-term rate. Balduzzi, Das, Foresi, and Sundaram (2000) propose models in which the factors are the short-term rate and the central tendency of the short-term rate. While models with these different emphases can sometimes be recast into factor models of more recognizable form, they are valuable for connecting the factors and parameters of the model with economic quantities. Since all models are simplifications of reality, the more intuition that can be used to parameterize a model and to check its reasonableness, the more useful the model is likely to be.

Some modeling approaches do not begin and end with the short-term rate process. Duffie and Kan (1996), for example, show how to use yields as factors. Rather than posit a multi-factor model for short rates and then find a parameterization that generates desired yield behavior, Duffie and Kan (1996) allow users to make assumptions about yield behavior directly. The cost of the approach is that working out the arbitrage pricing of other contingent claims is not so simple as having the risk-neutral short-rate process immediately available.

Some models with relatively many factors are gaining popularity as a way to capture the true correlation between rates across the term structure. *String models*, for example, directly model the evolution of many forward rates, including their volatility and correlation structure. Along with the benefits of many factors, these models are typically much more flexible than the models described in this Part with respect to matching market prices of traded options. See, for example, Longstaff, Santa-Clara, and Schwartz (2001). Recent *market models*, like Brace, Gatarek, and Musiela (1997), model forward rates in a way that allows many options to be priced in an internally consistent manner and, at the same time, in a manner consistent with simpler and popular models used to price individual options.

Models need enough flexibility so that they can be calibrated to capture the essence of market behavior. At the same time, models need enough structure to be useful for valuation and hedging. Model 1, a one-factor model without drift, says that almost all bonds and swaps are vastly mispriced and that any security can be perfectly hedged with one other security by calculating the impact of parallel shifts. At the other extreme, a model with very many factors used to fit all observed rates and volatilities says that all securities are fairly priced. In this extreme case, since each observed rate is a factor the only true hedge of a bond or swap position is to sell the position. Also, hedging derivatives in this extreme framework might require simultaneous purchases and sales of very many different securities. In summary, the most useful models reflect users' views about the future behavior of the term structure and about the set of security prices that fairly reflect that future behavior. An appropriate model matches its complexity and the complexity of its hedging strategies to the needs of the application at hand. To the extent the user is wrong in these judgements the model provides less than optimal results, but therein lies the challenge.

APPENDIX 13A
CLOSED-FORM SOLUTION FOR SPOT RATES IN THE TWO-FACTOR MODEL

A formula for spot rates from the two-factor model described in this chapter may be used to understand the relationships between model parameters and the shape of the term structure. The spot rate of term T, $\hat{r}(T)$, implied by the equations (13.1) through (13.4), is given by the following expression:

$$
\begin{aligned}
\hat{r}(T) = {}& \theta_x + \frac{1-e^{-k_x T}}{k_x T}\left(x_0 - \theta_x\right) + \theta_y + \frac{1-e^{-k_y T}}{k_y T}\left(y_0 - \theta_y\right) \\
& - \frac{\sigma_x^2}{2k_x^2}\left(1 + \frac{1-e^{-2k_x T}}{2k_x T} - 2\frac{1-e^{-k_x T}}{k_x T}\right) - \frac{\sigma_y^2}{2k_y^2}\left(1 + \frac{1-e^{-2k_y T}}{2k_y T} - 2\frac{1-e^{-k_y T}}{k_y T}\right) \\
& - \frac{\rho\sigma_x\sigma_y}{k_x k_y}\left(1 - \frac{1-e^{-k_x T}}{k_x T} - \frac{1-e^{-k_y T}}{k_y T} + \frac{1-e^{-(k_x+k_y)T}}{(k_x+k_y)T}\right)
\end{aligned} \tag{13.12}
$$

CHAPTER 14

Trading with Term Structure Models

This chapter describes how term structure models may be used to identify potentially rich and cheap securities and how they may be used to construct trades to take advantage of perceived mispricings. While it is important to understand the relationships among a model, measures of relative value, factor hedges, and realized profit or loss, these matters make up only a small part of a successful trading or investment operation. Other crucial elements of success have little to do with the particular features of a model. Experience with models in general signals when a model's results are likely to be reliable and when they are not. Knowledge of supply and demand forces for particular securities indicates when these securities will converge to model value and when they will stay cheap or rich for a long time. Discipline to bear reasonable amounts of risk given the extent of the mispricing and the risks involved protects a trading or investment account from disaster in the event of adverse surprises. In short, despite the scientific look of this chapter, term structure models are not black boxes that offer trading or investment success.

After reviewing the CMT swap example introduced in Chapter 9 and used in this chapter, the text discusses a popular measure of relative value, namely option-adjusted spread. The presentation then relates the profit and loss from a trade to various model quantities and this relative value measure. A trading case study follows to illustrate concepts and to describe by example how term structure models are used to derive hedge ratios. The final sections of this chapter present certain debates regarding the proper use of term structure models in trading contexts.

EXAMPLE REVISITED: PRICING A CMT SWAP

For expositional purposes this chapter continues with the example of a stylized constant maturity Treasury (CMT) swap introduced in Chapter 9. To review, the risk-neutral tree for the six-month rate is:

$$
\begin{array}{ccc}
 & & 6.00\% \\
 & {}^{.6489}\nearrow & \\
 & 5.50\% & \\
{}^{.8024}\nearrow & & {}^{.3511}\searrow \\
5.00\% & & 5.00\% \\
{}^{.1976}\searrow & & {}^{.6489}\nearrow \\
 & 4.50\% & \\
 & & {}^{.3511}\searrow \\
 & & 4.00\%
\end{array}
$$

Under this tree the cash flows of $1,000,000 of the stylized CMT swap are

$$
\begin{array}{ccc}
 & & 5,000 \\
 & \nearrow & \\
 & 2,500 & \\
\nearrow & & \searrow \\
0 & & 0 \\
\searrow & & \nearrow \\
 & -2,500 & \\
 & & \searrow \\
 & & -5,000
\end{array}
$$

(As in previous chapters, dollar signs are omitted from trees for readability.) Then, discounting the cash flows using the risk-neutral rates, the tree for the model values of the CMT swap is

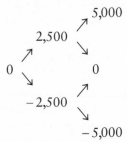

$$
\begin{array}{ccc}
 & & 5,000 \\
 & \nearrow & \\
3,157.66 + 2,500 = 5,657.66 & & \\
\nearrow & & \searrow \\
3,616\ .05 & & 0 \\
\searrow & & \\
 & -1,717.87 - 2,500 = -4,216.87 & \nearrow \\
 & & \searrow \\
 & & -5,000
\end{array}
$$

OPTION-ADJUSTED SPREAD

Option-adjusted spread (OAS) is a measure of the market price of a security relative to its model value. Say that the market price of the CMT swap is \$3,613.25, \$2.80 less than the model price. The OAS of the CMT swap is the spread that when added to all the short rates in the risk-neutral tree for discounting purposes produces a model price equal to the market price. In this example, the OAS is 10 basis points. To see this, note that the perturbed rate tree for discounting purposes is

$$
\begin{array}{ccc}
 & & 6.10\% \\
 & 5.60\% & \nearrow^{.6489} \\
 & \nearrow^{.8024} & \searrow_{.3511} \\
5.10\% & & 5.10\% \\
 & \searrow_{.1976} & \nearrow^{.6489} \\
 & 4.60\% & \\
 & & \searrow_{.3511} \\
 & & 4.10\%
\end{array}
$$

Since this tree is for discounting only, the cash flows stay the same. The new valuation tree, using the perturbed rate tree for discounting, is

$$
\begin{array}{ccc}
 & & 5,000 \\
3,156.13 + 2.500 = 5,656.13 & \nearrow & \\
 \nearrow & & \searrow \\
3,613.25 & & 0 \\
 \searrow & & \nearrow \\
-1,716.03 - 2,500 = -4,216.03 & & \\
 & & \searrow \\
 & & -5,000
\end{array}
$$

The resulting value is the market price of \$3,613.25. Hence the OAS of the CMT swap is 10 basis points, or the CMT swap is 10 basis points cheap. Were the OAS negative, the CMT swap would be rich.

The sensitivity of model price to a one-basis point decrease in OAS will be called *DVOAS*. In this example, DVOAS of the CMT swap equals about 28 cents. This can be calculated analogously to DV01 (see Chapter 5): Set the OAS first to one and then to minus one basis point and divide the resulting price change by two. In this example, DVOAS is not particularly sensitive to the level of OAS, so the DVOAS approximately equals the difference between the model and market price, or \$2.80, divided by the OAS of 10 basis points.

Discussion of OAS as a measure of value continues in the next section. This section closes with a note on the name option-adjusted spread. This term arose because the concept of OAS was first developed to analyze the embedded call options in mortgage-backed securities and callable bonds. The name is now a misnomer, however, because OAS can be and is calculated for securities that, like the CMT swap, have no option features. Nevertheless, because the term is so widely used, it is used here as well.

PROFIT AND LOSS (P&L) ATTRIBUTION

Term structure models are important not only for valuation and hedging but also for analyzing the performance of trades and trading strategies. In particular, it is good practice to compare the actual performance of a trade with its performance predicted by the model being used for valuation and hedging. Aside from occasionally revealing errors in reported market prices, calculated P&L, or even hedge ratios, this comparison allows an investment or trading operation to assess its valuation and hedging framework on a regular basis.

P&L attribution is the process by which total realized P&L is broken down and separated into meaningful components. The starting point of the process is the price function of any security. In the case of a model with one factor, x, the price of a security may be denoted $P(x, t, \text{OAS})$. In fact, by the definition of OAS, $P(x, t, \text{OAS})$ is identical to the market price of the security. Using a first-order Taylor approximation, the change in the price of the security is

$$dP = \frac{\partial P}{\partial x} dx + \frac{\partial P}{\partial t} dt + \frac{\partial P}{\partial \text{OAS}} d\text{OAS} \tag{14.1}$$

Dividing by the price and taking expectations,

$$E\left[\frac{dP}{P}\right] = \frac{1}{P}\frac{\partial P}{\partial x} E[dx] + \frac{1}{P}\frac{\partial P}{\partial t} dt \tag{14.2}$$

Since OAS is assumed to be a constant spread over the life of the security, equation (14.2) assumes that the expected change in the OAS is zero.

As discussed in Chapter 10, if expectations are taken with respect to the risk-neutral process, then, for any security priced according to the model,

$$E\left[\frac{dP}{P}\right] = rdt \tag{14.3}$$

(Taking expected values with respect to the true probabilities would add a risk premium term to the right-hand side of the equation.) But equation (14.3) does not apply to securities that are not priced according to the model, that is, to securities with an OAS that is not equal to zero. For these securities, by definition, the cash flows are discounted not at the short-term rate but at the short-term rate plus the OAS. Equivalently, the expected return under the risk-neutral probabilities is not the short-term rate but the short-term rate plus the OAS. Hence, the more general form of (14.3) is

$$E\left[\frac{dP}{P}\right] = (r + \text{OAS})dt \tag{14.4}$$

Finally, substituting (14.2) and (14.4) into (14.1) and rearranging terms gives a breakdown of the return of a security into its component parts:

$$\frac{dP}{P} = (r + \text{OAS})dt + \frac{1}{P}\frac{\partial P}{\partial x}\left(dx - E[dx]\right) + \frac{1}{P}\frac{\partial P}{\partial \text{OAS}}d\text{OAS} \tag{14.5}$$

Defining DV01_x to be the derivative of the price with respect to the factor and using the definition of DVOAS, (14.5) may be written to give the components of the change in price (i.e., of the P&L):

$$dP = (r + \text{OAS})Pdt + \text{DV01}_x\left(dx - E[dx]\right) + \text{DVOAS} \times d\text{OAS} \tag{14.6}$$

In words, the return of a security or its P&L may be divided into a component due to the passage of time, a component due to changes in the factor, and a component due to the change in the OAS. These components are often called *carry*, *factor exposure*, and *convergence*. The term convergence is used since, for models with predictive power, the OAS tends to zero or, equivalently, the security price tends toward its fair value according to the model.

The two decompositions (14.5) and (14.6) highlight the usefulness of OAS as a measure of the value of a security with respect to a particular model. According to the model, a long position in a cheap security earns superior returns in two ways. First, it earns the OAS over time intervals in which the security does not converge to its fair value. Second, it earns the DVOAS times the extent of any convergence.

To further highlight the role of OAS, consider the implications of equation (14.6) for a hedged position financed with short-term borrowing. A hedged position means that the portfolio has no factor risk (i.e., $\partial P/\partial x = 0$). A position financed with short-term borrowing means that the value of the position is borrowed at the short-term rate at a cost $rPdt$. Substituting the hedging condition into (14.6) and subtracting the financing cost, the P&L of a financed and hedged position is[1]

$$dP = \text{OAS} \times Pdt + \text{DVOAS} \times d\text{OAS} \qquad (14.7)$$

In words, the P&L is simply the carry due to OAS plus any profits from convergence to fair value.

One subtlety in the analysis of this section needs to be addressed. Writing the derivative with respect to the factor in equations (14.5) and (14.6) more fully,

$$\frac{\partial P}{\partial x} = \frac{\partial P(x,t,\text{OAS})}{\partial x} \qquad (14.8)$$

In words, this derivative is the change in the market price of the security for a change in the factor assuming the current OAS. When hedging, however, it might be better to hedge changes in the model price. This would mean using the derivative

$$\left.\frac{\partial P}{\partial x}\right|_{\text{OAS}=0} = \frac{\partial P(x,t,0)}{\partial x} \qquad (14.9)$$

instead of (14.8) for hedging purposes. The pros and cons of hedging to the market and hedging to the model will be discussed in the last section of this chapter.

---

[1]This development assumes that the short-term rate in the market (i.e., the rate at which borrowing is effected) equals the short-term rate in the model (i.e., the rate in the equations of the text). If these two rates are not equal, as may very well be the case for equilibrium models, equation (14.7) would require an additional term to account for the difference.

P&L ATTRIBUTIONS FOR A POSITION IN THE CMT SWAP

To illustrate the results of the previous section, return to a $1,000,000 face amount position in the CMT swap. To begin, verify that if the CMT swap trades at an OAS of 10 basis points when the short rate is 5%, it earns an expected return under the risk-neutral probabilities of 5.10%; that is, verify equation (14.4). Using the risk-neutral probabilities and the OAS-adjusted tree of CMT values, the annualized expected return of the CMT swap is

$$2\left[\frac{.8024 \times \$5,656.13 + .1976 \times \left(-\$4,216.03\right)}{\$3,613.25} - 1\right] = 5.10\% \qquad (14.10)$$

Next, verify that a hedged position in the CMT swap earns 5.10% without any risk. This is a much stronger statement than (14.10), which says that the expected return of the CMT swap is 5.10%. Note that the return of the CMT swap in the up state is

$$2\left[\frac{\$5,656.13}{\$3,613.25} - 1\right] = 113.1\% \qquad (14.11)$$

while the return in the down state is

$$2\left[\frac{-\$4,216.03}{\$3,613.25} - 1\right] = -433.4\% \qquad (14.12)$$

While an expected return of 5.10% is more attractive than the six-month rate of 5%, few investors would be willing to take an outright long position in the CMT swap that may return 113.1% or –433.4%. Many traders, however, would take a hedged position in the CMT swap that earns 5.10% for certain. (It should not be forgotten, of course, that the CMT swap exists because some market participants find that its purchase conveniently reduces the existing interest risk of their portfolios.)

A hedged position may be constructed using the techniques of Chapter 9. First, the tree for $1,000 face of a 1.5-year zero constructed in Chapter 9 is repeated here:

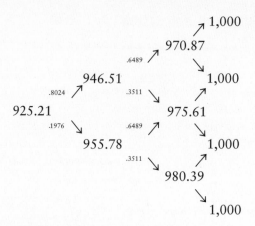

Second, the tree for $1,000 face of a six-month zero is simply

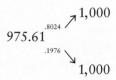

Third, to solve for the portfolio of six-month and 1.5-year zeros that replicates the CMT swap trading at an OAS of 10 basis points, define $F_{.5}$ and $F_{1.5}$ as the required face amounts. Then write the two conditions of replication:

$$F_{.5} + .94651F_{1.5} = \$5,656.13$$
$$F_{.5} + .95578F_{1.5} = -\$4,216.03$$

$$(14.13)$$

Solving these equations, $F_{.5}=\$1,012,984.30$ and $F_{1.5}=-\$1,064,257.85$. Note that the replicating portfolio is short 1.5-year zeros because the CMT swap gains value when rates rise and loses value when rates fall.

    Fourth, consider the following hedged strategy. Buy $1,000,000 face of the CMT swap. Hedge the interest rate exposure by invoking the result of the previous paragraph and buying $1,064,257.85 face of the 1.5-year zeros for $1,064,257.85×.92521 or $984,662.35. Finally, borrow the cost of the hedging securities for six months at the market rate of 5%.[2] Since

---

[2]Equivalently, sell six-month zeros to raise the necessary funds.

the cost of the hedging securities has been borrowed, the outlay for this portfolio on date 0 is just the price of the CMT swap or $3,613.25. The payoff of the hedged portfolio in the up state of date 1 is[3]

$$\$5,656.13 + \$1,064,257.85 \times .94651 - \$984,662.35(1 + .05/2) = \$3,705.39 \quad (14.14)$$

while the payoff in the down state is

$$-\$4,216.03 + \$1,064,257.85 \times .95578 - \$984,662.35(1 + .05/2) = \$3,705.39 \quad (14.15)$$

The values in the up and down states are, of course, the same since $1,064,257.85 face of 1.5-year zeros, by construction, hedges the interest rate risk of the CMT swap.[4] Since these values are the same, the certain return on the hedge portfolio is

$$2\left[\frac{\$3,705.39}{\$3,613.25} - 1\right] = 5.10\% \quad (14.16)$$

In conclusion, the hedged portfolio does earn the short-term rate plus the OAS with certainty.

As a final illustration of the results of the previous section, verify that a hedged and financed position in the CMT swap obeys equation (14.7) so that it earns a P&L equal to $.001 \times \$3,613.25 \times \frac{1}{2}$ or $1.81. The position described in the previous paragraphs is a hedged position. To finance the position, borrow the outlay of $3,613.25 at 5%. Subtracting the repayment of the loan from the date 1 payoff of $3,705.39 leaves

$$\$3,705.39 - \$3,613.25 \times (1 + .05/2) = \$1.81 \quad (14.17)$$

So a hedged and financed position does obey equation (14.7).

---

[3]Given the large face amounts involved, to replicate this result the 1.5-year zero coupon prices must be taken to more places. The value in the up state is .94650763 while the value in the down state is .95578372.

[4]With a time step of six months, a six-month zero has no interest rate risk. Therefore, the quantity of six-month zeros in the replicating portfolio serves only to borrow or lend cash. The six-month zeros play no role in hedging interest rate risk.

TRADING CASE STUDY: Trading 2s-5s-10s in Swaps with a Two-Factor Model

This case study uses the V2 model of Chapter 13 to illustrate how a term structure model might be used in a particular trade, namely a butterfly in swaps.[5]

The V2 model, like any term structure model, has parameters and factors. The parameters of this model are the coefficients of mean reversion, the target levels of the factors, the risk premium, the volatility of the factors, and the correlation of the two factors. These are parameters in the sense that the model assumes that these values are constant. By contrast, the model assumes that the factors x and y change constantly according to the assumed processes.

To be consistent with these model assumptions, only the factors may be changed regularly by the user of the model. In this section, for example, the values x_0 and y_0 are changed each day so that the two- and 10-year rates in the model fit or match those in the market. In other words, the unobservable factors are inferred from market prices. This does not mean that, in practice, the parameters of the model should never be changed. If the financial markets change in a way that makes the existing parameters stale (e.g., if the Federal Reserve becomes active after a period of dormancy or if the term structure of volatility reshapes), the parameters may have to be changed to maintain reasonable model performance. Some practitioners take this logic a step further and change parameters to fit market quantities on a daily basis. The pros and cons of this practice are discussed in the next section.

Figure 14.1 graphs the market and model swap rate curves from two to 10 years on February 14, 2001, and May 15, 2001. Since the factors are used each day to fit the two- and 10-year rates, these rates are fair by construction. The figure shows that, according to the

---

[5]Swaps are discussed in detail in Chapter 18. For the purposes of this chapter the reader should think of swaps as fixed coupon par bonds. To "receive in" a swap should, for now, be interpreted as buying a fixed coupon par bond and to "pay in" a swap should, for now, be interpreted as selling a fixed coupon par bond.

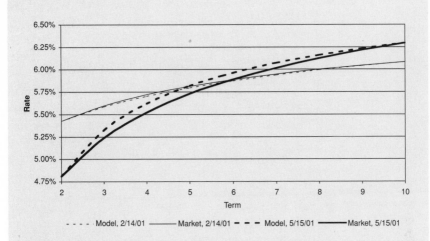

FIGURE 14.1   Market and Model Swap Rates on February 14, 2001 and May 15, 2001

model, the entire swap curve is essentially fair on February 14, 2001. On May 15, 2001, however, intermediate market yields are low relative to the model, implying that intermediate market swap prices are too high. Table 14.1 reports the OAS, in basis points, for each swap on the two dates. A positive number means the market swap price is too low (the swap is cheap), while a negative number means that the market swap price is too high (the swap is rich). Table 14.1 repeats the message of Figure 14.1: Intermediate swaps are rich. If the model is correct, the OAS magnitudes on May 15, 2001, indicate the presence of substantial trading opportunities. For example, the (yield-based) DV01 of a five-year swap on May 15, 2001, was about 4.29 cents per $100 face value. A trader capturing 8 basis points of OAS in the five-year swap on $100,000,000 face amount would make $343,200.

Figure 14.1 and Table 14.1 highlight the effect of choosing to fit the factors to the two- and 10-year rates. Since these rates are fair by construction, the OAS of all other rates must be interpreted as values relative to the two- and 10-year rates. The statement that the five-year rate is 8.8 basis points rich really means that if a trader pays in the five-year and hedges with the two- and 10-year, then the trader will

TABLE 14.1 Option-Adjusted
Spread of Swap Rates on February
14, 2001, and May 15, 2001

	OAS (bps)	
Term	2/14/01	5/15/01
2	0.0	0.0
3	0.9	−8.6
4	1.7	−9.9
5	1.7	−8.8
6	1.5	−7.4
7	1.0	−5.7
8	0.7	−3.7
9	0.4	−1.6
10	0.0	0.0

earn 8.8 basis points. If, however, the hedge is long securities that are not fair but rich or cheap, the trader will not earn those 8.8 basis points. Consider, for example, paying in the five-year, receiving in three-year swaps with an OAS of −8.6 basis points, and receiving in nine-year swaps with an OAS of −1.6 basis points. Since the model predicts that long positions in these rich hedging securities will lose money, the total position is expected to earn substantially less than the 8.8 basis points of cheapness in the 5-year.

Before continuing with the case, it is worth examining the import of the assumption that the two- and 10-year rates are fair. Say that the correctly calibrated and fitted true model of the term structure shows that the two- and 10-year rates are each four basis points rich and that the five-year is 12.8 basis points rich. This means that the V2 is wrong in the sense that a long position in the five-year earns an expected return of 12.8 basis points above its risk-adjusted fair return rather than 8.8 basis points. The V2 model is not wrong, however, with respect to the richness of the five-year relative to the two- and 10-year: Both V2 and the true model show the five-year as 8.8 basis points rich relative to the two- and 10-year. Changing the example slightly, however, shows the full risk of assuming that the two- and

10-year rates are fair. Say the true model reveals that the two-year rate is fair but that the 10-year rate is four basis points rich. In this case the V2 model will be misleading. It concludes that there is nothing to be gained by paying in the 10-year and receiving in the two-year, while that trade is actually expected to earn four basis points. Furthermore, the V2 model is likely to value intermediate swaps relative to the two- and 10-year differently from the true model. In short, the choice of how to fit the model factors to market quantities can have a significant impact on model performance.

Presented with the OAS results of the V2 model on May 15, 2001, a trader has to decide whether or not to believe the results and whether or not to act upon them. Given the activity of the Federal Reserve at that time, a trader might feel that the fair level of the five-year depends on the slope of the curve from three months to two years as well as on the two- and 10-year rates. In other words, the trader might feel that with an active Federal Reserve another factor is required for proper hedging. Alternatively the trader might feel that mortgage-related accounts have needed and will continue to need to pay in five-year swaps. In that case, the trader might postpone any contemplated trade until the payers seem to be done or might execute the trade in relatively small size. Similarly, the trader might feel that the five-year sector is under pressure because other players have losing positions in similar trades and are being forced by internal risk controls to liquidate these positions. Once again, the trader might postpone a trade until the liquidation seems done or else trade in small size.

Assuming that the trader believes the model and fitting choices adequate and the time ripe, the richness of the intermediate swaps suggests several trades. If a trader thinks that the curve from two to 10 years will steepen, meaning that shorter swaps will outperform longer swaps, a good trade is to receive in the two-year swap and pay in the five-year swap. This picks up 8.8 basis points of relative value in addition to any profit from having correctly predicted the steepener. By contrast, receiving in the five-year swap and paying in a 10-year swap also profits from a steepener but gives up 8.8 basis points of relative value. If, on the other hand, the trader thinks that the curve will flatten, meaning that longer swaps will outperform shorter swaps, a good trade is to pay in the five-year and receive in the 10-year, again picking up 8.8 basis points in relative value above any profit from the expected flattening.

For the purposes of this case it is assumed that the trader has no view on the curve and, therefore, wants to lock in the 8.8 basis point richness of the five-year under any yield curve scenario. Since the model being used is a two-factor model, a comprehensive hedge requires two swaps to trade against the five-year. In theory, any two swaps can serve this purpose: a one-year and a three-year, a two-year and a 10-year, or a two-year and a 30-year. The first choice is a particularly bad idea. While the model does say that any two swaps can perfectly hedge the interest rate risk of the five-year swap, there is no reason to test the model that severely. A portfolio with a swap maturing in less than five years and a swap maturing in more than five years will probably be less exposed to model imperfections than portfolios in which both swaps mature in either more or less than five years. The choice of hedging with the two- and 30-year swaps often offers more relative value than a narrower butterfly but is more subject to model imperfections. A two-factor model is more likely to perform badly, for example, in predicting relative movements of the two-, five-, and 30-year rates than of the four-, five-, and six-year rates. As a compromise among these various considerations, the trader chooses to hedge by receiving in two- and 10-year swaps.

The next step is to find the specific portfolio of two- and 10-year swaps that hedges the five-year swap. The exposure of this portfolio to changes in the x factor must equal the exposure of the five-year to changes in the x factor, and the exposure of this portfolio to changes in the y factor must equal the exposure of the five-year to changes in the y factor. Table 14.2 gives the derivative of each swap price with respect to changes in the factors.[6] As conventional for dollar sensitivities, these derivatives are quoted in cents per 100 face of swaps. For comparison purposes, the (yield-based) DV01 of each swap[7] is also

---

[6]Note that the derivatives are calculated at model prices (i.e., at an OAS of zero), and not at market prices. This issue will be discussed in the last section of this chapter.

[7]This is the DV01 of the fixed side of the swap only. See Chapter 18.

TABLE 14.2   Swap Sensitivities to Factors and Swap DV01s

Term	dP/dx	dP/dy	DV01
2	1.8646	0.4808	1.8853
5	4.0689	0.4864	4.2853
10	6.5495	0.4843	7.3384

recorded. While certainly not equivalent to a parallel shift, a change in the x factor is comparable to a parallel shift. As a result, the derivatives with respect to the x factor are of the same order of magnitude as DV01. Letting F_2 and F_{10} denote the required face amount of two- and 10-year swaps, the hedging condition with respect to the x factor is

$$\frac{1.8646}{100}F_2 + \frac{6.5495}{100}F_{10} = 4.0689 \qquad (14.18)$$

and with respect to the y factor risk is

$$\frac{.4808}{100}F_2 + \frac{.4843}{100}F_{10} = .4864 \qquad (14.19)$$

Solving (14.18) and (14.19), $F_2 = 54.10$ and $F_{10} = 46.72$.

As mentioned in Chapter 8, butterflies are often quoted with risk weights where the weights are percentages of the DV01 of the center position. With the weights just computed, the DV01 of the two-year, as a fraction of the DV01 of the 5-year, is

$$\frac{54.10 \times .018853}{4.2853} = 23.8\% \qquad (14.20)$$

while the risk weight of the 10-year is

$$\frac{46.72 \times .073384}{4.2853} = 80.0\% \qquad (14.21)$$

A term structure model implies risk weights from the assumptions made about the possible future shapes of the term structure. In this case the risk weights sum to 103.8%, meaning that paying on 100 face of the five-year and receiving on the hedging portfolio results in an excess DV01 of 3.8% of 4.2853 or .16 cents. This finding might be interpreted as showing that the total position is not market neutral. But that interpretation runs counter to the purpose of the term structure model. No position in two securities hedges a third security under all possible yield curve moves. The V2 model incorporates a particular set of shifts and there is no reason to expect that hedging against these shifts will also hedge against a parallel shift. Therefore, the fact that the DV01 of a position hedged according to the model differs from zero does not imply that the position bears market risk.

As described in the previous sections, once a hedged position has been established there will be P&L due to carry and due to changes in OAS. But, by the definition of a hedged position, there will be no P&L due to changes in the factors. This by no means implies, however, that all models perfectly hedge against changes in the term structure. The OAS values of a poor model will experience high volatility relative to the volatility of the factors as the model's inability to capture yield curve changes is erroneously attributed to changes in OAS. Consequently, the OAS values from a poor model will not be good indicators of cheapness or richness. The OAS values of a good model, by contrast, will experience low volatility relative to the volatility of the factors as most yield curve changes are explained by changes in the factors.

An analysis of the performance of the model from this perspective is beyond the scope of this case. To give a flavor for the judgment required in this type of analysis, however, Figure 14.2 plots several one-day changes in the swap curve against the corresponding model predicted changes. (It is a coincidence that all three examples are essentially sell-offs, that is, increases in yield.)

For the relatively small change in the slope of the yield curve from February 13 to 14, the model predicts a close to linear change in yields. The actual change, however, saw the intermediate sector selling

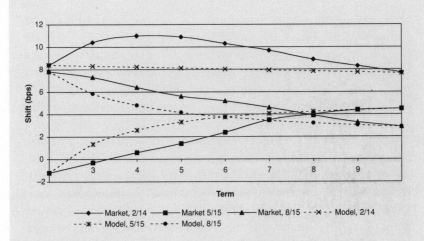

FIGURE 14.2 Basis Point Changes in Market and Model Yields over Selected Dates

off more than indicated by that linear prediction. The change from May 14 to 15 is a steepening sell-off, while the change from August 14 to August 15 is a flattening sell-off. In both cases, however, the actual yield moves are closer to linear than predicted by the model. In other words, the model erroneously predicts that a large change in the slope of the curve manifests itself predominantly in the shorter end of the intermediate terms. The characteristics of the model's predictions may be traced back to the assumed factor structures discussed in Chapter 13.

The fact that the model does not accurately describe changes in the yield curve may be due to several causes. First, the factor structure of the existing model might be inaccurate. Second, the model might be missing a factor. As mentioned earlier, when the Federal Reserve is active, it could very well be that predicting changes in the five-year rate requires changes not only in the two- and 10-year rates, but in the three-month rate as well. Third, the market prices in the intermediate terms might be moving too much. If this is the case, the difference between market and model changes along with the resulting OAS changes represent trading opportunities. An understanding of the economic environment, of the relative supply and demand in various sectors, and of the model being used are all necessary to decide on the combination of these three factors that best suits the facts.

Returning to the butterfly trade, the composition of the hedging portfolio will change over time and with the level of rates. The trader has to weigh the advantages of rehedging against the accompanying transaction costs. Since the composition of a hedged butterfly typically changes slowly, this section assumes for simplicity that the butterfly portfolio remains unchanged until August 15, 2001.

On August 15, the OAS of the five-year according to the model was .7. Since the 5-year moved from 8.8 basis points rich to .7 basis points cheap, the butterfly trade should have made a substantial profit. Table 14.3 shows that this is indeed the case and describes the P&L of the trade from May 15 to August 15. The column listing rates on May 15 gives the two-, five-, and 10-year rates on May 15. Since by August 15 the swaps have matured for a quarter of a year, the column listing rates on August 15 gives the 1.75-, 4.75-, and 9.75-year rates.[8] Price changes then emerge from straightforward yield calculations. For an order of magnitude approximation, the reader might simply multiply the original DV01 by the change in yield, in basis points. For the five-year, for example, this rough approximation for the price change per 100 face is

TABLE 14.3 Profit and Loss from 2s-5s-10s from May15 to August 15

	Face ($millions)	5/15 Rate	8/15 Rate	100 Face Price Change	100 Face Interest	P&L ($)
2-Year leg	54.10	4.809%	4.204%	1.00387	1.20224	1,193,470
5-Year leg	−100.00	5.727%	5.290%	1.80788	1.43181	−3,239,689
10-Year leg	46.72	6.295%	5.815%	3.52030	1.57375	2,380,123
Position P&L:						333,904

---

[8]Since these rates are not directly observable in the market, they are calculated by quadratic interpolation of the nearest three observable rates. So, for example, the 4.75-year rate was calculated by quadratic interpolation of the four-, five-, and six-year rates.

$$\frac{4.2853}{100} \times 10,000 \times \left(5.290\% - 5.727\%\right) = -1.87 \qquad (14.22)$$

Since the position has been held for three months, the interest component of P&L is simply one-fourth of the coupon of the par swap on May 15 (i.e., of its yield on May 15). For the five-year, for example, the interest per 100 face is $^{4.809}/_4$ or 1.202. Finally, the P&L column scales the preceding columns for position size.[9]

Since the average DV01 of the five-year over the life of the trade is about 4.22, a profit of $333,904 on $100,000,000 face represents a gain of about 8 basis points. This is approximately equal to but smaller than the calculated OAS change of .7–(–8.8) or 9.5 basis points. Discrepancies of this sort should be explored to understand the behavior of the model and, if necessary, make changes to improve it.

---

[9]Since the total proceeds from the trade are relatively small, financing is a very small part of the P&L of the trade. For expositional simplicity the details are omitted.

FITTING MODEL PARAMETERS

This section examines an issue raised in the case study, namely the practice of fitting model parameters to market quantities. Most market participants would agree that parameters have to be changed from time to time to reflect changes in market conditions. The real debate is about whether the model should reflect observable market quantities as closely as possible at all times and, consequently, whether or not parameters should be changed frequently, perhaps even daily, to achieve this close match. In the V2 model, for example, some might advocate changing the parameter θ_x each day to match the 30-year rate or changing the volatility of the y factor each day to match a short-expiry option price.

Consider the following sequence of events. On day 0 a quantitative researcher sets a volatility parameter in a model equal to 100 basis points per year. A trader using the output of the model notices that a particular butterfly is 10 basis points cheap and decides to purchase that butterfly, that is, go long the center and short the wings. On day 1 the center cheapens relative to the wings and the trade loses money. In addition, the quantitative researcher decides to change the volatility parameter to 110 basis points per year. It so happens that the increased convexity advantage of the wings is worth exactly the cheapening of the center so that the model reports again that the butterfly is 10 basis points cheap. The trader has not only lost money, but the OAS of the trade has stayed the same. This is bad news: One source of consolation when losing money is that an even better trading opportunity is available. If OAS is unchanged, however, the loss is not accompanied by an improvement in the opportunity set.

It is easy to describe what happened in this story from a technical point of view. The P&L attribution described earlier in this chapter is not valid if the parameters change. In that situation there will be P&L terms due to changes in parameters in addition to terms due to changes in factors and changes in the OAS.

Assume that the researcher and trader agree that volatility has in fact changed—that is, that 100 basis points per year was the best estimate of future realized volatility on day 0, and that 110 basis points per year is the best estimate of future realized volatility on day 1. In this case changing the parameter is appropriate and, in retrospect, the trader should have hedged the trade's exposure to the volatility parameter. This is analogous to the practice of pricing stock options with the Black-Scholes model (that assumes constant volatility) but hedging against changes in volatility nonetheless. In any case, the P&L attribution system should indicate that the trader lost money not due to factor or OAS changes but due to changes in the volatility parameter.

Now assume instead that the trader does not believe that true volatility has changed but that small, random price movements or temporary supply and demand disturbances have led to the change in model parameterization. In this case it is probably not appropriate to change the volatility parameter, and it is probably appropriate to signal that the OAS of the butterfly has increased. The trader may very well choose to hedge volatility in a model with constant volatility, but might not want that volatility parameter changing frequently. Put another way, the trader might believe that the P&L should be attributed to OAS.

Changing volatility is a particularly good example of the need to fit parameters because many practitioners have not found it worthwhile in the term structure context to use models with stochastic volatility (i.e., models that assume volatility follows a process of their own). A less convincing example of the need to fit parameters might be a parameter of mean reversion. First, since it would be hard to find an economic rationale for frequent changes to this parameter, changes to this parameter might be covering up serious model deficiencies. Second, since mean reversion parameters are so intimately connected with term structure movements, it is not clear why changing a mean reversion parameter frequently is better than adding another factor. Adding another factor has the advantage of internal consistency, and changes in that factor are probably easier to interpret than changes in a mean reversion coefficient.

While some argument can probably be advanced for fitting any parameter, the cumulative effect of fitting many parameters makes a model difficult to use. Hedging a portfolio becomes much more complicated as changes to many parameters have to be hedged at the same time. P&L attribution also becomes more complicated as there is an additional term for each parameter. These complexity issues grow particularly fast with time-dependent parameters. A user who feels that the problem at hand demands the flexibility of fitting many parameters might be advised to switch to one of the multi-factor approaches mentioned in Chapter 13 rather than trying to force multi-factor behavior onto a low-dimensional model.

HEDGING TO THE MODEL VERSUS HEDGING TO THE MARKET

As mentioned several times in this chapter, when using a term structure model one can calculate factor exposures either at model values (i.e., at an OAS of zero), or at market values (i.e., at the prevailing OAS). As usual, the choice depends on the application at hand and is explored in this section.

The important issues can be easily explained with the following very simple example. Consider two zero coupon bonds maturing in 10 years that are identical in every respect but trade separately. Furthermore, assume that for some reason, presumably temporary, one bond yields 5% while the other yields 5.10%. To take advantage of this obvious mispricing a trader decides to buy the bond yielding 5.10% and sell the bond yielding 5%. What hedge ratio should be used?

The model hedge ratio is equal face amounts. The two securities are identical, and, therefore, their model prices respond to any change in the environment in the same way. An arbitrage argument is equivalent. Buying the zero yielding 5.10% and selling an equal face amount of the zero yielding 5% will generate cash today without generating any future cash payments. A third equivalent argument is to find the face amounts that set the portfolio DV01 to zero, calculating DV01 at the model yield. Whatever the model yield is, it is the same for both securities. Therefore, the two DV01 values are the same and the hedged portfolio consists of equal face amounts.

The market hedge ratio sets the portfolio DV01 to zero, with calculations at market yields. Using equation (6.23), the DV01 values of the two bonds are

$$\frac{10}{100\left(1+.05/2\right)^{21}} = .059539 \tag{14.23}$$

and

$$\frac{10}{100\left(1+.051/2\right)^{21}} = .058932 \tag{14.24}$$

Consequently, the market hedge is to sell .058932/.059539 or .9898 of the bonds yielding 5% against the purchase of every unit of bond yielding 5.10%.

If an investor or trader plans to hold the zeros until they sell at the same yield or until they mature, the model hedge ratio is best. This hedge ratio guarantees that at the horizon of the trade the P&L will be independent of the level of interest rates. In fact, at the horizon of the trade the positions cancel and there is no cash flow at all. By contrast, the P&L of the market hedge depends on the interest rate at the horizon. If, for example, both yields suddenly equalize at 6%, the price of both zeros is 55.3676 and the liquidation of the position generates (1–.9898)×55.3676 or .5648. But if yields suddenly equalize at 4%, the price of both zeros is 67.2971 and the liquidation of the position generates (1–.9898)×67.2971 or .6864.

A market maker, on the other hand, might not plan to hold the zeros for very long. The trade has no risk if held to maturity, but many market makers cannot hold a trade for that long. Furthermore, at times before maturity the trade might very well lose money, as the spread between the yield could increase well beyond the original 10 basis points. For this trader the market hedge might be best. If both yields rise or fall by the same number of basis points, the P&L is, by construction, zero. With the model hedge, if both yields fall by the same amount the trade records a loss: The DV01 of the short position is greater than the DV01 of the long position. For 100 face of each, for example, a sudden (admittedly unrealistic) fall of 100 basis points would result in a loss of 6.4 cents:

$$\frac{100}{\left(1+.041/2\right)^{20}} - \frac{100}{\left(1+.051/2\right)^{20}} - \left[\frac{100}{\left(1+.04/2\right)^{20}} - \frac{100}{\left(1+.05/2\right)^{20}}\right] = -.064 \quad (14.25)$$

In summary, hedging to the model ensures that P&L at convergence or at maturity is independent of rates but exposes the position to P&L fluctuations before then. Hedging to the market immunizes P&L to market moves without any convergence but exposes the position to P&L variance if there is any convergence. In the context of relative value trades, like the butterfly analyzed in the case study, the point of the trade is to hold until convergence. Therefore, as assumed in the case, the trade should be hedged to model.

This discussion suggests yet another possibility for hedging, somewhere between the market and model hedges. Say that a trader decides to put on a trade and hold it until the OAS falls to 5 basis points. In that case the P&L can be immunized against rate changes by hedging using derivatives that assume an OAS of 5 basis points. This reasoning is particularly appropriate for securities, like mortgages, that tend to trade cheap relative to most model specifications.

Selected Securities

CHAPTER 15

Repo

REPURCHASE AGREEMENTS AND CASH MANAGEMENT

Suppose that a corporation has accumulated cash to spend on constructing a new facility. While not wanting to leave the cash in a non-interest-bearing account, the corporation would also not want to risk these earmarked funds on an investment that might turn out poorly. Balancing the goals of revenue and safety, the corporation may very well decide to extend a short-term loan and simultaneously take collateral to protect its cash. Holding collateral makes it less important to keep up-to-the-minute information on the creditworthiness of the borrower. If the borrower does fail to repay the loan, the corporation can sell the collateral and keep the proceeds.

Municipalities are another example of entities with cash to lend for short terms. A municipality collects taxes a few times a year but pays money out over the whole year. Tax revenues cannot, of course, be invested in risky securities, but the cash collected should not lie idle, either. Short-term loans backed by collateral again satisfy both revenue and safety considerations.

Repurchase agreements, or *repos*, allow entities to effect this type of loan. Say that a corporation has $100 million to invest. In an overnight repurchase agreement the corporation would purchase $100 million worth of securities from the borrower and agree to sell them back the next day for a higher price. If the *repo rate* were 5.45%, the agreement would specify a repurchase price of

$$\$100,000,000 \times \left(1 + \frac{.0545}{360}\right) = \$100,015,139 \qquad (15.1)$$

Since the corporation pays $100 million on one day and receives that sum plus another $15,139 the next day, the corporation has effectively made a loan at an actual/360 rate of 5.45%.

If the corporation were willing to commit the funds for a week, it might enter into a *term* repurchase agreement in which it would agree to repurchase the securities after seven days. In that case, if the seven-day rate were also 5.45%, the repurchase price would be

$$\$100,000,000 \times \left(1 + \frac{7 \times .0545}{360}\right) = \$100,105,972 \qquad (15.2)$$

Once again, the corporation has effectively made a loan at 5.45%, this time for seven days, collecting interest of $105,972.

The legal status of a repurchase agreement has not been definitively settled as a securities trade or as collateralized borrowing. Were repo declared to be collateralized borrowing, the right to sell a borrower's collateral immediately in the event of a default might be restricted in order to protect the borrower's other creditors.[1] It is for this reason that participants in the repo market are usually careful to avoid the terms borrowing or lending. This chapter, however, neglects the legal treatment of repurchase agreements in the event of insolvency and does not differentiate between a repurchase agreement and a secured loan.

Before concluding this section, the discussion focuses on repo collateral. First, because the typical lender of cash in the repo market values safety highly, only securities of great creditworthiness and liquidity are accepted as collateral. The most common choices are U.S. Treasury securities and, more recently, mortgages guaranteed by the U.S. government. Second, even holding U.S. Treasuries as collateral, a lender faces the risk that the borrower defaults at the same time U.S. Treasury prices decline in value. In that eventuality, selling the collateral might not fully cover the loss of the loan amount. Therefore, repo agreements include *haircuts* requiring the borrower of cash to deliver securities worth more than the amount of the loan. Furthermore, repo agreements often include *repricing* provisions requiring the borrower of cash to supply extra collateral in declining markets and allowing the borrower of cash to withdraw collateral

---

[1] See Stigum (1989).

in advancing markets. For simplicity, this chapter ignores haircuts and repricing provisions.

REPURCHASE AGREEMENTS AND FINANCING LONG POSITIONS

The previous section describes typical lenders of cash in the repo market; This section describes the typical borrowers of cash, namely, financial institutions in the business of making markets in U.S. government securities. Say that a mutual fund client wants to sell $100 million face amount of the U.S. Treasury's $5^7/_8$s of November 15, 2005, to a trading desk. The trading desk will buy the bonds and eventually sell them to another client. Until that other buyer is found, however, the trading desk needs to raise money to pay the mutual fund. Rather than draw on the scarce capital of its financial institution for this purpose, the trading desk will *repo* or *repo out* the securities, or *sell the repo*. This means it will borrow the purchase amount from someone, like the corporation described in the previous section, and use the $5^7/_8$s of November 15, 2005, that it just bought as collateral. Assume for now that the repo rate for this transaction is 5.10%. (A later section discusses the determination of repo rates.)

To be more precise, assume that the trade just described takes place on February 14, 2001, for settle on February 15, 2001. The bid price of the $5^7/_8$s of November 15, 2005, is 103-18, and the accrued interest is 1.493094.[2] Hence, the amount due the mutual fund on February 15, 2001, is

$$\$100,000,000 \times \left(103 + \frac{18}{32} + 1.493094\right)\% = \$105,055,594 \quad (15.3)$$

The trading desk will borrow this amount[3] from the corporation on February 15, 2001, *overnight* (i.e., for one day) at the market repo rate of 5.10%. On the same day, the desk will deliver the $100 million face amount of the bonds as collateral. Figure 15.1 charts these cash and repo trades.

---

[2]In a coupon period of 181 days, 92 days have passed.
[3]In this simple example, the corporation is willing to lend exactly the amount required by the trading desk. In reality, a financial institution's repo desk will make sure that the institution as a whole has borrowed the right amount of money to finance its security holdings.

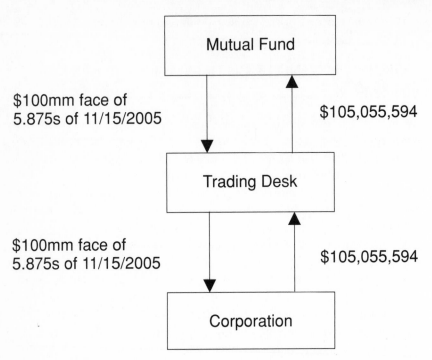

FIGURE 15.1 A Trading Desk Selling the Repo to Finance a Customer Bond Sale

On February 16, 2001, when the repo matures, the desk will owe the corporation the principal of the loan, $105,055,594, plus interest of

$$\$105,055,594 \times \frac{.051}{360} = \$14,883 \qquad (15.4)$$

After making this total payment of $105,070,477, the desk will take back the $5^7/_8$s it had used as collateral. Put another way, the cost of financing the overnight position in the bonds is $14,883.

Suppose that on February 16, 2001, another client, a pension fund, decides to buy the $5^7/_8$s. To keep the example relatively simple, assume that the bid price of the $5^7/_8$s is still 103-18. Assume that the bid-ask spread for these bonds is one tick so that the asking price is 103-19. Finally, note that the accrued interest has increased by one day of interest to 1.509323. The trading desk will then unwind its position as follows.

For $100 million of the $5^7/_8$s the pension fund will pay

$$\$100,000,000 \times \left(103 + \frac{19}{32} + 1.509323\right)\% = \$105,103,073 \qquad (15.5)$$

The desk will use $105,070,477 of these proceeds to pay off its debt to the corporation, take back the $100 million face of the $5^7/_8$s it had used as collateral, and deliver these bonds to the pension fund. Figure 15.2 charts this sequence of trades. Note that the trading desk makes $32,596 on these trades, the difference between the proceeds from the sale to the pension fund ($105,103,073) and the loan repayment to the corporation ($105,070,477). The sources of this profit are examined in the section on *carry*.

If a client does not emerge to purchase the $100 million bonds, the trading desk will have to finance its position again. In other words, the

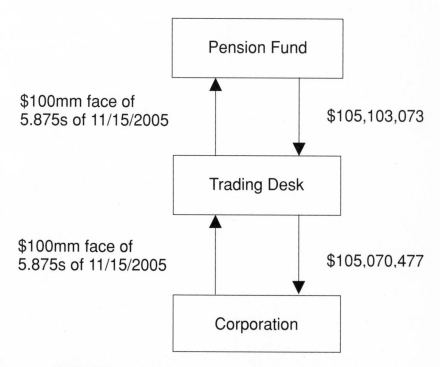

FIGURE 15.2 A Trading Desk Unwinding the Trade of Figure 15.1

desk will have to sell the repo again. It might simply extend the term of the original agreement with the corporation or sell the repo to another repo player, like a municipality.

REVERSE REPURCHASE AGREEMENTS AND SHORT POSITIONS

Rather than wanting to sell the $5^7/_8$s of November 15, 2005, as in the previous section, assume that the mutual fund wants to buy the bonds from a trading desk. Also assume that the trading desk doesn't happen to have that bond in inventory. The trading desk may very well sell the bonds anyway (i.e., go short the bonds), planning to buy them from another client at a later time. When the trade settles and the mutual fund pays for the bonds, the trading desk is obliged to deliver the $5^7/_8$s. But since the desk never had the $5^7/_8$s in the first place, it will have to borrow them from somewhere. The usual solution is to do a *reverse repurchase agreement*, to *reverse* or *reverse in* the securities, or to *buy the repo*. The trading desk finds some party that owns the $5^7/_8$s, perhaps another investment bank; lends that bank the cash received from the mutual fund; takes the $5^7/_8$s as collateral; and, finally, delivers that collateral to the mutual fund.

To be more precise, assume again that the trade takes place on February 14, 2001, for settlement on February 15, 2001, and that prices and bid-ask spreads are as assumed in the previous section. The mutual fund buys $100 million face amount of the bonds for

$$\$100,000,000 \times \left(103 + \frac{19}{32} + 1.493094\right)\% = \$105,086,844 \qquad (15.6)$$

On the settlement date, the trading desk receives this from the mutual fund; lends it to the other investment bank;[4] takes $100 million face amount of the $5^7/_8$s as collateral; and delivers that collateral to the mutual fund. Figure 15.3 charts this transaction.

---

[4]Since this section ignores haircuts and other transaction costs, the text is not careful about the exact amount borrowed or lent against a fixed amount of collateral. For example, the text is inconsistent about whether the bid or ask price is used in determining the loan amount because the haircut arrangement will have a large impact on this determination.

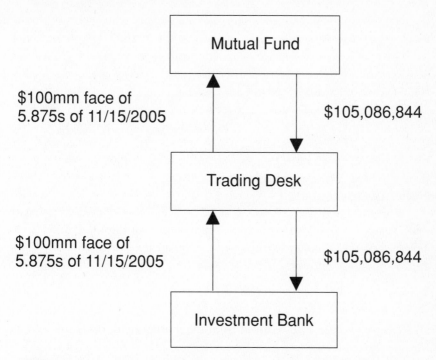

FIGURE 15.3   A Trading Desk Buying the Repo to Short a Bond to a Customer

Note that there is no difference between a reverse repurchase agreement from the point of view of the trading desk and a repurchase agreement from the point of view of the other investment bank. Nevertheless, the term reverse repo is useful to emphasize that the lender of cash is motivated by the need to borrow particular bonds.

Suppose that on February 15, 2001, a pension fund wants to sell $100 million face amount of the $5\frac{7}{8}$s to the trading desk at the bid price of 103-18 and accrued interest of 1.509323 for total proceeds of $105,071,823. Upon settlement the next day, the trading desk pays this amount to the pension fund; takes delivery of the bonds; and hands over the bonds to the other investment bank in exchange for the loan repayment of

$$\$105,086,844 \times \left(1 + \frac{.0510}{360}\right) = \$105,101,731 \qquad (15.7)$$

Figure 15.4 illustrates this unwinding of the original cash and reverse repo trade. Note that the trading desk made $29,908 in this trade: It collected $105,101,731 from the investment bank and paid $105,071,823 to the pension fund. The next section discusses why the desk made less in this trade than in the trade of the previous section.

The purchase and delivery of securities that had been sold and borrowed is called *covering* a short. Had the trading desk not found a client on February 15, 2001, wishing to sell the bonds, the desk would have had to *roll* its short position. The desk can roll its short either by extending its repo with the other investment bank or by finding another entity, like a commercial bank, willing to lend the $5^7/_8$s.

While this and the previous section describe how trading desks may find themselves both borrowing and lending cash in the repo market, on average across the money market, brokers and dealers are net borrowers of cash to finance their inventories.

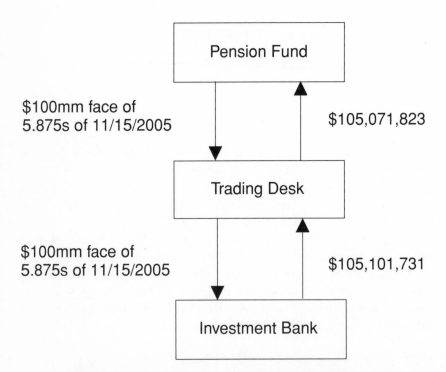

FIGURE 15.4   A Trading Desk Unwinding the Trade of Figure 15.3

CARRY

Practitioners like to divide the profit or loss of a trade into a component due to price changes and a component due to *carry*. Carry is defined as the interest earned on a position minus the cost of financing the position. To be more precise, define the following variables:

$P(0), P(d)$: Flat prices per dollar principal on the trade date and d days later

$AI(0), AI(d)$: Accrued interest on the trade date and d days later

r: Repo rate

c: Coupon rate

D: Actual days between last and next coupon payments

Then, the P&L from purchasing the bond and selling it d days later is

$$
\begin{aligned}
P \& L &= P(d) + AI(d) - \big(P(0) + AI(0)\big)\big(1 + rd/360\big) \\
&= P(d) - P(0) + AI(d) - AI(0) - \big(P(0) + AI(0)\big)\big(rd/360\big) \\
&= P(d) - P(0) + cd/D - \big(P(0) + AI(0)\big)\big(rd/360\big) \qquad (15.8) \\
&= \text{Price change} + \text{Interest income} - \text{Financing cost} \\
&= \text{Price change} + \text{Carry}
\end{aligned}
$$

To illustrate, return to the trade described in Figures 15.1 and 15.2. The P&L from the trade may be broken down as follows. The market for the bond did not change over the day, but because of the bid-ask spread the price change contribution to P&L is

$$
\$100,000,000 \times \big(1/32\big)\% = \$31,250 \qquad (15.9)
$$

The interest income from the position over the day is

$$
\$100,000,000\big(1.509323 - 1.493094\big)\% = \$16,229 \qquad (15.10)
$$

Finally, the cost of financing the position is given in equation (15.4) as $14,883. Hence, the carry is $16,229–$14,883 or $1,346, and the total profit is $31,250+$1,346 or $32,596.

Intuitively, the carry in this trade is positive because the coupon rate of the bond, 5.875%, is greater than the repo rate, 5.10%. The difference between the two rates is not perfectly indicative of carry, however, as can be seen from the third equation line of (15.8). First, interest income is earned on the face value, while the repo rate is applied to the full price. Second, interest income is calculated using an actual/actual day count, while repo interest is calculated using a 30/360 day count.

The trade just described makes more money for the desk than the trade described in Figures 15.3 and 15.4 because carry hurts the latter trade. In that trade, since the desk shorts the bond, it pays the coupon rate and receives the repo rate. The breakdown of the P&L is the $31,250 from the bid-ask spread minus a carry of $1,342 for a total profit of $29,908.

Carry is particularly useful for computing breakeven price changes. For example, an investor might plan to purchase the $5^7/_8$s of November 15, 2005, for an invoice price of 105.103073 and hold them for 30 days. If the 30-day term rate for financing the bonds is 5.10%, how big a price decline can occur before the investment shows a loss? Since the relevant coupon period has 181 days, the accrued interest per $100 million face amount is

$$\$100,000,000 \times \tfrac{1}{2} \times 5\tfrac{7}{8}\% \times \tfrac{30}{181} = \$486,878 \tag{15.11}$$

and the financing cost is

$$\$100,000,000 \times 105.103073\% \times 5.10\% \times \tfrac{30}{360} = \$446,688 \tag{15.12}$$

for a carry of $40,190. Therefore, so long as the price of the bond does not fall by more than about 4 cents per 100 face value over the 30-day period, the investment will prove profitable.

Similarly, carry is useful for calculating breakeven holding periods. For example, a trader might plan to short the $5^7/_8$s of November 15, 2005, at an invoice price of 105.055594 in the expectation that the price will eventually fall to 105. If the financing rate is certain to stay at 5.10%, how quickly does the price have to fall to 105 before the trade loses money? To answer this question, assume that the answer is d days. Then the carry of the position, which will be negative, is

$$-\$100,000,000 \times \tfrac{1}{2} \times 5\tfrac{7}{8}\% \times \tfrac{4}{181} + \$105,055,594 \times 5.10\% \times \tfrac{d}{360} \quad (15.13)$$

If the price does fall to 105, the price change component of the profit from the short position will be

$$\$100,000,000 \times (105.055594 - 105)\% = \$55,594 \quad (15.14)$$

The negative carry will just offset this profit if

$$-\$100,000,000 \times \tfrac{1}{2} \times 5\tfrac{7}{8}\% \times \tfrac{4}{181} + \$105,055,594 \times 5.10\% \times \tfrac{d}{360} = -\$55,594 \quad (15.15)$$

that is, if d is about 41 days. If the target price is realized before 41 days have elapsed the trade makes money. If the target price is realized after 41 days, then, despite the correct prediction that the price would fall to 105, the trade loses money.

Positive carry trades have the desirable property that they earn money as they go. But this by no means implies that the expected return of a positive carry trade is greater than that of a negative carry trade. Consider the choice between investing in a premium bond or in a discount bond where the repo rate for both is between the coupon rates. The premium bond offers positive carry, but its price will be pulled down toward par. The discount bond suffers from negative carry, but its price will be pulled up toward par. Clearly, carry considerations alone are not sufficient to determine which bond earns the higher expected return nor which furnishes the better return per unit of risk borne. In the examples of this chapter, the trading desk made more money on its positive carry trade, Figures 15.1 and 15.2, than on its negative carry trade, Figures 15.3 and 15.4, because of the arbitrary assumption that the bond price did not change from one day to the next. A more complete analysis would be required to reveal the full risk and return characteristics of each trade.

Viewing carry from a theoretical standpoint, Part Three showed that the expected return of any fairly priced portfolio equals the short-term rate plus an appropriate risk premium. This required expected return is the same whether it comes in the form of positive carry and a relatively small or negative expected price change or in the form of negative carry and a relatively large expected price change.

GENERAL COLLATERAL AND SPECIALS

Investors using the repo market to earn interest on cash balances with the security of U.S. Treasury collateral do not usually care about which particular Treasury securities they take as collateral. These investors are said to accept *general collateral* (GC). Other participants in the market, however, do care about the specific issues used as collateral. Commercial and investment banks engaging in repurchase agreements to finance particular security holdings have to deliver those particular securities as collateral. Also, trading operations that are short particular securities need to take those particular securities as collateral. These parties require *special collateral*.

The collection of these needs and interests constitutes supply and demand for general collateral and for individual issues. The repo market equilibrates the supply and demand for general collateral to emerge with a GC interest rate for repurchase agreements in which the lender of cash will accept any Treasury security as collateral. The repo market also equilibrates the supply and demand for individual securities or *specials* to emerge with a set of special rates for repurchase agreements in which the lender of cash must take particular Treasury securities as collateral. Table 15.1 lists the GC rate and a set of special rates for repurchase agreements settling on February 15, 2001.[5]

The general collateral rate on February 15, 2001, was 5.44%, 6 basis points below the fed funds target rate[6] of 5.50%. The GC rate is typically below the fed funds target rate because loans through repurchase agreement are effectively secured by collateral, while loans in the fed funds market are not. The spread between the fed funds target rate and the GC rate varies with the supply and demand for U.S. Treasury collateral.

Typically, and as shown in Table 15.1, the most recently issued Trea-

---

[5]Purchases and sales of the 5s of February 15, 2011, did not settle until February 15, 2001. Therefore, there is no overnight repo for these bonds from February 14, 2001, to February 15, 2001, and these bonds are not included in Table 15.1. Starting from the next day, however, this bond issue did trade in the overnight repo market as the new 10-year bond. The same is true for the 5.375s of February 15, 2031, the new 30-year settling on February 15, 2001.

[6]The fed funds rate is the rate at which banks lend money to one another. The Federal Reserve sets a fed funds target rate and keeps the fed funds rate close to that target. See Chapter 17.

TABLE 15.1 Selected Repo Rates for Settlement on February 15, 2001

General collateral rate:			5.440%
Treasury Issue			Special Repo Rate
Coupon	Maturity	Comment	
6.000%	07/31/02		5.150%
5.750%	10/31/02		5.200%
5.625%	11/30/02	Double-old 2-year	5.350%
5.125%	12/31/02	Old 2-year	4.750%
4.750%	01/31/03	On-the-run 2-year	4.880%
5.500%	02/28/03		5.150%
6.500%	05/15/05		5.200%
6.750%	05/15/05	Old 5-year	5.350%
6.500%	08/15/05		5.200%
5.750%	11/15/05	On-the-run 5-year	3.850%
5.875%	11/15/05		5.100%
5.625%	02/15/06		5.300%
6.500%	02/15/10	Old 10-year	5.350%
5.750%	08/15/10	On-the-run 10-year	4.250%
6.125%	08/15/29	Old 30-year	5.350%
6.250%	05/15/30	On-the-run 30-year	5.350%

sury securities trade special in the repo market. *On-the-run* (OTR) refers to the most recently issued security of a particular maturity, *old* refers to the next most recent, and *double-old* to the issue before that. That these issues typically trade special indicates that there is usually a strong demand to short these issues and, therefore, a need to borrow them through the repo market. Someone taking the OTR five-year as collateral is willing to lend money overnight at 3.85%, 159 basis points below the GC rate, in order to cover or initiate a short sale. (No investor without a particular interest in the OTR five-year would take it as collateral and earn 3.85% instead of taking general collateral and earning 5.44%.) Conversely, the owner of the OTR five-year enjoys the advantage of borrowing money at 159 basis points below GC by lending this bond. The next section discusses *current* issues and their special rates in more detail.

Some issues trade special because they are close substitutes for on-the-run issues. The 6.50s of May 15, 2005, and the 5.875s of November 15, 2005, mature on the same day as the old five-year and the OTR five-year, respectively. These issues trade somewhat special because some traders short these issues instead of the most recent issues. The extent to which special repo rates are below GC is entirely a question of supply and demand for collateral of specific issues. For example, the 6.50s of May 15, 2005, trade 15 basis points more special than the old five-year, while the 5.875s of November 15, 2005, trade 125 basis points less special than the OTR five-year.

Other issues trade special for reasons not apparent without understanding who owns and who has shorted particular issues. Arbitrage traders deciding that a particular sector of the Treasury market is rich relative to swaps[7] might form a large *short base* (i.e., a constituency that shorts a particular bond or set of bonds) in that sector and cause the issues in that sector to trade special. A large sale of a particular security from the dealer community to an investor that does not participate in the repo market might suddenly make it difficult for shorts to borrow that security and, therefore, might cause that security to trade special.

While not shown in Table 15.1, there is also a market for term GC and special rates. This market allows borrowers and lenders of cash to lock in a fixed rate over longer time periods, though typically less than a few months. With respect to GC, the term market allows participants to avoid overnight interest rate risk and the risk arising from changes in the supply and demand for U.S. Treasury collateral. The term market for specials also allows participants to avoid these risks and, in addition, to reduce risks arising from the fluctuating supply and demand of collateral in particular securities.

SPECIAL REPO RATES AND THE AUCTION CYCLE

Current issues tend to be more liquid. This means that their bid-ask spreads are particularly low and that trades of large size can be conducted relatively quickly. This phenomenon is partly self-fulfilling. Since everyone expects a recent issue to be liquid, investors and traders who demand liquidity and who trade frequently flock to that issue and thus endow it with the anticipated liquidity. Also, the dealer community, which trades as

---

[7]See Chapter 18.

part of its business, tends to own a lot of a new issue until it *seasons* and is distributed to buy-and-hold investors.

The extra liquidity of newly issued Treasuries makes them ideal candidates not only for long positions but for short positions as well. Most shorts in Treasuries are for relatively brief holding periods: a trading desk hedging the interest rate risk of its current position, a corporation or its underwriter hedging an upcoming sale of its own bonds, or an investor betting that interest rates will rise. All else being equal, holders of these relatively brief short positions prefer to sell particularly liquid Treasuries so that, when necessary, they can cover their short positions quickly and at relatively low transaction costs.

Investors and traders long an on-the-run security for liquidity reasons require compensation to sacrifice liquidity by lending those securities in the repo market. At the same time, investors and traders wanting to short the on-the-run securities are willing to pay for the liquidity of shorting these securities when borrowing them in the repo market. As a result, the on-the-run securities tend to trade special in the repo market.

Figures 15.5, 15.6, and 15.7 graph the *special spread* of the five-, 10-, and 30-year on-the-run security over time. This special spread is defined as the overnight general collateral rate minus the overnight special rate of the then on-the-run security. The vertical lines indicate Treasury auctions in that maturity. These are either auctions of new on-the-run securities, in which case the on-the-run security changes over the vertical line, or *reopenings* of existing on-the-run securities (i.e., auctions that increase the size of an already existing issue), in which case the same security is featured on both sides of the vertical line.

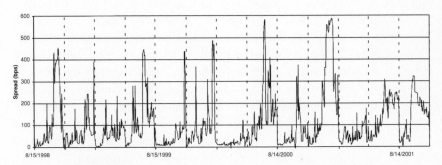

FIGURE 15.5 Special Spreads for the On-the-Run Five-Year

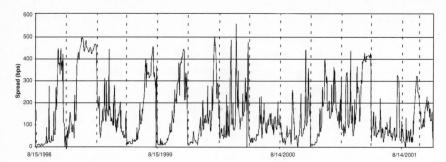

FIGURE 15.6   Special Spreads for the On-the-Run 10-Year

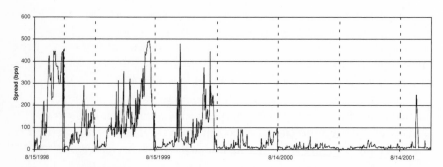

FIGURE 15.7   Special Spreads for the On-the-Run 30-Year

Several lessons may be drawn from these graphs. First, the special spreads are quite volatile on a daily basis, reflecting supply and demand for special collateral on that day. Second, special spreads can be quite large: Spreads of 200 to 400 basis points are quite common.

Third, while the cycle of on-the-run special spreads is far from regular, these spreads tend to be small immediately after auctions and to peak before auctions. It takes some time for a short base to develop. Immediately after an auction of a new on-the-run security, shorts can stay in the previous on-the-run security or shift to the new on-the-run. This substitutability tends to depress special spreads. Also, immediately after a reopening auction the extra supply of the on-the-run security tends to depress special spreads. In fact, a more careful examination of data on special spreads indicates that special spreads for reopened issues do not get as wide as special spreads of new issues. In any case, as time passes after an auction, shorts tend to migrate toward the on-the-run security and its special spread tends to rise.

Fourth, the OTR 30-year seems to have stopped trading special in the repo market. This process began as government surpluses made it seem likely that the Treasury would eventually cancel the issuance of new 30-year bonds. The market anticipated that as a result the sector as a whole would become less liquid, and, perhaps in a self-fulfilling manner, so it did. Interest in shorting the 30-year fell concurrently with this fall in liquidity, and special spreads shrank. To finish the story, in the fall of 2001, despite the possible disappearance of government surpluses, the Treasury did cancel the sale of new 30-year bonds.

By graphing special spreads rather than rates, Figures 15.5 through 15.7 do hide one factor that limits special spreads. Consider a trader who is short the OTR 10-year and needs to borrow it through a repurchase agreement. If for some reason the bond cannot be borrowed, the trader will *fail* to deliver it and, consequently, not receive the proceeds from the sale. In effect, the trader will lose one day of interest on the proceeds. On the other hand, if the bond can be borrowed, the trader will deliver the bond, receive the proceeds, and lend them at the special repo rate. But if the repo rate is 0%, there is no point in bothering with the repo agreement: Earning 0% on the proceeds is the equivalent of having failed to deliver the bond. And certainly the trader will prefer to fail rather than accept a special rate less than 0%. Therefore, the special rate cannot fall below 0%, and, equivalently, the special spread cannot be greater than the GC rate. In the fall of 2001, for example, with the GC rate near 2%, the maximum special spread was about 200 basis points. In short, Figures 15.5 through 15.7 are slightly misleading since special spreads are not completely comparable over time when the level of rates is changing.

LIQUIDITY PREMIUMS OF RECENT ISSUES

Recent issues tend to trade at higher prices than otherwise similar issues. Some of this premium is due to the demand for shorts and the resulting financing advantage, that is, the ability to borrow money at less than GC rates when using these bonds as collateral. Any additional premium, which might be called a pure liquidity premium, is due to the liquidity demands from long positions. Market participants often refer to the sum of the financing advantage and the pure liquidity premium—that is, to the entire premium of a recent issue relative to an otherwise similar issue—as the liquidity premium. Table 15.2 illustrates the magnitude of these premiums with pairs of bonds in each of the two-, five-, 10-, and 30-year sectors for February 15, 2001, settle.

The table illustrates the liquidity premiums in the two- and five-year sectors by comparing the yield of the on-the-run Treasury with that of another bond maturing on the same date. The yield of the two-year was almost six basis points below that of the otherwise comparable bond, and the yield of the five-year was five basis points below its comparable bond.[8]

The table illustrates the liquidity premiums in the 10- and 30-year sectors by comparing the yields on when-issued[9] (WI) securities, those about to become the new on-the-run securities, with the yields on existing on-the-run securities, those about to become old bonds. The WI 10- and 30-year bonds traded at about a 12-basis point premium to the OTR 10- and 30-year bonds. These numbers actually understate liquidity premiums because the OTR issues command a premium themselves relative to surrounding issues.

TABLE 15.2   Examples of Liquidity Premium for Settlement on February 15, 2001

Coupon	Maturity	Comment	Yield
4.750%	01/31/03	On-the-run 2-year	4.821%
5.500%	01/31/03		4.878%
5.750%	11/15/05	On-the-run 5-year	4.970%
5.875%	11/15/05		5.020%
5.750%	08/15/10	On-the-run 10-year	5.238%
5.000%	02/15/11	When-issued 10-year	5.121%
6.250%	05/15/30	On-the-run 30-year	5.553%
5.375%	02/15/31	When-issued 30-year	5.433%

---

[8]These yields are not perfectly comparable because of the coupon effect described in Chapter 3. This effect is very small, however, relative to the liquidity premium.
[9]Bonds to be sold by the Treasury trade on a when-issued basis for a short time before they are actually issued. The 5s of February 15, 2011, for example, although not issued until February 15, 2001, traded some time before then for settlement on February 15, 2001.

To appreciate the interplay between pure liquidity premiums and special repo rates, it is important to differentiate the sources of these two effects. A pure liquidity premium arises because of a large demand to hold a particular bond relative to the supply of that bond available for trading. A bond trades special because of a large demand to short the bond relative to the supply of bonds available in the repo market, that is, relative to the number of bonds in the hands of those willing to lend bonds. Since the sources of pure liquidity premium and special repo rates are different, these effects can surface in various permutations. A typical on-the-run issue, highly valued for its liquidity and attracting a large short base, commands a pure liquidity premium and trades special. Recently, however, the 30-year on-the-run issue is valued for liquidity but few market participants seem interested in shorting it. As a result, the OTR 30-year does command a pure liquidity premium but does not trade special. Yet another permutation arises for seasoned issues that just happen to attract a large short base relative to their supply in the repo market. These bonds do not command a liquidity premium but do trade special.

APPLICATION: Valuing a Bond Trading Special in Repo

The financing advantage of a bond that trades special comprises an important part of the return from buying or shorting that bond. Say that a money manager is considering purchasing one of the two five-year bonds listed in Table 15.2, either the 5.75s or the 5.875s of November 15, 2005. The (yield-based) DV01 of the two bonds is quite similar, but the 5.75s are five basis points more expensive. Is it worth paying a five-basis point premium for the on-the-run issue? First, the manager must make a subjective decision about how much to value liquidity. A manager who plans on trading the security frequently or who wants to be able to turn the position back into cash with minimum effort, even in a crisis, will value liquidity relatively highly. On the other hand, a manager who plans to hold the security to maturity will value liquidity hardly at all. For the sake of discussion, assume that the manager values the extra liquidity of the OTR five-year at one basis point. The question then becomes whether the financing advantage of the OTR five-year bond justifies a premium of four basis points.

The answer depends, of course, on how special the OTR five-year will trade over the manager's horizon and on how much of a yield premium the OTR five-year will command at the end of that horizon. Say that the manager assumes that over the next 90 days the OTR five-year will trade at an average of 100 basis points through the 5.875s in the repo market and that at the end of that time the yield spread between the two will decline from five to three basis points.

Under these assumptions, a rough calculation of the advantage of the OTR five-year might proceed as follows. The financing advantage of the OTR five-year bond is

$$\frac{.01 \times 90}{360} = .25\% \tag{15.16}$$

of face value. The interest disadvantage of the OTR five-year bond, with a coupon 12.5 basis points below that of the 5.875s, is worth approximately

$$\frac{.00125 \times 90}{365} = .0308\% \tag{15.17}$$

of face value. Finally, with a DV01 of 4.261, the anticipated loss of 2 basis points on the OTR five-year relative to the 5.875s is worth

$$2 \times .04261\% = .0852\% \tag{15.18}$$

of face value. Putting these pieces together, the advantage of the OTR five-year is

$$.25\% - .0308\% - .0852\% = .134\% \tag{15.19}$$

At the DV01 of 4.261, the percentage of face value given by equation (15.19) is equivalent to .134%/.04261% or about 3.1 basis points. But, putting aside the one basis point of liquidity value to the manager, the OTR five-year is trading four basis points rich to the 5.875s. So, using the preferences and assumptions of this money manager, the 5.875s are the preferred investment. By the same set of calculations, however, another money manager with the same financing assumptions but a liquidity valuation of about two basis points would find the OTR five-year and the 5.875s fairly priced relative to one another.

Any trade or hedge involving a security that is trading special requires the same set of assumptions and calculations as in this example. How much is liquidity worth? How will special spreads behave? How will the premium change over time? The case study in Appendix 18A will review a trade based on the conclusion that the premium commanded by the OTR five-year bond was too high relative to the prices of other securities.

APPLICATION: Disruption in the Specials Market after September 11, 2001

The terrorist attack on the World Trade Center disrupted the specials market in two ways. First, the resulting confusion and the destruction of records caused many government bond transactions to fail, meaning that bonds sold were not delivered. Second, heightened uncertainty and credit concerns caused many participants in the repo markets to *pull* their securities from the repo market. The combination of these forces caused a severe shortage of on-the-run collateral, particularly in the five- and 10-year sectors. Table 15.3 summarizes the situation with average repo rates on September 20.

Note that the GC rate was 1.75% while the fed funds rate at the time was 3%. The widespread shortage of Treasury collateral widened the spread between fed funds and GC to 125 basis points. While on-the-run special rates do occasionally hit the low relative levels of Table 15.3, it is rare for all of them to do so simultaneously and to stay there for an extended period of time.

In response to the shortage of collateral, the Treasury made a surprise announcement on the morning of October 4, 2001. It would auction $6 billion of the OTR 10-year at 1:00 p.m. that day. This was unprecedented in two ways. First, the Treasury usually keeps to a strict issuance calendar. Second, the Treasury almost always gives much more notice of auctions. These policies are designed to foster market stability, but on October 4 the Treasury judged that drastic action was required.

Figure 15.8 shows the price response of the 10-year futures contract[10] to the surprise

TABLE 15.3   Selected Repo Rates on September 20, 2001

Treasury Issue			
		General collateral rate:	1.750%
Coupon	Maturity	Comment	Special Repo Rate
3.875%	07/31/03	Old 2-year	0.750%
3.625%	08/31/03	On-the-run 2-year	0.650%
5.750%	11/15/05	Old 5-year	0.400%
4.625%	05/15/06	On-the-run 5-year	0.100%
5.000%	02/15/11	Old 10-year	0.600%
5.000%	08/15/11	On-the-run 10-year	0.350%
6.250%	05/15/30	Old 30-year	1.900%
5.375%	02/15/31	On-the-run 30-year	1.750%

---

[10]See Chapter 20 for a discussion of bond and note futures contracts.

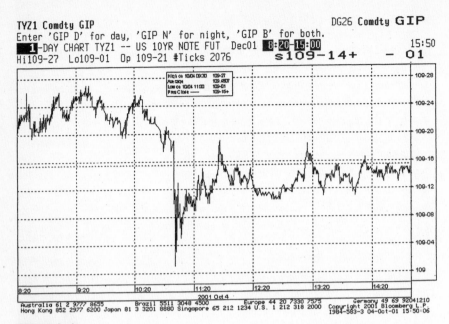

FIGURE 15.8 Intraday Prices of TY21 on October 4, 2001
Source: Copyright 2002 Bloomberg L.P.

announcement. Prices in that sector of the Treasury market fell dramatically to accommodate the coming supply. The spread between the OTR and old 10-year notes also experienced a large one-day move, falling from about 5.2 basis points to about 3.7 basis points. Finally, the special spread of the OTR 10-year note fell about 100 basis points that day. This is visible in Figure 15.6: The last vertical line of the graph represents this surprise auction.

CHAPTER 16

Forward Contracts

$\mathbf{S}$pot trades or contracts are agreements to buy and sell some asset for immediate delivery so that the cash and the asset change hands immediately. By contrast, forward and futures contracts are agreements to trade an asset for delivery on some particular date in the future.[1] The price at which the asset will be traded is fixed today, but the exchange of cash and the asset takes place in the future. While explicit forward contracts are not so prevalent as futures contracts, an understanding of forward contracts is essential in fixed income markets. First, the common practice of combining a spot position with borrowing or lending creates the economic equivalent of a forward contract. Second, futures contracts are more easily understood after first understanding forward contracts. Third, option contracts may usefully be viewed as derivatives of forward contracts. Consequently, in many ways this chapter prepares for subsequent chapters in this part.

DEFINITIONS

A forward contract is an agreement to buy or sell a security in the future at a price specified at the time of the agreement. The *forward price* refers to that agreed-upon price. The terms *forward date, expiration date, delivery date,* or *maturity date* refer to the date of that future purchase or sale. The *underlying security* is the security that will be bought or sold on the expiration date. Finally, the *buyer* of the contract, who is *long* the forward,

---

[1]Most trades in fixed income markets are for delivery in one or two days and, while rarely referred to as forward trades, are technically forward trades. True spot transactions (i.e., trades that settle the same day as the trade) are differentiated using the term *cash settle*.

agrees to buy the underlying security on the expiration date from the *seller* of the contract, who is *short* the forward.

When a forward contract is negotiated, the forward price is set such that the buyer and seller are willing to enter into the agreement without any exchange of cash. This implies that at the initiation of the contract the *value* of the forward contract is zero. Over time the value of a position in the forward may rise or fall. Increases in the price of the underlying security tend to benefit the buyer of the forward contract, who committed to purchase the security when its price was relatively low. In this situation the value of the forward contract tends to be positive, meaning that the short would have to pay the long to exit the contract. Conversely, decreases in the price of the underlying security tend to benefit the seller of the forward. In this situation the value of the forward tends to be negative, meaning that the long would have to pay the short to exit the contract. Note that the value of a forward contract is not the same as the forward price: The forward price is the price at which the underlying security will be traded on the delivery date.

FORWARD PRICE OF A DEPOSIT OR A ZERO COUPON BOND

Begin with the following example of a forward contract:

Forward contract transaction date: November 15, 2001
Underlying security: $1,000,000 face of a deposit maturing on June 18, 2002
Forward date: March 20, 2002
Forward price: 99.4347

This agreement requires that on March 20, 2002, the buyer of the forward buy a $1,000,000 deposit maturing on June 18, 2002, for 99.4347% of face value. Equivalently, the buyer will deposit $994,347 on March 20, 2002, and will receive $1,000,000 on June 18, 2002. Note that this is conceptually the same as buying $1,000,000 face of a zero coupon bond maturing on June 18, 2002, for a payment of $994,347 on March 20, 2002.

Some additional data are required for the example:

Price of a zero maturing on June 18, 2002, as of November 15, 2001: 98.7149

Price of a zero maturing on March 20, 2002, as of November 15, 2001: 99.2761

Number of days from March 20, 2002, to June 18, 2002: 90

With this additional data the forward price of 99.4347 can be derived by arbitrage arguments. Let the forward price be P_{fwd} and consider the following set of transactions:

On November 15, 2001:

Buy the forward contract at P_{fwd}.

Short the zero maturing on June 18, 2002, for 98.7149.

Invest the proceeds from the short sale in the zero maturing on March 20, 2002. More specifically, with the proceeds of 98.7149 purchase 98.7149/.992761 or 99.4347 face of the zero maturing on March 20, 2002.

⇒**No net cash payment or receipt.**

On March 20, 2002:

Buy the zero maturing on June 18, 2002, via the forward contract for P_{fwd}.

Deliver the zero to cover the original short sale.

Collect 99.4347 from the investment in the zero maturing on March 20, 2002.

⇒**Cash flow is 99.4347–P_{fwd}.**

Since the cash flow on November 15, 2001, is zero, if the cash flow on March 20, 2002, is positive then these transactions generate an arbitrage profit. Similarly, if the cash flow on March 20, 2002, is negative then the transactions can be reversed to generate an arbitrage profit (i.e., sell the forward and buy the June 18, 2002, zero on November 15, 2001, etc.). Therefore, the only forward price that does not admit an arbitrage opportunity is 99.4347.

Since investing in the shorter-maturity zero is the same as lending cash, the preceding demonstration shows that a long forward position can be hedged perfectly by selling the underlying zero and lending the proceeds. In other words, a long forward position is equivalent to buying the zero and borrowing the purchase amount. Intuitively, borrowing the purchase price to the forward date essentially locks in the cost of the bond as of the forward date.

In general, the forward price of a zero or a deposit may be derived as follows. Let T be the time to the forward date and let $d(t,T)$ be the discount factor or zero price as of time t to time T. Let $P(t)$ denote the price of the underlying security at time t, and let $P_{fwd}(t,T)$ be the forward price at time t for delivery at time T. According to the discussion in the previous paragraphs, the forward price equals the cash flow from selling the underlying security and investing the proceeds to the forward date. Mathematically,

$$P_{fwd}(t,T) = P(t)/d(t,T) \qquad (16.1)$$

USING FORWARDS TO HEDGE BORROWING COSTS OR LOAN PROCEEDS

Buying the forward contract described in the previous section locks in the price of a 90-day zero for delivery on March 20, 2002. Using an actual/360 convention to quote an interest rate (see Chapter 4), a forward price of 99.4347 corresponds to a forward rate r such that

$$\frac{1}{1 + {}^{90}r\!/_{360}} = 99.4347\% \qquad (16.2)$$

or

$$r = 2.274\% \qquad (16.3)$$

Expressing the forward price in terms of a forward rate means that buying the forward contract locks in a lending rate of 2.274%, while selling the forward contract locks in a borrowing rate of 2.274%.

Institutions expecting a temporary cash surplus or deficiency often wish to reduce the uncertainty of their ultimate loan proceeds or borrowing costs. Consider the case of a corporation that finalizes its capital expenditure program on November 15, 2001. It is scheduled to raise $100,000,000 on March 20, 2002, but does not plan to spend the money until June 18, 2002. If the corporation does not hedge, the rate it receives over the 90 days subsequent to March 20, 2002, depends on the prevailing 90-day rate on March 20, 2002. If that rate happens to be 2.75% it will have

$$\$100,000,000\left(1 + {}^{.0275 \times 90}\!/_{360}\right) = \$100,687,500 \qquad (16.4)$$

on June 18, 2002, to spend on capital projects. But, if the rate happens to be 1.75% it will have only

$$\$100,000,000\left(1 + {}^{.0175 \times 90}\!/_{360}\right) = \$100,437,500 \qquad (16.5)$$

to spend. Rather than face this uncertainty, however, the corporation can buy a forward contract on November 15, 2001, at 2.274%. In that case, regardless of the rate on March 20, 2002, the corporation will have

$$\$100,000,000\left(1 + {}^{.02274 \times 90}\!/_{360}\right) = \$100,568,500 \qquad (16.6)$$

for its capital expenditure program.

FORWARD PRICE OF A COUPON BOND

This section derives the forward price of a coupon bond and begins with the following example:

Forward contract transaction date: November 26, 2001
Underlying security: 100 face amount of the 5.50s of May 15, 2009
Forward date: March 28, 2002
Price of 5.50s of May 15, 2009, for November 27, 2001, settle: 103.6844
Accrued interest for November 27, 2001, settle: .1823
Repo rate from November 27, 2001, to March 28, 2002: 1.80%
Accrued interest for March 28, 2002, settle: 2.0207
Number of days from November 27, 2001, to March 28, 2002: 121

Again denoting the forward price by P_{fwd}, it can be demonstrated that P_{fwd} equals 102.4744, a *drop* of 1.21 relative to the spot price. Consider the following set of transactions.

On November 26, 2001 (repo and cash settle November 27, 2001):

Buy the forward contract at P_{fwd}.
Sell the bond for 103.6844+.1823 or 103.8667.
Buy the repo[2] at 1.80%.
⇒**No net cash payment or receipt.**

On March 28, 2002:

Buy the bond via the forward for P_{fwd}+2.0207.
Return bond/collect repo loan proceeds of $103.8667(1+^{.018 \times 121}/_{360})$ or
    104.4951.
⇒**Cash flow is 104.4951–(P_{fwd}+2.0207) or 102.4744–P_{fwd}.**

Note that, by convention, the forward price is quoted as a flat price: The invoice price of the transaction on the delivery date equals the forward price plus accrued interest.

The preceding transactions imply that an arbitrage opportunity does not exist if and only if P_{fwd}=102.4744. Furthermore, they imply that a long forward position in the bond can be replicated by buying the bond spot and selling the repo. Once again, borrowing the purchase price to the forward date essentially locks in the cost of the bond as of the forward date.

To derive a more general expression for the forward price of coupon bonds, let $P(0)$ denote the bond price at initiation of the forward contract, let r denote the repo rate, and let d denote the number of days between the expiration and initiation dates of the forward agreement. Furthermore, let $AI(0)$ and $AI(d)$ denote the accrued interest of the bond at the initiation and expiration dates of the contract, respectively. Finally, assume for the moment that there are no coupon payments over the term of the forward contract. According to the arbitrage pricing argument, the forward invoice price must equal the loan proceeds from the repo agreement. Mathematically,

$$P_{fwd} + AI(d) = \left(P(0) + AI(0)\right)\left(1 + rd/360\right) \tag{16.7}$$

---

[2]See Chapter 15.

Rewriting (16.7),

$$P_{fwd} = \big(P(0) + AI(0)\big)\big(1 + rd/360\big) - AI(d)$$
$$= P(0) - \Big[AI(d) - AI(0) - \big(P(0) + AI(0)\big)rd/360\Big] \qquad (16.8)$$
$$= P(0) - \text{Carry}$$

Carry in (16.8) is defined as in Chapter 15, namely as interest income minus the financing cost.

The last equation of (16.8) says that when carry is positive the forward price is less than the spot price. But, as discussed in Chapter 15, carry is usually positive when the coupon rate exceeds the repo rate. Therefore, equation (16.8) implies that when the coupon rate exceeds the repo rate the forward price is usually below the spot price. This is certainly true in the example of this section: The coupon rate is 5.50%, the repo rate is 1.80%, the spot price is 103.68, and the forward price is 102.47. Of course, if the term structure of interest rates is inverted, so that short-term rates exceed long-term rates, the repo rate of a bond may exceed its coupon rate and the bond forward price may exceed its spot price.

For reasons that will become clear in subsequent chapters, it is convenient to write the forward price of a deposit or zero coupon bond in a form slightly different from the forward price of a coupon bond. But, equations (16.1) and (16.8) are really the same. If the time to the delivery date corresponds to d days, then the discount factor in equation (16.1) is $1/(1 + {}^{rd}/_{360})$ and that equation may be rewritten as

$$P_{fwd} = P(0)\big(1 + rd/360\big) \qquad (16.9)$$

This is the same as (16.8) when the coupon rate and, therefore, accrued interest equal zero.

FORWARD YIELD AND FORWARD DV01

The forward yield of a bond is the one rate that when used to discount the cash flows of a bond from the forward date to the maturity date gives the forward invoice price of the bond. Put another way, the forward yield is the yield-to-maturity as of the forward date that produces the forward invoice price.

In the example of the previous section, the spot yield of the 5.50s of May 15, 2009, is 4.904% and the forward yield is 5.081%. Analogous to the treatment of spot and forward rates in Chapter 2, it is useful to think of the spot yield as a blend of the repo rate and the forward yield. In the example, the spot yield of 4.904% from November 27, 2001, to May 15, 2009, is a mix of the 1.80% repo rate from November 27, 2001, to the forward date March 28, 2002, and of the 5.081% forward yield from March 28, 2002, to May 15, 2009. This intuition explains why a repo rate below the spot yield leads to a forward yield above the spot yield.

The *forward DV01* is the DV01 as of the forward date using the forward yield. Relative to the spot DV01, the forward DV01 is impacted primarily by the shortening of maturity from the trade date to the forward date and secondarily by the difference between the spot yield and forward yield.

FORWARD PRICES WITH INTERMEDIATE COUPON PAYMENTS

The derivation of a forward price is more complicated if the underlying bond pays a coupon over the term of the forward contract. To illustrate the pricing of forwards in this situation, consider the following contract:

Forward contract transaction date: November 26, 2001

Underlying security: 100 face amount of the 6.50s of February 15, 2010

Forward date: March 28, 2002

Price of 6.50s of February 15, 2010, for November 27, 2001, settle: 110.0031

Accrued interest for November 27, 2001, settle: 1.8370

Repo rate from November 27, 2001, to March 28, 2002: 1.80%

Accrued interest for March 28, 2002, settle: .7362

Number of days from November 27, 2001, to February 15, 2002: 80

Number of days from February 15, 2002, to March 28, 2002: 41

The following set of transactions can be used to deduce the arbitrage-free forward price.

On November 26, 2001 (repo and cash settle November 27, 2001):

Buy the forward contract at P_{fwd}.
Sell the bond for 110.0031+1.8370=111.8401.
Buy the repo at 1.80%
⇒**No net cash payment or receipt.**

On February 15, 2002:

Repo proceeds have grown to $111.8401(1+.018\times80/_{360})$ or 112.2875.
Pay the bond owner a coupon payment of $6.5/_2$ or 3.25 from the repo proceeds, leaving 112.2875–3.25 or 109.0375. Continue to invest these proceeds through repo at 1.80%.
⇒**No net cash payment or receipt.**

On March 28, 2002:

Buy the bond via the forward for P_{fwd}+.7362.
Return bond/collect repo loan proceeds of $109.0375(1+.018\times41/_{360})$ or 109.2610.
⇒**Cash flow is 109.2610–(P_{fwd}+.7362) or 108.5248–P_{fwd}.**

Since these transactions generate no cash flows on November 26, 2001, or February 15, 2002, an arbitrage profit is available unless the cash flow on March 29, 2002, also equals zero. This implies that the forward price must be 108.5248.

The transactions on February 15, 2002, require some elaboration. First, a bond owner who lends a bond through a repurchase agreement continues to receive that bond's coupon payments. The trader who borrowed and sold the bond in this example must make the February 15, 2002, coupon payment to the lender of the bond. Second, as discussed in Chapter 15, the amount of money lent on the collateral of a bond is roughly equal to the value of that bond as measured by the invoice price. Furthermore, a coupon payment reduces the invoice price by exactly the coupon payment. Therefore, it is reasonable to reduce the loan balance extended on the collateral of the bond by the coupon payment on the coupon payment date. For these two reasons, the trader short the bond pays the original bond owner a coupon payment from the repo loan proceeds.

To derive the forward price algebraically when there is an intermediate coupon payment, let c be the annual coupon payment. Let d_1 be the number of days between the initiation of the forward contract and the coupon date, and let d_2 be the number of days between the coupon payment and the expiration of the forward contract as in the following diagram:

Then $d=d_1+d_2$ is, as before, the number of days from initiation to expiration of the forward contract. The forward invoice price must equal the terminal loan proceeds from the repurchase agreement:

$$P_{fwd} + AI(d) = \left[\left(P(0) + AI(0)\right)\left(1 + rd_1/360\right) - c/2\right]\left(1 + rd_2/360\right) \quad (16.10)$$

Equation (16.10) may be expressed in two more convenient ways. First,

$$P_{fwd} = \left[\left(P(0) + AI(0)\right) - \frac{c/2}{1 + rd_1/360}\right]\left(1 + rd_1/360\right)\left(1 + rd_2/360\right) - AI(d)$$

$$\approx \left[\left(P(0) + AI(0)\right) - \frac{c/2}{1 + rd_1/360}\right]\left(1 + rd/360\right) - AI(d) \quad (16.11)$$

Note that the coupon payment is discounted by the number of days from the initiation of the agreement to the coupon payment date. The second line of equation (16.11) ignores the relatively small terms of interest on interest and concludes that the forward price equals the original proceeds minus the present value of the intermediate coupon payment, all future valued to the delivery date, minus accrued interest as of the delivery date. This interpretation shows more clearly how the case of an intermediate coupon is a generalization of equation (16.7). Here, the present value of the intermediate cash flow must be subtracted from original proceeds. In fact, it can be shown that if there are many intermediate coupon payments before the delivery date, the forward price equals the original proceeds minus the present value of all the intermediate payments, all future valued to the delivery date, minus accrued interest as of the delivery date.

The second useful expression of equation (16.10) relates the forward price to the spot price and carry with an intermediate coupon. As in

(16.11), the second line of (16.12) ignores the relatively small interest on interest terms:

$$
\begin{aligned}
P_{fwd} &= \left(P(0) + AI(0)\right)\left(1 + rd_1/360\right)\left(1 + rd_2/360\right) - \left(c/2\right)\left(1 + rd_2/360\right) - AI(d) \\
&\approx \left(P(0) + AI(0)\right)\left(1 + rd/360\right) - \left(c/2\right)\left(1 + rd_2/360\right) - AI(d) \\
&\approx P(0) - \left[AI(d) + \left(c/2\right)\left(1 + rd_2/360\right) - AI(0) - \left(P(0) + AI(0)\right)rd/360\right] \qquad (16.12) \\
&\approx P(0) - \text{Carry}
\end{aligned}
$$

Note that in the case of an intermediate coupon the interest income over the period includes the actual coupon payment invested to the delivery date. For example, in the case of the 6.50s of February 15, 2011, the interest received is

$$
.7362 + \frac{6.5}{2}\left(1 + \frac{.018 \times 41}{360}\right) - 1.8370 = 2.155863 \qquad (16.13)
$$

VALUE OF A FORWARD CONTRACT

The value of a forward contract changes with the value of the underlying security. Continuing with the example of the 6.50s of February 15, 2011, the forward price on November 26, 2001, for delivery on March 28, 2002, is 108.5248. Therefore, a trader buying a forward contract on November 26, 2001, locks in a purchase price of 108.5248 on March 28, 2002. If the price of the bond on March 28, 2002, turns out to be 108, the trader will suffer a loss on that day of .5248: The trader will pay 108.5248 through the forward contract to purchase a bond worth only 108.[3] In other words, the value of the contract on the delivery date is −.5248. Alternatively, if the price of the bond on the delivery date turns out to be 109, the trader will reap a profit of .4752. In this case the value of the contract is .4752.

The value of the forward contract on dates before delivery can be as easily determined. Continuing with the 6.50s of February 15, 2011, assume that the forward price on January 15, 2002, for delivery on March 28, 2002, is 108. A trader who sold a forward contract on January 15,

---

[3]The accrued interest on March 28, 2002, cancels out of this calculation. The trader pays the accrued interest when buying the bond through the forward contract but collects the accrued interest when selling the bond in the market.

2002, incurs the obligation to sell the bond for 108 on March 28, 2002. Combined with a long position requiring the purchase of the bond for 108.5248 on March 28, 2002, the net position would be a certain payment of .5248 on March 28, 2002. Hence, as of January 15, 2002, the value of the long forward position can be described in one of two ways. First, as of January 15, 2002, the future value of the long forward position to March 28, 2002, is .5248. Second, the present value of the long forward position on January 15, 2002, is the present value of .5428 discounted from March 28, 2002, to January 15, 2002.

Mathematically, let $P_{fwd}(t,T)$ be the forward price at time t for delivery at time T. Then, as of time t, a contract initiated at time 0 has a time T future value of

$$P_{fwd}(t,T) - P_{fwd}(0,T) \qquad (16.14)$$

Equivalently, if the discount factor from time t to time T is $d(t,T)$, then, as of time t, the present value of the forward contract is

$$d(t,T)\left[P_{fwd}(t,T) - P_{fwd}(0,T)\right] \qquad (16.15)$$

FORWARD PRICES IN A TERM STRUCTURE MODEL

Chapter 17 will compare the pricing of forward and futures contracts. In preparation, this section returns to the risk-neutral trees of Part Three to express forward prices in that context.

Assume that the risk neutral rate process from dates 0 to 2 is given by the following tree:

Also assume that the prices of a particular security in the three states of date 2 have been computed using the later dates of the tree (not shown here). These three prices depend, of course, on the different values of the short-term rate on date 2 and are denoted P_2^{uu}, P_2^{ud}, and P_2^{dd}. For simplicity, assume that the security makes no cash flows between dates 0 and 2.

To find the forward price of the security for delivery on date 2, find the price of the security today, find the discount factor to date 2, and then invoke equation (16.1). Using the methods of Part Three, the price of the security today, $P(0)$, may be computed backward along the tree starting from date 2. Writing this out algebraically,

$$P(0) = \frac{1}{1+r_0} \left[.6 \times \frac{.5P_2^{uu} + .5P_2^{ud}}{1+r_1^u} + .4 \times \frac{.5P_2^{ud} + .5P_2^{dd}}{1+r_1^d} \right] \qquad (16.16)$$

Or, rearranging terms,

$$P(0) = .3\frac{P_2^{uu}}{(1+r_0)(1+r_1^u)} + .3\frac{P_2^{ud}}{(1+r_0)(1+r_1^u)} + .2\frac{P_2^{ud}}{(1+r_0)(1+r_1^d)} + .2\frac{P_2^{uu}}{(1+r_0)(1+r_1^d)} \qquad (16.17)$$

Each term of equation (16.17) is the probability of reaching a particular price times that price and discounted along the path to that price. In the first term, for example, the probability of moving up and then up again to the price of P_2^{uu} is .6×.5 or .3. Discounting P_2^{uu} along that path means discounting using r_0 and r_1^u. In general, the price of a security may be written as

$$P(0) = E\left[\frac{P(M)}{\prod_{m=0}^{M-1}(1+r_m)} \right] \qquad (16.18)$$

where M is a fixed number of dates from today and the product notation is standard:

$$\prod_{m=0}^{M-1}(1+r_m) = (1+r_0)(1+r_1)\cdots(1+r_{M-1}) \qquad (16.19)$$

In words, equation (16.18) says that the price today equals the expected discounted value of its future value—in particular, of its value on date M. This equation also reveals the reason for using the term expected discounted value rather than discounted expected value.

The discount factor to date 2 implied by the tree is the same, of course, as the price of a zero coupon bond maturing on date 2. But a zero coupon bond maturing on date 2 is one in every state; that is, $P_2^{uu} = P_2^{ud} = P_2^{dd} = 1$. Substituting these values into equation (16.17), the discount factor as of date 0 may be written as

$$d(0,2) = .3 \frac{1}{(1+r_0)(1+r_1^u)} + .3 \frac{1}{(1+r_0)(1+r_1^u)} + .2 \frac{1}{(1+r_0)(1+r_1^d)} + .2 \frac{1}{(1+r_0)(1+r_1^d)} \quad (16.20)$$

Or, more generally,

$$d(0,M) = E\left[\frac{1}{\prod_{m=0}^{M-1}(1+r_m)} \right] \quad (16.21)$$

Finally, from equation (16.1), $P_{fwd} = P(0)/d(0,M)$ where $P(0)$ and $d(0,M)$ are given by equations (16.18) and (16.21), respectively.

CHAPTER 17

Eurodollar and Fed Funds Futures

Futures contracts on short-term rates are extremely useful for hedging against risks arising from changes in short-term rates and for speculating on the direction of these rates. This usefulness stems from the great liquidity of many interest rate futures contracts relative to that of the underlying assets and from the relatively small amount of capital needed to establish futures positions relative to spot positions of equivalent risk.

This chapter describes the pricing of Eurodollar and fed funds futures and how these contracts are used for hedging exposures to short-term rates. An important part of the discussion is the *mark-to-market* feature of futures contracts which distinguishes them from the forward contracts described in Chapter 16.

LIBOR AND EURODOLLAR FUTURES

LIBOR, the *London Interbank Offered Rate*, is the rate at which banks are willing to lend to counterparties with credits comparable to those of strong banks. The rate varies with term, is quoted on an actual/360 basis, and assumes T+2 settlement (i.e., settlement two days after the trade). LIBOR rates are particularly important in financial markets because many other rates are keyed off LIBOR. For example, borrowing rates are often quoted as a spread to LIBOR, so that one company might be allowed to borrow money at LIBOR+150, that is, at 150 basis points above LIBOR. Also, *Eurodollar futures*, discussed in this chapter, and the floating side of swaps, discussed in Chapter 18, set off three-month LIBOR.

Eurodollar futures are extremely liquid securities that allow investors and traders to manage exposure to short-term rates. The underlying security of the oldest of these contracts is a $1,000,000 90-day LIBOR deposit. While these contracts mature in March, June, September, and December over the next 10 years, the most liquid mature in the next few years. Table 17.1 lists the first few contracts, their expiration dates, and their prices as of November 30, 2001. The table also lists the *futures rates*, defined as 100 minus the corresponding prices. Notice that the symbols are a concatenation of "ED" for a 90-day Eurodollar contract, a month (H for March, M for June, U for September, and Z for December), and a year. Hence, EDH2 is a 90-day Eurodollar futures contract expiring in March 2002.[1]

To describe how Eurodollar futures work, focus on EDH2. On its expiration date of March 18, 2002, the contract price is set at 100 minus 100 times the futures exchange set of 3-month LIBOR. So, for example, if the set is 1.75% on March 18, 2002, the final contract price is 100–100×1.75% or 98.25. Note that, given T+2 settlement of deposits and the 3-month term, this rate of 1.75% represents the 3-month deposit rate starting on March 20, 2002.

To avoid confusion it is important to note that the contract price is meaningful only as the convention for quoting a 90-day rate: A price of

TABLE 17.1   Eurodollar Futures as of November 30, 2001

Symbol	Expiration	Price	Rate(%)
EDZ1	12/17/01	98.0825	1.9175
EDH2	03/18/02	97.9500	2.0500
EDM2	06/17/02	97.5000	2.5000
EDU2	09/16/02	96.9450	3.0550
EDZ2	12/16/02	96.3150	3.6850
EDH3	03/17/03	95.8400	4.1600
EDM3	06/16/03	95.4050	4.5950
EDU3	09/15/03	95.0850	4.9150
EDZ3	12/15/03	94.7750	5.2250
EDH4	03/15/04	94.6350	5.3650
EDM4	06/14/04	94.4650	5.5350
EDU4	09/13/04	94.3300	5.6700

---

[1]When a contract expires, a new contract with the same symbol is added to the end of the contract list. For example, when EDZ1 expires in December, 2001, a new EDZ1 is listed, this one maturing in December, 2011.

98.25 means that the 90-day rate is 1.75%. The contract price is not the price of a 90-day zero at the contract rate. At a rate of 1.75%, the price of a 90-day zero is not 98.25 but $1/(1+^{1.75\% \times 90}/_{360})$ or 99.5644%.

On any day before expiration, market forces determine the settle prices of futures contracts. The second column of Table 17.2 records the settlement price of EDH2 from November 15, 2001, to November 30, 2001. The third and fourth columns record the corresponding futures rates and rate changes, in basis points.

If EDH2 were a forward contract, a rate of 2.275% on November 15, 2001, would indicate the rate at which investors could commit to borrow or lend money on March 20, 2002, for 90 days. An increase of the rate by 9.5 basis points to 2.37% on November 16, 2001, would constitute a loss to lenders who, by buying contracts, committed to lend the previous day at 2.275%. Similarly, the increase in rate would constitute a gain to borrowers who, by selling contracts, committed to borrow the previous day at 2.275%. Since the notional amount of one contract is $1,000,000, the change in the contract rate would indicate that the interest on the forward loan changed by

$$\$1,000,000\left(\frac{2.37\% \times 90}{360} - \frac{2.275\% \times 90}{360}\right) = \$1,000,000\frac{.095\% \times 90}{360}$$
$$= \$25 \times 9.5$$
$$= \$237.50$$

(17.1)

TABLE 17.2 Settlement Prices of EDH2 and Mark-to-Market from a Long of One Contract

Date	Price	Rate(%)	Change (bps)	Mark-to-Market
11/15/01	97.7250	2.2750		
11/16/01	97.6300	2.3700	−9.50	−$237.50
11/19/01	97.7400	2.2600	11.00	$275.00
11/20/01	97.7050	2.2950	−3.50	−$87.50
11/21/01	97.6400	2.3600	−6.50	−$162.50
11/23/01	97.6250	2.3750	−1.50	−$37.50
11/26/01	97.6150	2.3850	−1.00	−$25.00
11/27/01	97.7850	2.2150	17.00	$425.00
11/28/01	97.7900	2.2100	0.50	$12.50
11/29/01	97.9400	2.0600	15.00	$375.00
11/30/01	97.9500	2.0500	1.00	$25.00

According to the second line of equation (17.1), the change in the interest payment equals $25 per basis point.

Once again, if EDH2 were a forward contract then the $237.50 would represent the additional interest received on June 18, 2002, as a result of the increase in the contract rate. With a futures contract, however, the $237.50 is paid immediately by the longs to the shorts as a *mark-to-market* payment.[2] The fifth column of Table 17.2 shows the mark-to-market payment each day resulting from a long position of one contract.

When a Eurodollar futures contract expires and the last mark-to-market payment is made and received, the long and short have no further obligations. In particular, the long does not have to buy a 90-day deposit from the short at the rate implied by the final settlement price. Futures contracts that do not require delivery of the underlying security at expiration are said to be *cash settled*.[3] Futures contracts that do require delivery of an underlying security, like the note and bond futures discussed in Chapter 20, are said to be *physically settled*.

The mark-to-market feature reveals a critical difference between forward and futures contracts. Because forward contracts are not marked-to-market, any value, positive or negative, accumulates over time until final settlement at expiration. Futures contracts, however, pay or collect value changes as they occur. As a result, after each day's mark-to-market a futures contract has zero value. In fact, a futures contract is essentially like rolling over one-day forward contracts where each new forward price is that day's futures settlement price.

The fact that forward contracts can accumulate value over time while futures contracts can accumulate only one day of value may very well explain the historical predominance of futures contracts over forward contracts. Since gains in a forward contract can become quite substantial before the losing party need make any payment, there is a relatively large risk that a party with substantial accumulated losses will disappear or become insolvent and fail to make the required payments. With at most one day of value in a futures contract, however, the side with a gain will sacri-

---

[2] These payments are also called *variation margin* to distinguish them from the initial and maintenance margins required by futures exchanges.
[3] Note that this usage of the phrase is different from the other usage, mentioned in Chapter 16, meaning same-day settle.

fice a relatively small sum in the event the losing party fails to make a mark-to-market payment. In modern times much of the credit risk of futures contracts even over a single day is alleviated by having the futures exchange, with solid credit, stand as the counterparty for all contracts. This arrangement not only minimizes the risk of default but also saves the time and expense of examining the credit quality of many different potential counterparties.

HEDGING WITH EURODOLLAR FUTURES

Chapter 16 described how forward contracts on deposits can hedge the rate risk of plans to lend or borrow on future dates. Futures contracts can be used in the same way. Recall the example in Chapter 16 of a corporation scheduled to raise $100,000,000 on March 20, 2002, but planning to spend that money on June 18, 2002. On November 15, 2001, that corporation might buy 100 EDH2 contracts, each with a face value of $1,000,000, to hedge the interest on its future loan of $100,000,000. Assume that it buys these 100 contracts sometime during the day on November 15, 2001, for 97.726, corresponding to a rate of 2.274%. If the contract expires at 97.25, corresponding to a rate of 2.75%, the corporation will be able to lend $100,000,000 from March 20,2002, to June 18, 2002, at 2.75% and collect interest on June 18, 2002, of $687,500. See equation (16.4). However, the corporation loses 10,000×(2.75%–2.274%) or 47.6 basis points on its 100 contracts. At $25 per basis point that loss, realized as the sum of all mark-to-market receipts and payments, totals 100×$25×47.6 or $119,000. Subtracting this loss from the interest received leaves $568,500: exactly the amount locked in by a forward contract at 2.274%. See equation (16.6). Hence, the total cash collected by the company from the initiation of its futures position at 2.274% to the maturity of its loan equals the amount of cash locked in by a forward contract at 2.274% as of the maturity of the loan.

The futures hedge also works if rates fall after November 15, 2001. If the contract expires at a price of 98.25, corresponding to a rate of 1.75%, the corporation will lend its $100,000,000 at 1.75% and collect interest of only $437,500. See equation (16.5). However, the corporation gains10,000×(2.274%–1.75%) or 52.4 basis points on its 100 contracts for a total of 100×$25×52.4 or $131,000. Adding this gain to the interest received gives $568,500. Again, the total cash collected by the company equals the amount of cash locked in by a forward contract at 2.274%.

TAILS: A CLOSER LOOK AT HEDGING WITH FUTURES

While it is true that the corporation discussed in the previous section could hedge its total cash flows by buying 100 EDH2 contracts, this hedge is conceptually flawed. The cash flows received or paid from the futures contracts occur between November 15, 2001, and March 18, 2002, while the interest from the loan is received on June 18, 2002. So while the sum of the cash flows always equals $568,500, the timing of the cash flows and, therefore, the value of the cash flows on any fixed date are not precisely hedged. More concretely, any mark-to-market gains from the futures position may be reinvested to June 18, 2002, and any mark-to-market losses from the futures position must be financed to June 18, 2002, before being added or subtracted from the interest on the loan.

The following extreme examples demonstrate that a long position of 100 EDH2 does not really hedge the lending risk faced by the corporation. Assume that the term structure in the short end is flat and that the price of EDH2 changes only once, on November 15, 2001. In the first scenario of the previous section, the company purchases the contracts sometime during the day of November 15, 2001, at 97.726, and the contract immediately and dramatically falls to and settles at 97.25. After that, short-term rates remain at 2.75% to June 18, 2002. In this case, the total loss of $119,000 from the EDH2 position is realized on November 15, 2001. To finance this loss, the corporation must borrow $119,000 at 2.75% to June 18, 2002. Equivalently, to compare this loss with the interest on the loan, the loss must be future valued to June 18, 2002. Therefore, noting that there are 215 days between November 15, 2001, and June 18, 2002, the loss in terms of dollars on June 18, 2002, is

$$\$119,000\left(1 + {.0275 \times 215}/{360}\right) = \$120,954 \tag{17.2}$$

Subtracting these losses from the interest of $687,500 on June 18, 2002, leaves $566,546, $1,954 short of the $568,500 locked in by the forward hedge.

In the second scenario of the previous section, after the corporation purchases its contracts, EDH2 settles up to 98.25 on November 15, 2001.

The mark-to-market gain of $131,000 is immediately realized and reinvested for 215 days:

$$\$131,000\left(1 + {}^{.0175 \times 215}\!/_{360}\right) = \$132,369 \tag{17.3}$$

Adding this to the loan proceeds of $437,500 gives a total of $569,869 as of June 18, 2002, $1,369 above the $568,500 locked in by the forward hedge.

The discrepancies between the forward and futures hedge are not large in this example for two reasons. First, the level of rates is low so that timing differences do not have the value implications they would have at higher rate levels. Second, the time between the contract initiation and the ultimate receipt of cash flows is relatively short. If the contract were EDH6, for example, instead of EDH2, the difference between the two hedges could be substantially larger.

Relative to the forward hedge in the example, the shortfall in the case of rising rates (i.e., $1,954) exceeds in magnitude the surplus in the case of falling rates (i.e., $1,369). This is not a coincidence. When rates rise and the futures position suffers a loss, this loss has to be financed at relatively high rates. On the other hand, when rates fall and the futures position enjoys a gain, this gain is reinvested at relatively low rates. This asymmetry working to the detriment of long futures positions is the key to the pricing of futures versus the pricing of forwards explored in the following sections.

Since the hedge of 100 contracts leaves something to be desired, industry practice is to *tail* the hedge. Consider the P&L of the forward and future contracts on November 15, 2001. As pointed out previously, a decrease of one basis point in the forward rate generates P&L in a forward contract as of June 18, 2002. Therefore, a forward contract on $1,000,000 of a 90-day deposit would gain $25 per basis point as of June 18, 2002. On the other hand, a one basis point decrease in the futures rate generates an immediate mark-to-market gain of $25 for each EDH2 contract. The improved hedge ratio equates the present value of these two gains. Letting N_{fut} be the number of futures contracts to replace each forward contract and r the actual/360 rate from November 15, 2001, to June 18, 2002,

$$\frac{25}{1 + 215r/360} = 25N_{fut} \tag{17.4}$$

or

$$N_{fut} = \frac{1}{1 + 215r/360} \qquad (17.5)$$

In words, the number of futures contracts equals the number of forward contracts discounted from the cash flow date to the present.[4] With a flat term structure at 2.274%, the number of futures contracts in the example as of November 15, 2001, is

$$\frac{100}{1 + 2.274\% \times 215/360} = 98.66 \qquad (17.6)$$

Since contracts have to be bought in whole numbers, the corporation would buy 99 instead of 100 contracts. This hedge is said to have a *tail* of one contract. As mentioned earlier, because of the low level of rates and the short horizon of the trade, the tailed hedge is not very different from the simpler hedge. Chapter 20 will present an example of a more significant tail in the context of Treasury note futures.

Note that the hedge computation in equation (17.6) depends on the time to the date of the cash flow. In general, as the cash flow date approaches the present value effect gets smaller and the tail is reduced. Put another way, the calculated number of futures held to replicate each forward contract increases every day toward one. Since contracts have to be bought in whole numbers, however, the number of contracts actually bought has to change less often. In the preceding example, where the tail is particularly small, an actual hedge would jump at some point from 99 to 100 contracts and stay there to expiration.

A common approximation of the tail arises from the mathematical approximation $1/(1+x) \approx 1-x$ for small values of x. Applying this to equation (17.5), the number of futures contracts equals a fraction $1 - rd/360$ of the

---

number of forward contracts where d is the number of days to the date of the cash flow. In the preceding example, the approximation is $1-^{2.274\%\times215}\!/_{360}$ or 98.64%.

FUTURES ON PRICES IN A TERM STRUCTURE MODEL

A futures contract that based its final settlement price on the then prevailing price of a 90-day zero or deposit would be classified as a futures on a price. The Treasury note and bond contracts to be discussed in Chapter 20, for example, are futures on prices. But, as pointed out in the first section of this chapter, the final settlement of Eurodollar futures contracts are based on the rate of a 90-day deposit. Since 90-day deposits are of very short term, it turns out that the difference between a futures on the deposit price and a futures on the deposit rate is small. Nevertheless, it is conceptually useful to handle each case separately. This section explains the difference between the pricing of forward contracts and the pricing of futures contracts on prices. The next (very brief) section describes the pricing of futures contracts on rates.

Chapter 16 described the pricing of forward contracts in term structure models. To review results, denoting the price of a security today by $P(0)$ and the forward price for delivery on date M by P_{fwd}, Chapter 16 showed that

$$P(0) = E\left[\frac{P(M)}{\prod_{m=0}^{M-1}(1+r_m)}\right] \tag{17.7}$$

$$d(0,M) = E\left[\frac{1}{\prod_{m=0}^{M-1}(1+r_m)}\right] \tag{17.8}$$

and

$$P_{fwd} = P(0)/d(0,M) \tag{17.9}$$

To review the setup in Chapter 16, the risk-neutral process from dates 0 to 2 is assumed to be given by the following tree:

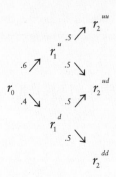

The prices of a particular security in the three states of date 2 are denoted P_2^{uu}, P_2^{ud}, and P_2^{dd}. And, for simplicity, it is assumed that the security makes no cash flows between dates 0 and 2.

To derive the futures price of a security in this context, begin by noting that the futures price for immediate delivery is, by definition, the same as the spot price of the security. Hence, at expiration of a futures contract, the futures price equals the spot price at that time. This reasoning may be applied to construct a tree for the futures price of a security at delivery (i.e., on date 2). Let F_m^i denote the futures price on date m, state i, immediately after the mark-to-market payment due on date m, but, to be consistent with previous notation, let $F(0)$ denote the current futures price. Then,

$$F_2^{uu} = P_2^{uu}$$
$$F_1^{u}$$
$$.6 \quad .5$$
$$F(0) \qquad F_2^{ud} = P_2^{ud}$$
$$.4 \quad .5$$
$$F_1^{d}$$
$$.5$$
$$F_2^{dd} = P_2^{dd}$$

As of the up state on date 1, the futures price is denoted F_1^u. If the price of the underlying moves to P_2^{uu} on date 2, then that will be the date 2 futures price, and the mark-to-market on a long position of one contract will be $P_2^{uu}-F_1^u$. Similarly, if the price moves to P_2^{ud} on date 2, then the mark-to-market will be $P_2^{ud}-F_1^u$. Since the tree has been assumed to be the risk-neutral pricing tree, the value of the contract in the up state of date 1 must equal the expected discounted value of its cash flows. But, by the definition of futures contracts, the value of a futures contract after its mark to market payment must equal zero. Putting these two facts together,

$$\frac{.5 \times \left(P_2^{uu} - F_1^u\right) + .5 \times \left(P_2^{ud} - F_1^u\right)}{1 + r_1^u} = 0 \tag{17.10}$$

Then, solving for the unknown futures price,

$$F_1^u = .5 \times P_2^{uu} + .5 \times P_2^{ud} \tag{17.11}$$

Since the same logic applies to the down state of date 1,

$$F_1^d = .5 \times P_2^{ud} + .5 \times P_2^{dd} \tag{17.12}$$

As of date 0, setting the expected discounted mark-to-market payment equal to zero implies that

$$\frac{.6 \times \left(F_1^u - F(0)\right) + .4 \times \left(F_1^d - F(0)\right)}{1 + r_0} = 0 \tag{17.13}$$

Or,

$$F(0) = .6 \times F_1^u + .4 \times F_1^d \tag{17.14}$$

Substituting (17.11) and (17.12) into (17.14),

$$\begin{aligned} F(0) &= .3 \times P_2^{uu} + .3 \times P_2^{ud} + .2 \times P_2^{ud} + .2 \times P_2^{dd} \\ &= .3 \times P_2^{uu} + .5 \times P_2^{ud} + .2 \times P_2^{dd} \end{aligned} \tag{17.15}$$

In words, under the risk-neutral process the futures price equals the expected price of the underlying security as of the delivery date. More generally,

$$F(0) = E\left[P(M)\right] \tag{17.16}$$

FUTURES ON RATES IN A TERM STRUCTURE MODEL

The final settlement price of a Eurodollar futures contract is 100 minus the 90-day rate. Therefore, the final contract prices are not P_2^{uu}, P_2^{ud}, and P_2^{dd}, as in the previous section, but rather $100-r_2^{uu}$, $100-r_2^{ud}$, and $100-r_2^{dd}$. Following the logic of the previous section after this substitution, the futures price equals the expected value of these outcomes. Denoting the rate on date M by $r(M)$ and the futures price based on the rates as $F^R(0)$,

$$
\begin{aligned}
F^R(0) &= E\big[100 - r(M)\big] \\
&= 100 - E\big[r(M)\big]
\end{aligned}
\tag{17.17}
$$

Defining the futures rate on date 0, r_{fut}, to be 100 minus the futures price,

$$
r_{fut} = 100 - F^R(0) = E\big[r(M)\big]
\tag{17.18}
$$

THE FUTURES-FORWARD DIFFERENCE

This section brings together the results of Chapter 16 and of the two previous sections to be more explicit about the difference between forward and futures prices and between futures and forward rates.

By the definition of covariance, for two random variables G and H,

$$
Cov(G, H) = E\big[G \times H\big] - E\big[G\big] \times E\big[H\big]
\tag{17.19}
$$

Letting $G = P(M)$ and $H = 1/\prod(1+r_m)$, equation (17.19) becomes

$$
Cov\left(P(M), \frac{1}{\prod(1+r_m)}\right) = E\left[\frac{P(M)}{\prod(1+r_m)}\right] - E\big[P(M)\big]E\left[\frac{1}{\prod(1+r_m)}\right]
\tag{17.20}
$$

In words, this covariance equals the expected discounted value minus the discounted expected value. Substituting (17.7), (17.8), and (17.16) into equation (17.20) and rearranging terms,

$$
F(0) = \frac{P(0)}{d(0,M)} - Cov\left(P(M), \frac{1}{\prod(1+r_m)}\right)\Big/ d(0,M)
\tag{17.21}
$$

Finally, substitute (17.9) into (17.21) to obtain

$$
F(0) = P_{fwd} - Cov\left(P(M), \frac{1}{\prod(1+r_m)}\right)\Big/ d(0,M)
\tag{17.22}
$$

Combining (17.22) with the meaning of the covariance term, the difference between the forward price and the futures price is proportional to the difference between the expected discounted value and the discounted expected value.

Since the price of the security on date M is likely to be relatively low if rates from now to date M are relatively high and the price is likely to be relatively high if rates from now to date M are relatively low, the covariance term in equation (17.22) is likely to be positive.[5] If this is indeed the case, it follows that

$$F(0) < P_{fwd} \tag{17.23}$$

The intuition behind equations (17.22) and (17.23) was mentioned in the section about tails. Assume for a moment that the futures and forward price of a security are the same. Daily changes in the value of the forward contract generate no cash flows while daily changes in the value of the futures contract generate mark-to-market payments. While mark-to-market gains can be reinvested and mark-to-market losses must be financed, on average these effects do not cancel out. Rather, on average they make futures contracts less desirable than forward contracts. As bond prices tend to fall when short-term rates are high, when futures suffer a loss this loss has to be financed at relatively high rates. But, when futures enjoy a gain, this gain is reinvested at relatively low rates. On average then, if the futures and forward prices are the same, a long futures position is not so valuable as a long forward position. Therefore, the two contracts are priced properly relative to one another only if the futures price is lower than the forward price, as stated by (17.23).

The discussion to this point is sufficient for note and bond futures, treated in detail in Chapter 20. For Eurodollar futures, however, it is more

---

[5]This discussion does not necessary apply to forwards and futures on securities outside the fixed income context. Consider, for example, a forward and a future on oil. In this case it is more difficult to determine the covariance between the discounting factor and the underlying security. If this covariance happens to be positive, then equation (17.23) holds for oil. But if the covariance is zero, then forward and futures prices are the same. Similarly, if the covariance is negative, then futures prices exceed forward prices.

common to express the difference between futures and forward contracts in terms of rates rather than prices.

Given forward prices of zero coupon bonds, forward rates are computed as described in Chapter 2. If P_{fwd} denotes the forward price of a 90-day zero, the simple interest forward, r_{fwd} is such that

$$P_{fwd} = \frac{1}{1 + 90 \times r_{fwd}/360} \tag{17.24}$$

The Eurodollar futures rate is given by (17.18). To compare the futures and forward rates, note that

$$F(0) = E[P(M)] = E\left[\frac{1}{1 + 90 \times r(M)/360}\right] \tag{17.25}$$

where the first equality is (17.16) and the second follows from the definitions of $P(M)$, $r(M)$, and simple interest. Using a special case of Jensen's Inequality,[6]

$$E\left[\frac{1}{1 + 90 \times r(M)/360}\right] > \frac{1}{1 + 90 \times E[r(M)]/360} \tag{17.26}$$

Finally, combining (17.18), (17.23), (17.24), (17.25), and (17.26),

$$P_{fwd} = \frac{1}{1 + 90 \times r_{fwd}/360} > F(0) > \frac{1}{1 + 90 \times r_{fut}/360} \tag{17.27}$$

This equation shows that the difference between forwards and futures on rates has two separate effects. The first inequality represents the difference between the forward price and the futures on a price. This difference is properly called the *futures-forward* effect. The second inequality represents the difference between a futures on a price and a futures on a rate which, as evident from (17.26), is a convexity effect. The sum, expressed as the difference between the observed forward rates on deposits and Eurodollar futures rates, will be referred to as the total futures-forward effect.

---

[6]See equation (10.6).

It follows immediately from (17.27) that

$$r_{fut} > r_{fwd} \tag{17.28}$$

According to (17.28), the futures rate exceeds the forward rate or, equivalently, the total futures-forward difference is positive. But, since the futures-forward effect depends on the covariance term in equation (17.22), the magnitude of this effect depends on the particular term structure model being used. It is beyond the mathematical level of this book to compute the futures-forward effect for a given term structure model. However, to illustrate orders of magnitude, results from a particularly simple model are invoked. In a normal model with no mean reversion, continuous compounding, and continuous mark-to-market payments, the difference between the futures rate and the forward rate of a zero due to the pure futures-forward effect is

$$\sigma^2 t^2 / 2 \tag{17.29}$$

where σ^2 is the annual basis point volatility of the short-term rate and t is the time to expiration, in years, of the forward or futures contract. In the same model, the difference due to the convexity effect is

$$\sigma^2 \beta t / 2 \tag{17.30}$$

where β is the maturity, in years, of the underlying zero. The total difference between the futures and forward rates is the sum of (17.29) and (17.30). In the case of Eurodollar futures on 90-day deposits, β is approximately .25 and the convexity effect is approximately $\sigma^2 t / 8$. Note that, except for very small times to expiration, the difference due to the pure futures-forward effect is larger than that due to the convexity effect and, for long times to expiration, the contribution of the convexity effect to the difference is negligible.

Figure 17.1 graphs the total futures-forward effect for each contract as of November 30, 2001, in the simple model described assuming that volatility is 100 basis points a year across the curve. The graph illustrates that, as evident from equation (17.29), the effect increases with the square of time to contract expiration.

EDH2 matures on December 20, 2002, about .3 years from the pricing date. For this contract, the total futures-forward effect in basis points is practically zero:

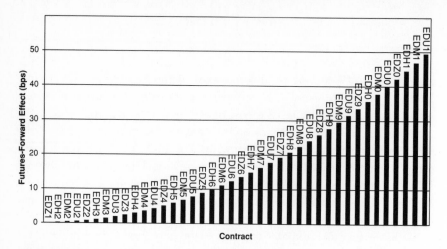

FIGURE 17.1 Futures-Forward Effect in a Normal Model with No Mean Reversion and an Annual Volatility of 100 Basis Points

$$10,000 \times \left[\frac{.01^2 \times .3^2}{2} + \frac{.01^2 \times .3}{8} \right] = .0825 \tag{17.31}$$

The effect is not trivial, though, for later-maturing contracts. EDZ6 matures on December 20, 2006, about 5.05 years from the pricing date. In this case the total futures-forward effect in basis points is

$$10,000 \times \left[\frac{.01^2 \times 5.05^2}{2} + \frac{.01^2 \times 5.05}{8} \right] = 13.4 \tag{17.32}$$

And, as can be seen from the graph, for the contracts with the longest expiry the effect approaches 50 basis points.

The terms (17.29) and (17.30) explicitly show that the total futures-forward effect increases with interest rate volatility. The pure futures-forward effect arises because mark-to-market gains are invested at low rates while mark-to-market losses are financed at high rates. With no interest rate volatility there are no mark-to-market cash flows and no investment or financing of those flows. The convexity effect also disappears without volatility, as demonstrated in Chapter 10.

TED SPREADS

As discussed in Part Three, making judgments about the value of a security relative to other securities requires that traders and investors select some securities that they consider to be fairly priced. Eurodollar futures are often, although certainly not always, thought of as fairly priced for two somewhat related reasons. First, they are quite liquid relative to many other fixed income securities. Second, they are immune to many individual security effects that complicate the determination of fair value for other securities. Consider, for example, a two-year bond issued by the Federal National Mortgage Association (FNMA), a government-sponsored enterprise (GSE). The price of this bond relative to FNMA bonds of similar maturity is determined by its supply outstanding, its special repo rate, and the distribution of its ownership across investor classes. Hence, interest rates implied by this FNMA bond might be different from rates implied by similar FNMA bonds for reasons unrelated to the time value of money. With 90-day Eurodollar futures, by contrast, there is only one contract reflecting the time value of money over a particular three-month period. Also, there is no limit to the supply of any Eurodollar futures contract: whenever a new buyer and seller appear a new contract is created. In short, the prices of Eurodollar contracts are much less subject to the idiosyncratic forces impacting the prices of particular bonds.

TED spreads[7] use rates implied by Eurodollar futures to assess the value of a security relative to Eurodollar futures rates or to assess the value of one security relative to another. The idea is to find the spread such that discounting cash flows at Eurodollar futures rates minus that spread produces the security's market price. Put another way, it is the negative of the option-adjusted-spread (OAS) of a bond when Eurodollar futures rates are used for discounting.

As an example, consider the FNMA 4s of August 15, 2003, priced as of November 30, 2001, to settle on the next business day, December 3, 2001. The next cash flow of the bond is on February 15, 2002. Referring to Table 17.1, EDZ1 indicates that the three-month futures rate starting

---

[7]TED spreads were originally used to compare T-bill futures, which are no longer actively traded, and Eurodollar futures. The name came from the combination of T for Treasury and ED for Eurodollar.

from December 19, 2001, is 1.9175%. Assume that the rate on the *stub*—the period of time from the settlement date to the beginning of the period spanned by the first Eurodollar contract—is 2.085%. (This stub rate can be calculated from various short-term LIBOR rates.) Since there are 16 days from December 3, 2001, to December 19, 2001, and 58 days from December 19, 2001, to February 15, 2002, the discount factor applied to the first coupon payment using futures rates is

$$\frac{1}{\left(1 + .02085\% \times 16 \big/_{360}\right)\left(1 + .019175\% \times 58 \big/_{360}\right)} \tag{17.33}$$

Subtracting a spread s, this factor becomes

$$\frac{1}{\left(1 + (.02085\% - s) \times 16 \big/_{360}\right)\left(1 + (.019175\% - s) \times 58 \big/_{360}\right)} \tag{17.34}$$

The next coupon payment is due on August 15, 2002. Table 17.3 shows the relevant Eurodollar futures contracts and rates required to discount the August 15, 2002, coupon. Adding a spread to these rates, this factor is

$$\frac{1}{\left(1 + (2.085\% - s) \times 16 \big/_{360}\right)\left(1 + (1.9175\% - s) \times 91 \big/_{360}\right)\left(1 + (2.05\% - s) \times 91 \big/_{360}\right)\left(1 + (2.50\% - s) \times 57 \big/_{360}\right)} \tag{17.35}$$

Proceeding in this way, using the Eurodollar futures rates from Table 17.1, the present value of each payment can be expressed in terms of the TED spread.[8] The next step is to find the spread such that the sum of these present values equals the full price of the bond.

TABLE 17.3 Discounting the August 15, 2002, Coupon Payment

From	To	Days	Symbol	Rate(%)
12/3/01	12/19/01	16	STUB	2.0850
12/19/01	03/20/02	91	EDZ1	1.9175
3/20/02	06/19/02	91	EDH2	2.0500
6/19/02	08/15/02	57	EDM2	2.5000

---

[8]Since February 15, 2003, falls on a weekend, the coupon payment due on that date is deferred to the next business day, in this case February 17, 2003. This actual payment date is used in the TED spread calculation.

The price of the FNMA 4s of August 15, 2003, on November 30, 2001, was 101.7975. The first coupon payment and the accrued interest calculation differ from the examples of Chapter 4. First, these agency bonds were issued with a *short first coupon*. The issue date, from which coupon interest begins to accrue, was not August 15, 2001, but August 27, 2001. Put another way, the first coupon payment represents interest not from August 15, 2001, to February 15, 2002, as is usually the case, but from August 27, 2001, to February 15, 2002. Consequently, the first coupon payment will be less than half of the annual 4%. Second, unlike the U.S. Treasury market, the U.S. agency market uses a 30/360-day count convention that assumes each month has 30 days. Table 17.4 illustrates this convention by computing the number of days from August 27, 2001, to February 15, 2002. Note the assumption that there are only three days from August 27, 2001, to the end of August, that there are 30 days in October, and so on.

The coupon payment on February 15, 2001, is assumed to cover the 168 days computed in Table 17.4 out of a six-month coupon period of 180 days. At an annual rate of 4%, the semiannual coupon payment is, therefore,

$$\frac{4\%}{2}\frac{168}{180} = 1.8667\% \tag{17.36}$$

TABLE 17.4 Example of the 30/360 Convention: The Number of Days from August 27, 2001, to February 15, 2002

From	To	Days
8/27/01	08/30/01	3
9/1/01	09/30/01	30
10/1/01	10/30/01	30
11/1/01	11/30/01	30
12/1/01	12/30/01	30
1/1/02	01/30/02	30
2/1/02	02/15/02	15
Total		168

All subsequent coupon payments are, as usual, 2% of face value.

To determine the accrued interest for settlement on December 3, 2001, calculate the number of 30/360 days from August 27, 2001, to December 3, 2001. Since this comes to 96 days, the accrued interest is

$$\frac{4\%}{2}\frac{96}{180} = 1.0667\% \qquad\qquad (17.37)$$

To summarize, for settlement on December 3, 2001, the price of 101.7975 plus accrued interest of 1.0667 gives an invoice price of 102.8642. The first coupon payment of 1.8667, later coupon payments of 2, and the terminal principal payment are discounted using the discount factors, described earlier, which depend on the TED spread s. Solving produces a TED spread of 15.6 basis points.

The interpretation of this TED spread is that the agency is 15.6 basis points rich to LIBOR as measured by the futures rates. Whether these 15.6 basis points are justified or not requires more analysis. Most importantly, is the superior credit quality of FNMA relative to that of the banks used to fix LIBOR worth 15.6 basis points on a bond with approximately two years to maturity? Chapter 18 will treat this type of question in more detail.

As mentioned earlier, a TED spread may be used not only to measure the value of a bond relative to futures rates but also to measure the value of one bond relative to another. The FNMA 4.75s of November 14, 2003, for example, priced at 103.1276 as of November 30, 2001, had a TED spread of 20.5 basis points. One might argue that it does not make sense for the 4.75s of November 14, 2003, to trade 20.5 basis points rich to LIBOR while the 4s of August 15, 2003, maturing only three months earlier, trade only 15.6 basis points rich.[9] The following section describes how to trade this difference in TED spreads.

Discounting a bond's cash flows using futures rates has an obvious theoretical flaw. According to the results of Part One, discounting should be done at forward rates, not futures rates. But, as shown in the previous section, the magnitude of the difference between forward and futures rates is relatively small for futures expiring shortly. The longest futures rate required to discount the cash flows of the 4.75s of November 14, 2003, is

---

[9]The two bonds finance at equivalent rates in the repo market.

EDU3 expiring on September 15, 2003, that is, about 1.8 years from the settlement date of December 3, 2001. Using the simple model mentioned in the previous section with a volatility of 100 basis points in order to record an order of magnitude, (17.29) and (17.30) combine to produce a total futures-forward difference for EDU3 of about 1.8 basis points. In addition, when using TED spreads to compare one bond to a similar bond, discounting with futures rates instead of forward rates uses rates too high for both bonds. This means that the relative valuation of the two bonds is probably not very much affected by the theoretically incorrect choice of discounting rates.

APPLICATION: Trading TED Spreads

A trader believes that the FNMA 4s of August 15, 2003, are too cheap to LIBOR at a TED spread of 15.6 basis points, or, equivalently, that the TED spread should be higher. To take advantage of this perceived mispricing the trader plans to buy $100,000,000 face of the bonds and to sell Eurodollar futures. How many of each futures contract should be sold? The procedure is as follows.

1. Decrease a futures rate by one basis point.
2. Keeping the TED spread unchanged, calculate the value of $100,000,000 of the bond with this perturbed rate and subtract the market price of the position. In other words, calculate the bucket risk of the position with respect to that futures rate.
3. Divide the bucket risk by $25, the value of one basis point to a position of one Eurodollar contract.
4. Repeat steps 1 to 3 for all pertinent futures rates.

For example, decreasing EDU2 from 3.055% to 3.045% while keeping the TED spread at 15.6 basis points raises the invoice price of the bond from 102.8642 to 102.866685. On a position of $100,000,000 this price change is worth

$$\$100,000,000\times\left(102.866685\%-102.8642\%\right)=\$2,485 \tag{17.38}$$

Therefore, to hedge against a change in EDU2 of one basis point, sell $\$2,485/\$25$ or about 99 contracts. Repeating this exercise for each contract gives the results in Table 17.5.

Intuitively, since the value of the bonds is about $103,000,000, hedging a forward rate

TABLE 17.5 Hedging $100,000,000 of FNMA 4s of August 15, 2003, with Eurodollar Futures

Contract Symbol	Number to Sell
STUB	18
EDZ1	103
EDH2	102
EDM2	101
EDU2	99
EDZ2	99
EDH3	97
EDM3	62

with a $1,000,000 futures contract requires about 103 contracts. Stub risk, of course, an exposure of only 16 days, requires only 18 contracts: $103 \times {}^{16}/_{91}$ equals 18. The full 103 contracts of EDZ1 are required, but the tail reduces the required number of contracts with later expirations. The tail on the EDH3, for example, reduces the hedge by six contracts. The reduced amount of EDM3 is mostly because the contract is required to cover only 57 days of risk and partly because of the tail. (The relevant number of days for the stub and EDM3 calculations appear in Table 17.3.)

Summing the number of contracts in Table 17.5, 681 contracts should be sold against the bonds. Imagine that all Eurodollar rates increase by one basis point but that the price of the 4s of August 15, 2003, stays the same. The short position in Eurodollar futures will make $681 \times 25 or $17,025, while the bond position will, by assumption, not change in value. At the same time, by the definition of a TED spread, the TED spread of the bond will increase from 15.6 to 16.6 basis points. In this sense the trade described profits $17,025 for each TED spread basis point.

The same caveat with respect to valuing bonds using TED spreads must be made with respect to hedging bonds with Eurodollar futures contracts. If volatility were to increase, the futures-forward difference would increase. But if forward rates rise relative to futures rates, a position long bonds and short futures will lose money. This is an unintended exposure of the trade described arising from hedging bond prices or forwards with futures. Again, however, for relatively short-term securities the effect is usually small.

The other trade suggested by the previous section is to buy the 4s of August 15, 2003, at a TED of 15.6 basis points and sell the 4.75s of November 14, 2003, at a TED of 20.5 basis points. This trade is typically designed not to express an opinion about the absolute level of TED spreads but, rather, to express the opinion that the TED of the 4.75s of November 15, 2003, is too high relative to that of the 4s of August 15,2003. In trader jargon, this trade is usually intended to express an opinion about the *spread of spreads*.

To construct a spread of spreads trade, first calculate the DV01 values of the two bonds. In this case the values are 1.67 for the 4s of August 15, 2003, and 1.91 for the 4.75s of November 15, 2003, implying a sale of $87,434,600 4.75s against a purchase of $100,000,000 4s. Next, calculate the Eurodollar futures position required to put on a TED spread trade for each leg of the position. Third, net out the Eurodollar futures positions. Table 17.6 shows the results of these steps. Viewing the trade as a combination of two TED spreads makes it clear that the trade will make money if the TED of the 4s of August 15, 2003, rises and if the TED of the 4.75s of November 15, 2003, falls. But it is the hedging of the DV01 of the bonds that makes the trade a pure bet on the spread of spreads. The DV01 hedge forces the sum of the net Eurodollar futures contracts to equal approximately zero.[10] This means that if bond prices do not change but all futures rates increase or decrease by one basis point, so that both TED spreads increase or decrease by one basis point, then the trade will not make or lose money. In other words, the trade makes or loses

TABLE 17.6   Spread of Spreads Trade

Buy $100,000,000 FNMA 4s of August 15, 2003
Sell $87,434,600 FNMA 4.75s of November 15, 2003

Contract Symbol	Futures to Sell vs. 8/03s	Futures to Buy vs. 11/03s	Net Purchase
STUB	18	16	−2
EDZ1	103	91	−12
EDH2	102	90	−12
EDM2	101	89	−12
EDU2	99	88	−11
EDZ2	99	87	−12
EDH3	97	86	−11
EDM3	62	84	22
EDU3		53	53

---

[10]The net futures position is not exactly zero because DV01 is based on the change of semiannually compounded rates rather than 30/360 rates. If the bond holdings are set so that the net futures position is exactly zero, then the trade will be exactly neutral with respect to parallel shifts in futures rates but not exactly neutral with respect to equal changes in bond yields.

money only if the TED spreads change relative to one another, as intended. Without the DV01 hedge, the net position in Eurodollar futures contracts would not be zero and the trade would make or lose money if bond prices stayed the same while all futures rates rose or fell by one basis point.

Chapter 18 will present *asset swap spreads* that measure the value of a bond relative to the swap curve and asset swap trades that trade bonds against swaps. While asset swap spreads are a more accurate way to value a bond relative to LIBOR, TED spreads are still useful for two reasons. First, for bonds maturing within a few years, TED spreads are relatively accurate. Second, for bonds of relatively short maturity, TED spread trades are easier to execute than asset swap trades because Eurodollar futures of relatively short maturity are more liquid than swaps of relatively short maturity.

FED FUNDS

In the course of doing business, banks often find that they have cash balances to invest or cash deficits to finance. The market in which banks trade funds overnight to manage their cash balances is called the *federal funds* or *fed funds* market. While only banks can borrow or lend in the fed funds market, the importance of banks in the financial system causes other short-term interest rates to move with the fed funds rate.

The Board of Governors of the Federal Reserve System ("the Fed") sets monetary policy in the United States. An important component of this policy is the *targeting* or *pegging* of the fed funds rate at a level consistent with price stability and economic well-being. Since banks trade freely in the fed funds market, the Fed cannot directly set the fed funds rate. But, by using the tools at its disposal, including buying and selling short-term securities or repo on short-term securities, the Fed has enormous power to influence the fed funds rate and to keep it close to the desired target.

The Federal Reserve calculates and publishes the weighted average rate at which banks borrow and lend money in the fed funds market over each business day. This rate is called the *fed funds effective rate*. Figure 17.2 shows the time series of the fed funds target rate against the effective rate from January 1994 to September 2001. For the most part, the Fed succeeds in keeping the fed funds rate close to the target rate. The average difference between the two rates over the sample period is only 2.2 basis points.

While the fed funds rate is usually close to the target rate, Figure

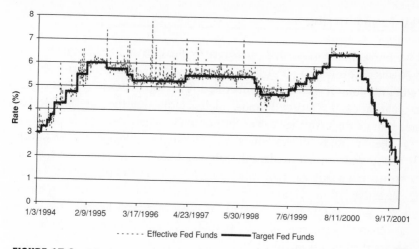

FIGURE 17.2   The Fed Funds Effective Rate versus the Fed Funds Target Rate

17.2 shows that the two rates are sometimes very far apart. Sometimes this happens because temporary, sharp swings in the demand or supply of funds are not, for one reason or another, counterbalanced by the Fed. Other times, the Fed decides to abandon its target temporarily in pursuit of some other policy objective. During times of financial upheaval, for example, the value of liquidity or cash rises dramatically. Individuals might rush to withdraw cash from their bank accounts. Banks, other financial institutions, and corporations might be reluctant to lend cash, even if it were secured by collateral. (See the application at the end of Chapter 15.) As a result, otherwise sound and creditworthy institutions might become insolvent as a consequence of not being able to raise funds. At times like these the Fed "injects liquidity into the system" by lending cash on acceptable collateral. As a result of this action, the fed funds effective rate might very well drop below the stated target rate. There are two particularly recent and dramatic examples of this in Figure 17.2. First, the Fed injected liquidity in anticipation of Y2K problems that never, in fact, materialized. This resulted in the fed funds rate on December 31, 1999, being about 150 basis points below target. Second, to contain the financial disruption following the events of September 11, 2001, the Fed injected liquidity and the fed funds rate fell to about 180 basis points below target.

FED FUNDS FUTURES

Like Eurodollar futures, *fed funds futures* provide another means by which to hedge exposure to short-term interest rates. Table 17.7 lists the liquid fed funds contracts as of December 4, 2001. Note that the symbol is a concatenation of "FF" for fed funds, a letter indicating the month of the contract, and a digit for the year of the contract.

The fed funds futures contract is designed as a hedge to a $5,000,000 30-day deposit in fed funds. First, the final settlement price of a fed funds contract in a particular month is set to 100 minus 100 times the average of the effective fed funds rate over that month. In November 2001, for example, the average rate was 2.087% so the contract settled at 97.913. Second, since changing the rate of a $5,000,000 30-day loan by one basis point changes the interest payment by

$$\$5,000,000 \times \frac{.0001 \times 30}{360} = \$41.67 \qquad (17.39)$$

the mark-to-market payment of the contract is set at $41.67 per basis point.

To see how the fed funds futures contract works as a hedge, consider the case of a small regional bank that has surplus cash of $5,000,000 over the month of November 2001. The bank plans to lend this $5,000,000 overnight in the fed funds market over the month but wants to hedge the risk that a falling fed funds rate will reduce the interest earned in the fed funds market. Therefore, the bank buys one November fed funds futures contract at the close of business on October 31, 2001, for 97.79, implying a rate of 2.21%.

TABLE 17.7   Fed Funds Futures as of December 4, 2001

Symbol	Expiration	Price	Rate
FFZ1	12/31/01	98.155	1.845
FFF2	01/31/02	98.235	1.765
FFG2	02/28/02	98.290	1.710
FFH2	03/31/02	98.245	1.755
FFJ2	04/30/02	98.200	1.800
FFK2	05/30/02	98.100	1.900

Recalling that the average fed funds rate in November 2001 was 2.087, over the month the bank earns interest of[11]

$$\$5,000,000 \times \frac{2.087\% \times 30}{360} = \$8,695.83 \qquad (17.40)$$

Also, an average rate of 2.087% implies a final settlement price of 97.913, so the bank gains 97.913–97.79 or 12.3 basis points on its fed funds contract. At \$41.67 per basis point, the total gain comes to 12.3×\$41.67 or \$512.54. Together with the interest payment then, the bank earns \$9,208.37. But this is almost exactly the interest implied by the 2.21% rate of the fed funds futures contract purchased on October 31, 2001:

$$\$5,000,000 \times \frac{2.21\% \times 30}{360} = \$9,208.33 \qquad (17.41)$$

Hence, by combining lending in the fed funds market and trading in fed funds futures, the bank can lock in the lending rate implied by the fed funds contracts.

Note that the hedge is easy to calculate for any other amount of surplus cash. If the bank has \$20,000,000 to invest, for example, the hedge would be to buy four fed funds contracts: Since each contract has a notional amount of \$5,000,000, four contracts are required to hedge an investment of \$20,000,000.

To hedge over a month with 28 or 31 days, the number of contracts has to be adjusted very slightly. The contract value of \$41.67 per basis point is based on 30 days of interest. To hedge a loan with 28 days of interest requires $^{28}/_{30}$ times the amount of the investment. So, hedging a \$100,000,000 investment over February requires $20 \times (^{28}/_{30})$ or 19 contracts. Similarly,

---

[11]This hedging example implicitly assumes that the bank does not earn interest on interest on its fed funds lending. This is consistent with the assumption of the fed funds contract that the relevant interest rate is the average of effective fed funds over the month. To the extent that the bank does earn interest on interest, the fed funds contract setting is not consistent with the lending context and the hedge works less precisely. And, while discussing approximations, since fed funds futures are usually liquid for only the next five months or so, tails are not usually big enough to warrant attention.

hedging a $100,000,000 investment over December requires $20\times(^{31}/_{30})$ or 21 contracts.

This hedging example uses a bank because only banks can participate in the fed funds market. But, as mentioned earlier, many short-term rates are highly correlated with the fed funds rate. Therefore, other financial institutions, corporations, and investors can use fed funds futures to hedge their individual short-term rate risk. For example, in October 2001 a corporation discovers that it needs to borrow money over the month of December. To hedge against the risk that rates rise and increase the cost of borrowing, the company can sell December fed funds futures. While this hedge will protect the corporation from changes in the general level of interest rates, fed funds futures will not protect against corporate borrowing rates rising relative to fed funds nor, of course, against that particular corporation's borrowing rate rising relative to other rates. The difference between the actual risk (e.g., changes in a corporation's borrowing rate) and the risk reduced by the hedge (e.g., changes in the fed funds rate) is an example of *basis risk*.

APPLICATION: Fed Funds Contracts and Predicted Fed Action

Under the chairmanship of Alan Greenspan the Fed has established informal and unofficial rules under which it changes the fed funds target rate. In particular, the Fed usually changes the target by some multiple of 25 basis points only after announcing the change at the conclusion of a regularly scheduled Federal Open Market Committee (FOMC) meeting. But this rule is not always followed: On April 18, 2001, the Fed announced a surprise cut in the target rate from 5% to 4.5%. For the most part, however, the current policy of the Fed is to take action on FOMC meeting dates.

The prices of fed funds futures imply a particular view about the future actions of the Fed. Consider the following data as of December 4, 2001.

1. The fed funds target rate is 2%.
2. The average fed funds effective rate from December 1, 2001, to December 4, 2001, was 2.025%.
3. The next FOMC meeting is scheduled for December 11, 2001.
4. The December fed funds contract closed at an implied rate of 1.845%.

What is the fed funds futures market predicting about the result of the December FOMC meeting?

Assuming that the Fed will not change its target before the next FOMC meeting, a reasonable estimate for the fed funds effective rate from December 5, 2001, to December 10, 2001, is 2%. (An expert in the money market might be able to refine this estimate by one or two basis points by considering conditions in the banking system.) From December 11, 2001, to December 31, 2001, the rate will be whatever target is set at the FOMC meeting. Let that new target rate be r. Then, the average December fed funds rate combines four days (December 1, 2001, to December 4, 2001) at an average of 2.025%, six days (December 5, 2001, to December 10, 2001) at an average of 2%, and 21 days (December 11, 2001, to December 31, 2001) at an average of r. Setting this average equal to the implied rate from the December fed funds futures gives the following equation:

$$\frac{4 \times 2.025\% + 6 \times 2\% + 21 \times r}{31} = 1.845\% \qquad (17.42)$$

Solving, r=1.766%. This means that the market expects a cut in the target rate by about 25 basis points, from 2% to about 1.75%.[12]

The fact that 1.766% is slightly above 1.75% might mean that the market puts some very small probability on the event that the Fed will not lower its target rate. Assume, for example, that with probability p the Fed leaves the target rate at 2% and that with probability $1-p$ it lowers the target rate to 1.75%. Then an expected target rate of 1.766% implies that

$$p \times 2\% + (1 - p) \times 1.75\% = 1.766\% \qquad (17.43)$$

Solving, p=6.4%. To summarize, one interpretation of the December fed funds contract price is that the market puts a 6.4% probability on the target rate being left unchanged and a 93.6% probability on the target rate being cut to 1.75%.

Another interpretation of the December contract price is that the market assumes that the Fed will cut the target rate to 1.75% on December 11, 2001. But, for technical reasons, the market expects that the effective funds will trade, on average, 1.6 basis points above the target rate from December 11, 2001, to December 31, 2001. In any case, the analysis of the December contract price reveals that the market puts a very high probability on a 25-basis point cut on December 11, 2001.

This exercise can be extended to extract market opinion about subsequent meetings. After the December meeting, the three scheduled FOMC meeting dates[13] are for January 30,

---

[12]This calculation ignores any risk premium or convexity in the price of the December fed funds contract. Given the very short term of the rate in question, this simplification is harmless.

[13]When the FOMC meets for two days, the announcement about the target rate is expected on the second day.

2002, March 19, 2002, and May 7, 2002. Table 17.7 lists the fed funds futures prices through the May contract. Table 17.8 shows a scenario for changes in the target rate that match the futures prices to within a basis point.[14]

Many fixed income strategists thought the expected changes in the target rate implied by fed funds futures as of December 4, 2001, were not reasonable. As can be seen from Table 17.8, the fed funds rate was expected to fall over the subsequent two meetings but then rise over the next two meetings. (The same conclusion emerges from simply observing that rates implied by futures declined through the February contract and then increased.) According to some this view represented a wildly optimistic prediction that by March 2002 the U.S. economy would have rapidly emerged from a recession and that the Fed would then raise rates to fight off inflation. According to others the view expressed by fed funds futures ignored the reluctance of the Fed to switch rapidly from a policy of lowering rates to a policy of raising rates.

Other commentators thought that the March, April, and May fed funds contracts at the beginning of December were not reflecting the market's view of future Fed actions at all. The dramatic sell-off in the bond market at the time had caused large liquidations of long positions, particularly in a popular speculative security, the March Eurodollar contract. The selling of this security depressed its price relative to expectations of future rates and dragged down the prices of the related fed funds futures contracts along with it. According to these commentators, this was the cause of the relatively high rates implied by the March through May contracts in Table 17.7.

TABLE 17.8 Scenario for Fed Target Rate Changes, in Basis Points, Matching Fed Funds Futures as of December 4, 2001

Meeting Date	Expected Action
12/11/01	−23
01/30/02	−6
03/19/02	9
05/7/02	12

---

[14]Like the analysis of the December contract alone, this analysis ignores risk premium and convexity. The simplification is still relatively harmless as the relevant time span is only six months.

APPENDIX 17A
HEDGING TO DATES NOT MATCHING FED FUNDS
AND EURODOLLAR FUTURES EXPIRATIONS

The examples showing how to hedge with fed funds and Eurodollar futures have all assumed that the deposit or security being hedged starts and matures on the same dates as some futures contract. In practice, of course, the hedging problem is usually more complicated. This section uses one example to illustrate the relevant issues.

As part of a larger position established on November 10, 2001, a trader will be lending $50,000,000 on an overnight basis from November 10, 2001, to March 30, 2002. In addition, some combination of fed funds and Eurodollar futures will be used to hedge the risk that rates may fall over that period.

To hedge the risk from November 10, 2001, through the end of November the trader will buy November fed funds futures. How many contracts should be bought? Even though the trade is at risk in November for the remaining 20 days only, the correct hedge is to buy 10 fed funds futures contracts against the $50,000,000 lending program. To see this, assume that the overnight rate falls by 10 basis points on November 10, 2001, and remains at that level for the rest of the month. Since fed funds futures settle based on an average rate over the month, by close of business on November 10, 2001, the average for the first 10 days of November has already been set. Equivalently, only the average for the last 20 days is affected. Therefore, the average rate for the November fed funds contract will fall not by 10 basis points but by $(^{20}/_{30}) \times 10$ or 6.67 basis points. This implies a profit of 41.67×6.67 or about $277.80 per contract and a profit of $2,778 on all 10 contracts. But that is the cost of a 10-basis point drop in the lending rate on $50,000,000 over the 20 days from November 10, 2001, to November 30, 2001: $50,000,000 \times (^{20 \times .001}/_{360})$ or $2,778. In summary, since the interest rate sensitivity of both the November contract and the November portion of the lending program falls as November progresses, the correct hedge, even when put on in the middle of the month, is to cover the face amount for the entire month.

Having covered the risk in November, the trader still needs to cover the 119 days of risk from December 1, 2001, to March 30, 2002.[15] Since EDZ1 covers the 90 days from December 19, 2001, to March 19, 2002, one possi-

---

[15]One-month LIBOR contracts also trade and they mesh with the three-month contracts. This means that the trader could buy a November LIBOR contract and the

ble hedge is to buy $50 \times {}^{119}/_{90}$ or approximately 66 EDZ1. The problem with this hedge is that, as mentioned earlier, there is a Fed meeting on December 11, 2001. If views about Fed action were to change, EDZ1 would fully reflect that, even though the lending program from December 1, 2001, to December 19, 2001, would be unaffected. This is the problem with *stacking* the risk from December 1, 2001, to December 19, 2001, onto a Eurodollar future covering the period December 19, 2001, to March 19, 2002.

Another solution is to buy 19 days' worth of protection from December fed funds futures—that is, $({}^{50}/_5) \times ({}^{19}/_{30})$ or about six contracts—and then some EDZ1. The problem here is that both the December fed funds contract and EDZ1 cover the period from December 19, 2001, to the end of December. Therefore, the hedge will again be too sensitive to the days after the Fed meeting relative to the sensitivity of the lending program being hedged.

When implementing this second hedge, the trader will have to adjust holdings of the December fed funds contract as December progresses. Consider the situation on December 10, 2001. Only nine days of risk remain to be covered by the fed funds futures, while the original hedge faced 19 days. Hence, by December 10, 2001, the trader will have had to pare down the number of December contracts from six to $({}^{50}/_5) \times ({}^9/_{30})$ or three contracts.

No matter which decision the trader makes—to buy 66 EDZ1 or a combination of FFZ1 and EDZ1—the hedge will have to be adjusted when EDZ1 expires on December 17, 2001. EDZ1 protected against changes in forward rates from December 19, 2001, to March 19, 2002, but once the contract expires, the protection expires with it. Therefore, on December 17, 2001, the trader will have to buy fed funds futures to hedge against rates falling in December and subsequent months.

In light of the stacking and maintenance difficulties of hedging with Eurodollar futures, the trader might consider buying December through March fed funds futures. In this example the fed funds futures will probably be liquid enough for the purpose for two reasons. First, the last contract expiration is not very far away. Second, when the Fed is actively changing the fed funds target rate the liquidity of fed funds futures tends to be high. Conveniently, this means that when stacking risk with Eurodollar futures is particularly problematic the fed funds futures solution becomes especially easy to implement.

December Eurodollar contract to hedge December seamlessly. In the third week of November, however, the LIBOR contract will expire and the trader will be left with a problem analogous to the one described in the text.

CHAPTER 18

Interest Rate Swaps

SWAP CASH FLOWS

From nonexistence in 1980, swaps have grown into a very large and liquid market in which participants manage their interest rate risk. For discussion, consider the following interest rate swap depicted in Figure 18.1. On November 26, 2001, no cash is exchanged, but two parties make the following agreement. Party A agrees to pay 5.688% on $100,000,000 to party B every six months for 10 years while party B agrees to pay three-month LIBOR on $100,000,000 to party A every three months for 10 years. Since three-month LIBOR was set at 2.156% on November 26, 2001, the first of the LIBOR payments is based on a rate of 2.156%. Subsequent payments, however, depend on the future realized values of three-month LIBOR.

In the terminology of the swap market, 5.688% is the *fixed rate*, and three-month LIBOR is the *floating rate*. Party A *pays fixed* and *receives floating*, party B *receives fixed* and *pays floating*, and the $100,000,000 is called the *notional amount*. The word notional is used rather than principal because the $100,000,000 is never exchanged: This amount is used only to compute the interest payments of the swap. Finally, the last payment date is the *maturity* or *termination* date of the swap.

Panel I of Table 18.1 lists the current value of three-month LIBOR and

FIGURE 18.1 Example of an Interest Rate Swap

TABLE 18.1   Two Years of Cash Flows from the Perspective of the Fixed Payer

Fixed rate: 5.688%
Notional amount ($):   100,000,000

Panel I		Panel II				
Date	3-Month LIBOR	Date	Actual Days	Floating Receipt($)	30/360 Days	Fixed Payment($)
11/26/01	2.156%	11/28/01				
02/26/02	2.000%	02/28/02	92	550,883	90	
05/26/02	1.900%	05/28/02	89	494,444	90	2,844,000
08/26/02	2.000%	08/28/02	92	485,556	90	
11/26/02	2.100%	11/29/02	93	516,667	91	2,859,800
02/26/03	2.200%	02/28/03	91	530,833	89	
05/28/03	2.300%	05/28/03	89	543,889	90	2,828,200
08/26/03	2.400%	08/28/03	92	587,778	90	
		11/28/03	92	613,333	90	2,844,000

assumed levels for the future. (These assumed levels are used only to illustrate the calculation of cash flows.) Panel II lists the first two years of cash flows from the point of view of the fixed payer under the swap agreement.

As swaps typically settle T+2, this swap is assumed to settle two business days after the trade, on November 28, 2001, meaning that the swap is on from November 28, 2001, to November 28, 2011. Floating payment dates, therefore, are on the 28th day of the month every three months, unless that day is a holiday. Similarly, fixed payment dates are on the 28th day of the month every six months unless that day is a holiday. Short-term LIBOR loans or deposits also settle two business days after the trade date. For example, three-month LIBOR on May 26, 2002, covers the three-month period starting from May 28, 2002.

Floating rate cash flows are determined using the actual/360 convention, so, for example, the floating cash flow due on May 28, 2002, is

$$\$100,000,000 \times \frac{2\% \times 89}{360} = \$494,444 \qquad (18.1)$$

Note that the interest rate used to set the May 28, 2002, cash flow is three-month LIBOR on February 26, 2002. For this reason the dates in Panel I are called *set* or *reset* dates.

Fixed rate cash flows are determined using the 30/360 convention, so, for example, the fixed cash flow due on November 29, 2002, is

$$\$100,000,000 \times \frac{5.688\% \times (90+91)}{360} = \$2,859,800 \qquad (18.2)$$

Unlike bonds, swap cash flows include interest over a holiday. A bond scheduled to make a payment of \$2,844,000 on Thanksgiving, November 28, 2002, would make that exact payment on November 29, 2002. A similarly scheduled swap payment is postponed for a day as well, but increases to \$2,859,800 to account for the extra day of interest.

VALUATION OF SWAPS

Unlike the cash flows from U.S. Treasury bonds, the cash flows from swaps are subject to default risk: A party to a swap agreement may fail to make a promised payment. A discussion of this topic is deferred to the last section of this chapter. For now, however, assume that parties will not default on any swap obligation.

The valuation of swaps without default risk is made much simpler by the following fiction. Treat the swap as if the fixed-rate payer pays the notional amount to the floating-rate payer on the termination date and as if the floating-rate payer pays the notional amount to the fixed-rate payer on the termination date. This fiction does not alter the cash flows because the payments of the notional amounts cancel. But this fiction does allow the swap to be separated into the following recognizable fixed and floating legs. Including the final notional amount, the fixed leg of the swap resembles a bond: Its cash flows are six-month interest payments at the fixed rate of the swap and a final principal payment. Similarly, including the final notional amount, the floating leg of the swap resembles a floating rate note, to be described in the next section.

By including the payment of a notional amount, the fixed leg of a swap may be valued using the methods of Part One but with a swap curve instead of a bond curve.[1] Figure 18.2 graphs the *par swap curve* as of November 26, 2001. The par swap curve is analogous to a par yield curve in a

---

[1]This is market convention but requires further discussion. See the last section of this chapter.

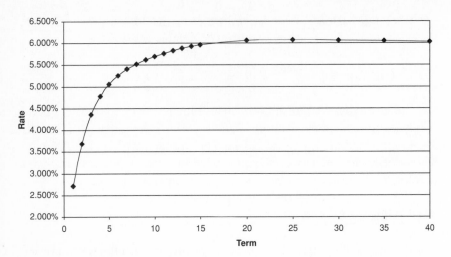

FIGURE 18.2 Par Swap Curve on November 26, 2001

government bond market. Employing the methods of Part One, the collection of par swap rates may be used to extract discount factors, spot rates, or forward rates. Then the fixed leg of any swap may be valued with those discount factors or rates. Also, all the techniques of Part Two may be applied to measure the interest rate risk of a swap's fixed leg.

To value and measure the sensitivity of the floating leg of a swap the discussion turns to floating rate notes.

FLOATING RATE NOTES

A *floating rate note* or *floater* makes periodic payments that are keyed off some rate *index* before returning principal at par. For example, 100 face of a 10-year floating rate note keyed off three-month LIBOR and maturing on November 28, 2011, would make payments for 10 years, computed in the same way as those appearing in the floating column of Table 18.1, and then return the 100 principal amount. For simplicity of exposition, however, this section assumes that set and payment dates all occur on the 28th of the month. The results presented here do not change under a more precise development that differentiates between set and payment dates.

Since the cash flows of a floater depend on the level of interest rates over time, it would seem that valuing a floater requires a term structure model. As it turns out, for many floating rate notes this is not the case and their valuation is quite straightforward.

The key to valuing floaters is to start at the maturity date and work backward. Continuing with the example, on November 28, 2011, the floating rate note pays 100 in principal plus an interest payment of

$$100 \times \frac{L[08/28/2011] \times d}{360} \qquad (18.3)$$

where $L[t]$ is three-month LIBOR as of date t and d is the number of days from the previous payment date, August 28, 2011, to November 28, 2011. To value this three-month cash flow as of August 28, 2011, discount by the three-month rate as of the valuation date; that is, discount by $L[08/28/2011]$.[2] It follows that the value of the total cash flow is

$$\frac{100 + 100 \times L[08/28/2011] \times d/360}{1 + L[08/28/2011] \times d/360} = 100 \qquad (18.4)$$

In words, on August 28, 2011, the ex-coupon value of the floating rate note (i.e., the value not including the August 28, 2011, payment) must equal par. This valuation does not depend on the value of LIBOR on that date. Intuitively, as of the set date the floater earns the fair interest rate on three-month money for three months. And the value of a note earning the fair rate of interest over the single period of its life is simply par.

The exercise can be repeated to value the floater on the previous set date, namely May 28, 2011. Since the floater is worth par on August 28, 2011, ex-coupon, its value on August 28, 2011 including the payment is

$$100 + 100 \times \frac{L[05/28/2011] \times d}{360} \qquad (18.5)$$

where d is now the number of days from May 28, 2011, to August 28, 2011. To value the cash flow in (18.5) as of May 28, 2011, discount by three-month LIBOR as of May 28, 2011:

---

[2]Again, this is market convention but is discussed further in the last section of this chapter.

$$\frac{100 + 100 \times L[05/28/2011] \times d/360}{1 + L[05/28/2011] \times d/360} = 100 \qquad (18.6)$$

Continuing in this fashion, it can be shown that the value of the floating rate note on all set dates is par. In particular, the value of the floating rate note on the first set date—that is, at the time of issue—is par.

Having discovered the value of the floater on set dates, it is easy to write down the value of the floater between set dates. For example, using Table 18.1 the first payment on \$100,000,000 of the floating rate note is \$550,883 on February 28, 2002. As of December 31, 2001, the first payment date is 59 days away, and on that date, ex-coupon, the note is worth par. Therefore, if $\hat{L}$ is the appropriate LIBOR discount rate as of December 31, 2001, the value of the floater on December 31, 2001, is

$$\frac{\$100,550,883}{1 + 59 \times \hat{L}/360} \qquad (18.7)$$

The duration properties of floating rate notes can be deduced from (18.7). Despite the fact that the maturity of the floater is 10 years, the price of the floating rate note depends only on the short-term rate and its effect on the present value of the next payment date. Put another way, since the floating rate note is always worth par on set dates, it behaves like a zero coupon bond maturing on the next payment date. Hence, by the arguments of Chapter 6, its duration is approximately equal to the time to the next payment date, that is, .25 years. Unlike the case of a fixed coupon bond, a change in interest rates does not affect the value of all the payments of a floater. The provision resetting each floating payment to reflect a fair market rate at the time of reset makes the value of later payments on the floater immune to changes in interest rates. Only the first payment which has been fixed and the par value at the next payment date have values that are subject to interest rate risk.

VALUATION OF SWAPS, CONTINUED

Under the fiction that the floating-rate payer pays the notional amount at maturity, the floating leg of a swap is equivalent to a floating rate note. And, as discussed earlier, under the fiction that the fixed-rate payer pays the notional amount at maturity, the fixed leg of a swap is equivalent to a fixed coupon bond. Therefore, applying the results of Parts One and Two for the fixed leg and of the previous section for the floating leg, both legs of a swap can be valued.

Most swaps exchange the fixed rate against the floating rate *flat* (i.e., without any spread). Some swaps, however, provide for a spread off the floating rate. For example, a swap might provide for a fixed rate of 5.698% against a floating rate of LIBOR plus 10 basis points for 10 years. This swap is no harder to value than the swaps against LIBOR flat. Since the 10-basis point spread to LIBOR is fixed over the life of the swap, it must be valued like any other fixed stream of cash flows. Abstracting from the differences between the fixed and floating payment conventions, the spread to LIBOR can be subtracted from the fixed rate: receiving 5.698% and paying LIBOR+10 basis points is approximately the same as receiving 5.688% and paying LIBOR flat. In any case, spreads to the floating rate do not particularly complicate valuation.

Denote the values of the fixed and floating legs of the swap by V_{Fixed} and V_{Float}. Then, the value of a swap to the fixed receiver/floating payer is $V_{Fixed}-V_{Float}$, and the value of a swap to the floating receiver/fixed payer is $V_{Float}-V_{Fixed}$. Since no payment is exchanged at the initiation of the swap, the swap is only fair if its net value to each party equals zero, that is, $V_{Fixed}-V_{Float}$ equals zero. Also, the previous section showed that at the initiation of a swap the floating leg at LIBOR flat is worth par: $V_{Float}=100$. Putting these two observations together, it must be the case that at the initiation of the swap the fixed leg is also worth par: $V_{Fixed}=100$. But, by definition, this can be true only if the fixed rate of the swap at initiation equals the par swap rate. Hence, the par swap rate curve graphed in Figure 18.2 is the fixed rate of swap agreements against LIBOR flat entered into on November 26, 2001.

As interest rates change and as time passes, the value of the swap may become positive or negative. If $V_{Fixed}-V_{Float}>0$, then the value of the swap is positive to the fixed receiver but negative to the fixed payer. This means that if the parties wish to *terminate* the swap, so that neither party need make any more payments to the other, the fixed payer will have to make a positive payment of $V_{Fixed}-V_{Float}$ to the fixed receiver. Conversely, if $V_{Float}-V_{Fixed}>0$, then the value of the swap is positive to the fixed payer but negative to the fixed receiver. If the swap were terminated, the fixed receiver would make a positive payment of $V_{Float}-V_{Fixed}$ to the fixed payer.

NOTE ON THE MEASUREMENT OF FIXED
AND FLOATING INTEREST RATE RISK

Strictly speaking, it is correct to say that the DV01 of a swap from the perspective of the fixed receiver is the DV01 of the fixed leg minus the DV01 of the floating leg. But this observation is not used much in practice. The DV01 of the fixed leg depends on the swap rate curve out to the maturity of the swap, whereas the DV01 of the floating leg depends on LIBOR out to the first payment date. Hence, adding these DV01 values for a 10-year swap, for example, mixes 10-year risk with three-month risk. While this is technically correct in the DV01 model of parallel shifts, this aggregation of risk does not constitute good hedging practice. For this reason it is common in the industry to manage the interest rate risk of the fixed and floating legs separately. The fixed side of a swap is hedged with other swaps or bonds, and the floating side of a swap is hedged with Eurodollar or fed funds futures, see Chapter 17, or other short-term securities.

Another measure of risk used in the swap markets is *PV01*, normally meant to mean the change in the value of a swap for a one-basis point change in its fixed rate. Writing a bond pricing equation in terms of discount factors reveals that PV01 equals the sum of the discount factors used to discount the fixed cash flows.

SWAP SPREADS

Chapter 2 describes the conditions under which it turns out better to have rolled over investments in short-term securities rather than having made an investment in a long-term security. The reasoning there may be used to describe the conditions under which it turns out better to have received floating on a swap versus having received fixed. The par swap rate may be thought of as composed of a series of three-month forward rates. If the realised values of three-month LIBOR turn out to be above the forward rates, then it will have been better to receive floating and pay fixed than to pay floating and receive fixed. Conversely, if the realised values of three-month LIBOR turn out to be below the forward rates, then it will have been better to pay floating and receive fixed. In the intermediate cases, when some realised values of three-month LIBOR turn out to be above and some turn out to be below the forward rates, then a more detailed calculation is required to determine which side of the swap turns out better.

The same considerations that relate long-term rates in government bond markets to the evolution of short-term rates also apply to the swap market. Expectations, risk premium, and convexity, as described in Chapter 10, may be used to understand the shape of the swap curve with respect to the evolution of three-month LIBOR. The critical difference between the government bond and swap context is the credit component of the short-term rate in the swap context. A three-month government bond rate depends on general economic conditions while three-month LIBOR depends on both general economic conditions and on three-month bank credit spreads.

While three-month LIBOR depends on the credit of the banking sector and swap rates depend on the evolution of three-month LIBOR, it is not true that the 10-year swap rate should equal the yield on a 10-year bond issued by a financially solid bank. To understand this point requires a bit more detail about how three-month LIBOR is set. The *British Bankers' Association* (BBA), the body responsible for setting LIBOR, starts with a list of banks with strong credit ratings. Every day it polls those banks about the three-month rate, drops the highest and lowest responses, and averages the rest. If a bank on the list has credit problems, it is supposed to be dropped from the list and replaced with another bank. Given this procedure for setting three-month LIBOR, the 10-year swap rate should be substantially below the 10-year obligation of a particular bank. The 10-year swap rate reflects views on a *rolling* three-month credit (i.e., on the three-month credit of banks that are on the polling list over time). Since banks are supposed to be dropped from the list after some credit deterioration, three-month LIBOR should never reflect the credit quality of banks with very serious credit problems. The yield on a 10-year bank obligation, however, reflects the possibility that a particular bank might experience credit problems, and perhaps severe credit problems, in the future. The more aggressive the BBA is in dropping banks with financial problems, the lower the swap rate relative to the yield of individual bank obligations. The less aggressive, the closer the swap rate is to those individual bank yields. Furthermore, the less correlated the credit of banks in the banking system, the lower the swap rate relative to the yield of individual bank obligations as substitutions of one bank for another on the LIBOR list are worth a lot in terms of credit. The more correlated the credit of banks in the banking system, the closer the swap rate to individual bank note yields as substitutions of one bank for another are not worth very much in terms of credit.

Since swap rates reflect three-month rolling bank credit, they should certainly exceed government bond rates. *Swap spreads* are simply the difference between swap rates and government bond yields of a particular maturity. One problem in defining swap spreads is that a 10-year swap, for example, matures in exactly 10 years while, at most times, there is no government bond with exactly 10 years to maturity. By convention, therefore, the 10-year swap spread is defined as the difference between the 10-year swap rate and the 10-year on-the-run government bond. Swap spreads of other maturities are defined analogously. Given the importance of both the swap and government bond markets, swap spreads are closely watched indicators of fixed income market pricing. Figure 18.3 graphs some history of the 10-year swap spread.

The fall in swap spreads in the early 1990s reflected the recovery of the banking sector from its problems in the 1980s. The rise in swap spreads in the late 1990s, on the other hand, can be best explained by a perceived scarcity in the supply of U.S. Treasury securities relative to demand. This recent history illustrates the roles of both credit and the supply and demand for Treasuries and swaps in the determination of swap spreads.

While quoted swap spreads are useful for investigating broad themes, as in the brief discussion of Figure 18.3, in the small these data can be misleading. The problem derives from quoting swap spreads using on-the-run

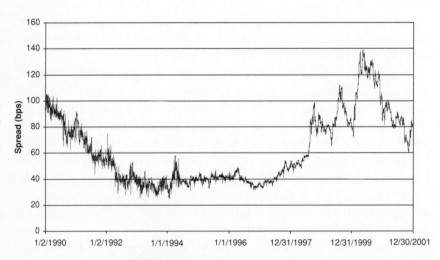

FIGURE 18.3 Ten-Year Swap Spreads

Treasury securities. As discussed in Chapter 15, liquidity premiums and special financing have a large impact on the yield of on-the-run government bonds. This means that the swap spread is not a clean measure of the credit of the banking system and of demand and supply in the swap and government bond markets. Possible solutions to this problem are measuring swap spreads with respect to fitted yields from an off-the-run government curve or explicitly adjusting on-the-run yield for financing and liquidity. As both of these solutions require a good deal of subjective judgement, adjusted swap spreads tend to be used by individual trading desks and houses rather than being widely quoted in the marketplace.

MAJOR USES OF INTEREST RATE SWAPS

While many corporations prefer floating rate debt, the market for long-term floating rate notes in the U.S. is very small. Corporations with very strong credit ratings may effectively pay a floating rate by issuing and rolling over short-term obligations, like *commercial paper*. Even among these particularly creditworthy corporations, however, some wish to avoid *liquidity risk*, that is, the risk that credit rating deteriorates and, sometimes quite suddenly, short-term obligations can no longer be refinanced (i.e., rolled over). A solution for these corporations is to issue fixed rate debt and then receive fixed and pay floating in a swap. The net effect of the fixed debt and the swap is floating rate funding. This solution for creating floating rate debt synthetically is also used by corporations who prefer floating rate debt and do not possess the credit stature to issue short-term obligations.

Perhaps the largest use of swaps is related to the mortgage market. Agencies or Government-sponsored enterprises (GSEs) like the *Federal National Mortgage Association* (FNMA) and the *Federal Home Loan Mortgage Corporation* (FHLMC), among other activities, sell fixed rate debt and buy mortgages. As the net interest rate risk of the resulting portfolios changes over time, with the level of rates, and with the shape of the curve, these GSEs use swaps to control their interest rate risk. Mortgage servicers, who collect fees for collecting and processing mortgage payments, are also exposed to interest rate risk from their business activities and hedge with swaps. Chapter 21 will describe the interest rate risk of mortgages and an application in that chapter will discuss the effect of mortgage hedging on the swap market.

A last example of the use of swaps is that of a corporation hedging future debt issuance. Once a corporation has decided to sell bonds to fund its capital expenditures or operations, it may want to hedge against rising interest rates from the time of its decision to the actual sale of the bonds. To hedge the future issuance of 10-year debt, for example, it can pay fixed on a 10-year swap at the time of its decision and unwind the swap at the time of its bond sale.[3] If rates have risen over that period, the corporation will have to pay a higher coupon rate on its debt but will have gained from its swap position. Of course, if rates have fallen then the corporation will not benefit from selling debt at a lower rate because that gain will be offset by losses from its swap position. An advantage of using swaps rather than Treasuries for this purpose is that swaps hedge not only changes in the general level of rates but also, at least to some extent, changes in *credit spreads* (i.e., the differences between yields on corporate and on government debt). The magnitude of the correlation between swap rates and credit spreads is a matter of empirical debate, and this correlation is important in deciding to hedge corporate debt with Treasuries or with swaps. Even if the correlation is high, substantial basis risk remains when hedging changes in corporate rates with swaps. First, swap rates reflect banking credit specifically rather than general corporate credits. Second, swap rates cannot possibly hedge the risk that the credit spread of a particular corporation might change relative to the general level of credit spreads.

ASSET SWAP SPREADS AND ASSET SWAPS

Chapter 17 discussed the convenience of measuring the value of bonds, like agency securities, relative to rate curves that are not contaminated by individual security effects. TED spreads, based on Eurodollar futures rates, serve this function for relatively short-term bonds. For longer-term bonds, market participants rely on *asset swap spreads*. The asset swap spread of a bond is the spread such that discounting the bond's cash

---

[3]Rather than pay fixed on a swap, a corporation may sell Treasuries to hedge changes in the level of rates and purchase a *spread lock*, which makes money if swap spreads widen, to hedge credit spreads. While it seems that these transactions skirt the swap market, the dealer selling the spread lock has to pay fixed in swaps to hedge its own risk. The effective use of the swap market, therefore, is essentially as described in the text.

flows by swap rates plus that spread gives the bond price. Asset swap spreads are, for the most part, a measure of a bond's credit risk relative to the credit risk built into the swap curve. But security-specific pricing effects, like special financing or supply and demand imbalances, are also captured by asset swap spreads. The example of this section and the agency case study in the next section focus on the credit risk component of asset swap spreads while the appendix, a case study of OTR five-year Treasuries compared with old five-year Treasuries, focuses on security-specific effects.

Consider the following example. Assume that the swap curve is flat at 6.10% and that the yield of the FNMA 6.25s of May 15, 2029, is 6.25%. By the definition of yield, discounting the bond's cash flows by 6.25% gives the bond price. Therefore, discounting at the flat swap rates of 6.10% plus a spread of 15 basis points also gives the bond price. Hence the asset swap spread of the bond in this example is 15 basis points.[4]

The next section discusses the reasonableness of an asset swap spread of 15 basis points for the FNMA security. For now, however, assume that an investor believes that the bond is cheap relative to swaps and wants to profit from the large spread. A common choice is an *asset swap*, a series of transactions depicted in Figure 18.4.

The investor buys $100 million face of the FNMA 6.25s of May 15, 2029, at par and finances the position by selling the repo. The investor then engages to pay 6.25% fixed on $100 million notional amount in exchange for LIBOR plus 15 basis points. Note that this is a fair swap: Since 6.10% is the par swap rate, paying 6.10% is fair against LIBOR flat. But then paying 6.25% against LIBOR plus 15 basis points must also be fair.[5]

The asset swap depicted in Figure 18.4 has the following consequences. The coupon payments from the bond cancel the fixed payments to the swap. The principal payment from the bond at maturity cancels the repo indebtedness at that time. And the floating payments total LIBOR

---

[4]Only in the very special case of a flat swap rate curve does the asset swap spread equal the difference between the bond yield and the swap rate.

[5]Once again, the text simplifies by ignoring the difference in payment conventions between the fixed and floating legs of the swap. The section continues to use this simplification without further comment.

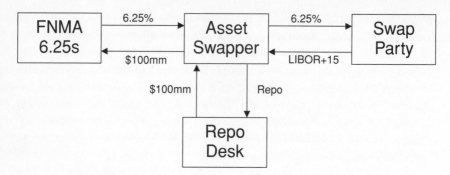

FIGURE 18.4   Asset Swap of the FNMA 6.25s of May 15, 2029

plus 15 basis points minus the repo rate.[6] The investor receives this periodic payment so long as the agency security does not default. If the agency does default, then the coupon payments from the bond cease but the fixed payments to the swap are still due. Intuitively, the asset swap spread is a measure of the credit risk of the bond relative to the swap curve while LIBOR minus repo is a measure of the credit risk of the swap curve. Therefore, an asset swap allows an investor to earn the full credit spread of a bond so long as that bond does not default.

The example in Figure 18.4 is particularly simple because the bond is assumed to sell at par. To explore the slightly more difficult case, change the example slightly to assume that the swap rate curve is flat at 5.90% and the yield of the FNMA 6.25s of May 15, 2029, is 6.05%. The asset swap spread remains equal to 15 basis points but the price of the FNMA bonds becomes 102.683. The problem with structuring the asset swap as before is that the floating rates lose comparability. The $102.683 million cost of the bond will have to be financed at the repo rate, while the LIBOR plus 15 basis points will be earned on the notional amount of $100 mil-

---

[6]At the initiation of the asset swap this net rate is earned on $100 million. If bond yields then fall, however, a higher bond value must be financed so the repo rate is paid on a higher amount. Similarly, if swap rates fall, then, as explained in the last section of this chapter, the investor must put up cash on which he earns approximately LIBOR. Therefore, if bond yields and swap rates fall together, the investor continues to earn LIBOR plus 15 minus repo, but on an amount greater than $100 million. Conversely, if bond yields and swap rates increase together, the investor earns LIBOR plus 15 minus repo on an amount less than $100 million.

lion. The solution is to execute a swap agreement that includes an up-front payment of $2.683 million, as depicted in Figure 18.5.

Since the swap rate curve is now assumed to be flat at 5.90%, it is fair to pay 5.90% against LIBOR flat. Also, at that swap rate, it is the case that a flow of 19.7 basis points on $100 million notional is worth $2.683 million.[7] In other words, paying 5.90% plus 19.7 or 6.097% against LIBOR flat and receiving an up-front payment of $2.683 million is a fair swap. But then paying an additional 15.3 basis points on the fixed side and receiving the same on the floating side is also fair and gives rise to the swap in Figure 18.5: Pay 6.25%, receive an up-front payment of $2.683 million, and receive LIBOR plus 15.3 basis points.

Apart from this swap the investor buys the FNMA 6.25s of May 15, 2029, for $102.683 million. He applies the $2.683 million received from the swap to this purchase and finances the remaining $100 million at the repo rate. The net cash flow from the asset swap trade, therefore, is LIBOR plus 15.3 basis points minus repo on $100 million.

Note that the net flow is slightly bigger in the asset swap depicted in

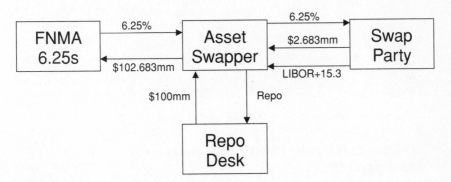

FIGURE 18.5 Asset Swap of the FNMA 6.25s of May 15, 2029. Bonds at a Premium

---

[7]The magnitudes make intuitive sense as follows. On the agency bond yielding 6.05%, a coupon rate of 6.25% (i.e., 20 basis points above the yield) is worth 2.683% of par. Since the swap rate is below the bond yield, the DV01 of the swap is higher than that of the bond. Therefore, a fixed flow of slightly less than 20 basis points produces the same 2.683% of par on the swap. The exact flow turns out to be 19.7 basis points.

Figure 18.5 than in that depicted in Figure 18.4. When the bond is selling at a premium, an event of default costs more. Put another way, the 6.25% coupon stream at risk is worth more in the second case, when the swap rate is 5.90%, than in the first case, when the swap rate is 6.10%.

Asset swaps are designed as buy-and-hold trades. The focus is on the periodic payments over the life of the bond and swap rather than on the return to any particular horizon. But the trade does make or lose money as rates and spreads move. First, since the bond yield differs from the swap rate, the DV01 of the bond differs from the DV01 of the fixed leg of the swap. Therefore, rising or falling rates before maturity will have a P&L impact. Second, the trade experiences P&L as the asset swap spread changes. If, in these examples, the yield of the bond increases and the swap rate stays the same, then the asset swap spread increases and the trade shows a loss. Similarly, if the asset swap spread narrows, the trade shows a gain. While it is true that an investor could, in theory, plan to hold the trade until maturity, collect the spread, and ignore interim P&L fluctuation, almost all investors are, in reality, limited in the amount of interim losses they can accumulate. This does not necessarily mean that the asset swap is a poor way to set up the trade. It does mean that the issues raised in Chapter 14 are relevant here. Hedging with current DV01 values, as in the case study in Appendix 18A, minimizes current P&L fluctuation but not interest rate risk at maturity. At the other extreme, by perfectly offsetting fixed cash flows, the asset swap minimizes interest rate risk at maturity but not interim P&L fluctuation.

TRADING CASE STUDY: 30-Year FNMA Asset Swap Spreads

The U.S. government created FNMA to facilitate the growth of the U.S. mortgage market. This agency is now private but continues to have close enough ties to the government to be called a government-sponsored enterprise and continues to play an extremely important role in the mortgage market. Most market participants believe that debt issued by FNMA has minimal credit risk. This view is mostly due to the size and value of its assets relative to its debt. But there is also a widespread belief that, despite the absence of any explicit guarantee, the U.S. government would not allow such a crucial institution in the U.S. economy to default on its obligations.

The examples of the previous section, with the asset swap spread of the 6.25s of May 15, 2029, at 15 basis points, reflect market conditions in late August 2001. But is a spread of 15 basis points reasonable for an agency security? Since most market participants believe that agency debt is extremely unlikely to default, the periodic flows from asset swaps are extremely likely to be realized over the life of the trade. The superior credit of FNMA relative to that of strong banks also means that the repo rate on agencies should be well below LIBOR. Therefore, the periodic flow from an asset swap of the 6.25s of May 15, 2029, is 15 basis points plus the positive difference between LIBOR and the repo rate. Many argued that this was an excellent trading opportunity. In fact, given the solidity of FNMA's credit, many argued further that the fair asset swap spread was negative. An asset swap spread equal to zero still offers a positive periodic payment to the asset swap: LIBOR minus the repo rate. Only a negative asset swap spread produces the minimal return to the asset swap trade justified by the small probability that FNMA might default.

Figure 18.6 graphs the recent history of the asset swap spread of the FNMA 6.25s of May 15, 2029. The spread was negative until early 2001. It then hovered around zero until July 2001, at which time it widened dramatically. A convincing explanation of this price action was not easily found. Almost no one made the argument that the cheapening of the bonds resulted from a perception that FNMA's credit had weakened. In any case, as the cheapening persisted, positioning started to play an important role. Many investors and traders had reasoned along the lines of the previous paragraph, had taken account of recent history, and had bought the agency against swaps at asset swap spreads of 0, 10, 15, and so on. As spreads continued to widen, these positions lost a good deal of money and forced liquidations that, in turn, widened the spreads even further.

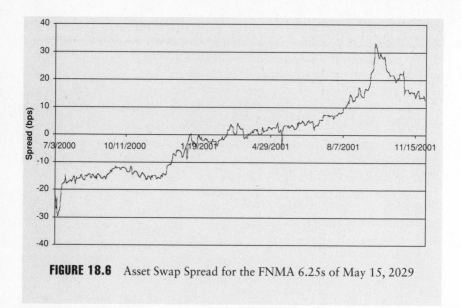

FIGURE 18.6   Asset Swap Spread for the FNMA 6.25s of May 15, 2029

ON THE CREDIT RISK OF SWAP AGREEMENTS

In discussing the determination of swap rates, this chapter has taken account of the credit risk built into three-month LIBOR but has assumed that parties to the swap agreement will never default on their obligations to one another. This section discusses the implications of default by parties to the swap agreement.

It is not correct to view a swap as a position in a fixed rate note and an opposite position in a floating rate note when considering the implications of default. Default on either a fixed or a floating rate note may result in a loss of principal. In a swap agreement, however, no principal payment is ever made or received. Furthermore, interest rate swap agreements typically absolve one party from payments if the other party defaults on a payment. Therefore, in the event of default the loss in a swap agreement is limited to the value of the swap, if positive. If $V_{Fixed}-V_{Float}>0$ the fixed receiver is subject to a loss of $V_{Fixed}-V_{Float}$, while if $V_{Float}-V_{Fixed}>0$ the floating receiver is subject to a loss of $V_{Float}-V_{Fixed}$. For an order of magnitude approximation to these values at risk, multiply the net DV01 of the swap by the change in rates since the initiation of the swap agreement. For example, the fixed leg of the $100 million swap to November 15, 2005, in the previous section had a DV01 of .04158 and any swap floating leg at LIBOR flat has a DV01 of approximately .0025. This net DV01 of .04158–.0025 or .03908 implies that a parallel shift in swap rates of as many as 50 basis points puts at most

$$\$100,000,000 \times \frac{.03908}{100} \times 50 = \$1,954,000 \qquad (18.8)$$

at risk. This value would, of course, be larger for a swap with a longer maturity or for a bigger change in swap rates. But the order of magnitude of the loss is very much below that of a default on a principal amount of $100,000,000. Thus the default risk of a swap is in no way comparable to the default risk of a note, and the notional amount of a swap is an order of magnitude larger than the resulting value at risk.

In practice, the credit risk of swaps is even lower than that suggested by the previous paragraph. Swap agreements usually require cash margin, which earns interest at a short-term rate, to cover negative swap values. If the value of a swap is –$X to party A and +$X to party B, party A will have posted $X to party B as margin. If party A defaults, party B may keep the margin and terminate the swap. (There is, of course, no reason for party B to default on the swap. Whatever the financial situation of party B, it should assign the swap to some third party[8] and collect the value of the swap rather than default.)

Given the relatively low credit risk of swaps, the market convention is not to discriminate across credits with price. In other words, if party A with an extremely strong credit rating and party B with an acceptable credit rating both approach party C to do a particular swap, parties A and B will usually be quoted about the same swap rate. Party C differentiates between the credits by imposing stricter credit terminations and margin requirements on party B than on party A. Also, party C will accept a lower total swap exposure to party B than to party A; that is, party B will have a smaller *credit line* than party A.

The market convention of achieving low default risk on swaps through contractual provisions and credit allocation means that observable swap

---

[8]Party B can assign a swap to a new party C so long as party A and party C agree to accept each other's credit.

rates reflect the rates on swap agreements with little perceived risk of default. To some extent this justifies pricing swaps as if there were no risk of counterparty default. To the extent that these contractual provisions do not fully eliminate the risk of default, however, it is not strictly correct to price swaps in this way. Similarly, to the extent that swap dealers do business with equal and inferior credits, they are exposed to credit risk for which they must be compensated by the profitability of the business.

Having discussed the credit issues of swap agreements, it becomes clear that there is an internal inconsistency in the convention for pricing swaps presented in the previous sections. On the one hand it is assumed that there is no risk of counterparty default: The cash flows are assumed to be as specified in the swap agreement and fictional notional amounts are added to the fixed and floating sides. On the other hand, all cash flows are discounted at LIBOR or swap rates (i.e., at rates containing the rolling credit risk of strong banks). If counterparty default risk is significant, then cash flows should be adjusted for the potential of default and be discounted at a rate appropriate for that particular counterparty. If default risk is insignificant, then the promised cash flows should be discounted at default-free rates—that is, at government bond rates. In this light the market convention must be viewed as a compromise. The default risk of a swap agreement is perceived small enough to assume that promised cash flows are received and to discount these cash flows at a rate appropriate for a very strong credit, namely the rolling credit of financially sound banks.

APPENDIX 18A
TRADING CASE STUDY: Five-Year On-the-Run/ Off-the-Run Spread of Spreads

On January 17, 2001, the OTR five-year Treasury bond seemed to be priced rich relative to the old five-year Treasury bond. Table 18.2 gives details.

The yield on the OTR five-year, maturing November 15, 2005, was 11.9 basis points below that of the old five-year, maturing May 15, 2005. This yield spread is a bit difficult to assess on its own because it does not control for the term structure of interest rates between the two maturity dates. If, for example, the term structure of

TABLE 18.2   Yields and Spreads of 5s and Old 5s as of January 17, 2001

Coupon	Maturity	Description	Yield	Swap Rate to Maturity	Spread (bps)	Bond DV01	Swap DV01
5.750%	11/15/05	OTR 5-year	4.852%	5.765%	−91.3	0.04352	0.04158
6.750%	05/15/05	Old 5-year	4.971%	5.725%	−75.4	0.04005	0.03782
	Spread (bps)		−11.9	4.0			
	Spread of spreads (bps)		−15.9				

interest rates in that maturity region was very downward-sloping, then it may have made perfect sense for the bond with an extra six months of maturity to trade at a yield lower by 11.9 basis points.

One way to control for curve is to look at the slope of the swap curve. Table 18.2 reports that the par swap rate to November 15, 2005, was four basis points above the par swap rate to May 15, 2005. In other words, the swap curve sloped upward in that range of maturity. Making the strong assumption that the slope of the Treasury curve should approximately equal the slope of the swap curve over this six-month maturity region, the OTR five-year of November 15, 2005, should have traded at a yield four basis points above that of the old five-year of May 15, 2005. The fact that the yield of the OTR five-year was 11.9 basis points below that of the old five-year then implies that the yield of the OTR was 15.9 basis points too low.

The same argument can be made in terms of swap spreads. Using the data in Table 18.2, the OTR was 91.3 basis points rich relative to swaps. At the same time the old five-year was 75.4 basis points rich relative to swaps.[9] Note that these differences between bond and swap yields do not measure value as precisely as asset swap spreads. But, as will become apparent, the trade described in this appendix is more closely related to yield spreads than to asset swap spreads. In any case, did it make sense for bonds so close in maturity to trade 15.9 basis points apart in spreads to the swap curve? After all, both bonds are

---

[9]Whether these spreads are reasonable in absolute magnitude given the rolling credit risk of the banking sector is a question not discussed in this case.

U.S. Treasuries and the swap curve over the six months in question reflects the same rolling bank credit risk over slightly different periods. In other words, was a *spread of spreads* of 15.9 basis points too large?

Two factors that have not been accounted for in Table 18.2 are liquidity premium and special financing. Both these effects can be incorporated by constructing the trade on a forward basis. Assume that an experienced trader made the following argument in January, 2001. On May 8, 2001, a new five-year bond will start to trade in the when-issued market. Soon after that time the 5.75s of November 15, 2005, will become the old five-year and the 6.75s of May 15, 2005, will become the double-old five-year. From experience, the spread of spreads between an old five-year and a double-old five-year, due to financing and liquidity effects, should be about 3 basis points. Therefore, the question is really whether the spread of spreads forward to May 8, 2001, is more than 3 basis points rich. Table 18.3 supplies the relevant data for this question.

Before proceeding with an analysis of the forward trade, it is important to understand exactly how constructing the trade on a forward basis accounts for special financing from the trade date to the forward date. According to Table 18.3, the repo rate from January 17, 2001, to May 8, 2001, for the OTR five-year was substantially below that for the old five-year. The resulting financing advantage explained, at least in part, why the spot yield of the OTR five-year was so far below that of the old five-year. But since this financing advantage was not expected to be so large after some seasoning, that is, from May 8, 2001, on, as it had been from January 17, 2001, to May 8, 2001, the forward yield spread

TABLE 18.3   Yields and Spreads for 5s and Old 5s as of January 17, 2001, Forward to May 8, 2001

Coupon	Maturity	Description	Repo to Forward Date	Forward Yield	Swap Rate to Forward Date	Forward Swap Rate	Forward Spread (bps)	Bond Forward DV01	Swap Forward DV01
5.750%	11/15/05	OTR 5-year	3.814%	4.929%	5.522%	5.779%	−85.0	0.04086	0.03927
6.750%	05/15/05	Old 5-year	5.006%	4.963%	5.522%	5.737%	−77.4	0.03742	0.03544
		Forward spread (bps)	−3.4			4.2			
		Forward spread of spreads (bps)	−7.6						

of the bonds was not so large as the spot yield spread. In other words, the market priced the bonds from May 8, 2001, under the assumption that the OTR and old five-year would not then trade so differently in the special repo market. Table 18.3 quantifies this effect, showing that the forward yield spread was only 3.4 basis points, 8.5 basis points below the 11.9 spot yield spread reported in Table 18.2.

A direct calculation of the relative financing advantage of the OTR five-year makes the same point as computing the difference between the spot and forward yield spreads. The spread between the OTR five-year and the old five-year term repo rates to May 8, 2001, is 5.006%-3.814% or 119.2 basis points. Therefore, the cost of financing 100 worth of the OTR five-year relative to the cost of financing 100 worth of the old five-year over the 111 days between January 17, 2001, and May 8, 2001, is

$$100 \times \frac{1.192\% \times 111}{360} = .3675 \qquad (18.9)$$

Dividing by the DV01 of the OTR five-year, given in Table 18.2, measures this financing cost in terms of the yield of the OTR five-year:

$$\frac{.3675}{.04352} = 8.4 \qquad (18.10)$$

As was to be shown, these 8.4 basis points essentially explain the difference between the spot yield spread of 11.9 basis points and the forward yield spread of 3.4 basis points.

The relationship between the spot and forward spreads of the swaps was quite different from that of the bonds. Since the swap rate to the forward date is, by definition, the same for both the November 15, 2005, and the May 15, 2005, swaps,[10] the 4.2-basis point difference between the forward swap rates in Table 18.3 was essentially the same as the 4.0-basis point difference between the spot swap rates in Table 18.2.

Return now to the forward trade and Table 18.3. The forward spread of spreads to May 8, 2001, equals −7.6 basis points. In other

---

[10]Succinctly, all swaps finance at LIBOR. Including the fictional notional amounts, receiving fixed and paying floating is analogous to buying a bond and financing it at LIBOR every quarter.

words, the OTR five-year was 7.6 basis points rich to the old five-year on a forward spread basis. But since the trader believed that the OTR five-year would be only 3 basis points rich to the old five-year on May 8, 2001, the OTR five-year was, on a forward basis, 4.6 basis points too rich relative to the old five-year.

The following six trades can be executed in an attempt to capture these 4.6 basis points.

1. Sell $100,000,000 of the 5.75s of November 15, 2005.
2. Buy the repo to May 8, 2001, at 3.814%.
3. Receive fixed on $100,000,000×.04086/.03927 or about $104.05 million November 15, 2005, swaps forward to May 8, 2001.
4. Buy $100,000,000×.04086/.03742 or about $109.19 million of the 6.75s of May 15, 2005.
5. Sell the repo to May 8, 2001, at 5.006%.
6. Pay fixed on

$$\left(\$100,000,000 \times \frac{.04086}{.03742} \right) \times \frac{.03742}{.03544} = \$109.19 \times \frac{.03742}{.03544} \qquad (18.11)$$

or about $115.29 million May 15, 2005, swaps forward to May 8, 2001.

Steps 1 through 3 essentially sell the OTR five-year on an asset swap basis forward to May 8, 2001. The forward DV01 of the swap position is equated to that of the bond so that the value of the forward asset swap is immune to parallel changes in forward bond yields and forward swap rates. The asset swap makes money only if the OTR five-year cheapens relative to swaps and loses money only if it richens relative to swaps. Similarly, steps 4 through 6 essentially buy the old five-year on an asset swap basis forward to May 8, 2001. Neither steps 1 through 3 nor steps 4 through 6 is literally an asset swap since the fixed cash flows do not cancel. But these positions are similar in spirit to asset swaps in that they make or lose money with changes in asset swap spreads.

Note that step 4 sets the forward DV01 of the old five-year equal to the forward DV01 of the OTR five-year. As a result, each asset swap trade has the same exposure to changes in swap spread. But this implies that the combination of the two asset swap trades generates P&L only from movements in the spread of spreads and not from equal moves of each asset swap spread. In short, the proposed trade generates P&L only in response to changes in the quantity that is perceived to be mispriced, namely the spread of spreads.

Table 18.4 reports the relevant yields and swap rates on May 8, 2001. The spread of spreads fell so that the OTR five-year was 2.9 basis points rich to the old five-year. On January 17, 2001, that spread had been sold forward to May 8, 2001, at 7.6 basis points. Therefore, on a position short $100,000,000 5.75s of November 15, 2005, with a forward DV01 of .04086, the profit from the trade was approximately

$$\$100,000,000 \times \frac{.04086}{100} \times (7.6 - 2.9) = \$192,042 \qquad (18.12)$$

Table 18.5 presents a more accurate summary of the P&L of the trade by security. The P&L of each part of the trade equals the change in forward price, as a percent of par, times the face value. The total P&L comes to $192,985, quite close to the estimate in (18.12) from using the DV01 of the OTR five-year position and the change in the spread of spreads.

TABLE 18.4 Yields and Spreads for 5s and Old 5s as of May 8, 2001

Coupon	Maturity	Description	Yield	Swap Rate to Maturity	Spread (bps)
5.750%	11/15/05	OTR 5-year	4.725%	5.385%	−66.0
6.750%	05/15/05	Old 5-year	4.644%	5.275%	−63.1
	Spread (bps)		8.1	11.0	
	Spread of spreads (bps)		−2.9		

TABLE 18.5 Summary P&L of Forward Spread of Spreads Trade

Position	Face ($millions)	1/17/01 Forward Price	5/8/01 Price	P&L ($)
OTR 5	−100.00	103.2874	104.1263	−838,900
Swap to 11/15/2005	104.05	99.9428	101.5051	1,625,584
Old 5	109.19	106.4366	107.6398	1,313,774
Swap to 05/15/2005	−115.29	99.9549	101.6094	−1,907,473
Total:				192,985

Comparing Tables 18.2 and 18.4 shows that the term structure steepened dramatically from January 17, 2001, to May 8, 2001. The swap curve from May 15, 2005, to November 15, 2005, steepened 7 basis points, from 4 to 11. The spread of the two Treasury bond yields in the table moved 20 basis points, from −11.9 to 8.1. Of these 20 basis points, 7 may be regarded as a steepening of the Treasury curve while the remaining 13 may be regarded as the looked-for cheapening of the OTR five-year to the old five-year. In this particular example, therefore, a trade that sold the OTR five-year and bought the old five-year without any swaps would have done particularly well, benefiting from both the relative cheapening of the OTR five-year and the steepening. However, had the Treasury and swap curves flattened instead, the OTR versus old trade without swaps would have done worse than the spread of spreads trade and might even have lost money. In short, the spread of spreads trade is less subject to curve risk and, therefore, is a purer bet on the richness of the OTR five-year than is the OTR versus old trade. This conclusion is, of course, subject to the caveat that in the maturity region of interest the Treasury and swap curves flatten or steepen together. If the Treasury curve were to flatten and the swap curve to steepen, then the spread of spreads trade could do very badly indeed.

CHAPTER 19

Fixed Income Options

Many readers are likely to be familiar with equity options. This chapter seeks to present issues of particular relevance to fixed income markets without excessively repeating material usually covered in the context of equity options. To this end the chapter begins with a brief review of some option basics and continues with a more fixed income focus.

DEFINITIONS AND REVIEW

A *call* option on a bond gives the right to purchase that bond at a fixed *strike* or *exercise* price. If the call is *European* in style, this right may be exercised on one particular date called the *expiration*, or *exercise* date. An example from a later section is a European call option to buy the 5s of February 15, 2011, at 99-18¼ on July 15, 2002. If the price of the 5s of February 15, 2011, on July 15, 2002, turns out to be 98, then the value of the right to purchase the bond at 99-18¼ is zero. If, however, the price of the bond on July 15, 2002, turns out to be 100, then the value of the call option is

$$100 - \left[99 + 18\,\tfrac{1}{4}/32\right] = .4297 \tag{19.1}$$

Note that the amount paid for the bond in the example is actually 99-18¼ plus accrued interest. However, since that bond can then be sold for 100 plus accrued interest, the accrued interest does not appear in equation (19.1).

In general, if the price of the bond at expiration is P and the strike price is K, then the value of the call option at expiration is

$$\max(P - K, 0) \tag{19.2}$$

Figure 19.1 graphs this function for a call option on the 5s of February 15, 2011, struck at 99-18$^{1}/_{4}$. Since the value of the call option is zero or positive, a simple arbitrage argument shows that the price of the call option before expiration must be positive. Put more simply, one has to pay for the right but not the obligation to purchase a bond at a fixed price. This implies, by the way, that purchasing an option loses money, *ex post*, if the bond price does not rally enough to compensate for the initial cost of the option.

A *put* option gives the right to sell a bond at the strike price. Consider a put on the 5s of February 15, 2011, struck at 99-18$^{1}/_{4}$ and expiring on July 15, 2011. If the price of the bond at expiration is greater than 99-18$^{1}/_{4}$, then the right to sell the bond at 99-18$^{1}/_{4}$ is worthless. Alternatively, if the price of the bond at expiration is below the strike price, for example at 98, then the put option is worth

$$99 + 18\,{}^{1}\!/_{4}/32 - 98 = 1.5703 \tag{19.3}$$

More generally, the value of a put at expiration is

$$\max(K - P, 0) \tag{19.4}$$

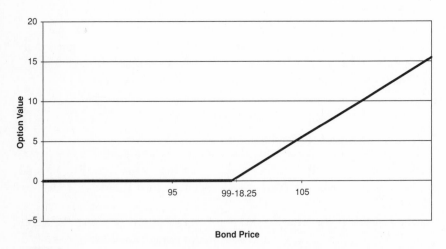

FIGURE 19.1   Value of a 99-18.25 Call Option on the 5s of February 15, 2011, at Expiration

Figure 19.2 graphs this function for a put option on the 5s of February 15, 2011, struck at 99-18$^1/_4$. By arbitrage arguments the price of the put must be positive. Furthermore, a purchase of a put will lose money, *ex post*, if the price of the bond does not fall enough to compensate for the initial cost of the put.

It follows from the expiration values in Figures 19.1 and 19.2 that, at any time before expiration, the value of a call option increases with the price of the underlying bond and the value of a put decreases with the price. Higher volatility increases the values of both puts and calls. This fact is due to the asymmetric payoffs depicted in Figures 19.1 and 19.2. In the case of calls, higher volatility raises the likelihood of large price increases (relative to the strike) that translate to larger, positive payoffs. While the likelihood of large price declines also increases, the payoff from a large decline is no different from the payoff from a small decline: Both are zero. Similarly, puts benefit from a greater likelihood of large price declines but do not suffer from the concomitant greater likelihood of large price increases.

Calls and puts can be combined into portfolios to create a great many payoff functions. One important combination is a *straddle*, achieved by a

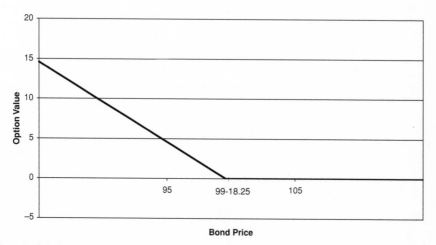

FIGURE 19.2 Value of a 99-18.25 Put Option on the 5s of February 15, 2011, at Expiration

position in one call and one put with the same strike. Figure 19.3 graphs the expiration value of a straddle on the 5s of February 15, 2011, struck at 99-18¼. Unlike call options that benefit from rising bond prices and put options that benefit from falling prices, straddles benefit from both rising and falling prices, that is they benefit mostly from changes in bond prices or, equivalently, from volatility. By arbitrage arguments the price of a straddle must be positive. Therefore, a straddle will lose money, *ex post*, if the absolute change in the bond price is not large enough to compensate for the initial cost of the straddle.

A *Bermudan* call or put option allows for exercise on some fixed set of dates. A typical Bermudan option on a bond would allow the holder to exercise on any coupon payment date. An *American* call or put option allows for exercise at any time on or before the expiration date.

PRICING AMERICAN AND BERMUDAN BOND OPTIONS IN A TERM STRUCTURE MODEL

By way of introducing arbitrage-free pricing, Chapter 9 described the pricing of European bond options. Basically, either (19.2) or (19.4) is used to determine the value of the option at expiration and then the standard tree methodology is used to determine the value of the option on

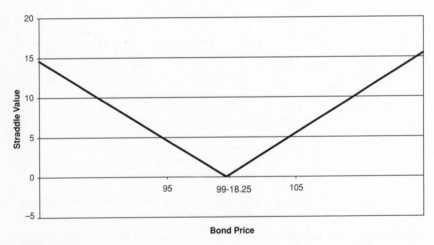

FIGURE 19.3   Value of a 99-18.25 Straddle on the 5s of February 15, 2011, at Expiration

earlier dates. This section, therefore, focuses on the pricing of American and Bermudan options.

The following example prices an option to call 100 face of a 1.5-year, 5.25% coupon bond at par on any coupon date. Assume that the risk-neutral interest rate process over six-month periods is as in the example of Chapter 9:

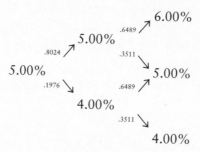

With this tree and the techniques of Part Three, the price tree for a 5.25% coupon bond maturing in 1.5 years may be computed to be

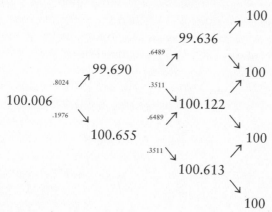

Note that all the prices in the tree are ex-coupon prices. So, for example, on date 2, state 2, the bond is worth 100.122 after the coupon payment of 2.625 has been made.

The value of the option to call this bond at par is worthless on the maturity date of the bond since the bond is always worth par at maturity. On any date before maturity the option has two sources of value. First, it can be exercised immediately. If the price of the bond is P and the strike price is K, then the value of immediate exercise, denoted V_E, is

$$V_E = \max(P - K, 0) \tag{19.5}$$

Second, the option can be held to the next date. The value of the option in this case is like the value of any security held over a date, namely the expected discounted value in the risk-neutral tree. Denote this value by V_H.

The option owner maximizes the value of the option by choosing on each possible exercise date whether to exercise or to hold the option. If the value of exercising is greater the best choice is to exercise, while if the value of holding is greater the best choice is to hold. Mathematically, the value of the option, V, is given by

$$V = \max(V_E, V_H) \tag{19.6}$$

For more intuition about the early exercise decision, consider the following two strategies. Strategy 1 is to exercise the option and hold the bond over the next period. Strategy 2 is not to exercise and, if conditions warrant next period, to exercise then. The advantage of strategy 1 is that purchasing the bond entitles the owner to the coupon earned over the period. The advantages of strategy 2 are that the strike price does not have to be paid for another period and that the option owner has another period in which to observe market prices and decide whether to pay the strike price for the bond. With respect to the advantage of waiting to decide, if prices fall precipitously over the period then strategy 2 is superior to strategy 1 since it would have been better not to exercise. And if prices rise precipitously then strategy 2 is just as good as strategy 1 since the option can still be exercised and the bonds bought for the same strike price of 100. To summarize, early exercise of the call option is optimal only if the value of collecting the coupon exceeds the combined values of delaying payment and of delaying the decision to purchase the bond at the fixed strike price.[1]

Returning to the numerical example, the value of immediately exercising the option on date 2 is .613, .122, and 0 in states 0, 1, and 2, respectively. Furthermore, since the option is worthless on date 3, the value of the option on date 2 is just the value of immediate exercise.

---

[1] In the stock option context, the equivalent result is that early exercise of a call option is not optimal unless the dividend is large enough.

On date 1, state 0, the value of immediate exercise is .655. The value of holding the option is

$$\frac{.6489 \times .122 + .3511 \times .613}{1 + .045/2} = .288 \tag{19.7}$$

Therefore, on date 1, state 0, the owner of the option will choose to exercise and the value of the option is .655. Here, it is worth more to exercise the option on date 1 and earn a coupon rate of 5.25% in a 4.50% short-term rate environment than to hold on to the option.

On date 1, state 1, the bond sells for less than par so the value of immediate exercise equals zero. The value of holding the option is

$$\frac{.6489 \times 0 + .3511 \times .122}{1 + .055/2} = .042 \tag{19.8}$$

Hence the owner will hold the option, and its value is .042.

Finally, on date 0, the value of exercising the option immediately is .006. The value of holding the option is

$$\frac{.8024 \times .042 + .1976 \times .655}{1 + .05/2} = .159 \tag{19.9}$$

The owner of the option will not exercise, and the value of the option on date 0 is .159. In this situation, earning a coupon of 5.25% in a 5% short-term rate environment is not sufficient compensation for giving up an option that could be worth as much as .655 on date 1.

The following tree for the value of the option collects these results. States in which the option is exercised are indicated by option values in boldface.

$$
\begin{array}{ccccccc}
& & & & & & 0 \\
& & & & 0.000 & & \\
& & & 0.042 & & & 0 \\
& & 0.159 & & \mathbf{0.122} & & \\
& & & \mathbf{0.655} & & & 0 \\
& & & & \mathbf{0.613} & & \\
& & & & & & 0 \\
\end{array}
$$

Put options are priced analogously. The only change is that the value of immediately exercising a put option struck at K when the bond price is P equals

$$V_E = \max(K - P, 0) \tag{19.10}$$

rather than (19.5). The advantage of early exercise for a put option (i.e., the right to sell) is that the strike price is received earlier. The disadvantages of exercising a put early are giving up the coupon and not being able to wait another period before deciding whether to sell the bond at the fixed strike price.

Before concluding this section it should be noted that the selection of time steps takes on added importance for the pricing of American and Bermudan options. The concern when pricing any security is that a time step larger than an instant is only an approximation to the more nearly continuous process of international markets. The additional concern when pricing Bermudan or American options is that a tree may not allow for sufficiently frequent exercise decisions. Consider, for example, using a tree with annual time steps to price a Bermudan option that permits exercise every six months. By omitting possible exercise dates the tree does not permit an option holder to make certain decisions to maximize the value of the option. Furthermore, since on these omitted exercise dates an option holder would never make a decision that lowers the value of the option, omitting these exercise dates necessarily undervalues the Bermudan option.

In the case of a Bermudan option the step size problem can be fixed either by reducing the step size so that every Bermudan exercise date is on the tree or by augmenting an existing tree with the Bermudan exercise dates. In the case of an American option it is impossible to add enough dates to reflect the value of the option fully. While detailed numerical analysis is beyond the scope of this book, two responses to this problem may be mentioned. First, experiment with different step sizes to determine which are accurate enough for the purpose at hand. Second, calculate option values for smaller and smaller step sizes and then extrapolate to the option value in the case of continuous exercise.

APPLICATION: FNMA 6.25s of July 19, 2011, and the Pricing of Callable Bonds

The *Federal National Mortgage Association* (FNMA) recently reintroduced its *Callable Benchmark Program* under which it regularly sells *callable* bonds to the public. On July 19, 2001, for example, FNMA sold an issue with a coupon of 6.25%, a maturity date of July 19, 2011, and a *call* feature allowing FNMA to purchase these bonds on July 19, 2004, at par. This call feature is called an *embedded call* because the option is part of the bond's structure and does not trade separately from the bond. In any case, until July 19, 2004, the bond pays coupons at a rate of 6.25%. On July 19, 2004, FNMA must decide whether or not to exercise its call. If FNMA does exercise, it pays par to repurchase all of the bonds. If FNMA does not exercise, the bond continues to earn 6.25% until maturity at which time principal is returned. This structure is sometimes referred to as "10NC3," pronounced "10-non-call-three," because it is a 10-year bond that is not callable for three years. These three years are referred to as the period of *call protection*.

The call feature of the FNMA 6.25s of July 19, 2011, is a particularly simple example of an embedded option. First, FNMA's option is European; it may call the bonds only on July 19, 2004. Other callable bonds give the issuer a Bermudan or American call after the period of call protection. For example, a Bermudan version might allow FNMA to call the bonds on any coupon date on or after the *first call date* of July 19, 2004, while an American version would allow FNMA to call the bonds at any time after July 19, 2004. The second reason the call feature of the FNMA issue is particularly simple is that the strike price is par. Other callable bonds require the issuer to pay a premium above par (e.g., 102 percent of par). In the Bermudan or American cases there might be a schedule of call prices. An old rule of thumb in the corporate bond market was to set the premium on the first call date equal to half the coupon rate. After the first call date the premium was set to decline linearly to par over some number of years and then to remain at par until the bond's maturity. The pricing technique of the previous section is easily adapted to a schedule of call prices.

The rest of this section and the next discuss the price behavior of callable bonds in detail. The basic idea, however, is as follows. If interest rates rise after an issuer sells a bond, the issuer wins in the sense that it is borrowing money at a relatively low rate of interest. Conversely, if rates fall after the sale then bondholders win in the sense that they are investing at a relatively high rate of interest. The embedded option, by allowing the issuer to purchase the bonds at some fixed price, caps the amount by which investors can profit from a rate decline. In fact, an embedded call at par cancels any price appreciation as of the call date although investors do collect an above-market coupon rate before the call. In exchange for giving up some or all of the price appreciation from a rate decline, bondholders receive a higher coupon rate from a callable bond than from an otherwise identical noncallable bond.

To understand the pricing of the callable bond issue, assume that there exists an otherwise identical noncallable bond—a noncallable bond issued by FNMA with a coupon rate of 6.25% and a maturity date of July 19, 2011. Also assume that there exists a separately traded European call option to buy this noncallable bond at par. Finally, let P_C denote the price of the callable bond, let P_{NC} denote the price of the otherwise identical noncallable bond, and let C denote the price of the European call on the noncallable bond. Then,

$$P_C = P_{NC} - C \tag{19.11}$$

Equation (19.11) may be proved by arbitrage arguments as follows. Assume that $P_C < P_{NC} - C$. Then an arbitrageur would execute the following trades:

Buy the callable bond for P_C.
Buy the European call option for C.
Sell the noncallable bond for P_{NC}.

The cash flow from these trades is $P_{NC} - C - P_C$, which, by assumption, is positive.

If rates are lower on July 19, 2004, and FNMA exercises the embedded option to buy its bonds at par, then the arbitrageur can unwind the trade without additional profit or loss as follows:

Sell the callable bond to FNMA for 100.
Exercise the European call option to purchase the noncallable bond for 100.
Deliver the purchased noncallable bond to cover the short position.

Alternatively, if rates are higher on July 19, 2004, and FNMA decides not to exercise its option, the arbitrageur can unwind the trade without additional profit or loss as follows:

Allow the European call option to expire unexercised.
Deliver the once callable bond to cover the short position in the noncallable bond.

Note that the arbitrageur can deliver the callable bond to cover the short in the noncallable bond because on July 19, 2004, FNMA's embedded option expires. That once callable bond becomes equivalent to the otherwise identical noncallable bond.

The preceding argument shows that the assumption $P_C < P_{NC} - C$ leads to an initial cash flow without any subsequent losses, that is, to an arbitrage opportunity. The same argument in reverse shows that $P_C > P_{NC} - C$ also leads to an arbitrage opportunity. Hence the equality in (19.11) must hold.

The intuition behind equation (19.11) is that the callable bond is equivalent to an otherwise identical noncallable bond minus the value of the embedded option. The value of the option is subtracted from the noncallable bond price because the issuer has the option. Equivalently, the value of the option is subtracted because the bondholder has sold the embedded option to the issuer.

Along the lines of the previous section, a term structure model may be used to price the European option on the otherwise identical noncallable bond. After that, equation (19.11) may be used to obtain a value for the callable bond. While the discussion to this point assumes that the embedded option is European, equation (19.11) applies to other option styles as well. If the option embedded in the FNMA 6.25s of July 19, 2011, were Bermudan or American, then a term structure model would be used to calculate the value of that Bermudan or American option on a hypothetical noncallable FNMA bond with a coupon of 6.25% and a maturity date of July 19, 2011. Then this Bermudan or American option value would be subtracted from the value of the noncallable bond to obtain the value of the callable bond.

Combining equation (19.11) with the optimal exercise rules described in the previous section reveals the following about the price of the callable bond. First, if the issuer calls the bond then the price of the callable bond equals the strike price. Second, if the issuer chooses not to call the bond (when it may do so) then the callable bond price is less than the strike price. To prove the first of these statements, note that if it is optimal to exercise, then, by equation (19.6), the value of the call option must equal the value of immediate exercise. Furthermore, by equation (19.5), the value of immediate exercise equals the price of the noncallable bond minus the strike. Putting these facts together,

$$C = P_{NC} - K \tag{19.12}$$

But substituting (19.12) into (19.11),

$$P_C = P_{NC} - C = P_{NC} - \left(P_{NC} - K\right) = K \tag{19.13}$$

To prove the second statement, note that if it is not optimal to exercise, then, by equation (19.6), the value of the option is greater than the value of immediate exercise given by equation (19.5). Hence

$$C > P_{NC} - K \tag{19.14}$$

Then, substituting (19.14) into (19.11),

$$P_C = P_{NC} - C < P_{NC} - \left(P_{NC} - K\right) = K \tag{19.15}$$

By market convention, issuers pay for embedded call options through a higher coupon rate rather than by selling callable bonds at a discount from par. On July 19, 2001, for example, when FNMA sold its 6.25s of July 19, 2011, for approximately par, the yield on 10-year FNMA bonds was approximately 5.85%. FNMA could have sold a callable bond with a coupon of 5.85%. In that case the otherwise identical noncallable bond would be worth about par, and the callable bond, by equation (19.11), would sell at a discount from par. Instead, FNMA chose to sell a callable bond with a coupon of 6.25%. The otherwise identical noncallable bond was worth more than par but the embedded call option, through equation (19.11), reduced the price of the callable bond to approximately par.

GRAPHICAL ANALYSIS OF CALLABLE BOND PRICING

This section graphically explores the qualitative behavior of callable bond prices using the FNMA 6.25s of July 19, 2011, for settle on July 19, 2001, as an example. Begin by defining two reference bonds. The first is the otherwise identical noncallable bond referred to in the previous section—an imaginary 10-year noncallable FNMA bond with a coupon of 6.25% and a maturity of July 19, 2011. The second reference bond is an imaginary three-year noncallable FNMA bond with a coupon of 6.25% and a maturity of July 19, 2004.[2] Assuming a flat yield curve on July 19, 2001, the dashed line and thin solid line in Figure 19.4 graph the prices of these reference bonds at different yield levels. When rates are particularly low the 10-year bond is worth more than the three-year bond because the former earns an above-market rate for a longer period of time. Conversely, when rates are particularly high the three-year bond is worth more because it earns a below-market rate for a shorter period of time. Also, the 10-year bond's price-yield curve is the steeper of the two because its DV01 is greater.

The thick solid line in the figure graphs the price of the callable bond using a particular pricing model. While the shape and placement of this curve depends on the model and its parameters, the qualitative results described in the rest of this section apply to any model and any set of parameters.

---

[2]If the call price of the FNMA 6.25s of July 19, 2011, were 102 instead of 100, the three-year reference bond would change. For the analysis of this section to apply, this reference bond would pay 3.125 every six months, like the callable bond, but would pay 102 instead of 100 at maturity. While admittedly an odd structure, this reference bond can be priced easily.

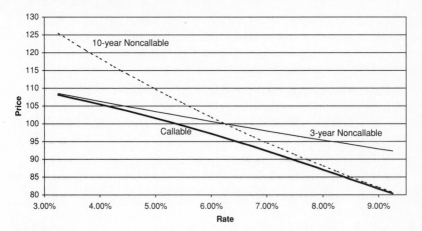

FIGURE 19.4   Price-Rate Curves for the Callable Bond and the Two Noncallable
Reference Bonds

The four qualitative features of Figure 19.4 may be summarized as
follows.

1. The price of the callable bond is always below the price of the three-
   year bond.
2. The price of the callable bond is always below the price of the 10-year
   bond.
3. As rates increase, the price of the callable bond approaches the price of
   the 10-year bond.
4. As rates decrease, the price of the callable bond approaches the price
   of the three-year bond.

The intuition behind statement 1 is as follows. From July 19, 2001, to
July 19, 2004, the callable bond and the three-year bond make exactly the
same coupon payments. However, on July 19, 2004, the three-year bond
will be worth par while the callable bond will be worth par or less: By the
results at the end of the previous section, the callable bond will be worth
par if FNMA calls the bond but less than par otherwise. But if the cash
flows from the bonds are the same until July 19, 2004, and then the three-
year bond is worth as much as or more than the callable bond, then, by arbitrage, the three-year bond must be worth more as of July 19, 2001.

Statement 2 follows immediately from the fact that the price of an option is always positive. Since $C>0$, by (19.11) $P_C<P_{NC}$. In fact, rearranging (19.11), $C=P_{NC}-P_C$. Hence the value of the call option is given graphically by the distance between the price of the 10-year bond and the price of the callable bond in Figure 19.4.

Statement 3 is explained by noting that, when rates are high and bond prices low, the option to call the bond at par is worth very little. More loosely, when rates are high the likelihood of the bond being called on July 19, 2004, is quite low. But, this being the case, the prices of the callable bond and the 10-year bond will be close.

Finally, statement 4 follows from the observation that, when rates are low and bond prices high, the option to call the bond at par is very valuable. The probability that the bond will be called on July 19, 2004, is high. This being the case, the prices of the callable bond and the three-year bond will be close.

Figure 19.4 also shows that an embedded call option induces negative convexity. For the callable bond price curve to resemble the three-year curve at low rates and the 10-year curve at high rates, the callable bond curve must be negatively convex.

Figure 19.5 illustrates the negative convexity of callable bonds more dramatically by graphing the duration of the two reference bonds and that of the callable FNMA bonds. The duration of the 10-year bond is, as expected, greater than that of the three-year bond. Furthermore, the 10-year

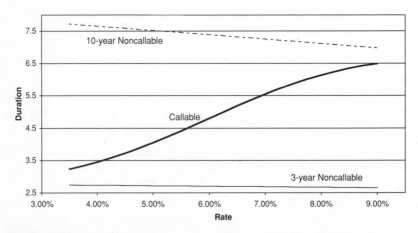

FIGURE 19.5 Duration-Rate Curves for the Callable Bond and the Two Noncallable Reference Bonds

duration curve is steeper than that of the three-year because longer bonds are generally more convex. See Chapter 6.

When rates are high the duration of the callable bond approaches the duration of the 10-year bond. However, since the callable bond may be called and, in that eventuality, may turn out to be a relatively short-term bond, the duration of the callable bond will be below that of the 10-year bond. When rates are low the duration of the callable bond approaches the duration of the three-year bond. Since, however, the callable bond may not be called and thus turn out to be a relatively long-term bond, the duration of the callable bond will be above that of the three-year bond. In order for the duration of the callable bond to move from the duration of the three-year bond when rates are low to the duration of the 10-year bond when rates are high, the duration of the callable bond must increase with rates. But this characteristic is akin to negative convexity.

The analysis of Figures 19.4 and 19.5 helps explain why FNMA has chosen to issue callable bonds. FNMA owns a great amount of mortgages that, as will be explained in Chapter 21, are negatively convex. By selling only noncallable debt, FNMA would find itself with negatively convex assets and positively convex liabilities. As explained in the context of Figure 5.9, a position with that composition would require constant monitoring and frequent hedging. By selling some callable debt, however, FNMA can ensure that its negatively convex assets are at least partially matched by negatively convex liabilities.

Using data over the six-month period subsequent to the issuance of the FNMA 6.25s of July 19, 2011, Figure 19.6 shows that the theoretical analysis built into Figures 19.4 and 19.5 holds in practice. Figure 19.6 graphs the price of the noncallable FNMA 6s of May 15, 2011, and the price of the callable FNMA 6.25s of July 19, 2011, as a function of the yield of the noncallable bond. Because of the embedded call, the callable bond does not rally as much as the noncallable bond as rates fall. Also, the empirical duration of the callable bond is clearly lower than that of the noncallable bond. Finally, some negative convexity seems to be present in the data but the effect is certainly mild.

A NOTE ON YIELD-TO-CALL

As defined in Chapter 3, the yield-to-maturity is the rate such that discounting a bond's cash flows by that rate gives the market price. For a

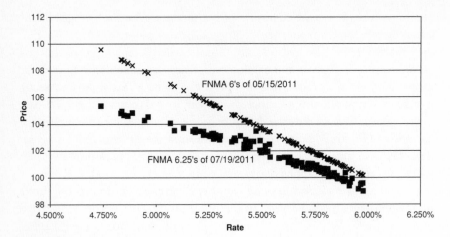

FIGURE 19.6   Prices of the Noncallable FNMA 6s of May 15, 2011, and the
Callable 6.25s of July 19, 2011

callable bond, with cash flows that may be earned to the first call date, to
maturity, or to some date in between, there is no obvious way to define a
yield. In response, some market participants turn to *yield-to-call*.

To calculate the yield-to-call, assume that the bond will definitely be
called at some future date. The most common assumption is that the call
will take place on the first call date but, in principle, any call date may be
used for the calculation. To distinguish among these assumptions practitioners refer to yield-to-first-call, to first par call, to November 15, 2007,
call, and so on. In any case, the assumption of a particular call scenario
gives a particular set of cash flows. The yield-to-call is the rate such that
discounting these cash flows by that rate gives the market price.

Some practitioners believe that bonds may be priced on yield-to-call
basis when rates are low and on a yield-to-maturity basis when rates are
high. These practitioners also tend to believe that the price of a callable
bond is bracketed by price using yield-to-call and price using yield-to-maturity. Figure 19.4 shows these rules of thumb to be misleading. At any
given yield the price of the callable bond on a yield-to-maturity basis is
simply the price of the 10-year bond. Similarly, at any given yield the price
of the callable bond on a yield-to-call basis is simply the price of the three-
year bond. At any yield level the price of the callable bond is below both
the price on a yield-to-call basis and the price on a yield-to-maturity basis.

Hence both of these price calculations overestimate the price of the callable bond, and the prices from the two approaches do not bracket the price of the callable bond.

The intuition behind the overestimation of the callable bond price using either yield-to-call or yield-to-maturity is that the issuer of the bond has an option. Assuming that the issuer will not exercise this option optimally underestimates the issuer's option and overestimates the value of the callable bond. The yield-to-call calculation makes this error by assuming that the issuer acts suboptimally by committing to call the bond no matter what subsequently happens to rates. The yield-to-maturity calculation makes the error by assuming that the issuer commits not to call the bond no matter what subsequently happens to rates.

SWAPTIONS, CAPS, AND FLOORS

Swaptions (i.e., options on swaps) are particularly liquid fixed income options. A *receiver swaption* gives the owner the right to receive fixed in an interest rate swap. For example, a European-style receiver might give its owner the right on May 15, 2002, to receive fixed on a 10-year swap at a fixed rate of 5.75%. A *payer swaption* gives the owner the right to pay fixed in an interest rate swap. For example, an American-style payer might give its owner the right at any time on or before May 15, 2002, to pay fixed on a 10-year swap at a fixed rate of 5.75%.

Recall from Chapter 18 that the initial value of the floating side of a swap, including the fictional notional payment at maturity, is par. Also recall that the fixed side of a swap, including the fictional notional payment, is equivalent in structure to a bond with a coupon payment equal to the fixed rate of the swap. These observations imply that the right to receive fixed at 5.75% and pay floating for 10 years is equivalent to the right to receive a 5.75% 10-year bond for a price of par. In other words, this receiver option is equivalent to a call option on a 10-year 5.75% coupon bond. Similarly, the payer option just mentioned is equivalent to a put option on a 10-year 5.75% coupon bond. Therefore, the term structure models of Part Three combined with the discussion in this chapter may be used to price swaptions.

The swaption market is sufficiently developed to offer a wide range of option exercise periods and underlying swap expirations. Table 19.1 illustrates a subset of this range of offerings as of January, 2002. The rows

TABLE 19.1 Swaption Volatility Grid, January 2002

		Underlying Swap Maturity				
		1 year	2 Years	5 Years	10 Years	30 Years
	1 month	47.6%	40.3%	29.1%	25.2%	17.6%
	3 months	43.5%	37.8%	28.7%	25.2%	17.8%
Swaption	6 months	42.9%	35.0%	27.1%	24.0%	17.1%
Maturity	1 year	34.0%	29.0%	24.6%	22.2%	16.1%
	2 years	26.0%	24.4%	22.7%	20.9%	15.8%
	5 years	21.4%	20.9%	19.7%	18.1%	14.0%
	10 years	17.1%	16.8%	16.1%	15.1%	11.3%

represent option expiration periods, the columns represent swap expirations, and the entries record the yield volatility (see Chapter 12) implied by the respective swaptions prices and *Black's model*.[3] For example, a three-month option to enter into a 10-year swap is priced using a yield volatility of 25.2%.

Caps and *floors* are other popular interest rate options. Define a *caplet* as a security that, for every dollar of notional amount, pays

$$\frac{\max(L(t) - \overline{L}, 0) \times d}{360} \qquad (19.16)$$

d days after time t, where $L(t)$ is the specified LIBOR rate and $\overline{L}$ is the caplet rate or strike rate. As an example, consider a $10,000,000 caplet on three-month LIBOR struck at 2.25% and expiring on August 15, 2002. If three-month LIBOR on May 15, 2002, is 2.50%, then this caplet pays

$$\frac{\$10,000,000 \times (2.50\% - 2.25\%) \times 92}{360} = \$6,389 \qquad (19.17)$$

If, however, three-month LIBOR on May 15, 2002, is below 2.25%, for example at 2.00%, then the caplet pays nothing. This caplet, therefore, is a call on three-month LIBOR.

---

[3]Black's model for swaptions is closely related to the Black-Scholes stock option model. For further details see Hull (2000), pp. 543–547.

A cap is a series of caplets. For example, buying a two-year cap on February 15, 2002, is equivalent to seven caplets maturing on August 15, 2002, November 15, 2002, and so on, out to Februry 15, 2004. (By convention the caplet maturing on May 15, 2002, is omitted since the setting of LIBOR relevant for a May 15, 2002, payment, that is, LIBOR on February 15, 2002, is known at the time the cap is traded.)

A *floorlet* pays

$$\frac{\max\left(\overline{L} - L(t), 0\right) \times d}{360} \tag{19.18}$$

d days after time *t* and, therefore, is a put on LIBOR. A floor is a series of floorlets.

The payoffs to the other options described in this chapter are expressed in terms of bond prices while the payoffs to caps and floors depend directly on the level of interest rates. In any case, the tools of Part Three can be easily applied to value caps and floors. As of January, 2002, Table 19.2 presents volatility levels for caps on three-month LIBOR given their prices and a variant of the Black-Scholes option model.[4] For example, a five-year cap on three-month LIBOR is priced using a yield volatility of 26.8%.

Tables 19.1 and 19.2 reveal the difficulty of designing models for trading swaptions, caps, and floors. First, given the varying levels of liquidity of the options in these grids, decisions have to be made about how much influence each option should have in the modeling process. Second, a

TABLE 19.2   Three-Month LIBOR Cap Volatility, January 2002

Maturity	Yield Volatility
1 year	38.6%
2 years	34.9%
5 years	26.8%
10 years	23.1%

---

[4]See Hull (2000), pp. 537–543.

model with very few factors is not usually able to capture the rich structure of these volatility grids without a good deal of time dependence in the volatility functions. But, as described in Part Three, time-dependent volatility functions can sometimes strain credulity.

For the limited goal of quoting market prices, models that essentially interpolate the volatility grids are adequate, and relatively complex time-dependent volatility functions can be tolerated. For the more ambitious goals of pricing for value and for hedging, practitioners and academics are gravitating to multi-factor models that balance the competing objectives of describing market prices, of computational feasibility, and of economic and financial sensibility. See Chapter 13.

QUOTING PRICES WITH VOLATILITY MEASURES IN FIXED INCOME OPTIONS MARKETS

Market participants often use yield-to-maturity to quote bond prices because interest rates are in many ways more intuitive than bond prices. Similarly, market participants often use volatility to quote option prices because volatility is in many ways more intuitive than option prices. Chapter 3 defined the widely accepted relationship between yield-to-maturity and price. This section discusses the use of market conventions to quote the relationship between volatility and option prices.

Many options trading desks have their own proprietary term structure models to value fixed income options. If customers want to know the volatility at which they are buying or selling options, these trading desks have a problem. Quoting the volatility inputs to their proprietary models does not really help customers because they do not know the model and have no means of generating prices given these volatility inputs. Furthermore, the trading desk may not want to reveal the workings of its models. Therefore, markets have settled on various canonical models with which to relate price and volatility.

In the bond options market, Black's model, a close relative of the Black-Scholes stock option model, is used for this purpose. As discussed in Chapter 9, direct applications of stock option models to bonds may be reasonable if the time to option expiry is relatively short. Further details are not presented here other than to note that Black's model assumes that the price of a bond on the option expiration date is lognormally distributed with a mean equal to the bond's forward price.[5]

Figure 19.7 reproduces a Bloomberg screen used for valuing options using Black's model. The darkened rectangles indicate trader input values. The header under "OPTION VALUATION" indicates that the option is on the U.S. Treasury 5s of February 15, 2011. As of the trade date January 15, 2002, this bond was the double-old 10-year. The option expires in six months, on July 15, 2002. The current price of the bond is 101-8¼ corresponding to a yield of 4.827%. The strike price of the option is 99-18¼ corresponding to a yield of 5.063%. At the bottom right of the screen, repo rate is 1.58% which, given the bond price, gives a forward price of 99-18¼. The option is,

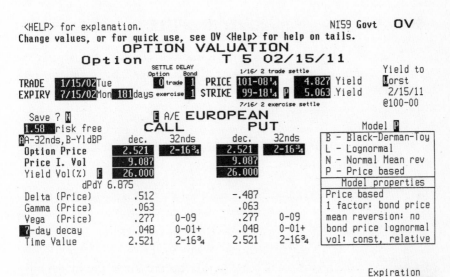

FIGURE 19.7 Bloomberg's Option Valuation Screen for Options on the 5s of February 15, 2001
Source: Copyright 2002 Bloomberg L.P.

---

[5]For more details, see Hull (2000), pp. 533–537.

therefore, an at-the-money forward (ATMF) option, meaning that the strike price equals the forward price. The risk-free rate equals 1.58%, used in Black's model to discount the payoffs of the option under the assumed lognormal distribution. Because the double-old 10-year was not particularly special on January 15, 2002, the repo rate and the risk-free rate are equal. If the bond were trading special, the repo rate used to calculate the bond's forward price would be less than the risk-free rate.

As can be seen above the words "CALL" and "PUT," the option is a European option. To the right is the model code "P" used to indicate the price-based or Black's model. Below this code is a brief description of the model's properties. It is a one-factor model with the bond price itself as the factor. There is no mean reversion in the process, the bond price is lognormal, and the volatility is constant. The description also indicates that the volatility is relative, that is, measured as a percentage of the bond's forward price.

The main part of the option valuation screen shows that at a percentage price volatility of 9.087% put and call prices equal 2.521.[6] This means, for example, that an option on $100,000,000 of the 5s of February 15, 2011, on July 15, 2002, at 99-18$^1/_4$ costs

$$\$100,000,000 \times \frac{2.521}{100} = \$2,521,000 \qquad (19.19)$$

The price volatility is labeled "Price I. Vol" for "Price Implied Volatility" because the pricing screen may be used in one of two ways. First, one may input the volatility and the screen calculates the option price using Black's model. Second, one may input the option price and the screen calculates the *implied volatility*—the volatility that, when used in Black's model, produces the input option price.

While Black's model is widely used to relate option price and volatility, percentage price volatility (or, simply, price volatility) is not so intuitive as volatility based on interest rates. Writing the percentage change in the forward price as $\Delta P_{fwd}/P_{fwd}$, the percentage change may be rewritten as

---

[6]At-the-money forward put and call prices must be equal by put-call parity.

$$\frac{\Delta P_{fwd}}{P_{fwd}} = \frac{y_{fwd}}{P_{fwd}} \frac{\Delta P_{fwd}}{\Delta y_{fwd}} \frac{\Delta y_{fwd}}{y_{fwd}} \approx \frac{y_{fwd}}{P_{fwd}} 10,000 \times DV01_{fwd} \frac{\Delta y_{fwd}}{y_{fwd}} \qquad (19.20)$$

Letting σ_p denote price volatility and σ_y denote yield volatility, it follows from equation (19.20) that

$$\sigma_P = \frac{y_{fwd}}{P_{fwd}} 10,000 \times DV01_{fwd} \sigma_y \qquad (19.21)$$

In the example of Figure 19.7,

$$9.087\% = \frac{5.063\%}{99 - 18\frac{1}{4}} 10,000 \times .06875\sigma_y \qquad (19.22)$$

Note that all of these inputs are on the Bloomberg screen. Since the strike is equal to the forward price, the yield corresponding to the strike is the forward yield. Also, the forward DV01 is computed next to the symbol "dPdY" (i.e., the derivative of price with respect to yield). Solving equation (19.22),

$$\sigma_y = 26\% \qquad (19.23)$$

as reported in the row labeled "Yield Vol (%)." The input "F," by the way, indicates that volatility should be computed using a forward rate, as done here.

Many market participants find yield volatility more intuitive than price volatility. With yields at 5.063%, for example, a yield volatility of 26% indicates that a one standard deviation move is equal to 26% of 5.063%. This also suggests measuring volatility in basis points: 26% of 5.063% is 131.6 basis points. Letting σ_{bp} denote basis point volatility, then, as explained in Chapter 12,

$$\sigma_{bp} = y_{fwd}\sigma_y \qquad (19.24)$$

It is crucial to note that while volatility can be quoted as yield volatility or as basis point volatility, Black's model takes price volatility as input. In other words, it is price volatility that determines the probability distribution used to calculate option prices. To make this point more clearly, consider three models: Black's model with price volatility equal to 9.087%, a model with a lognormally distributed short rate and yield volatility equal to 26%, and a model with a normally distributed short rate and basis point volatility equal to 131.6 basis points. These three models are different. They will not always produce the same option prices even though the volatility measures are the same in the sense of equations (19.21) and (19.24).

Return now to the trading desk with a proprietary option pricing model. A customer inquires about an at-the-money forward option on the 5s of February 15, 2011, and the desk responds with a price of 2.521 corresponding to a Black's model volatility of 9.087%. The customer knows the price and has some idea what this price means in terms of volatility, whether by thinking about price volatility directly or by converting to yield or basis point volatility. But the customer cannot infer the price the trading desk would attach to a different option on the same bond nor certainly to an option on a different bond. Plugging in a price volatility of 9.087% on a Bloomberg screen to price other options on the 5s of February 15, 2011, will not produce the trading desk's price unless the trading desk itself uses Black's model.

SMILE AND SKEW

Assume that the market price is 2.521 for the ATMF option on the 5s of February 15, 2011, corresponding to a Black volatility of 9.087%. If Black's model were the true pricing model, an option on the 5s of February 15, 2011, with any strike expiring on July 15, 2002, could be priced using a volatility of 9.087%. The correct risk-neutral distribution of the terminal price, however, might have *fatter tails* than the lognormal price distribution assumed in Black's model. The tails of a distribution refer to the probability of relatively extreme events (i.e., events far from the mean). A distribution with fat tails relative to the lognormal price distribution has relatively higher probability of extreme events and relatively lower probability of the more central outcomes. The implication of fat tails for option pricing is that out-of-the-money forward (OTMF) options—options with strikes above or below the forward price—will be worth more than indicated by Black's model. Equivalently, since option prices increase with volatility, using Black's model to compute the implied volatility of an OTMF option will produce a volatility number higher than 9.087%. This effect is called a *smile* from the shape of a graph of Black implied volatility against strike.

If, relative to the lognormal price distribution, the correct pricing distribution attaches relatively high probabilities to outcomes above the forward price and relatively low probabilities to outcomes below the forward price, or vice versa, then the correct distribution is *skewed* relative to the lognormal price distribution. As a result the true distribution will generate option prices above Black's model for high strikes and below Black's model for low strikes, or vice versa. Equivalently, the implied volatility computed from Black's model will be higher than 9.087% for high strikes and below 9.087% for low strikes, or vice versa.

In general, of course, the correct risk-neutral distribution can differ in arbitrary ways from the lognormal price distribution of Black's model, and the implied volatility computed by Black's model for options with different strikes can take on many different patterns. Figure 19.8 graphs two examples. The horizontal axis gives the strike of call options on the 5s of February 15, 2011, and the vertical axis gives the implied volatility of call options computed using Black's model.

The curve labeled "Normal Model" generates option prices using a one-factor model with normally distributed short rates, an annualized volatility of 146 basis points, and mean reversion with a half-life of about 23 years. The model was calibrated so that the ATMF call option has a price of 2.521. Note that this curve is relatively flat, meaning that the implied volatility of call options with various strikes is not far from 9.087%.

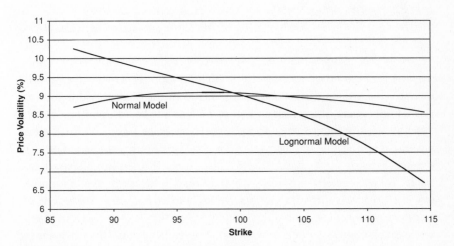

FIGURE 19.8 Black's Model Implied Volatility as a Function of Strike for a Normal and a Lognormal Short-Rate Model

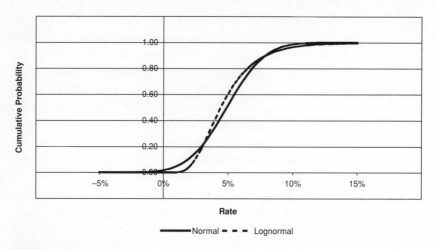

FIGURE 19.9   Cumulative Normal and Lognormal Distribution Functions Based
on Example in Figure 12.3

This is not very surprising because normally distributed rates imply lognormally distributed bond prices, as assumed in Black's model.

By contrast, the curve labeled "Lognormal Model" demonstrates substantial skew. This one-factor model with no mean reversion and a yield
volatility of 27.66% gives an ATMF option price of 2.521, but the implied
volatility of call options with other strikes is very different from 9.087%.
In particular, call options with low strikes are associated with relatively
high Black volatility and call options with high strikes are associated with
relatively low Black volatility. Equivalently, the lognormal model values
the low-strike options more and the high-strike options less than Black's
model. This is not surprising given the shape of the normal and lognormal
probability density functions in Figure 12.3 or the corresponding cumulative normal and lognormal distribution functions in Figure 19.9. The lognormal distribution attaches relatively low probability to low levels of
interest rates (i.e., to high prices). Therefore, the lognormal short-rate
model values high-strike options less than Black's lognormal price (approximately normal short-rate) model. Also, the lognormal distribution attaches relatively high probability to high rates (i.e., to low prices) so that
the lognormal model values low-strike options more than Black's model.

CHAPTER 20

Note and Bond Futures

Futures contracts on government bonds are important for the longer-maturity part of the market for the same reasons that futures on short-term deposits are important for the short end. Futures on bonds are very liquid and require relatively little capital to establish sizable positions. Consequently, these contracts are often the instruments of choice for hedging risks arising from changes in longer-term rates and for speculating on the direction of these rates.

Unlike the futures contracts described in Chapter 17, futures contracts on bonds contain many embedded options that greatly complicate their valuation. This chapter addresses the relevant issues in the context of U.S. Treasury futures, but the treatment applies equally well to futures traded in European markets. In fact, the options embedded in European futures contracts are simpler than those embedded in U.S. contracts.

MECHANICS

This section describes the workings of U.S. note and bond futures contracts.[1] The section after next explains the motivations behind the design of these contracts.

Futures contracts on U.S. government bonds do not have one underlying security. Instead, there is a *basket* of underlying securities defined by some set of rules. The 10-year note contract expiring in March, 2002 (TYH2), for example, includes as an underlying security any U.S. Treasury note that matures in 6.5 to 10 years from March 1, 2002. This rule includes all of the securities listed in Table 20.1. The rule excludes, however,

---

[1]For a more detailed treatment see Burghardt, Belton, Lane, and Papa (1994).

TABLE 20.1   The Deliverable Basket into
TYH2

Coupon	Maturity	Conversion Factor
4.75%	11/15/08	0.9335
5.50%	05/15/09	0.9718
6.00%	08/15/09	0.9999
6.50%	02/15/10	1.0305
5.75%	08/15/10	0.9838
5.00%	02/15/11	0.9326
5.00%	08/15/11	0.9297

the 9.125s of May 15, 2009: While this bond matures in a little less than 7.25 years from March 1, 2002, it was issued as a U.S. Treasury bond rather than a U.S. Treasury note.[2] The conversion factors listed in the table are discussed shortly.

The seller of a futures contract, or the *short*, commits to sell or *deliver* a particular quantity of a bond in that contract's basket during the *delivery month*. The seller may choose which bond to deliver and when to deliver during the delivery month. These options are called the *quality option* and the *timing option*, respectively. The buyer of the futures contract, or the *long*, commits to buy or *take delivery* of the bonds chosen by the seller at the time chosen by the seller. For TYH2 the delivery month is March 2002. Delivery may not take place before the *first delivery date* of March 1, 2002, nor after the *last delivery date* of March 28, 2002. The *contract size* of TYH2 is $100,000, so the seller delivers $100,000 face amount of the chosen bonds to the buyer for each contract the seller is short.

Market forces determine the futures price at any time. Each day, the exchange on which the futures trade determines a *settlement price* that is usually close to the price of the last trade of the day. Mark-to-market payments, described in Chapter 17, are based on daily changes in the settlement price. Table 20.2 lists the settlement prices of TYH2 from November

---

[2]U.S. Treasury notes are issued with an original term of 10 years or less. U.S. Treasury bonds are issued with an original term greater than 10 years. This distinction is rarely of any importance and this chapter continues to use the term bond to mean any coupon bond.

TABLE 20.2 Settlement Prices of TYH2 and Mark-to-Market from a Long of One Contract

Date	Price	Change (32nds)	Mark-to-Market
11/15/01	106-25		
11/16/01	105-24	−33	−$1,031
11/19/01	106-23	31	$969
11/20/01	105-31+	−23.5	−$734
11/21/01	105-07+	−24	−$750
11/23/01	104-28+	−11	−$344
11/26/01	104-27+	−1	−$31
11/27/01	105-14	18.5	$578
11/28/01	105-13	−1	−$31
11/29/01	106-25	44	$1,375
11/30/01	106-30+	5.5	$172

15 to November 30, 2001, along with the mark-to-market payments arising from a long position of one contract. To illustrate this calculation, the settlement price falls from November 19 to November 20, 2001, by 23.5 ticks (i.e., 32nds). On the $100,000 face amount of one contract the loss to a long position is $100,000×($^{23.5}/_{32}$)/100 or $734.

The price at which a seller delivers a particular bond to a buyer is determined by the settlement price of the futures contract and by the *conversion factor* of that particular bond. Let the settlement price of the futures contract at time t be $F(t)$ and the conversion factor of bond i be cf^i. Then the delivery price is $cf^i \times F(t)$ and the invoice price for delivery is this delivery price plus accrued interest: $cf^i \times F(t) + AI^i(t)$. The conversion factors for TYH2 are listed in Table 20.1. If, for example, the futures settlement price is 100, any delivery of the 4.75s of November 15, 2008, will occur at a flat price of .9335×100 or 93.35. At the same time any delivery of the 6.5s of February 15, 2010, will occur at a flat price of 1.0305×100 or 103.05.

Each contract trades until its *last trade date*. The settlement price at the end of that day is the *final settlement price*. This final settlement price is used for the last mark-to-market payment and for any deliveries that have not yet been made. The last trade date of TYH2 is March 19, 2002. Any delivery from then on, through the last delivery date of March 28, 2002, is based on the final settlement price determined on March 19, 2002. This feature of U.S. futures contracts gives rise to the *end-of-month option* discussed in the penultimate section of this chapter.

The quality option is the most significant embedded option in futures contracts. To simplify the presentation, the timing and end-of-month options are ignored until discussed explicitly. Ignoring these two options is equivalent to assuming that the first delivery date, the last trade date, and the last delivery date are one and the same. In fact, this simplification accurately describes the government bond futures contracts that trade in Europe.

COST OF DELIVERY AND THE DETERMINATION OF THE FINAL SETTLEMENT PRICE

The *cost of delivery* measures how much it costs a short to fulfill the commitment to deliver a bond through a futures contract. Having decided to deliver bond i, the short has to buy the bond at its market price and then deliver it at the futures price. If the price of bond i at time t is $P^i(t)$, then

$$\text{Cost of Delivery} = P^i(t) + AI^i(t) - \left(cf^i \times F(t) + AI^i(t) \right)$$
$$= P^i(t) - cf^i \times F(t) \tag{20.1}$$

The short will minimize the cost of delivery by choosing which bond to deliver from among the bonds in the delivery basket. The bond that minimizes the cost of delivery is called the *cheapest-to-deliver* or the CTD. Table 20.3 illustrates cost of delivery calculations for TYH2 as of March 28, 2002, assuming that all bonds yield 5% and that the final settlement price is 105.6215. For example, the cost of delivering the 6s of August 15, 2009, is

$$106.107 - .9999 \times 105.6215 = .496 \tag{20.2}$$

In the example of Table 20.3, the 4.75s of November 15, 2008, are the bonds with the lowest cost of delivery, which in this case is zero. The next to CTD are the 5.5s of May 15, 2009, with a cost of delivery of 32 cents.

Since this section ignores the timing and end-of-month options, the determination of the final settlement price is quite simple:

TABLE 20.3 Cost of Delivery Calculations Assuming Yields of 5%

Futures price: 105.6215

Coupon	Maturity	Price	Conversion Factor	Cost of Delivery	Price/ Factor
4.75%	11/15/08	98.598	0.9335	0.000	105.6215
5.50%	05/15/09	102.962	0.9718	0.319	105.9501
6.00%	08/15/09	106.107	0.9999	0.496	106.1174
6.50%	02/15/10	109.671	1.0305	0.828	106.4249
5.75%	08/15/10	105.081	0.9838	1.170	106.8109
5.00%	02/15/11	99.995	0.9326	1.492	107.2213
5.00%	08/15/11	99.995	0.9297	1.798	107.5558

$$F(T) = \frac{P^{CTD}(T)}{cf^{CTD}} \tag{20.3}$$

where T denotes the last delivery date.

Equation (20.3) is proved by showing that there is an arbitrage opportunity if (20.3) does not hold.

First assume that $F(T) > P^{CTD}(T)/cf^{CTD}$ or, equivalently, that $cf^{CTD} \times F(T) - P^{CTD}(T) > 0$. In this case a trader could buy the CTD, sell the contract, and deliver the CTD. The profit from this trade is

$$cf^{CTD} \times F(T) - P^{CTD}(T) \tag{20.4}$$

But, by assumption, (20.4) is positive and, therefore, the trade described constitutes an arbitrage opportunity. Hence it cannot be the case that $F(T) > P^{CTD}(T)/cf^{CTD}$.

Next assume that $F(T) < P^{CTD}(T)/cf^{CTD}$ or, equivalently, that $P^{CTD}(T) - cf^{CTD} \times F(T) > 0$. In this case a trader could sell the CTD, buy the contract, and take delivery of the bond delivered by the short. Denoting the delivered bond as bond j, the profit from this strategy is

$$P^j(T) - cf^j \times F(T) \tag{20.5}$$

By the definition of CTD, the cost of delivering bond j must be greater than the cost of delivering the CTD. Hence,

$$P^j(T) - cf^j \times F(T) \geq P^{CTD}(T) - cf^{CTD} \times F(T) \qquad (20.6)$$

where equality holds if bond j is the CTD. But, by assumption, the right-hand side of (20.6) is positive. Therefore $P^j(T)-cf^j{\times}F(T)$ is positive, and the trade constitutes an arbitrage opportunity. Hence it cannot be the case that $F(T){<}P^{CTD}(T)/cf^{CTD}$. Ruling out these two assumed inequalities proves that equation (20.3) must hold.

Having determined the final settlement price is (20.3), the relationships among all the bonds in the basket, the CTD, and the futures price as of the last delivery date can be summarized neatly. First, it follows immediately from (20.3) that

$$P^{CTD}(T) - cf^{CTD} \times F(T) = 0 \qquad (20.7)$$

In words, the cost of delivering the CTD on the last delivery date is zero. Second, combining (20.3) with the CTD condition in (20.6) and rearranging terms, for any bond j that is not the CTD,

$$\frac{P^j(T)}{cf^j} > \frac{P^{CTD}(T)}{cf^{CTD}} = F(T) \qquad (20.8)$$

Equation (20.8) says that the CTD is the bond with the smallest ratio of price to conversion factor and that the futures price equals this minimum ratio. Furthermore, the futures price is less than or equal to the price of any bond divided by its conversion factor. Intuitively, the short uses the delivery option to minimize the value of the short position, that is to minimize the value of the futures contract. In particular, the short delivers the bond with the minimum ratio of price to conversion factor and, given that rule, the futures price equals that minimum. The last column of Table 20.3 illustrates the validity of equation (20.8) for the example of this section.

MOTIVATIONS FOR A DELIVERY BASKET AND CONVERSION FACTORS

The design of bond futures contracts purposely avoids a single underlying security. One reason for this is that if the single underlying bond should lose liquidity, perhaps because it has been accumulated over time by buy-and-hold investors and institutions, then the futures contract would lose its liquidity as well. Another reason for avoiding a single underlying bond is the possibility of a *squeeze*. To illustrate this problem, assume for the moment that only one bond were deliverable into a futures contract. Then a trader might be able to profit by simultaneously purchasing a large fraction of that bond issue and a large number of contracts. As parties with short positions in the contract scramble to buy that bond to deliver or scramble to buy back the contracts they have sold,[3] the trader can sell the holding of both bonds and contracts at prices well above their fair values. But by making shorts hesitant to take positions, the threat of a squeeze can prevent a contract from attracting volume and liquidity.

The existence of a basket of securities effectively avoids the problems of a single deliverable only if the cost of delivering the next to CTD is not that much higher than the cost of delivering the CTD. In the example of Table 20.3, the difference between the cost of delivering the CTD and the cost of delivering the next to CTD is 32 cents. If a trader squeezes the 4.75s of November 15, 2008, then the most that can be extracted from shorts in the contract is 32 cents: If the trader tries to extract more, then shorts would purchase and deliver the 5.50s of May 15, 2009, instead.

The difference between the cost of delivering the CTD and the cost of delivering the next to CTD is as small as it is because of the conversion factors. To see this, imagine that all the conversion factors were equal to one so that any bond in the basket could be delivered at the futures price. In this special case, (20.8) shows that, on the delivery date, the bond with the lowest price would be CTD and the futures price would equal this lowest price. In the example of Table 20.3, the CTD would still be the 4.75s of November 15, 2008, but the futures price would be 98.598. The 5s of February 15, 2011, and the 5s of August 15, 2011, would tie for the next to CTD at a price of 99.995. The cost of delivering either of these would be 99.995–98.598 or 1.397, much more than the 32-cent cost of delivering the next to CTD when the actual conversion factors are used.

The large difference between delivering the CTD versus the next to CTD when all conversion factors are one arises because the same credit is given for delivering the low-coupon 4.75s of November 15, 2008, as the 5s of August 15, 2011. Actual conversion factors reduce the differences in delivery costs across bonds by adjusting delivery prices for coupon rates. For

---

[3]The penalty for failing to deliver to the futures exchange is quite severe.

TYH2 the *notional coupon* of the contract is 6%. The precise role of this coupon is discussed shortly, but the basic idea is to set the conversion factor of bonds with a coupon rate of 6% to one so that their delivery prices (i.e., the conversion factors times the futures price) are equal to the futures price. Bonds with a coupon rate below 6%, typically worth less than bonds with coupons equal to 6%, are assigned conversion factors less than one so that their delivery prices are below the futures price. Finally, bonds with a coupon rate above 6%, typically worth more than bonds with a coupon rate of 6%, are assigned conversion factors greater than one so that their delivery prices are above the futures price. The conversion factors in Table 20.3 clearly increase with coupon rate and approximately equal one at a rate of 6%.

Conversion factors are computed by the futures exchanges and are easily available. The precise rule for computing conversion factors is a bit complicated, but there is an approximate rule that is pretty accurate and, as will soon become clear, quite useful for intuition about futures contracts. The conversion factor of a bond is approximately equal to its price per dollar face amount as of the last delivery date with a yield equal to the notional coupon rate. Table 20.4 illustrates the accuracy of the approximation for TYH2.

To see why conversion factors set according to this rule reduce the differences in delivery costs across bonds, assume that the approximation just described holds exactly and that the term structure is flat at the notional coupon rate. Under these assumptions the price of each bond is the value of 100 face amount at a yield equal to the notional coupon rate and the

TABLE 20.4 Approximating Conversion Factors as the Unit Bond Price at a Yield Equal to the Notional Coupon

Coupon	Maturity	Conversion Factor	Approximation	Error
4.75%	11/15/08	0.9335	0.9324	−0.0011
5.50%	05/15/09	0.9718	0.9713	−0.0005
6.00%	08/15/09	0.9999	0.9999	0.0000
6.50%	02/15/10	1.0305	1.0310	0.0005
5.75%	08/15/10	0.9838	0.9836	−0.0002
5.00%	02/15/11	0.9326	0.9318	−0.0008
5.00%	08/15/11	0.9297	0.9290	−0.0007

conversion factor of each bond is the value of one face amount at a yield equal to the notional coupon rate. Equivalently, the ratio of the price of each bond to its conversion factor is 100 and, by the logic of the previous section, the futures price is also 100. But this implies that the cost of delivering each bond is zero and, therefore, that all bonds are jointly CTD. To summarize, if the term structure is flat at the notional coupon rate then conversion factors perfectly adjust delivery prices. No bond is preferable to any other with respect to delivery. Also, squeezes of individual bond issues are pointless since shorts are just as willing to deliver issues that have not been accumulated.

IMPERFECTION OF CONVERSION FACTORS AND THE DELIVERY OPTION AT EXPIRATION

Most of the time—that is, whenever the term structure is not flat at the notional coupon rate—conversion factors used in futures contracts do not perfectly adjust delivery prices. Figure 20.1 illustrates this point for three bonds in the TYH2 basket under the assumption of a flat term structure. The vertical axis graphs price divided by conversion factor, and the horizontal axis graphs yield. As discussed in the previous paragraph, at a yield of 6% the conversion factors perfectly adjust prices and the ratio of price to conversion factor equals 100 for all three bonds.

As yield moves away from the notional coupon it is no longer true that conversion factors perfectly adjust delivery prices. To understand why this is so, consider the slope of the price ratio–yield curves in Figure 20.1. Since the vertical axis is price divided by conversion factor, the slope of the curve for bond i on the delivery date T is

$$\frac{1}{cf^i}\frac{dP^i(T)}{dy} \tag{20.9}$$

But at a yield of 6% the conversion factor of a bond is approximately equal to its price per dollar face value. In light of this fact, (20.9) reveals that the slope of the price ratio–yield curve for a bond in Figure 20.1 is approximately proportional to that bond's duration.

As yield increases above the notional coupon rate the prices of all bonds fall, but the price of the bond with the highest duration, namely the

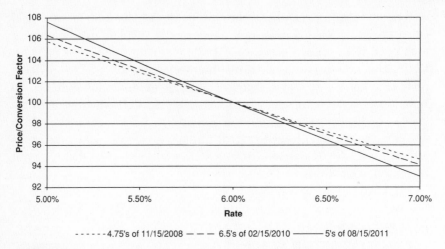

FIGURE 20.1 CTD Analysis for TYH2 at Delivery: A Flat Term Structure of Yields

5s of August 15, 2011, falls relative to the prices of other bonds. But, because conversion factors are fixed, the delivery price of the 5s of August 15, 2011, stays the same relative to that of all other bonds. In other words, as yields increase above the notional coupon rate, the cost of delivering the 5s of August 15, 2011, falls more than that of any other bond. Therefore, while all bonds are equally attractive to deliver at a yield of 6%, as yield increases the 5s of August 15, 2011, become CTD. Graphically, the ratio of the price to conversion factor of the 5s of August 15, 2011, falls below that of all other bonds.

As yield falls below the notional coupon rate, the prices of all bonds increase but the price of the bond with the lowest duration, namely the 4.75s of November 15, 2008, increases the least. At the same time, since the conversion factors are fixed the delivery price of the 4.75s of November 15, 2008, stays the same relative to those of other bonds. Therefore, while all bonds are equally attractive to deliver at a yield of 6%, as yield decreases the 4.75s of November 15, 2008, become CTD.

Figure 20.1 is a stylized example in that it assumes a flat term structure. It is for this reason that the CTD is either the 4.75s of November 15, 2008, or the 5s of August 15, 2011, but never the 6.50s of February 15, 2010, except, of course, at 6% when all bonds are jointly CTD. In reality, of course, the term structure can take on a wide variety of shapes that will affect the determination of the CTD. In general, anything that cheapens a bond relative to other bonds makes that bond more likely to be CTD. If, for example, the curve steepens, then long-duration bonds (e.g., the 5s of August 15, 2011) are more likely to be CTD. On the other hand, if the curve flattens, then short-duration bonds (e.g., the 4.75s of November 15, 2008) are more likely to be CTD. Figure 20.2 depicts a different shift in which the 6.50s of February 15, 2010, cheapen by 4 basis points (i.e., their yield increases by 4 basis points) relative to levels in Figure 20.1. As a result the 6.5s of February 15, 2010, become CTD when the general yield level is between about 5.60% and 6.20%. For lower yields the 4.75s of November 15, 2008, remain CTD, and for higher yields the 5s of August 15, 2011, remain CTD.

At any yield level the futures price at delivery is, according to equation (20.3), the ratio of the price of the CTD to its conversion factor. Graphically, the futures price is the lower envelope of the price ratio–yield curves. Figure 20.3 graphs the futures price corresponding to the price ratio–yield curves in Figure 20.2. Note that the futures price at delivery is negatively convex. As yield decreases the duration of the futures contract moves from resembling the relatively high duration of the 5s of August 15, 2011, to re-

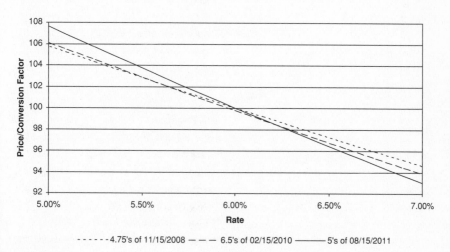

FIGURE 20.2 CTD Analysis for TYH2 at Delivery: A Flat Term Structure with a Cheapening of the 6.5s of February 15, 2010

sembling the intermediate duration of the 6.50s of February 15, 2010, to resembling the relatively low duration of the 4.75s of November 15, 2008. Hence, at delivery, the duration of the futures contract falls with yield; that is, the contract is negatively convex.

One way to think about the quality option at expiration is as the value of being able to deliver any of the three bonds depicted in Figure 20.3 rather than being forced to deliver the 5s of August 15, 2011. In the figure, this value is related to the difference between the price ratio of the 5s of August 15, 2011, and the futures price at any particular yield level. When yield is relatively high and the 5s of August 15, 2011, are the CTD, there is no difference in value between being able to choose which bond to deliver and being forced to deliver the 5s of August 15, 2011. The value of the option is higher when yield is in the intermediate range and the CTD is the 6.50s of February 15, 2010. Finally, the value of the option is highest when yield is relatively low and the CTD has moved all the way to the 4.75s of November 15, 2008.

The quality option at expiration may also be viewed with another bond as the benchmark. Say, for example, that the quality option is defined as the value of being able to deliver any bond rather than having to deliver the 6.50s of February 15, 2010. Then, at expiration, the option is worth

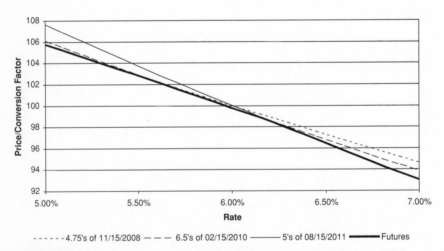

FIGURE 20.3 Futures Price for TYH2 at Delivery: A Flat Term Structure with a Cheapening of the 6.5s of February 15, 2010

nothing in the intermediate range of yield but has value for relatively high or relatively low levels of yield.

GROSS AND NET BASIS

Transactions in futures are usually either outright (i.e., buying or selling futures by themselves) or against forward bond positions in the form of *basis trades*. Basis trades essentially take a view that the futures contract is cheap or rich relative to the value of bonds in the delivery basket. These trades are important to arbitrageurs who profit from these trades but, from a market perspective, the potential for profit in these trades is the force that keeps a future contract near its fair value relative to cash bonds. This section defines basis trades and relates the profit from these trades to the change in a quantity called the *net basis*.

A long basis trade in bond i may be described as follows[4]:

Buy G^i face amount of deliverable bond i.
Sell the repo of bond i to the last delivery date.
Sell $cf^i \times G^i/100,000$ futures contracts.

The combination of buying the bond and selling the repo is equivalent to buying the bond forward to the last delivery date. Rewriting the description,

Buy G^i face amount of deliverable bond i forward to the last delivery date.
Sell $cf^i \times G^i/100,000$ futures contracts.

The analogous form of a short basis trade is the reverse set of transactions:

Sell G^i face amount of a deliverable bond i.
Buy the repo of bond i to the last delivery date.
Buy $cf^i \times G^i/100,000$ futures contracts.

---

[4]Practitioners also refer to a position in futures versus a spot bond position as a basis trade.

Or, equivalently,

> Sell G^i face amount of a deliverable bond i forward to the last delivery date.
> Buy $cf^i \times G^i/100,000$ futures contracts.

Note that buying or selling the basis in this form involves no cash outlay: The repo position finances or invests the bond proceeds, and the futures trade, by definition, requires no cash.[5]

Let $P^i(t)$ be the spot price of bond i at time t, let $P^i_{fwd}(t)$ be its time t forward price to the last delivery date, and let $F(t)$ be the futures price at time t. Then the *gross basis* and *net basis* of bond i at time t, $GB^i(t)$ and $NB^i(T)$ respectively, are defined as:

$$GB^i(t) = P^i(t) - cf^i \times F(t) \qquad (20.10)$$

$$NB^i(t) = P^i_{fwd}(t) - cf^i \times F(t) \qquad (20.11)$$

Using equation (16.8), the forward price may be written in terms of the spot price and carry. Using this fact to rewrite equation (20.11),

$$NB^i(t) = P^i(t) - \text{carry}^i(t) - cf^i \times F(t) = GB^i(t) - \text{carry}^i(t) \qquad (20.12)$$

The right-hand side of equation (20.12) explains the term net basis: It is the gross basis net of carry.

At delivery the forward price equals the spot price, or, equivalently, carry equals zero. Therefore, by inspection of (20.10) and (20.11) or of (20.12), the gross basis equals the net basis. Furthermore, by comparing these equations to (20.1), both measures equal the cost of delivery.

Table 20.5 reports the gross and net basis for all the bonds in TYH2 as of November 26, 2001. In accordance with market convention, basis values in the table are quoted in ticks or 32nds. As an example of the cal-

---

[5]This discussion, of course, abstracts from futures margin requirements and repo haircuts.

TABLE 20.5 TYH2 and Its Deliverable Basket as of November 26, 2001

Pricing date: 11/26/01
Last delivery date: 03/28/02
Futures price: 104-27.5

Coupon	Maturity	Conversion Factor	Price	Gross Basis	Repo	Forward Yield	Carry	Net Basis
6.000%	08/15/09	0.9999	106-19.5	56.3	1.80%	5.132%	42.7	13.6
6.500%	02/15/10	1.0305	109-31	61.2	1.80%	5.174%	47.3	13.8
5.500%	05/15/09	0.9718	103-20	55.1	1.80%	5.091%	38.7	16.4
4.750%	11/15/08	0.9335	99-13.5	49.1	1.80%	5.029%	31.5	17.6
5.750%	08/15/10	0.9838	105-2.375	61.2	1.80%	5.183%	40.4	20.9
5.000%	02/15/11	0.9326	99-26.125	64.8	1.65%	5.181%	35.1	29.7
5.000%	08/15/11	0.9297	99-28.5	76.9	1.00%	5.193%	42.1	34.8

culations, consider the 6s of August 15, 2009. Since the gross basis in decimals is

$$106 + 19.5/32 - .9999 \times (104 + 27.5/32) = 1.7605 \qquad (20.13)$$

the gross basis is 1.7605×32 or 56.3 ticks. The carry is given in ticks in the table, so the net basis is 56.3–42.7 or 13.6 ticks.

Chapter 17 showed that a futures position could be transformed into a forward position by adjusting the number of futures contracts according to the tail. For ease of exposition, it is now assumed that all basis position are properly tailed so that the text can treat a futures position as if it were a forward position. In other words, in the background of the discussion is an unmentioned tail adjustment. The case study at the end of the chapter explicitly describes this tail adjustment.

Neglecting the mark-to-market feature of the futures, that is, assuming that the futures position is properly tailed, the profit and loss (P&L) from a long basis trade initiated at time t and taken off at time t' is the profit of a long forward position in a bond minus the profit of a long futures position. Mathematically the P&L is

$$G^i \times \left[P^i_{fwd}(t') - P^i_{fwd}(t) \right] - G^i \times cf^i \times \left[F(t') - F(t) \right] \qquad (20.14)$$

Using the definition of net basis in equation (20.11), this P&L may be rewritten as

$$G^i \times \left[NB^i(t') - NB^i(t) \right] \qquad (20.15)$$

In words, (20.15) says that the P&L from the long basis position equals the size of the bond position times the change in the net basis.

QUALITY OPTION BEFORE DELIVERY

This section describes the quality option before the delivery date and relates the value of this option to net basis, both algebraically and graphically.

Continuing to assume that futures positions are properly tailed, the net basis at time t is the value of the quality option at delivery, with respect to bond i, that can be locked in as of date t. To see this, recall that on the delivery date T the cost of delivering bond i is $P^i(T) - cf^i \times F(T)$. Since a trader on date t can lock in a price of $P^i_{fwd}(t)$ for date T delivery of bond i and can lock in a futures price of $F(t)$ for date T delivery, the cost of delivery that can be locked in on date T is $P^i_{fwd}(t) - cf^i \times F(t)$. At the same time, the cost of delivering the CTD on the delivery date is, by definition, zero. Therefore, the cost of delivering a particular bond minus the cost of delivering the bond that is optimal to deliver is also $P^i_{fwd}(t) - cf^i \times F(t)$. Finally, by equation (20.11), this is just the net basis.

If the net basis of any bond is near zero, then the quality option embedded in the contract is nearly worthless and selling that bond forward is equivalent to selling the futures contract (again assuming proper tailing). Mathematically, this is a special case of equation (20.11). When the net basis equals zero, then $F(t) = P^i_{fwd}(t)/cf^i$.

The bonds in Table 20.5 are in order of ascending net basis. The bond with the lowest net basis, in this case the 6s of August 15, 2009, is usually called the CTD. Strictly speaking it is not correct to call any bond the CTD before the first delivery date. But the smaller the value of the quality option with respect to a particular bond, the lower the cost of committing to deliver that bond (i.e., of sacrificing the quality option). In this sense, the smaller the value of the quality option, the smaller the net basis, and the closer the bond is to being the CTD. In the same sense the 6s of August 15,

2009, and the 6.50s of February 15, 2010, with net bases within .2 ticks of each other, are essentially jointly CTD.

Figure 20.4 uses the data in Table 20.5 and a pricing model to illustrate the value of the quality option and the concept of CTD before delivery. On the vertical axis is the forward price divided by the conversion factor and on the horizontal axis is a parallel basis point shift in the forward yields relative to those in table 20.5. Unlike Figure 20.3, depicting the futures price on the delivery date, the futures price in Figure 20.4 is not equal to the minimum of the price to conversion factor ratios. In fact, the futures price is strictly less than all these ratios. Intuitively, before expiration the value of the quality option is positive and the minimum net basis is positive. The futures price is closest to the price of the 6.50s of February 15, 2010, divided by its conversion factor. This indicates that, of the three bonds portrayed, it is the CTD.

The discussion surrounding Figures 20.1 and 20.2 shows that yield levels above the notional coupon rate tend to make the short-duration bonds CTD. In Table 20.5 the levels of the forward yields to the delivery date are between 80 and 100 basis points below the notional coupon rate of 6%, but the shortest-duration bonds, that is, the 4.75s of November 15, 2008, and the 5.50s of May 15, 2009, are not CTD. The reason for this is that the curve is relatively steep: The forward yield of the 5s of August 15,

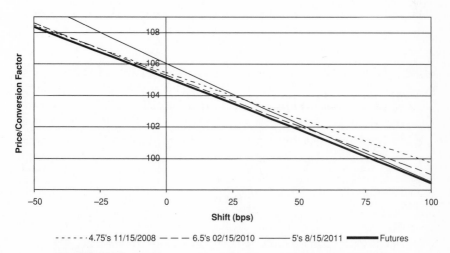

FIGURE 20.4   TYH2 and Its Deliverables as of November 26, 2001

2011, is over 16 basis points greater than that of the 4.75s of November 15, 2008. This curve shape richens the shorter-duration bonds relative to other bonds in the basket and pushes the CTD out to the 6s of August 15, 2009. If general yield levels were to fall further, the CTD would shift to the front end of the basket. If the curve were to steepen more, the CTD would shift to the back end of the basket.

Figure 20.5 graphs the net basis for three bonds in the TYH2 basket using the data in Table 20.5 and a pricing model. The net basis graphs behave like the quality options they represent. The net basis of the 4.75s of November 15, 2008, increases with rates since the 4.75s of November 15, 2008, move further away from being CTD as rates increase. In option parlance, the net basis of the 4.75s of November 15, 2008, behaves like a call on rates or, equivalently, like a put on bond prices. The net basis of the 5s of August 15, 2011, increases as rates fall since the 5s of August 15, 2011, move further away from being CTD as rates fall. This net basis, therefore, behaves like a put on rates or, equivalently, like a call on bond prices. Finally, the net basis of the 6.50s of February 15, 2010, increases when rates fall and when rates rise. The 6.50s of February 15, 2010, are very close to CTD at yield levels as of November 26, 2001. Any change in rates pushes

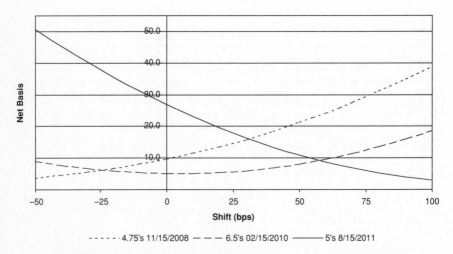

FIGURE 20.5   Net Basis, TYH2 Deliverables as of November 26, 2001

them away from CTD and raises their net basis. Thus, the net basis of a bond close to CTD behaves like a straddle on rates or prices.

Maintaining the assumption of parallel shifts of forward yields, Figure 20.6 graphs the DV01 of the futures contract and of the 6.5s of February 15, 2010. The intuition behind the negative convexity of the futures contract is explained in the section on the delivery option at expiration. However, along with Figure 20.4, this figure dramatically demonstrates that the interest rate behavior of a futures contract is quite different from the interest rate behavior of a bond. Furthermore, when hedging a bond with a futures contract or vice versa the hedge must be rebalanced as rates change.

SOME NOTES ON PRICING THE QUALITY OPTION IN TERM STRUCTURE MODELS

Having set up a term structure model in the form of a tree, pricing the quality option is straightforward. Start at the delivery date. At each node compute the price to conversion factor ratio for each bond. Find the bond with the minimum ratio and set the futures price equal to that ratio. This is the tree equivalent of Figure 20.3. Given these terminal values of

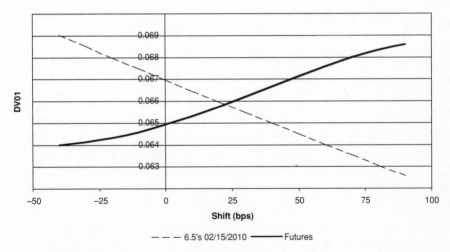

FIGURE 20.6   DV01 of TYH2 and DV01 of 6.5s of February 15, 2010

the futures price, prices on earlier dates can be computed along the lines described in Chapter 17.

The algorithm described in the previous paragraph assumes that the prices of the bonds are available on the last delivery date. For example, for TYH2 it assumes that the price of the 4.75s of November 15, 2008, is available at all nodes on March 28, 2002. These bond prices can be computed in one of two ways. If a model with a closed-form solution for spot rates is being used, these rates can be used to compute bond prices as of the delivery date. Otherwise, the tree has to be extended to the maturity date of the longest bond in the basket, and bond prices have to be computed using the usual tree methodology. Obviously the first solution is faster and less subject to numerical error, but each user must decide if a model with a closed-form solution is suitable for the purpose at hand.

As discussed in Part Three, pricing models usually assume that some set of securities is fairly priced. In the case of futures the standard assumption is that the forward prices of all the bonds in the deliverable basket are fair. Technically this can be accomplished by attaching an OAS to each bond such that its forward price in the model matches the forward price in the market. The assumption that bond prices are fair is popular because many market participants first uncover an investment or trade opportunity in bonds and then determine whether futures contracts should be used instead of some or all bonds in the trade. This is the case because futures are complex securities and, as a result, many investors and traders use futures only when they offer advantages in value, liquidity, or both. Separating the value of futures relative to bonds from the value of bonds themselves allows for a clean consideration of the costs and benefits of using futures.

Term structure models commonly used for pricing futures contracts fall into two main categories. First are one- or two-factor models of the types described in Part Three. The advantage of these models is that they are relatively easy to implement and, for the most part, flexible enough to capture the yield curve dynamics driving futures prices. With only one or two factors, however, these models cannot capture the empirical price movements of one bond relative to its neighboring bonds. So, for example, these models cannot capture a change like the relative cheapening of the 6.50s of February 15, 2010, depicted in Figure 20.2.

The second type of model used in practice allows for a richer set of relative price movements across the deliverable basket. These models essentially allow each bond to follow its own price or yield process. The cost of this flexibility is model complexity of two types. First, ensuring that these models are arbitrage-free takes some effort. Second, the user must specify parameters that describe the stochastic behavior of all bond prices in the basket. For TYH2, for example, a user might have to specify volatility for each of the seven bonds in the deliverable basket and their 21 correlation coefficients.

Futures traders often describe their models in terms of the *betas* of the bonds in the basket with respect to a benchmark bond in the basket. The benchmark is usually chosen as the longest bond in the basket but, if that bond is an on-the-run bond exhibiting a lot of idiosyncratic behavior, then the second to longest bond might be chosen as a benchmark. For TYH2, for example, the 5s of August 15, 2011, are a common benchmark. The beta of a bond represents the expected change in the yield of that bond given a one-basis point change in the yield of the benchmark. If the 4.75s of November 15, 2008, were assigned a beta of 1.02, it would mean that its yield is expected to increase or decrease by 2% more than the increase or decrease of the yield of the 5s of August 15, 2011. The beta of a particular bond can be thought of as the coefficient from a regression of changes in its yield on changes in the yield of the benchmark bond. Note that in a one-factor model the beta of a bond is simply the ratio of the volatility of that bond yield to the volatility of the benchmark bond yield.

MEASURES OF RATE SENSITIVITY

The sensitivity of a futures contract to changes in interest rates is often computed with respect to either spot yields or forward yields. To compute a DV01, for example, the spot yields of all the bonds in the basket may be shifted up and down by one basis point or the forward yields to the delivery date may be shifted up and down by one basis point. To understand the implications of this choice, recall from Chapter 16 that a change in the spot yield may be thought of as a simultaneous change in the repo rate and in the forward yield. Therefore, computing a DV01 by changing forward yields assumes that repo rates stay the same, while computing a DV01 by changing spot yields assumes that forward yields and repo rates move in parallel. Which of these assumptions is more useful for hedging is an empirical question in which historical analysis and expectations about the future play a role.

The discussion in the previous paragraph suggests that there is a family of one-factor measures of price sensitivity for futures contracts. It may be assumed that for every one-basis point move in the spot yield the repo rate moves by .25, .5, or some other fraction of a basis point. Once again, the correct choice is an empirical question.

A drawback of this one-factor approach is that repo rates and the yields of bonds in the basket are in very different parts of the yield curve and, as such, are far from perfectly correlated. A better solution than making an assumption about how much repo moves relative to spot yields is to measure exposures to spot yields and repo separately. In other words, compute both the change in futures price for a parallel shift in spot yields and the change in futures price for a parallel shift in repo rates. The first exposure may be hedged with cash bonds and the second with repo or Eurodollar and fed funds contracts. From this perspective the weakness of the one-factor approach stands out. Hedging a futures contract with cash bonds alone is, at least in part, a hedge of repo rates with bonds in the delivery basket, for example, a hedge of a three-month rate with 10-year bonds.

Since the futures price depends on the slope of the curve as well as on the level of interest rates, a one-factor approach in the bond sector may not be sufficient for many applications. An obvious solution is to use a two-factor model for both pricing and hedging. Another solution is to use a one-factor model for pricing and, for safety, to compute a derivative with respect to some measure of the slope of the term structure. To ensure that a futures position is not too exposed to the idiosyncratic risk of a particular bond, it may also be prudent to compute sensitivities with respect to changes in individual bond yields.

TIMING OPTION

The party short the futures contract may deliver at any time during the delivery month. The delivery period of TYH2, for example, extends from

March 1 to March 28, 2001. Consider the following two strategies for a trader with a short futures position during the delivery month. First, the early delivery strategy: Buy the CTD repo, deliver the CTD early, and stay short the CTD to the futures expiration date. Or second, the late delivery strategy: Stay short the futures contract until the expiration date. The determinants of the best policy are carry and option value. Under the early delivery strategy, the trader pays carry on the CTD and sacrifices any value left in the quality option. Under the late delivery strategy, the trader pays no carry and can switch bonds if the CTD changes. Clearly, if carry is positive, it is optimal to delay delivery. If carry is negative, however, then the carry advantage of delivering early must be weighed against the sacrifice of the quality option.

END-OF-MONTH OPTION

At the last trading date the final settlement price is set. A position long bond i, the current CTD, and short a matching face amount of futures contracts[6] is worth $cf^i \times \bar{F}$ where $\bar{F}$ is the final settlement price. If the price of the bond rises or falls but remains CTD, the value of the position stays fixed at this value. However, if bond prices change such that the CTD changes, that is, such that for some new CTD

$$P^{CTD} - cf^{CTD} \times \bar{F} < P^i - cf^i \times \bar{F} \tag{20.16}$$

then the short can sell the holding of bond i, buy the new CTD, and deliver the new CTD instead of bond i. This option to switch bonds after the last trading date is called the end-of-month option. The P&L from the switch is

---

[6]A basis position before the last trade date consists of a bond position and a conversion-factor-weighted number of futures contracts. After the last trade date the position must be adjusted to a matched number of futures contracts. Further discussion is too technical for the scope of this chapter. It should be noted, however, that the difference between these two hedge ratios is called a tail but has nothing to do with the financing tail introduced in Chapter 17 and discussed in this chapter.

$$cf^{CTD} \times \overline{F} + P^{i} - P^{CTD} - cf^{i} \times \overline{F} \qquad\qquad (20.17)$$

Before the last trade date the futures price reflects any cheapening of the CTD. After the last trade date, however, equation (20.17) shows that any cheapening of the CTD leads to greater and greater profits.

Despite this potential for great value, the end-of-month option does not turn out to be worth much in practice. First, since the end-of-month period is short, bond prices do not have the time to move very much. In TYH2, for example, the end-of-month period lasts less than seven business days.[7] Second, traders long bonds and short futures actively seek opportunities to profit by switching bond holdings. This attention tends to dominate trading of bonds in the deliverable basket. As a result, any time a bond begins to cheapen all the shorts express an interest in switching and the cheapening of the bond comes to an abrupt halt.

TRADING CASE STUDY: November '08 Basis into TYM0

On February 28, 2000, the 10-year note contract expiring in June 2000 (TYM0) appeared cheap in most models used by the industry. Table 20.6 gives some background information about the contract and prices at the time.

To take advantage of this cheapness, many traders sold the 4.75s of November 15, 2008, net basis at 7.45 ticks. Table 20.7 illustrates why many traders thought this was a good trade. The table is constructed using a horizon date of May 19, 2000. (The reason for this choice will become clear shortly.) The table lists several scenarios of

---

[7]The final settlement price is set on March 19, 2002. From March 20 to March 28, 2002, inclusive is seven business days, but the short has to give notice of the bond to be delivered before the last delivery day. This notification requirement shortens the time usable by the end-of-month option.

TABLE 20.6   TYM0 and Its Deliverable Basket as of February 28, 2000

Pricing date: 2/28/00
Last delivery date: 6/30/00
Futures price: 95-9

Coupon	Maturity	Conversion Factor	Price	Gross Basis	Repo	Forward Yield	Carry	Net Basis
4.750%	11/15/08	0.9195	87-24.625	5.1	5.55%	6.667%	−2.4	7.5
6.000%	8/15/09	1.0000	96-3	26.0	4.90%	6.637%	13.2	12.8
5.500%	5/15/09	0.9662	92-16.875	14.9	5.70%	6.632%	1.2	13.7
5.500%	2/15/08	0.9702	92-31.625	17.5	5.75%	6.692%	0.9	16.6
5.625%	5/15/08	0.9769	93-20.125	17.6	5.80%	6.681%	0.8	16.7
6.125%	8/15/07	1.0071	96-26.25	27.6	5.84%	6.716%	4.2	23.4
6.625%	5/15/07	1.0342	99-19.875	34.6	5.84%	6.734%	7.2	27.4
6.250%	2/15/07	1.0133	97-20.75	35.2	5.84%	6.723%	5.0	30.2
5.000%	2/15/10	1.0358	100-16	57.9	3.85%	6.550%	27.7	30.2

parallel shifts in forward yields for delivery on the last delivery date of TYM0 (i.e., June 30, 2000). The scenario of +20 basis points is the scenario in which forward yields of all deliverable bonds for June 30, 2000, delivery increase 20 basis points from the trade date of February 28, 2000, to the horizon date of May 19, 2000. The table also gives the futures price and the net basis of the 11/08s in the various scenarios according to a particular pricing model. This model price assumes that the futures price is fair relative to cash bonds on the horizon date. The row in Table 20.7 labeled "Basis P&L($)" gives the predicted P&L from selling $100,000,000 11/08 net basis on February 28, 2000, as of the horizon date May 19, 2000. As shown in (20.15), the P&L of a basis trade equals the change in the net basis times the face amount of bonds.[8] So, for example, in the +20 scenario the P&L is

$$\$100,000,000 \times \frac{(7.45 - .9)/32}{100} = \$204,688 \qquad (20.18)$$

---

[8]The tail held to realize this P&L is discussed at the end of the case.

TABLE 20.7 Scenario Analysis of Selling $100mm November '08 Basis into TYM0 as of February 28, 2000

Initial November '08 net basis:	7.45
Horizon date:	05/19/00
Futures option strike:	95
Futures option price:	1-16.5
Number of options:	47

Parallel Shift Scenario	-80	-60	-40	-20	0	20	40	60	80
Futures price	100.3666	99.2198	98.02	96.7683	95.4937	94.226	92.9756	91.7426	90.5241
November '08 net basis	13.2	7.1	3.2	1.5	1	0.9	0.9	0.9	1.1
Basis P&L($)	(179,688)	10,938	132,813	185,938	201,563	204,688	204,688	204,688	198,438
Call P&L, 100 face	3.851	2.704	1.504	0.253	(1.022)	(1.516)	(1.516)	(1.516)	(1.516)
Total P&L	1,308	138,034	203,518	197,813	153,532	133,453	133,453	133,453	127,203

Many traders thought that selling the 11/08 basis was a good trade based on data like that presented in the "Basis P&L($)" row of Table 20.7. The scenarios cover the most likely outcomes. There are 77 days from the trade date to the horizon date. Assuming a volatility of 100 basis points per year, the volatility over 77 days is $100\sqrt{77/365}$ or 46 basis points so a scenario span from −80 to +80 covers from about −1.74 to +1.74 standard deviations. The trade starts to lose money in a rally of a bit more than 60 basis points, but makes money for any smaller rally and any sell-off. In the context of the table, it is a matter of personal preference to determine if the potential gains are large enough for the risks borne.

A criticism of making a trading decision based on Table 20.7 is that the table does not really describe all of the risks involved in the basis trade. If the curve flattens, then one of the shortest bonds in the basket will become CTD and the net basis of the 11/08s will rise. If the curve steepens, then one of the longer bonds in the basket will become CTD and the net basis of the 11/08s will rise. Also, if the 11/08s for some reason cheapen relative to the other bonds in the basket, then the net basis of the 11/08s will rise. All these risks are not included in Table 20.7.

Some traders looking at the payoff profile of the basis in Table 20.7 did not like the dramatic drop in P&L after a rally of more than 40 basis points. To make the P&L profile look better, many traders bought 95 strike call options on TYM0 expiring on May 19, 2000, for 1.51 per 100 face amount of futures. The payoff from calls on 100 face of futures is given in Table 20.7. With a rally of 60 basis points, for example, the payoff is 99.2198–95–1.516 or 2.704. Choosing to purchase 47 calls (i.e., calls on 47 contracts covering 47×$100,000 or $4.7 million face) evens out the payoff profile nicely. The rally of 60 basis points makes the 47 calls worth

$$\$4,700,000 \times \frac{2.704}{100} = \$127,088 \qquad (20.19)$$

Adding this to the P&L of $10,938 from the net basis position alone gives a total P&L of $138,034. Finally, Table 20.7 gives the predicted

P&L profile with the options position. It is understandable that some traders would choose to sacrifice some upside in a sell-off to limit the loss in a large rally.

The option position also reduces risk in a way not shown in Table 20.7. If volatility were to rise over the trading horizon, the value of the quality option and therefore the net basis would rise as well. A long option position would at least partially offset this loss since option values increase with volatility. This argument applies strictly between the trade date and the horizon date. On the horizon date the net basis will be adversely affected by increased volatility but the expiring option will not benefit from that increased volatility. Nevertheless, as the case will show, preventing losses over the course of the trade can be as important as the final P&L profile.

It should now be clear that the P&L analysis was done to a May 19, 2000, horizon because the option on TYM0 expired on that date. Options on futures are set to expire before the first delivery date so that these options cannot expire after all delivery has taken place. This convention often makes basis trading difficult because delivery usually occurs on the last delivery date, more than a month after the relevant option has expired. A trader can correct for this mismatch by using bond options that mature later in the delivery month.[9] Unfortunately, however, these options are not exchange traded and are not so liquid as futures options.

Tables 20.8, 20.9, and 20.10 show how the trade worked out. Table 20.8 reports the forward yield of each bond in the basket for June 30, 2000, delivery on the trade date, on two intermediate dates of interest, and on the option expiration date. Table 20.9 reports the futures price, the net basis of each bond, and the option price on these same four dates. Table 20.10 reports the cumulative P&L components of the trade.

From the initiation of the trade to April 3, 2000, forward yields

---

[9] Another possibility is options on the next futures contract. For example, the contract after TYM0 is the September contract. This choice entails basis risk that has to be evaluated.

TABLE 20.8 Forward Yields for June 30, 2000, Delivery as of Selected Dates

Coupon	Maturity	Pricing Date: 2/28/00 Forward Yield	4/3/00 Forward Yield	2/28/00 to 4/3/00 Change	4/10/00 Forward Yield	4/3/00 to 4/10/00 Change	5/19/00 Forward Yield	2/28/00 to 5/19/00 Change
6.250%	02/15/07	6.7234	6.2505	−47.3	6.0814	−16.9	6.7656	4.2
6.625%	05/15/07	6.7344	6.2637	−47.1	6.1002	−16.4	6.7668	3.2
6.125%	08/15/07	6.7155	6.2514	−46.4	6.0915	−16.0	6.7530	3.8
5.500%	02/15/08	6.6920	6.2253	−46.7	6.0467	−17.9	6.7175	2.6
5.625%	05/15/08	6.6814	6.2035	−47.8	6.0144	−18.9	6.7083	2.7
4.750%	11/15/08	6.6670	6.1885	−47.9	5.9924	−19.6	6.6851	1.8
5.500%	05/15/09	6.6319	6.1579	−47.4	5.9584	−20.0	6.6354	0.3
6.000%	08/15/09	6.6370	6.1464	−49.1	5.9485	−19.8	6.6033	−3.4
6.500%	02/15/10	6.5502	6.0468	−50.3	5.8481	−19.9	6.5159	−3.4

TABLE 20.9 TYM0 Futures Price, Futures Options Price, and Net Basis Values as of Selected Dates

	Pricing Date:	2/28/00	4/3/00	4/10/00	5/19/00
	Futures price:	95-9	98-8.5	99-6.5	95-9.5
	Price of calls @95:	1.516	3.375	4.234	0.297
Coupon	Maturity	Net Basis	Net Basis	Net Basis	Net Basis
6.250%	02/15/07	30.2	13.3	12.1	22.7
6.625%	05/15/07	27.4	11.5	9.8	21.3
6.125%	08/15/07	23.4	9.9	8.8	16.3
5.500%	02/15/08	16.6	9.7	14.2	11.5
5.625%	05/15/08	16.7	13.9	21.3	11.3
4.750%	11/15/08	7.5	11.1	22.0	3.5
5.500%	05/15/09	13.7	19.2	32.6	12.5
6.000%	08/15/09	12.8	22.9	36.7	19.4
6.500%	02/15/10	30.2	47.3	63.5	37.4

fell approximately in parallel by 47 basis points. As a result the CTD moved toward the shorter end of the basket, to the 8/07s and 2/08s, and the 11/08 net basis rose to 11.06 for a loss of $112,813. The option position, however, gained $87,391, making the total loss only $25,422. On this date the models reported that the contract was still

TABLE 20.10   Cumulative P&L from the November '08 Basis Trade, with and without Futures Options

| Face amount basis: | | | −100,000,000 | | |
| Face amount calls: | | | 4,700,000 | | |

Date	11/15/08 Net Basis	Option Price	P&L from Net Basis	P&L from Options	Total P&L
2/28/00	7.45	1.516			
4/3/00	11.06	3.375	−112,813	87,391	−25,422
4/10/00	22.01	4.234	−455,000	127,781	−327,219
5/19/00	3.51	0.297	123,125	−57,281	65,844

cheap but that it had richened by about 1.5 ticks relative to cash. This implies that the loss would have been about $100,000,000 \times (^{1.5}/_{32})/100$ or $46,875 larger had the value of the futures contract not richened to approach its theoretically fair value.

From April 3 to April 10, 2000, the forward yields continued to fall by between 16 and 20 basis points. Over this period, however, the forward yield curve flattened by about 3 basis points. In addition, the models reported that the contract had cheapened about 2.5 ticks over these few days. The combination of these effects was disastrous for the trade. The flattening rally moved all the shorter-term bonds closer to CTD. The net basis of every bond from the 2/07s to the 5/08s fell below that of the 11/08s. The net basis of the 11/08s increased to over 22 for a loss on the net basis position of $455,000. The option position gained $127,781, mitigating the damage to a loss of $327,219.

Note that the loss of $327,219 is greater than any number in the predicted P&L of Table 20.7. Part of this is due to the steepening of the forward yield curve and part due to the additional cheapening of the futures contract. In any case, the trading lesson is that intermediate losses can be much greater than horizon losses. In other words, even if the analysis of Table 20.7 turned out to be correct, the losses in the interim could be great and perhaps too great to bear. In particular, a trader showing a loss of $455,000 or $327,219 on this trade might have been ordered to reduce or close the position. In that situation the trader would never see the results of Table 20.7. In fact, one explanation at the time for the cheapening of the futures contract from April 3, 2000, to April 10, 2000, was that many traders were forced to liquidate short basis positions. Since such liquidations entail selling futures and buying bonds, enough activity of this sort will cheapen the contract relative to bonds.

By May 19, 2000, the forward yield curve had returned to the levels of February 28, 2001, but had flattened by between 3 and 4 basis points. This yield curve move restored the 11/08s to CTD and reduced their net basis to 3.51. Even though the futures contracts returned to their original levels, the options lost most of their time value. The total P&L of the trade to its horizon turned out to be $65,844. Note that this profit is substantially below the predicted P&L of about $153,532. First, the forward yield curve did flatten, making the shorter-maturity bonds closer to CTD than predicted by the parallel shift scenarios. Second, while the model assumed that the futures contract would be fair relative to the bonds on May 19, 2000, it turned out that the contract was still somewhat cheap to cash on that date. A quick way to quantify these effects is to notice that the net basis of the 11/08s on the horizon date was 3.51 while it had been predicted to be close to 1. This difference of 2.51 ticks is worth $100,000,000 \times (2.51/32)/100$ or $78,438 in P&L. Adding this to the actual P&L of $65,844 would bring the total to $144,282, much closer to the predicted number. By the way, a trader can, at least in theory, capture any P&L shortfall due to the cheapness of the futures contract on the horizon date by subsequent trading.

Before concluding the case, the tail of this trade is described. By working with the net basis directly the case implicitly assumes that the tail was being managed. The conversion factor of the 11/08s was .9195, so, without the tail, the trade would have purchased about 920 contracts against the sale of $100,000,000 bonds. On February 28, 2000, there were 122 days to the last delivery date, and the repo rate for the 11/08s to that date was 5.55%. Hence, using the rule of Chapter 17, the tail was

$$920 \times \frac{.0555 \times 122}{360} = 17 \qquad (20.20)$$

contracts. In other words, only 920-17 or 903 contracts should have been bought against the bond position. On April 3, 2000, the required tail had fallen to 13 contracts, or, equivalently, the futures position should have increased to 920-13 or 907 contracts. Over that time period the futures price rose from 95-9 to 98-8$^1/_2$, making the tail worth about 2.98 per 100 face of contracts. Assuming an average tail of 15 contracts (i.e., $1,500,000 face), the tail in this trade turned out to be worth $44,765. In other words, had the tail not been managed, the P&L of the basis trade would have differed from the bond position times the change in net basis by about $44,765.

CHAPTER 21

Mortgage-Backed Securities

A *mortgage* is a loan secured by property. Until the 1970s banks made mortgage loans and held them until maturity, collecting principal and interest payments until the mortgages were paid off. This *primary market* was the only mortgage market. During the 1970s, however, the *securitization* of mortgages began. The growth of this *secondary market* substantially changed the mortgage business. Banks that might otherwise restrict their lending, because of limited capital or because of asset allocation decisions, can now continue to make mortgage loans since these loans can be quickly and efficiently sold. At the same time investors have a new security through which to lend their surplus funds.

Individual mortgages are grouped together in *pools* and packaged in a *mortgage-backed security* (MBS). In a *pass-through* security, interest and principal payments flow from the homeowner, through banks and servicing agents, to investors in the MBS. The issuers of these securities often guarantee the ultimate payment of interest and principal so that investors do not have to face the risk of homeowner default.

In striving to understand and value mortgage-backed securities, practitioners expend a great deal of effort modeling the aggregate behavior of homeowners with respect to their mortgages and analyzing the impact on a wide variety of MBS. This chapter serves as an introduction to this highly developed and specialized field of inquiry.[1]

BASIC MORTGAGE MATHEMATICS

The most typical mortgage structure is a fixed rate, *level payment* mortgage. Say that to buy a home an individual borrows from a bank $100,000

---

[1]For a book-length treatment see Hayre (2001).

secured by that home. To pay back the loan the individual agrees to pay the bank $599.55 every month for 30 years. The payments are called level because the monthly payment is the same every month. This structure differs from that of a bond, for example, which makes relatively small coupon payments every period and then makes one relatively large principal payment.

The interest rate on a mortgage is defined as the monthly compounded yield-to-maturity of the mortgage. In the example, the interest rate y is defined such that

$$\$599.55 \sum_{n=1}^{360} \frac{1}{\left(1+y/12\right)^n} = \$100,000 \tag{21.1}$$

Solving numerically, $y=6\%$.

The intuition behind this definition of the mortgage rate is as follows. If the term structure were flat at y, then the left-hand side of equation (21.1) equals the present value of the mortgage's cash flows. The mortgage is a fair loan only if this present value equals the original amount given by the bank to the borrower.[2] Therefore, under the assumption of a flat term structure, (21.1) represents a fair pricing condition. Mortgage pricing without the flat term structure assumption will be examined shortly.

While a mortgage rate can be calculated from its payments, the payments can also be derived from the rate. Let X be the unknown monthly payment and let the mortgage rate be 6%. Then the equation relating X to the rate is

$$X \sum_{n=1}^{360} \frac{1}{\left(1+.06/12\right)^n} = \$100,000 \tag{21.2}$$

Applying equation (3.3) to perform the summation, equation (21.2) may be solved to show that

$$X = \frac{\$100,000 \times .06/12}{1 - \dfrac{1}{\left(1+.06/12\right)^{360}}} = \$599.55 \tag{21.3}$$

---

[2]This section ignores the prepayment option and the possibility of homeowner default. Both are discussed in the next section.

The rate of the mortgage may be used to divide the monthly payments into its interest and principal components. These accounting quantities are useful for tax purposes since interest payments are deductible from income while principal payments are not. Let $B(n)$ be the outstanding principal balance of the mortgage after the payment on date n. The interest component of the payment on date $n+1$ is

$$B(n) \times \frac{y}{12} \qquad (21.4)$$

In words, the interest component of the monthly payment over a particular period equals the mortgage rate times the principal outstanding at the beginning of that period. The principal component of the payment is the remainder, namely

$$X - B(n) \times \frac{y}{12} \qquad (21.5)$$

In the example, the original balance is \$100,000. At the end of the first month, interest at 6% is due on this balance, implying that the interest component of the first payment is

$$\$100,000 \times \frac{.06}{12} = \$500.00 \qquad (21.6)$$

The rest of the monthly payment of \$599.55 pays down principal, implying that the principal component of the first payment is \$599.55–\$500.00 or \$99.55. This principal payment reduces the outstanding balance from the original \$100,000 to

$$\$100,000 - \$99.55 = \$99,900.45 \qquad (21.7)$$

The interest payment for the end of the second month will be based on the principal amount outstanding at the end of the first month as given in (21.7). Continuing this sequence of calculations produces an *amortization table*, selected rows of which are given in Table 21.1.

Early payments are composed mostly of interest, while later payments are composed mostly of principal. This is explained by the phrase "interest lives off principal." Interest at any time is due only on the then outstanding

TABLE 21.1 Selected Rows from an Amortization Table of a 6% 30-Year Mortgage

Payment Month	Interest Payment	Principal Payment	Ending Balance
			100,000.00
1	500.00	99.55	99,900.45
2	499.50	100.05	99,800.40
3	499.00	100.55	99,699.85
36	481.01	118.54	96,084.07
60	465.94	133.61	93,054.36
120	419.33	180.22	83,685.72
180	356.46	243.09	71,048.84
240	271.66	327.89	54,003.59
300	157.27	442.28	31,012.09
360	2.98	596.57	0.00

principal amount. As principal is paid off, the amount of interest necessarily declines.

The outstanding balance on any date can be computed through the amortization table, but there is an instructive shortcut. Discounting using the mortgage rate at origination, the present value of the remaining payments equals the principal outstanding. This is a fair pricing condition under the assumption that the term structure is flat and that interest rates have not changed since the origination of the mortgage.

To illustrate this shortcut in the example, after five years or 60 monthly payments there remain 300 payments. The value of these payments using the original mortgage rate for discounting is

$$\$599.55 \sum_{n=1}^{300} \frac{1}{\left(1+.06/12\right)^n} = \$599.55 \times \frac{1 - 1 / \left(1 + .06/12\right)^{300}}{.06/12} = \$93,054.36 \quad (21.8)$$

where the second equality follows from equation (3.3). Hence, the balance outstanding after five years is $93,054.36, as reported in Table 21.1.

To this point all cash flows have been discounted at a single rate. But Part One showed that each cash flow must be discounted by the rate appropriate for that cash flow's maturity. Therefore, the true fair pricing condition for a $100,000 mortgage paying X per month for N months is

$$X \sum_{n=1}^{N} d(n) = \$100,000 \tag{21.9}$$

where $d(n)$ is the discount factor applicable for cash flows on date n.

It is useful to think of equation (21.9) as the starting point for mortgage pricing. The lender uses discount factors or, equivalently, the term structure of interest rates, to determine the fair mortgage payment. Only then does the lender compute the mortgage rate as another way of quoting the mortgage payment.[3] This discussion is analogous to the discussion of yield-to-maturity in Chapter 3. Bonds are priced under the term structure of interest rates and then the resulting prices are quoted using yield.

The fair pricing condition (21.9) applies at the time of the mortgage's origination. Over time discount factors change and the present value of the mortgage cash flows changes as well. Mathematically, with $\widehat{N}$ payments remaining and a new discount function $\widehat{d}(n)$, the present value of the mortgage is

$$X \sum_{n=1}^{\widehat{N}} \widehat{d}(n) \tag{21.10}$$

The monthly payment X is the same in (21.10) as in (21.9), but the new discount function reflects the time value of money in the current economic environment.

The present value of the mortgage after its origination may be greater than, equal to, or less than the principal outstanding. If rates have risen since origination, then the mortgage has become a loan with a below-market rate and the value of the mortgage will be less than the principal outstanding. If, however, rates have fallen since origination, then the mortgage has become an above-market loan and the value of the mortgage will exceed the principal outstanding.

PREPAYMENT OPTION

A very important feature of mortgages not mentioned in the previous section is that homeowners have a *prepayment option*. This means that a

---

[3]The lender must also account for the prepayment option described in the next section and for the possibility of default by the borrower.

homeowner may pay the bank the outstanding principal at any time and be freed from the obligation of making further payments. In the example of the previous section, the mortgage balance at the end of five years is $93,054.36. To be free of all payment obligations from that time on the borrower can pay the bank $93,054.36.

The prepayment option is valuable when mortgage rates have fallen. In that case, as discussed in the previous section, the value of an existing mortgage exceeds the principal outstanding. Therefore, the borrower gains in a present value sense from paying the principal outstanding and being free of any further obligation. When rates have risen, however, the value of an existing mortgage is less than the principal outstanding. In this situation a borrower loses in a present value sense from paying the principal outstanding in lieu of making future payments. By this logic, the prepayment option is an American call option on an otherwise identical, nonprepayable mortgage. The strike of the option equals the principal amount outstanding and, therefore, changes after every payment.

The homeowner is very much in the position of an issuer of a callable bond. An issuer sells a bond, receives the proceeds, and undertakes to make a set of scheduled payments. Consistent with the features of the embedded call option, the issuer can pay bondholders some strike price to repurchase the bonds and be free of the obligation to make any further payments. Similarly, a homeowner receives money from a bank in exchange for a promise to make certain payments. Using the prepayment option the homeowner may pay the principal outstanding and not be obliged to make any further payments.

The fair loan condition described in the previous section has to be amended to account for the value of the prepayment option. Like the convention in the callable bond market, homeowners pay for the prepayment option by paying a higher mortgage rate (as opposed to paying the rate appropriate for a nonprepayable mortgage and receiving less than the face amount of the mortgage at the time of the loan). Therefore, the fair loan condition requires that at origination of the loan the present value of the mortgage cash flows minus the value of the prepayment option equals the initial principal amount. The mortgage rate that satisfies this condition in the current interest rate environment is called the *current coupon rate*.

When pricing the embedded options in government, agency, or corporate bonds, it is usually reasonable to assume that these issuers act in accordance with the valuation procedures of Chapter 19. More specifically, they exercise an option if and only if the value of immediate exercise exceeds the value of holding in some term structure model. If this were the case for homeowners and their prepayment options, the techniques of Chapter 19 could be easily adapted to value prepayable mortgages. In practice, however, homeowners do not seem to behave like these institutional issuers.

One way in which homeowner behavior does not match that of institutional issuers is that prepayments sometimes occur for reasons unrelated to interest rates. Examples include defaults, natural disasters, and home sales.

Defaults generate prepayments because mortgages, like many other loans and debt securities, become payable in full when the borrower fails to make a payment. If the borrower cannot pay the outstanding principal amount, the home can be sold to raise some, if not all, of the outstanding balance. Since issuers of mortgage-backed securites often guarantee the ultimate payment of principal and interest, investors in MBS expect to experience defaults as prepayments. More specifically, any principal paid by the homeowner, any cash raised from the sale of the home, and any balance contributed by the MBS issuer's reserves flow through to the investor as a prepayment after the event of default.[4]

Disasters generate prepayments because, like many other debt securities with collateral, mortgages are payable in full if the collateral is damaged or destroyed by fire, flood, earthquake, and so on. Without sufficient insurance, of course, it may be hard to recover the amount due. But, once again, MBS issuers ensure that investors experience these disasters as prepayments.

While defaults and disasters generate some prepayments, the most important cause of prepayments that are not directly motivated by interest rates is housing turnover. Most mortgages are *due on sale*, meaning that any outstanding principal must be paid when a house is sold. Since people often decide to move without regard to the interest rate, prepayments resulting from *housing turnover* will not be very related to the behavior of interest rates. Practitioners have found that the age of a

---

[4]The investor is protected from default but the homeowner is still charged a default premium in the form of a higher mortgage rate. This premium goes to the issuer or separate insurer who guarantees payment.

mortgage is very useful in predicting turnover. For example, people are not very likely to move right after they purchase a home but more likely to do so over the subsequent few years. The state of the economy, particularly of the geographic region of the homeowner, is also important in understanding turnover.

While housing turnover does not primarily depend on interest rates, there can be some interaction between turnover and interest rates. A homeowner who has a mortgage at a relatively low rate might be reluctant to pay off the mortgage as part of a move. Technically, paying off the mortgage in this case is like paying par for a bond that should be selling at a discount. Or, from a more pragmatic point of view, paying off a low-rate mortgage and taking on a new mortgage on a new home at market rates will result in an increased cost that a homeowner might not want to bear. This interaction between turnover and interest rates is called the *lock-in effect*.

Another interaction between turnover and interest rates surfaces for mortgages that are not due-on-sale but *assumable*. If a mortgage is assumable, the buyer of a home may take over the mortgage at the existing rate. If new mortgage rates are high relative to the existing mortgage rate, then the buyer and seller will find it worthwhile to have the buyer assume the mortgage.[5] In this case, then, the sale of the home will not result in a prepayment. Conversely, if new mortgage rates are low relative to the existing mortgage rate, then the mortgage will not be assumed and the mortgage will be repaid.

Having described the causes of prepayments not directly related to interest rates, the discussion turns to the main cause of prepayments, namely *refinancing*. Homeowners can exercise their prepayment options in response to lower interest rates by paying the outstanding principal balance in cash. However, since most homeowners do not have this amount of cash available, they exercise their prepayment options by refinancing their mortgages. In the purest form of a refinancing, a homeowner asks the original lending bank, or another bank, for a new mortgage loan sufficient to pay off the outstanding principal of the existing mortgage.

Ignoring transaction costs for a moment, the present value advantage

---

[5] In fact, a home with a below-market, assumable mortgage should be worth more than an identical home without such a mortgage.

of prepaying an above-market mortgage with cash is the same as the present value advantage of a pure refinancing. In both cases the existing mortgage payments are canceled. Then, in the case of a cash prepayment, the homeowner pays the principal outstanding in cash. In the case of a pure refinancing, the homeowner assumes a new mortgage in the size of that same principal outstanding. Furthermore, since the new mortgage rate is the current market rate, the value of the new mortgage obligation equals that principal outstanding. Hence, in terms of present value, the cash prepayment and the pure refinancing are equivalent.

In reality, homeowners do face transaction costs when refinancing. One explicit cost is the fee charged by banks when making mortgage loans. These are called *points* since they are expressed in a number of percentage points on the amount borrowed. This transaction cost raises no conceptual difficulties. The points charged by banks can simply be added to the outstanding principal amount to get the true strike price of the prepayment option. Then, the techniques of Chapter 19, in combination with a term structure model, can be used to derive optimal refinancing policies.

As it turns out, even when focusing on prepayments motivated solely by lower interest rates and even after accounting for points, homeowners do not behave in a way that justifies using the valuation procedures of Chapter 19. The main reason is that homeowners are not financial professionals. The cost to them of focusing on the prepayment problem, of making the right decision, and of putting together the paperwork can be quite large. Moreover, since homeowners vary greatly in financial sophistication or in access to such sophistication, the true costs of exercising the prepayment option vary greatly across homeowners.

Three well-known empirical facts about prepayments support the notion that the true costs of refinancing are larger than points and that these true costs vary across homeowners. First, refinancing activity lags interest rates moves; that is, it takes time before falling rates cause the amount of refinancing to pick up. Some of this delay is due to the time it takes banks to process the new mortgage loans, but some of the delay is no doubt due to the time it takes homeowners to learn about the possibility of refinancing and to make their decisions. Second, refinancing activity picks up after rates show particularly large declines and after rates hit new lows. This empirical observation has been explained as a *media effect*. Large declines and new lows in rates make newspapers report on the events, cause homeowners to talk to each other about the possibility of refinancing, and make it worthwhile for professionals in the mortgage business to advertise the benefits of refinancing. Third, mortgage pools that have been heavily refinanced in the past respond particularly slowly to lower levels of interest rates. This phenomenon has been called the *burnout effect*. The simplest explanation for this phenomenon is that homeowners with the lowest true costs of refinancing tend to refinance at the first opportunity for profitably doing so. Those homeowners remaining in the pool have particularly high true costs of refinancing and, therefore, their behavior is particularly insensitive to falling rates.

To summarize, some prepayments do not depend directly on the level of interest rates and those that do cannot be well described by the assumptions of Chapter 19. Therefore, practitioners have devised alternative approaches for pricing mortgage-backed securities.

OVERVIEW OF MORTGAGE PRICING MODELS

The earliest approaches to pricing mortgage-backed securities can be called *static cash flow models*. These models assume that prepayment rates can be predicted as a function of the age of the mortgages in a pool. Typical assumptions, based on empirical regularities, are that the prepayment rate increases gradually with mortgage age and then levels off at some constant prepayment rate. In a slightly more sophisticated approach, past behavior of prepayments as a function of age is used directly to predict future behavior.

Some practitioners like these models because they allow for the calculation of yield. Since assumed prepayments depend only on the age of the mortgages, the cash flows of the mortgage pool over time can be determined. Then, given that set of cash flows and a market price, a yield can be computed.

Despite this advantage, there are two severe problems with the static cash flow approach. First, the model is not a pricing model at all. Yes, given a market price, a yield may be computed. But a pricing model must provide a means of determining price in the first place. Static cash flow models cannot do this because they do not specify what yield is appropriate for a mortgage. A 30-year bond yield, for example, is clearly not appropriate because the scheduled cash flow pattern of a mortgage differs substantially from that of a bond and because the cash flows of a mortgage are really not fixed. The fact that prepayments change as interest rates change affects the pricing of mortgages but is not captured at all in static cash flow models.

The second, not unrelated problem with static cash flow models is that they provide misleading price-yield and duration-yield curves. Since these models assume that cash flows are fixed, the predicted interest rate behavior of mortgages will be qualitatively like the interest rate behavior of bonds with fixed cash flows. But, from the discussion of the previous section, the price-yield and duration-yield curves of mortgages should have more in common with those of callable bonds. The prepayment option alters the qualitative shape of these curves because mortgage cash flows, like those of callable bonds, are not fixed but instead depend on how interest rates evolve over time.

Another set of models may be called *implied models*. Recognizing the difficulties encountered by static cash flow models, implied models have a more modest objective. They do not seek to price mortgage-backed securities but simply to estimate their interest rate sensitivity. Making the assumption that the sensitivity of a mortgage changes slowly over time, they use recent data on price sensitivity to estimate interest rate sensitivity numerically. The technical procedure is the same as described in Part Two. Given two prices and two interest rate levels, perhaps of the 10-year swap rate, one can compute the change in the price of an MBS divided by the change in the interest rate and convert the result to the desired sensitivity measure. The hope is that averaging daily estimates over the recent past provides a useful estimate of an MBS' current interest rate sensitivity. A variation on this procedure is to look for a historical period closely matching the current environment and to use price and rate data from that environment to estimate sensitivity.

The implied models have several drawbacks as well. First, they are not pricing models. It should be mentioned, however, that investors with a mandate to invest in MBS might be content to take the market price as given and to use implied models for hedging and risk management. The second drawback is that the sensitivity of MBS to interest rates may change rapidly over time. As discussed, the qualitative behavior of mortgages is similar to that of callable bonds. And, as illustrated by Figure 19.5, the duration of callable bonds can change rapidly relative to that of noncallable bonds. Similarly, mortgage durations can change a great deal as relatively small changes in rates make prepayments more or less likely. Therefore, when one most needs accurate measures of interest rate sensitivity, recent implied sensitivities may prove misleading.

The third set of pricing models, called *prepayment models*, is the most popular among sophisticated practitioners. Often composed of two separate models—a turnover model and a refinancing model—this category of models uses historical data and expert knowledge to model prepayments as a function of several variables. More precisely, a prepayment model predicts the amount of prepayments to be experienced by a pool of mortgages as a function of the chosen input variables.

Prepayment models usually define an *incentive function*, which quantifies how desirable refinancing is to homeowners. This function can also be used to quantify the lock-in effect, that is, how averse a homeowner is to selling a home and giving up a below-market mortgage. Examples of incentive functions include the present value advantage of refinancing, the reduction in monthly payments as a result of refinancing, and the difference between the existing mortgage rate and the current coupon rate. While incentive functions always depend on the term structure of interest rates, the complexity of this dependence varies across models. An example of simple dependence would be using the 10-year swap rate to calculate the present value advantage of refinancing. An example of a complex dependence would be using the shape of the entire swap curve to calculate this present value advantage.

Lagged or past interest rates may be used to model the media effect. For example, both the change in rates over the past month and the level of rates relative to recent lows are proxies for the focus of homeowners on interest rates and on the benefits of refinancing.

Noninterest rate variables that enter into turnover and refinancing models may include any variable deemed useful in predicting prepayments. Some common examples of such variables, along with brief explanations of their relevance, are these:

- *Mortgage age*. Recent homeowners tend not to turn over or refinance as quickly as homeowners who have been in place for a while.
- *Points paid*. Borrowers who are willing to pay large fees in points so as to reduce their mortgage rates are likely to be planning to stay in their homes longer than borrowers who accept higher rates in exchange for paying only a small fee. Hence, mortgages with high points are likely to turn over and prepay less quickly than mortgages with low points.

- *Amount outstanding.* Borrowers with very little principal outstanding are not likely to bother refinancing even if the present value savings, as a percentage of amount outstanding, are high.
- *Season of the year.* Homeowners are more likely to move in certain seasons or months than in others.
- *Geography.* Given that economic conditions vary across states, both turnover and refinancing activity may differ across states. The predictive power of geography may decay quickly. In other words, the fact that people in California change residence more often than people in Kansas may be true now but is not necessarily a best guess of conditions five years from now.

One disadvantage of prepayment function models is that they are statistical models as opposed to models of homeowner behavior. The risk of such an approach is that historical data, on which most prepayment function models are based, may lose their relevance as economic conditions change. Unfortunately, theoretically superior approaches that directly model the homeowner decision process, the true costs of refinancing, the diversity of homeowners, and so on, have not proved particularly successful or gained industry acceptance.

IMPLEMENTING PREPAYMENT MODELS

It is possible that a prepayment function could be combined with the pricing trees of Part Three to value a pass-through security. Scheduled mortgage payments plus any `prepayments as predicted by the prepayment function would give the cash flow from a pool of mortgages on any particular date and state. And given a way to generate cash flows, pricing along the tree would proceed in the usual way, by computing expected discounted values. As it turns out, however, the complexity of prepayment models designed by the industry makes it difficult to use interest rate trees.

The tree technology assumes that the value of a security at any node depends only on interest rates or factors at that node. This assumption excludes the possibility that the value of a security depends on past interest rates—in particular, on how interest rates arrived at the current node. For example, a particular node at date 5 of a tree might be arrived at by two up moves followed by three down moves, by three down moves followed by two up moves, or by other paths. In all previous problems in this book the path to this node did not matter because the value of the securities under consideration depend only on the current state. The values of these securities are *path independent*. The values of mortgages, by contrast, are believed to be *path dependent*. The empirical importance of the burnout effect implies that a mortgage pool that has already experienced rates below 6% will prepay less quickly than a pool that has never experienced rates below 6% even though both pools currently face the same interest rates. The media effect is another example of path dependence. Say that the current mortgage rate is 6%. Then, in some implementations of the media effect, prepayments are higher if the mortgage rate has been well above 6% for a year than if the mortgage rate has recently fallen below 6%.

A popular solution to pricing path-dependent securities is *Monte Carlo simulation*. This procedure can be summarized as follows.[6]

Step 1: Using some term structure model that describes the risk-neutral evolution of the short rate, generate a randomly selected path over the life of the mortgage pool. An example follows assuming semiannual time steps:

Date 0: 4%
Date 1: 4.25%
Date 2: 3.75%
Date 3: 3.5%
Date 4: 3%

Step 2: Moving forward along this path, use the scheduled mortgage cash flows and the prepayment function to generate the cash flows from the mortgage pool until the principal has been completely repaid. Example:

Date 1: $10
Date 2: $12
Date 3: $15
Date 4: $80

Step 3: Find the value of the security along the selected interest rate path. More specifically, starting at the date of the last cash flow, discount all cash flows back to the present using the short rates. As with price trees,

---

[6]For a general overview of Monte Carlo methods for fixed income securities, see Andersen and Boyle (2000).

values on a particular date assume that the cash flows on that date have just been made. Example:

Date 4: $0

Date 3: $80/(1+$^{.035}$/$_2$)=$78.62

Date 2: ($78.62+$15)/(1+$^{.0375}$/$_2$)=$91.90

Date 1: ($91.90+$12)/(1+$^{.0425}$/$_2$)=$101.74

Date 0: ($101.74+$10)/(1+$^{.04}$/$_2$)=$109.55

Step 4: Repeat steps 1 through 3 many times and calculate the average value of the security across these paths. Use that average as the model price of the security.

To justify Monte Carlo simulation, recall equation (16.17) or equation (16.18). These equations say that a security may be priced as follows. First, discount each possible value of a security by the path of interest rates to that particular value. Second, using the probabilities of reaching each possible value, calculate the expected discounted value. This is very much like Monte Carlo simulation except that the development in Chapter 16 assumes that all possible paths are included when computing the expected value. In Monte Carlo simulation, by contrast, a subset of the possible paths is chosen at random. To the extent that the randomly selected subset is representative of all the paths and to the extent that this subset is a large enough sample of paths, Monte Carlo simulation will provide acceptable approximations to the true model price.

Step 1 uses a term structure model to generate rate paths. As in the case of interest rate trees, the term structure model may match the current term structure of interest rates in whole or in part. Since prepayment models are usually used to value mortgages relative to government bonds or swaps, practitioners tend to take the entire term structure as given.

Step 2 reveals the advantage of Monte Carlo simulations over interest rate trees. Since the paths are generated starting from the present and moving forward, a prepayment function that depends on the history of rates can be used to obtain cash flows. In the example, the cash flow of $15 on date 3 might have depended on any or all of the short-term rates on date 0, 1, or 2. By the way, while the short-term rate on date 4 is never used for discounting because the last cash flow is on date 4, this rate may very well have been used to compute that the cash flow on date 4 is $80. In particular, the 3% rate on date 4 might have triggered a prepayment of outstanding principal.

While the Monte Carlo technique of moving forward in time to generate cash flows has the advantage of handling path dependence, the approach is not suitable for all problems. Consider trying to price an American or Bermudan option one period before expiration using the Monte Carlo technique. Recall that this option price equals the maximum of the value of immediate exercise and the value of holding the option over the coming period. Given the interest rate at expiration and one period before expiration along a particular path, the value of exercising the option at expiration and at the period before expiration can be computed. But knowing the option value at expiration along a particular path is not enough to compute the value of holding the option. All possible option values at expiration are required for computing the value of holding the option from the period before expiration to expiration. This is the reason the tree methodology starts by computing all possible option values at expiration and then moves back to the period before expiration. In any case, without a good deal of extra effort, Monte Carlo techniques cannot be used to value optimally exercised Bermudan or American options.[7] Given, however, that homeowners do not optimally exercise their options, this sacrifice is certainly worthwhile in the mortgage context.

Just as the tree methodology can be used to calculate measures of interest rate sensitivity, so can the Monte Carlo method. The original term structure may be shifted up and down by a basis point. Then new paths may be generated and the pricing procedure repeated to obtain up and down prices. These up and down prices may be used to calculate numerical sensitivities. And taking the original price together with these two shifted prices allows for the numerical computation of convexity.

The computation of the option-adjusted spread of an MBS is analogous to that discussed in Chapter 14. In the case of Monte Carlo paths, each path is shifted by a varying number of basis points until, using the shifted rates for discounting, the model price of the MBS equals its market price. Note that, as in Chapter 14, the shifted rates are not used to recalculate the cash flows but only for discounting. This procedure preserves OAS as a model's prediction of the excess return to a hedged position in a seemingly mispriced security.

---

[7]A new technique to price early exercise provisions in a Monte Carlo framework is proposed in Longstaff and Schwartz (2001).

The assumptions of the prepayment function are clearly crucial in determining the model value of an MBS. But since the prepayment function is only an estimate of homeowner behavior, many practitioners like to calculate the sensitivity of model value to the parameters of the prepayment function. These sensitivities answer questions like the following: What happens to model value if homeowners refinance more or less aggressively than assumed in the model? What if turnover turns out to be higher or lower than assumed in the model? What if the burnout effect is stronger or weaker than assumed in the model? These sensitivities of model value to changes in model assumptions serve two purposes. First, they allow an investor or trader to judge whether the model OAS values are robust enough to justify taking sizable positions relative to government bonds or swaps. Second, these sensitivities allow an investor or trader to hedge prepayment model risks with other MBS. For example, while an individual MBS may have a large exposure to errors in the specification of turnover, it may be possible to create a portfolio of MBS such that the value of the portfolio is relatively insensitive to errors in turnover assumptions.

PRICE-RATE CURVE OF A MORTGAGE PASS-THROUGH

Figure 21.1 graphs the price of a 6%, 30-year, nonprepayable mortgage and, using a highly stylized prepayment model, the price of a pass-through on a pool of 6%, 30-year, prepayable mortgages. The term structure is assumed to be flat at the level given by the horizontal axis. The price-yield curve of the nonprepayable mortgage exhibits the usual properties of a security with fixed cash flows: It slopes downward and is positively convex.

According to the figure, the price of the pass-through is above that of the nonprepayable mortgage when rates are relatively high. This phenomenon is due to the fact that housing turnover, defaults, and disasters generate prepayments even when rates are relatively high. And when rates are high relative to the existing mortgage rate, prepayments benefit investors in the pass-through: A below-market fixed income investment is returned to these investors at par. Therefore, these seemingly suboptimal prepayments raise the price of a pass-through relative to the price of a nonprepayable mortgage. These prepayments are only seemingly suboptimal

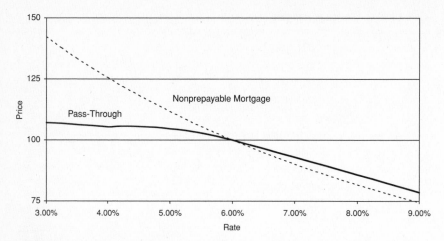

FIGURE 21.1 Price-Rate Curves for a Nonprepayable Mortgage and for a Pass-Through

because it may very well be optimal for the homeowner to move. But, from the narrower perspective of interest rate mathematics and of investors in the MBS, turnover prepayments in a high-rate environment raise the value of mortgages.

Apart from the price premium of the pass-through at relatively high rates described in the previous paragraph, the price-yield curve of the pass-through qualitatively resembles that of a callable bond. First, the pass-through does not rally as much as its nonprepayable counterpart when rates fall because homeowners prepay at par. Prepayments in a low-rate environment lower the value of mortgages. Second, for the same reason, the pass-through curve exhibits negative convexity. The only way for the pass-through to experience less of a rally than the nonprepayable mortgage is for the interest rate sensitivity of the pass-through to fall as rates fall.

Note that the price of the pass-through does rise above par at relatively low rates even though homeowners could free themselves of that above-par obligation by prepaying at par. This effect, of course, is due to the fact that homeowners do not exercise their prepayment option as aggressively as called for in Chapter 19.

APPLICATION: Mortgage Hedging and the Directionality of Swap Spreads

On several occasions in 2001 it was observed that swap spreads narrowed in sharp fixed income rallies and widened in sharp sell-offs. Many strategists believed that the activity of mortgage hedgers explained a good deal of this correlation. For illustration, Table 21.2 records two periods over which this phenomenon was observed and explained by market commentators as due to mortgage hedging. In the first example the 10-year Treasury rallied by 15 basis points and swap spreads narrowed by nearly 11 basis points. In the second example the 10-year Treasury sold off by 59 basis points and the swap spread widened by almost 7 basis points.

The argument made was along these lines. The total amount of MBS outstanding with 15- and 30-year mortgages as collateral was, at the time, about $2.25 trillion. With 10-year swap rates at about 5.75%, the duration of the portfolio of outstanding MBS is about 2.8. Furthermore, a 25-basis point increase in rates would raise this duration by about .5 years to 3.3, while a 25-basis point decrease in rates would lower it by about .5 years to 2.3. (Note the negative convexity of the MBS universe.) Therefore, if only 20% of the holders of MBS hedge their interest rate exposure, a 25-basis point change in rates creates a dollar basis point exposure of

$$20\% \times \$2,250,000,000,000 \times .5\% = \$2,250,000,000 \tag{21.11}$$

or $2.25 billion. If this were hedged exclusively with 10-year swaps, at a duration of about 7.525,[8] the face amount required would be

$$\frac{\$2,250,000,000}{.07525} = \$29,900,000,000 \tag{21.12}$$

TABLE 21.2 Ten-Year Rates and Spreads over Two Periods in 2001

Date	10-Year Swap Rate	10-Year Treasury Rate	Swap Spread (bps)
9/21/01	5.386%	4.689%	69.7
9/10/01	5.644%	4.839%	80.5
Change	−0.258%	−0.150%	−10.8
11/16/01	5.553%	4.893%	66.0
11/9/01	4.895%	4.303%	59.2
Change	0.658%	0.590%	6.8

---

[8]Apply equation (6.26) at a yield of 5.75%.

or about $30 billion.[9] To summarize: Given the size and convexity of the universe of MBS, and an estimate of how much of that market is actively hedged, a 25 basis point change in the swap rate requires a hedge adjustment of about $30 billion face amount of 10-year swaps.

The implication of these calculations for swap spreads is as follows. Assume that interest rates fall by 25 basis points. Since MBS duration falls, investors who hedge find themselves with not enough duration. To compensate they receive in swaps, probably with five- or 10-year maturity. And, as shown by the previous calculations, the amount they receive is far from trivial. As a result of this rush to receive, swap rates fall relative to Treasuries so that swap spreads narrow. If interest rates rise by 25 basis points the story works in reverse. MBS duration rises, investors who hedge find themselves with too much duration, they pay in swaps, swap rates rise relative to Treasuries, and swap spreads widen.

This argument does not necessarily imply that the effect on swap spreads is permanent. Since swaps are more liquid than mortgages, hedgers' first reaction is to cover their exposure with swaps. But, over time, they might unwind their swap hedge and adjust their holdings of mortgages. If this were the case, then the story for falling rates would end as follows. After mortgage hedgers receive in swaps to make up for lost duration, and widen swap spreads in the process, they slowly unwind their swaps and buy mortgages. In other words, they replace the temporarily purchased duration in swaps with duration in mortgages. The effect of this activity is to narrow swap spreads, perhaps back to their original levels, and richen mortgages relative to other assets.

There are a few points in the arguments of this section that require elaboration. First, why do market participants hedging the interest rate risk of MBS trade swaps instead of Treasuries? Before 1998 Treasuries were more commonly used to hedge MBS and the correlation between mortgage and Treasury rates justified that practice. The logic was that MBS cash flows, guaranteed by the agencies or other strong credits, are essentially free of default risk. Therefore, the correct benchmark for discounting and for hedging MBS is the Treasury market. Since 1998, however, swaps have gained in popularity as hedges for MBS at the expense of Treasuries. While the default characteristics of MBS have not changed much, the shift toward swaps might be explained by the following interrelated trends: the relative decline in the supply of Treasuries, the increase in idiosyncratic behavior of Treasury securities, and the deteriorating correlation between the Treasury and MBS markets.

---

[9]This calculation is a bit conservative because the duration of the swap, being positively convex, moves in the opposite direction of the duration of the mortgage. The change in the duration of the swap, however, at about .09 years for a 25 basis point shift, is relatively small.

The second point requiring elaboration is why traders and investors hedge mortgages with five- and 10-year swaps. Table 7.1 presented the key rate duration profile of a 30-year nonprepayable mortgage and showed that the 10-year key rate is quite influential. Put another way, the cash flow pattern of a nonprepayable mortgage makes the security quite sensitive to rates of terms less than 30 years despite the stated mortgage maturity of 30 years. The same argument applies with more force to mortgages with prepayment options, making five- and 10-year swaps sensible hedging securities.

Finally, if there is such a large demand to hedge long positions in mortgages, why isn't there a demand to hedge short positions in mortgages? In other words, if the duration of mortgages falls and investors hedging long positions need to buy duration, then market participants hedging short positions must need to sell duration. And, if this is the case, the two effects cancel and there should be no effect on swap spreads. The answer to this question is that the most significant market participants who short mortgages are homeowners, and homeowners simply do not actively hedge the interest rate risk of their mortgages.

MORTGAGE DERIVATIVES, IOs, AND POs

The properties of pass-through securities displayed in Figure 21.1 do not suit the needs of all investors. In an effort to broaden the appeal of MBS, practitioners have carved up pools of mortgages into different derivatives. One example is *planned amortization class* (PAC) bonds, which are a type of *collateralized mortgage obligation* (CMO). A PAC bond is created by setting some fixed prepayment schedule and promising that the PAC bond will receive interest and principal according to that schedule so long as the actual prepayments from the underlying mortgage pools are not exceptionally large or exceptionally small. In order to comply with this promise, some other derivative securities, called *companion* or *support* bonds, absorb the prepayment uncertainty. If prepayments are relatively high and PAC bonds receive their promised principal payments, then the companion bonds must receive relatively large prepayments. Alternatively, if prepayments are relatively low and PAC bonds receive the promised principal payments, then the companion bonds must receive relatively few prepayments. The point of this structure is that investors who do not like prepayment uncertainty—that is, who do not like the call feature of mortgage securities—can participate in the mortgage market through PACs. Dealers and investors who are comfortable with modeling prepayments and with controlling the accompanying interest rate risk can buy the companion or support bonds.

Other popular mortgage derivatives are *interest-only* (IO) and *principal-only* (PO) strips. The cash flows from a pool of mortgages or a pass-through are divided such that the IO gets all the interest payments while the PO gets all the principal payments. Figure 21.2 graphs the prices of the pass-through and of these two derivatives. As in Figure 21.1, a highly stylized prepayment model is used and the horizontal axis gives the level of a flat term structure. Since the cash flows from the pass-through are diverted to either the IO or the PO, the price of the IO plus the price of the PO equals the price of the pass-through.

When rates are very high and prepayments low, the PO is like a zero coupon bond, paying nothing until maturity. As rates fall and prepayments accelerate, the value of the PO rises dramatically. First, there is the usual effect that lower rates increase present values. Second, since the PO is like a zero coupon bond, it will be particularly sensitive to this effect. Third, as prepayments increase, some of the PO, which sells at a discount, is redeemed at par. Together, these three effects make PO prices particularly sensitive to interest rate changes.

The price-yield curve of the IO can be derived by subtracting the value of the PO from the value of the pass-through, but it is instructive to describe IO pricing independently. When rates are very high and prepayments low, the IO is like a security with a fixed set of cash flows. As rates fall and mortgages begin to prepay, the flows of an IO vanish. Interest lives off

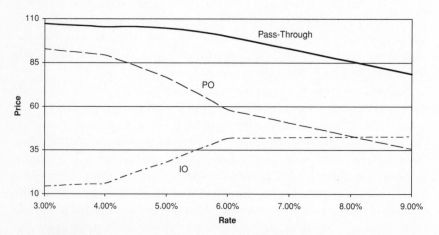

FIGURE 21.2   Price-Rate Curves for a Pass-Through, an IO, and a PO

principal. Whenever some of the principal is paid off there is less available from which to collect interest. But, unlike callable bonds or pass-throughs that receive principal, when exercise or prepayments cause interest payments to stop or slow the IO gets nothing. Once again, its cash flows simply vanish. This effect swamps the discounting effect so that when rates fall IO values decrease dramatically. The negative DV01 or duration of IOs, an unusual feature among fixed income products, may be valued by traders and portfolio managers in combination with more regularly behaved fixed income securities. For example, if the mortgage sector as a whole is considered cheap, as it often is, buying cheap IOs to hedge interest rate risk offers more value than selling fairly priced swaps.

EXERCISES

CHAPTER 1 Bond Prices, Discount Factors, and Arbitrage

1.1 Write down the cash flow dates and the cash flows of $1,000 face value of the U.S. Treasury 4s of April 30, 2003, issued on April 30, 2001.

1.2 Here is a list of bond transactions on May 15, 2001. For each transaction list the transaction price.

Bond	Price	Face Amount
10.75s of 5/15/2003	112-2⁵/₈	$10,000
4.25s of 11/15/2003	99-14+	$1,000
7.25s of 5/15/2004	107-4	$1,000,000

1.3 Use this list of Treasury bond prices as of May 15, 2001, to derive the discount factors for cash flows to be received in 6 months, 1 year, and 1.5 years.

Bond	Price
7.5's of 11/15/2001	101-25³/₄
7.5's of 05/15/2001	103-12¹⁵/₁₆
11.625's of 11/15/2002	110-21¹/₄

1.4 Suppose there existed a Treasury issue with a 7.5% coupon maturing on November 15, 2002. Using the discount factors derived in question 1.3, what would be the price of the 7.5s of November 15, 2002?

1.5 Say that the 7.5s of November 15, 2002, existed and traded at a price of 105 instead of the price derived in question 1.4. How could one earn an arbitrage profit by trading the 7.5s of November 15, 2002, and the three bonds listed in question 1.3? Using the prices listed in question 1.3, how much arbitrage profit is available in this trade?

1.6 Consider the following three bonds and bond prices:

Bond	Price
0s of 5/15/2002	*96-12*
7.5s of 5/15/2002	103-12$^{15}/_{16}$
15s of 5/15/2002	106-2

Do these prices make sense relative to one another? Why or why not?

CHAPTER 2   Bond Prices, Spot Rates, and Forward Rates

2.1 You invest $100 for two years at 5%, compounded semiannually. How much do you have at the end of the two years?

2.2 You invested $100 for three years and, at the end of those three years, your investment was worth $120. What was your semiannually compounded rate of return?

2.3 Using your answers to question 1.3, derive the spot rates for 6 months, 1 year, and 1.5 years.

2.4 Derive the relationship between discount factors and forward rates.

2.5 Using your answers to either question 1.3 or 2.3, derive the six-month rates for 0 years, .5 years, and 1 year forward.

2.6 Are the forward rates from question 2.5 above or below the spot rates of question 2.3? Why is this the case?

2.7 Question 1.3 gives the price of the 7.5s of November 15, 2001, and the 7.5s of May 15, 2002. The answer to question 1.4 gives the price of the 7.5s of November 15, 2002. Are these prices rising, falling, or both rising and falling with maturity? Why?

CHAPTER 3   Yield-to-Maturity

3.1 On May 15, 2001, the price of the 11.625s of November 15, 2002, was 110-21$^4/_4$. Verify that the yield-to-maturity was 4.2139%. Explain this yield relative to the spot rates from question 2.3.

3.2 On May 15, 2001, the price of the 6.75s of May 15, 2005, was 106-21$^1/_8$. Use a calculator or spreadsheet to find the yield of the bond.

3.3 Consider a 10-year par bond yielding 5%. How much of the bond's value comes from principal and how much from coupon payments? How does your answer change for a 30-year par bond yielding 5%?

3.4 Why would anyone buy a bond selling at a premium when after holding that bond to maturity it will be worth only par?

3.5 On May 15, 2001, the price and yield of the 11.625s of November 15, 2002, were 110-21$^1/_4$ and 4.2139%, respectively. Say that on November 15, 2001, the yield of the bond is still 4.2139%. Calculate the annualized return on the bond over that six-month period.

3.6 Consider the following bond yields on May 15, 2001:

Bond	Yield
5.25s of 8/15/2003	4.3806
5.75s of 8/15/2003	4.3838
11.125s of 8/15/2003	4.4717

Do these yields make sense relative to one another? Assume that the yield curve on May 15, 2001, was upward-sloping.

3.7 A 60-year-old retired woman is considering purchasing an annuity that pays $25,000 every six months for the rest of her life. Assume that the term structure of semiannually compounded rates is flat at 6%.

a. If the annuity cost $575,000 and the woman expects to live another 25 years, will she purchase the annuity? What if she expects to live another 15 years?

b. If law prohibits insurance companies from charging a different annuity price to men and to women and if everyone expects women to live longer than men, what would happen in the annuity market?

3.8 A state lottery advertises a jackpot of $1,000,000. In the fine print it is written that the winner receives 40 annual payments of $25,000. If the term structure is flat at 6%, what is the true value of the jackpot?

CHAPTER 4   Generalizations and Curve Fitting

4.1 The Treasury 5s of February 15, 2011, which were issued on February 15, 2001, are purchased on May 15, 2001, for a quoted price of 96-23$^1/_2$. What is the invoice price on $100,000 face amount?

4.2 Bank 1 offers 4.85% compounded monthly for a one-year investment. Bank 2 offers 5% compounded semiannually. Which bank offers the better investment?

4.3 Using simple interest and the actual/360 convention, how much interest is owed on a $1,000,000 loan from April 24, 2001, to May 2, 2001?

4.4 Is the discount function in Figure 1.2 concave or convex?

4.5 The following table gives spot rates for four terms:

Term	Spot Rate
2	4.32%
5	5.10%
10	5.74%
30	6.07%

Fit a cubic using equation (4.21) through these points. Graph the resulting spot rate function. Does this function seem reasonable? Why or why not?

4.6 A trader thinks that the 10.75s of August 15, 2005, are cheap relative to other bonds in that maturity sector. What risk does the trader face by buying that bond in the hope that its price will rise relative to other bonds in the sector? What if the trader buys that bond and sells the 6.5 of August 15, 2005?

4.7 What is the .75-year discount factor if the .75-year rate, continuously compounded, is 6%?

CHAPTER 5   One-Factor Measures of Price Sensitivity

The exercises for this chapter are built around a spreadsheet exercise. Set up a column of interest rates from 1.75% to 8.25% in 25 basis point increments. In the next column compute the price of a perpetuity with a face of 100 and a coupon of 5%: $100 \times {}^{.05}/_y$ where y is the rate in the first column. In the next column compute the price of a one-year bond with a face of 100 and an annual coupon of 5%: ${}^{105}/_{(1+y)}$.

5.1 Graph the prices of the perpetuity and the one-year bond as a function of the interest rate. Use the graph to determine which security is more sensitive to changes in rates. Use the graph to determine which security is more convex.

5.2 On the spreadsheet compute the DV01 of the perpetuity and of the one-year bond numerically for all of the rates in the first column. To compute the DV01 at a rate y, use the prices at the rates y plus 25 basis points and y minus 25 basis points. Do the results match your answer to question 5.1? How can you tell from these results which security has the higher convexity?

5.3 A trader buys 100 face of the perpetuity and hedges with the one-year bond. At a yield level of 5% what is the DV01 hedge? Why is the hedge so large? What is the hedge at a yield level of 2.50%? Explain why the hedge changes.

5.4 Calculate the duration of the perpetuity and of the one-year bond in the spreadsheet. At a yield level of 5% interpret the duration numbers in the context of a 10 basis point interest rate move for a fixed income portfolio manager.

5.5 Compute the convexity of the perpetuity and the one-year bond at all yield levels in the first column of your spreadsheet. To compute the convexity at y, compute the derivative using prices at y plus 25 basis points and at y. Then compute the derivative using prices at y and y minus 25 basis points.

5.6 Is the hedged position at a yield level of 5% computed for question 5.3 long or short convexity? First answer intuitively and then calculate the exact answer.

5.7 Estimate the price change of the perpetuity from a yield level of 5% to a level of 6% using its duration and convexity at 5%. How does this compare to the actual price change?

CHAPTER 6 Measures of Price Sensitivity Based on Parallel Yield Shifts

6.1 Order the following bonds by duration without doing any calculations:

Coupon	Maturity	Yield
4.25%	11/15/2003	4.4820%
11.875%	11/15/2003	4.5534%
4.625%	5/15/2006	4.9315%
6.875%	5/15/2006	5.0379%

6.2 Try to order the bonds listed in question 6.1 by DV01 without doing any calculations. This is not so straightforward as question 6.1.

6.3 Calculate the DV01 and modified duration for each of the following bonds as of May 15, 2001:

Coupon	Maturity	Yield	Price
8.75	5/15/2020	5.9653%	131-12$^7/_8$
8.125	5/15/2021	5.9857%	124-24$^1/_8$

Comment on the results.

6.4 In a particular trading session, two-year Treasury notes declined by $19 per $1,000 face amount while 30-year bonds fell $11 per $1,000 face amount. What lesson does this session have to teach with respect to the use of yield-based duration to hedge bond positions?

6.5 Calculate the Macaulay duration of 30-year and 100-year par bonds at a yield of 6%. Use the results to explain why Treasury STRIPS maturing in 20 to 30 years are in particularly high demand.

6.6 Bond underwriters often agree to purchase a corporate client's new bonds at a set price and then attempt to reoffer the bonds to investors. There can be a few days between the time the underwriter sets the price it will pay and the time it manages to sell all of its client's bonds. Underwriting fees often increase with the maturity of the bonds being sold. Why might this be so?

CHAPTER 7 Key Rate and Bucket Exposures

The following questions will lead to the design of a spreadsheet to calculate the two- and five-year key rate duration profile of four-year bonds.

7.1 Column A should contain the coupon payment dates from .5 to 5 years in increments of .5 years. Let column B hold a spot rate curve flat at 4.50%. Put the discount factors corresponding to the spot rate curve in column C. Price a 12% and a 6.50% four-year bond under this initial spot rate curve.

7.2 Create a new spot rate curve, by adding a two-year key rate shift of 10 basis points, in column D. Compute the new discount factors in column E. What are the new bond prices?

7.3 Create a new spot rate curve, by adding a five-year key rate shift of 10 basis points, in column F. Compute the new discount factors in column G. What are the new bond prices?

7.4 Use the results from questions 7.1 to 7.3 to calculate the key rate durations of each of the bonds.

7.5 Sum the key rate durations to obtain the total duration of each bond. Calculate the percentage of the total duration accounted for by each key rate for each bond. Comment on the results.

7.6 What would the key rate duration profile of a four-year zero coupon bond look like relative to those computed for question 7.4? How would your answer change for a five-year zero coupon bond?

CHAPTER 8   Regression-Based Hedging

You consider hedging FNMA 6.5s of August 15, 2004, with FNMA 6s of May 15, 2011. Taking changes in the yield of the 6s of May 15, 2011, as the independent variable and changes in the yield of the 6.5s of August 15, 2004, as the independent variable from July 2001 to January 2002 gives the following regression results:

Number of observations   131
R-squared   77.93%
Standard error   4.0861

Regression Coefficients	Value	t-Stat
Constant	–.7549	–2.1126
Change in yield of 6s of 5/15/2011	.9619	21.3399

8.1 What is surprising about the regression coefficients?

8.2 The DV01 of the 6.50s of August 15, 2004, is 2.796, and the DV01 of the 6s of May 15, 2011, is 7.499. Using the regression results given, how much face value of the 6s of May 15, 2011, would you sell to hedge a $10,000,000 face value position in the 6.50s of August 15, 2004?

8.3 How do the regression results given here compare with the regression results in Table 8.1? Explain the differences. How do the regression results given here make you feel about hedging FNMA 6.50s of August 15, 2004, with FNMA 6.5s of May 15, 2011?

CHAPTER 9   The Science of Term Structure Models

9.1 A fixed income analyst needs to estimate the price of an interest rate cap that pays $1,000,000 next year if the one-year Treasury rate exceeds 6% and pays nothing otherwise. Using a macroeconomic model developed in another area of the firm the analyst estimates that the one-year Treasury rate will exceed 6% with a probability of 25%. Since the current one-year rate is 5%, the analyst prices the cap as follows:

$$\frac{25\% \times \$1{,}000{,}000}{1.05} = \$238{,}095$$

Comment on this pricing procedure.

9.2 The following tree gives the true six-month rate process:

The prices of six-month, one-year, and 1.5-year zeros are 97.5610, 95.0908, and 92.5069. Find the risk-neutral probabilities for the six-month rate process. Assume, as in the text, that the risk-neutral probability of an up move from date 1 to date 2 is the same from both date 1 states. As a check to your work, write down the price trees for the six-month, one-year, and 1.5-year zeros.

9.3 Using the risk-neutral tree derived for question 9.2, price $100 face amount of the following 1.5-year *collared floater*. Payments are made every six months according to this rule: If the short rate on date i is r_i, then the interest payment of the collared floater on date $i+1$ is

$$\frac{1}{2}3.50\% \qquad \text{if } r_i < 3.50\%$$

$$\frac{1}{2}r_i \qquad \text{if } 6.50\% \geq r_i \geq 3.50\%$$

$$\frac{1}{2}6.50\% \qquad \text{if } r_i > 6.50\%$$

In addition, at maturity, the collared floater returns the $100 principal amount.

9.4 Using your answers to questions 9.2 and 9.3, find the portfolio of the originally one-year and 1.5-year zeros that replicates the collared floater from date 1, state 1, to date 2. Verify that the price of this replicating portfolio gives the same price for the collared floater at that node as derived for question 9.3.

9.5 Using the risk-neutral tree from question 9.2, price $100 notional amount of a 1.5-year *participating cap* with a *strike* of 5% and a *participation rate* of 40%. Payments are made every six months according to this rule: If the short rate on date i is r_i, then the cash flow from the participating cap on date $i+1$ is, as a percent of par,

$$\frac{1}{2}\left(r_i - 5\%\right) \qquad \text{if } r_i \geq 5\%$$

$$\frac{1}{2}40\%\left(r_i - 5\%\right) \quad \text{if } r_i \geq 5\%$$

There is no principal payment at maturity.

CHAPTER 10 The Short-Rate Process and the Shape of the Term Structure

10.1 On February 15, 2001, the yields on a 5-year and a 10-year interest STRIPS were 5.043% and 5.385%, respectively. Assuming that the expected yield change of each is zero and that the yield volatility is 95 basis points for both, use equation (10.27) to infer the risk premium in the marketplace. Hint: You will also need equations (6.24) and (6.36).

On May 15, 2001, the yields on a 5-year and 10-year interest STRIPS were 5.099% and 5.735%, respectively. Repeat the preceding exercise.

10.2 Describe as fully as possible the qualitative effect of each of these changes on 10- and 30-year par yields.

a. The market risk premium increases.

b. Volatility across the curve increases.

c. Volatility of the 10-year rate decreases while the volatility of the 30-year par rate stays the same.

d. The expected values of future short-term rates fall. Hint: Make assumptions about which future rates change in expected value.

e. The market risk premium falls and the volatility across the curve falls in such a way as to keep the 10-year yield unchanged.

CHAPTER 11   The Art of Term Structure Models: Drift

11.1 Assume an initial interest rate of 5%. Using a binomial model to approximate normally distributed rates with weekly time steps, no drift, and an annualized volatility of 100 basis points, what are the two possible rates on date 1?

11.2 Add a drift of 20 basis points per year to the model described in question 11.1. What are the two rates now?

11.3 Consider the following segment of a binomial tree with six-month time steps. All transition probabilities equal .5.

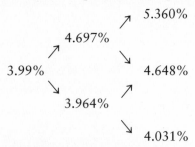

Does this tree display mean reversion?

11.4 What mean reversion parameter is required to achieve a half-life of 15 years?

CHAPTER 12   The Art of Term Structure Models: Volatility and Distribution

12.1 The yield volatility of a short-term interest rate is 20% at a level of 5%. Quote the basis point volatility and the Cox-Ingersoll-Ross (CIR) volatility parameter.

12.2 You are told that the following tree was built with a constant volatility. All probabilities equal .5. Which volatility measure is, in fact, constant?

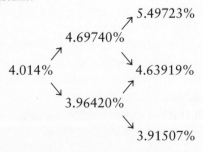

12.3 Use the closed-form solution in Appendix 12A to compute spot rates of various maturities in the Vasicek model with the parameters $\theta=10\%$, $k=.035$, $\sigma=.02$, and $r_0=4\%$. Comment on the shape of the term structure.

CHAPTER 13 Multi-Factor Term Structure Models

13.1 The following trees give the processes for the two factors of a term structure model:

$$
5\% \quad
\begin{array}{c}
\nearrow^{\frac{1}{2}} \; 6\% \\
\searrow_{\frac{1}{2}} \; 4\%
\end{array}
$$

$$
0\% \quad
\begin{array}{c}
\nearrow^{\frac{1}{2}} \; 1\% \\
\searrow_{\frac{1}{2}} \; -1\%
\end{array}
$$

The correlation of the changes in the factors is $-.5$. Finally, the short-term rate equals the sum of the factors. Derive the two-dimensional tree for the short-term rate.

CHAPTER 14 Trading with Term Structure Models

14.1 Question 9.3 required the calculation of the price tree for a collared floater. Repeat this exercise, under the same assumptions, but assuming that the option-adjusted spread (OAS) of the collared floater is 10 basis points.

14.2 Using the price trees from questions 9.3 and 14.1, calculate the return to a hedged and financed position in the collared floater from dates 0 to 1 assuming no convergence (i.e., the OAS on date 1 is also 10 basis points). Hint 1: Use all of the proceeds from selling the replicating portfolio to buy collared floaters. Hint 2: You do not need to know the composition of the replicating portfolio to answer this question.

Is your answer as you expected? Explain.

14.3 What is the return if the collared floater converges on date 1 so its OAS equals 0 on that date?

CHAPTER 15   Repo

The following data as of May 15, 2001, relates to the old 10-year Treasury bond and the on-the-run 10-year Treasury bond.

Coupon	Maturity	Yield	Price	Overnight Repo Rate	DV01
5.75%	8/15/2010	5.4709%	101-31⅞	3.80%	.07273
5%	2/15/2011	5.4346%	96-23+	0.10%	.07343

15.1 Calculate the carryover one day for $100 face of each of these bonds and comment on the difference. Note that there are 89 days between May 15, 2001, and August 15, 2001, and 181 days between February 15, 2001, and August 15, 2001.

15.2 Calculate the return to an investment in each bond if their respective yields fall by one basis point immediately after purchase.

15.3 By how many basis points does the yield spread between the two bonds have to change for the returns to be the same?

15.4 Explain whether or not it is likely for the yield spread to move in the direction indicated by your answer to question 15.3. Also explain the conditions under which a one-day investment in the on-the-run 10-year will be superior to an investment in the old 10-year and vice versa.

CHAPTER 16   Forward Contracts

16.1 For delivery dates in the near future, the forward prices of zero coupon bonds are above spot prices while the forward prices of coupon bonds are usually below spot prices. Explain.

16.2 For settle on November 27, 2001, the yield on the 4.75s of November 15, 2008, was 4.842% and the repo rate to March 28, 2002, was 1.80%. Approximate the forward yield of the 4.75s of November 15, 2008, to March 28, 2002, with as simple a calculation as you can devise. The actual forward yield was 5.023%.

16.3 Using the numbers in question 16.2, which is larger: the spot DV01 of the 4.75s of November 15, 2008, or its forward DV01 for delivery on March 28, 2002?

16.4 For settle on November 27, 2001, the price of the 5s of February 15, 2011 was 99-26$^1/_8$ and its repo rate to March 28, 2002, was 1.65%. Compute the forward price of the bond for March 28, 2002, delivery. You may assume that the repo rate curve is flat.

16.5 Say that on November 27, 2001, you bought the 5s of February 15, 2011, forward for March 28, 2002, delivery at the forward price computed for question 16.4. If the price of the 5s of February 15, 2011, on March 28, 2002, turns out to be 100, what is your profit or loss?

16.6 Which is larger: the three-month forward price of a then six-month zero or the six-month forward price of a then three-month zero?

CHAPTER 17 Eurodollar and Fed Funds Futures

For questions 17.1 to 17.5 use the following data. As of February 5, 2002, fed funds contracts traded at these levels:

February	98.250
March	98.250
April	98.275
May	98.195
June	98.145

17.1 A bank makes a loan of $50,000,000 on February 5, 2002, to be repaid on June 30, 2002. The bank plans to fund this loan with overnight borrowing. How many of each fed funds contract should it trade to hedge its interest rate exposure?

17.2 What cost of funds does the bank lock in by trading the contracts according to the answer to question 17.1? Quote the cost as an actual/360 rate and assume for simplicity that daily borrowing by the bank is not compounded while borrowing across months is compounded.

17.3 Say that the average fed funds rates realized each month are as follows:

February	1.75%
March	1.75%
April	1.75%
May	1.95%
June	2.00%

How much does the bank pay to finance its loan, and how much does it gain or lose from its fed funds position? Show that the net effect is to lock in the rate derived in question 17.2.

17.4 The most recent meeting of the FOMC was in January 2002, and the next two meetings are on March 19 and May 7. Assume that the only possible action on March 19 is to keep the fed funds target the same or to lower it by 25 basis points. What is the fed funds rate on February 5, 2002? What is the implied probability in the fed funds market of a 25 basis point reduction on March 19? You may ignore all other effects (e.g., risk premium).

17.5 Using your answer from question 17.4 for the expected fed funds rate before the May 7 FOMC meeting, what does the May fed funds contract say about the probability of an increase in rates at the May 7 meeting? Assume that the only two possible outcomes at that meeting are that the FOMC leaves the fed funds rate unchanged or that it increases that rate by 25 basis points.

17.6 A corporate lender makes the same loan as the bank in question 17.1, but wants to use Eurodollar futures instead of fed funds futures whenever possible and prudent. March Eurodollar futures expire on March 18, 2002, and June Eurodollar futures expire on June 17, 2002. What hedge of the loan uses February fed funds futures and March and/or June Eurodollar futures? Can you make an argument based on the FOMC meeting schedule given in question 17.4 for just ignoring the risk covered by the February fed funds contracts?

17.7 As of February 5, 2002, two Treasury bonds were priced as follows:

Coupon	Maturity	TED Spread	DV01
3.625	8/31/2003	31.1	1.53
4.500	11/15/2003	35.7	1.75

Qualitatively describe a spread of spreads trade suggested by these numbers. How much would a trade involving $100,000,000 of the 4.5s of November 15, 2003, make if the TED spread of the two bonds immediately equalized?

CHAPTER 18 Interest Rate Swaps

18.1 From the point of view of the fixed receiver, what are the exact cash flow dates and amounts of a $10,000,000 two-year swap at 5.75%

settling on February 15, 2002? Assume for the purposes of this question that the floating rate always sets at 2.50% over the life of the swap. Also assume that cash flow dates falling on weekends are made on the following business day. Why do the cash flows look so attractive to the fixed receiver?

18.2 Consider 100 face of a five-year floating rate note with semiannual resets. Assume that the term structure is flat at 5%. What is the DV01 of the series of floating coupons? Explain the surprising result.

18.3 One year ago you paid fixed on $10,000,000 of a 10-year interest rate swap at 5.75%. The nine-year par swap rate now is 6.25%, and the nine-year discount factor from the current swap rate curve is .572208. Assume that the next floating payment has just been set. Will you pay or receive money to terminate the swap? How much money will be exchanged in the termination?

18.4 "The FNMA 6.25s of May 15, 2029, should sell at an asset swap spread less than 15 basis points because the yield on an equivalent maturity bond of a financially strong bank is less than 15 basis points below the yield of that FNMA security." Comment on this reasoning.

18.5 On February 15, 2001, the 10-year swap spread was 96.5 basis points, and the overnight special spread of the on-the-run 10-year Treasury was 119 basis points. On May 15, 2001, the 10-year swap spread was 80.3 basis points, and the overnight special spread of the on-the-run 10-year was 422 basis points. Comment on the comparability of these two swap spreads.

CHAPTER 19   Fixed Income Options

19.1 Formalize the arbitrage argument that the value of a call option must be positive.

19.2 Graph the value at expiration of the following option combination: long one 95 strike option, short two 100 strike options, and long one 105 strike option.

19.3 The following diagram gives the tree for the price of a callable bond. The numbers above the tree give the call prices on particular dates. Circle the states in which the bond is optimally called.

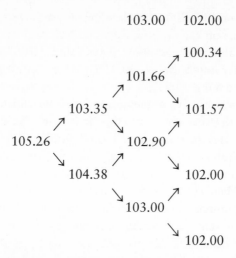

103.00   102.00

19.4 Consider a 5%, 10-year bond puttable at par by the holder after five years. In other words, the investor has the right to sell the bond to the issuer at par after five years. Describe the qualitative behavior of this bond as interest rates change.

19.5 Bond A matures in 15 years but is callable at par in 10 years. Bond B matures in six years but is callable at par in one year. At a yield approximately equal to the coupon rate, which bond's duration will change more rapidly as interest rates change?

19.6 What is the price volatility of a five-year zero coupon bond at a yield of 5% and a yield volatility of 25%?

CHAPTER 20   Note and Bond Futures

20.1 Using the conversion factors in Table 20.1, what is the delivery price of the 5.75s of August 15, 2010, if TYH2 expires at 102 and the bond price is then 101?

20.2 Using the data from question 20.1, what is the cost of delivering the 5.75s of August 15, 2010?

20.3 From the answer to question 20.2, are the 5.75s of August 15, 2010, cheapest to deliver (CTD)? Why or why not?

20.4 Recently it has often been true that only two bonds, the on-the-run five-year and the old five-year, have been eligible for delivery into the five-year futures contract. Describe how each of the following will impact which bond is CTD: yield level, slope of the term structure, on-the-run versus off-the-run premium.

20.5 According to Table 20.5 the net basis of the 6.5s of February 15, 2010, for delivery into TYH2 as of November 26, 2001, is 13.8. Say that a trader sold $50,000,000 face of these bonds forward to February 15, 2010, and bought a conversion-factor-weighted number of TYH2 contracts. Using the conversion factors in Table 20.5, how many contracts does the trader buy? If the 6.5s of February 15, 2010, are CTD at expiration, what is the trader's profit? You may ignore the tail (i.e., the difference between futures and forward contracts) for this question. When will the trader lose money on this trade?

20.6 A trader has a futures model that assumes there is only one delivery date. Knowing that there is a timing option, the trader computes both the model futures price assuming that delivery happens on the first delivery date and the model futures price assuming that delivery happens on the last delivery date. The trader then assumes that the true futures price should equal the smaller of these two prices. Comment on this procedure.

CHAPTER 21 Mortgage-Backed Securities

21.1 Assume that the term structure of monthly compounded rates is flat at 6%. Find the monthly payment of a 15-year, $100,000 mortgage.

21.2 An adjustable-rate mortgage (ARM) resets the interest rate every set period so that the borrower is essentially rolling over a short-term loan. How does the option to prepay an ARM compare to the option to prepay a fixed-rate mortgage?

21.3 Explain the intuition for each of the following results.

a. When interest rates fall, POs outperform 30-year Treasuries.

b. When interest rates rise by 100 basis points, mortgage pass-throughs fall by about 7%. When interest rates fall by 100 basis points, pass-throughs rise by 4%.

c. When interest rates decline, IOs and inverse IOs decline in price, but IOs suffer more severely. (An inverse IO receives no principal payments, like an IO, but receives interest payments that float inversely with the level of rates.)

REFERENCES AND SUGGESTIONS FOR FURTHER READING

Anderson, L., and P. Boyle. 2000. "Monte Carlo Methods for the Valuation of Interest Rate Securities." Pp. 367–402 in *Advanced Fixed Income Valuation Tools*, ed. N. Jegadeesh and B. Tuckman. New York: John Wiley & Sons, Inc.

Backus, D., S. Foresi, and C. Telmer. 2000. "Discrete-Time Models of Bond Pricing," Pp. 87–127 in *Advanced Fixed Income Valuation Tools*, ed. N. Jegadeesh and B. Tuckman. New York: John Wiley & Sons, Inc.

Balduzzi, P., S. Das, S. Foresi, and R. Sundaram. 2000. "Stochastic Mean Models of the Term Structure of Interest Rates." Pp. 128–161 in *Advanced Fixed Income Valuation Tools*, ed. N. Jegadeesh and B. Tuckman. New York: John Wiley & Sons, Inc.

Baygun, B., J. Showers, and G. Cherpelis. 2000. "Principles of Principal Components." Research Report, Salomon Smith Barney.

Black, F., and P. Karasinski. 1991. "Bond and Option Pricing When Short Rates Are Lognormal." *Financial Analysts Journal* (July–August): 52–59.

Brace, A., D. Gatarek, and M. Musiela. 1997. "The Market Model of Interest Rate Dynamics." *Mathematical Finance* 7: 127–155.

Brigo, D., and F. Mercurio. 2001. *Interest Rate Models: Theory and Practice*. Berlin: Springer-Verlag.

Burghardt, G., T. Belton, M. Lane, G. Luce, and R. McVey. 1991. *Eurodollar Futures and Options*. Chicago: Irwin Professional Publishing.

Burghardt, G., T. Belton, M. Lane, and J. Papa. 1994. *The Treasury Bond Basis*. New York: McGraw-Hill.

Chan, K., G. Karolyi, F. Longstaff, and A. Sanders. 1992. "An Empirical Comparison of Alternative Models of the Short-Term Interest Rate." *The Journal of Finance* 47: 1209–1228.

Duffie, D., and R. Kan. 1996. "A Yield-Factor Model of Interest Rates." *The Journal of Finance* 6: 379–406.

Golub, B., and L. Tilman. 2000. *Risk Management: Approaches for Fixed Income Markets.* New York: John Wiley & Sons, Inc.

Hayre, L., ed. 2001. *Salomon Smith Barney Guide to Mortgage-Backed and Asset-Backed Securities.* New York: John Wiley & Sons, Inc.

Heston, S., and G. Zhou. 2000. "Exploring the Relation between Discrete-Time Jump Processes and the Finite Difference Method." Pp. 347–366 in *Advanced Fixed Income Valuation Tools.* ed. N. Jegadeesh and B. Tuckman. New York: John Wiley & Sons, Inc.

Ho, T. 1992. "Key Rate Durations: Measures of Interest Rate Risks." *The Journal of Fixed Income* (September): 29–43.

Homer, S., and R. Sylla. 1996. *A History of Interest Rates.* 3rd ed., rev. New Brunswick, New Jersey: Rutgers University Press.

Hull, J. 2000. *Options, Futures, & Other Derivative Securities.* 4th ed. Upper Saddle River, New Jersey: Prentice-Hall, Inc.

Ibbotson Associates. 2001. *Stocks, Bonds, Bills, and Inflation: 2001 Yearbook.* Chicago: Ibbotson Associates, Inc.

Ilmanen, A. 2000. "Convexity Bias and the Yield Curve." In *Advanced Fixed Income Valuation Tools,* ed. N. Jegadeesh and B. Tuckman. New York: John Wiley & Sons, Inc.

Ingersoll, J. 1987. *Theory of Financial Decision Making.* Totowa, New Jersey: Rowman & Littlefield.

Longstaff, F., P. Santa-Clara, and E. Schwartz. 2001. "The Relative Valuation of Caps and Swaptions: Theory and Empirical Evidence." *The Journal of Finance* 56: 2067–2109.

Longstaff, F., and E. Schwartz. 1992. "Interest Rate Volatility and the Term Structure: A Two-Factor General Equilibrium Model." *The Journal of Finance* 47: 1259–1282.

Longstaff, F., and E. Schwartz. 2001. "Pricing American Options by Simulation: A Simple Least-Squares Approach." *Review of Financial Studies* 14: 113–147.

Rebonato, R. 1996. *Interest-Rate Option Models.* 2nd ed. New York: John Wiley & Sons, Inc.

Rebonato, R., and I. Cooper. 1995. "The Limitations of Simple Two-Factor Interest Rate Models." *The Journal of Financial Engineering* 5: 1–16.

Stigum, M. 1989. *The Repo and Reverse Markets.* Homewood, Illinois: Richard D. Irwin.

Stigum, M. 1990. *The Money Market.* 3rd ed. Homewood, Illinois: Richard D. Irwin.

Stigum, M., and F. Robinson. 1996. *Money Market and Bond Calculations.* Chicago: Richard D. Irwin.

Taleb, N. 1997. *Dynamic Hedging.* New York: John Wiley & Sons, Inc.

Vasicek, O. 1977. "An Equilibrium Characterization of the Term Structure." *Journal of Financial Economics* 5: 177–188.